THE RENAISSANCE IN EUROPE: A CULTURAL ENQUIRY

Challenges to Authority

THE RENAISSANCE IN EUROPE: A CULTURAL ENQUIRY

Challenges to Authority

EDITED BY PETER ELMER

Yale University Press, New Haven & London in association with The Open University

This publication forms part of an Open University course: AA305, *The Renaissance in Europe: A Cultural Enquiry*. Details of this and other Open University courses can be obtained from the Course Reservations Centre, PO Box 724, The Open University, Milton Keynes MK7 6ZS, United Kingdom: tel. +44 (0)1908 653231, e-mail ces-gen@open.ac.uk

Alternatively, you may visit the Open University website at http://www.open.ac.uk where you can learn more about the wide range of courses and packs offered at all levels by the Open University.

For availability of this or other components, contact Open University Worldwide Ltd, The Berrill Building, Walton Hall, Milton Keynes MK7 6AA, United Kingdom: tel. +44 (0)1908 858785; fax +44 (0)1908 858787; e-mail ouwenq@open.ac.uk; website http://www.ouw.co.uk

First published 2000 by Yale University Press in association with The Open University

Yale University Press
23 Pond Street
London
NW3 2PN

The Open University
Walton Hall
Milton Keynes
MK7 6AA

Edited, designed and typeset by The Open University

Printed and bound in the United Kingdom by The Alden Group, Oxford

Cover and colour printing by Spin Offset Ltd, Rainham, Essex

Colour reproduction by The Colour Assembly Ltd, London

British Library cataloguing in publication data
A catalogue record for this book is available from the British Library

Library of Congress cataloging in publication data
Card number 99-68042

ISBN 0-300-08215-0 (C)
ISBN 0-300-08220-7 (P)

010545/AA305bk3i1.1

1.1

To the memory of Tony Coulson 1944–2000

Contents

Preface

This is the third of three books in the series *The Renaissance in Europe: A Cultural Enquiry* which form the main texts of an Open University third-level course of the same name. This interdisciplinary course has been designed for students who are new to cultural history and the Renaissance as well as for those who have already undertaken some study in these areas. The purpose of this series is to introduce the idea of the Renaissance both as it developed during the fifteenth and sixteenth centuries and as it has since been interpreted. Through a wide-ranging series of case studies, we hope to provide a broad overview of current scholarship in the field of Renaissance studies. The subject is not tackled chronologically, although the earlier phases of the Renaissance tend to be considered in the first two volumes and the later in the third. Each book engages with different themes and aspects of the Renaissance and is self-sufficient and accessible to the general reader. This third book, *Challenges to Authority,* focuses on the fate of the classical revival in the sixteenth and early seventeenth centuries, with particular emphasis on the complex relationship between Renaissance values and the emergence of alternative sources of authoritative knowledge, including the Reformation and scientific innovation.

As part of the course, this book includes important teaching exercises which in most cases are followed by some discussion of the points raised. At the beginning of each chapter the expected outcomes for the reader are listed in the form of objectives. A bibliography has been prepared for each chapter and where applicable is followed by a source list for texts from the set Reader and Anthology (see below). At the end of the book is a glossary. Entries in the glossary are emboldened in the text, usually the first time they appear. The convention for dating adopted throughout the series is to use CE (Common Era) and BCE (Before Common Era) in preference to the more traditional AD and BC.

For each volume in the series there are set texts to which the reader will need access in order to engage fully with the material. Throughout the series references to the two volumes of source material are to the 'Reader' and the 'Anthology' followed by an extract number; page references to the Reader and Anthology are not usually given. References to other set texts are in the standard author/ date system except where specified. For this book the set texts are:

P. Elmer, N. Webb and R. Wood (eds) (2000) *The Renaissance in Europe: An Anthology*, New Haven and London, Yale University Press.

K. Whitlock (ed.) (2000) *The Renaissance in Europe: A Reader*, New Haven and London, Yale University Press.

Jacob Burckhardt (1990) *The Civilization of the Renaissance in Italy* , trans. S.G.C. Middlemore, introduction by Peter Burke, Harmondsworth, Penguin.

P. Corbin and D. Sedge (eds) (1999) W. Rowley, T. Dekker and J. Ford: *The Witch of Edmonton*, Manchester and New York, Manchester University Press.

Michel de Montaigne (1991) *The Complete Essays*, ed./trans. and introduction by M.A. Screech, Harmondsworth, Penguin.

Keith Whitlock (ed.) (2000) *The Life of Lazarillo de Tormes (La vida de Lazarillo de Tormes y de sus fortunas y adversidades)*, trans. D. Rowland, Warminster, Aris & Phillips.

The three books in the series are:

The Impact of Humanism, edited by Lucille Kekewich

Courts, Patrons and Poets, edited by David Mateer

Challenges to Authority, edited by Peter Elmer

The course editors were Julie Bennett, Christine Considine and Rachel Crease, picture research was carried out by Tony Coulson and Magnus John and the course secretary was Sam Horne. Roberta Wood was the course manager, Ruth Drage was the course designer, Ray Munns was the course artist and Robert Gibson was the compositor.

Introduction

BY PETER ELMER

Historians have long debated what is meant by the term
'Renaissance'. For some it is a distinctive period, for others a
momentous event, and for a third group a definable movement of
ideas and beliefs. Each choice has its problems and detractors. Those,
like Jacob Burckhardt, who envisage the Renaissance as primarily
denoting a specific period in the evolution of Europe – one
characterized by the emergence of the 'individual' – are forced to
confront the issue of deciding on an end date for the great period of
classical revival and emulation. More often than not, the decisive
break is identified as having taken place some time between 1520 and
1530 when that other great movement or epoch in western history,
the Reformation, took centre stage. Echoing Burckhardt, earlier
generations of Renaissance scholars were thus inclined to view the
onset of religious reform, both Catholic and Protestant, as essentially
antithetical to the secular and 'pagan' values of the Italian
Renaissance. In recent years, however, this view of the relationship
between the Renaissance and the Reformation has undergone
considerable revision. Today, a broad scholarly consensus suggests
that the Renaissance survived the onslaught of religious reform and
continued well into the seventeenth century when both movements
were faced with a further challenge to their authority, that of the
scientific revolution.

A central theme of this book, then, is the interaction in sixteenth-
century Europe between competing ideas and beliefs, some of which
owe their origin to the Renaissance preoccupation with the classical
past, while others reflect developments in the religious and
intellectual culture of the age which derive from alternative sources.
In Chapters 1–3 we explore this relationship in more detail by
focusing on the home of the Reformation, Germany. Here, we analyse
not just the debt of the German religious reformers such as Luther to
Renaissance humanism, but also the tensions between religious
reform and Renaissance values in the broader culture of the German
people. Chapter 1 is largely concerned with establishing the wider
context in which Luther's religious ideas developed, while Chapter 2
focuses on the way in which these ideas spread to the rest of the
German-speaking world. Throughout this discussion, Anne Laurence
points out not only the tension that existed between Protestant

reformers and fellow humanists – epitomized by the growing rift between Luther and Erasmus – but also that characterizing the debate in Catholic circles between moderates and conservatives which ultimately gave birth to the Counter-, or Catholic, Reformation. In Chapter 3 we conclude our study of the German Reformation by looking at the impact of reform on religious ritual and the musical and visual culture of Germany in the sixteenth century.

In Chapter 4 we shift the focus of our attention to post-Reformation Spain. Through a case study of one of the most popular texts in Spanish literature of this period, *Lazarillo de Tormes*, Keith Whitlock explores the debt of this vernacular, picaresque 'novel' to themes encountered in Chapters 1 and 2, namely humanism and the cause of religious reform in Catholic Spain. The example of Spain is particularly apposite given the bad press that, starting with Burckhardt, has characterized so much of the response of northern European and Protestant scholars to sixteenth-century Spain. Indeed, as Whitlock shows, the origins of Burckhardt's xenophobic reaction to the Spanish and his depiction of them as cultural barbarians owes much to the popular adaptation of humanist-inspired works such as *Lazarillo* by contemporary Protestant translators.

In Chapters 5–6 we encounter what many have seen as the other great challenge to traditional authority in this period, the beginnings of a new approach to science and the natural world that would ultimately lead to a new epoch in the history of the west, the age of the scientific revolution. Whereas traditional approaches to this subject have tended to portray scientific activity and belief in the sixteenth century as either rooted in an erroneous, classical past or enslaved to the dictates of the clergy, in Chapter 5 Peter Elmer tries to show how both humanism and religion played a vital role in reshaping attitudes to the natural world. Some of the great figures of sixteenth- and early seventeenth-century science such as Vesalius and Galileo are here shown not as isolated geniuses in their respective fields of anatomy and astronomy but rather as men typical of their age whose scientific work was the product of the distinctive religious, political and learned cultures they inhabited.

In Chapter 6 this theme is extended to a discussion of a realm of early modern thought which has all too often been perceived as an aberration of Renaissance science, magic and witchcraft. Just as the early religious reformers shared the humanists' passion for a return to original sources, however, so too did Renaissance magicians and demonologists rely heavily on classical and ancient texts in order to justify the widespread belief in occult powers, magic and the existence of witches. This so-called 'dark side' of the Renaissance is one that has too often been marginalized in accounts of the Renaissance, but is foregrounded here, in the case study by Peter Elmer of Gianfrancesco Pico della Mirandola's *Strix* (*The Witch*), in order to provide a more complete 'picture of the age'.

In Chapter 7 Richard Brown develops our understanding of the Renaissance preoccupation with witchcraft and demonology by looking at how such ideas were interpreted in the popular drama of early seventeenth-century England in his study of *The Witch of Edmonton*. In this play, unlike Pico's learned dialogue, we hear perhaps for the first time the authentic voice of the witch, as well as the popular fears that informed witch trials and prosecutions in this period. The play is of course a late product of English Renaissance drama and might be said to mark the end of the impact of the Renaissance on this particular literary form in England. In terms of both its contemporary setting and its subject matter it is a far cry from the work of Shakespeare and Marlowe. Moreover, in terms of its collaborative authorship it also challenges a number of assumptions about the nature of a literary text and the role of the author in the late Renaissance.

If one were to try to choose a single figure who best exemplifies the great variety of response to the Renaissance in sixteenth-century Europe most scholars would probably opt for Michel de Montaigne. In his celebrated *Essays*, an analysis of which forms the core of Anthony Lentin's concluding chapter, the great French scholar applied his classical scholarship to many, if not most, of the great issues of the day, as well as to some which seem extraordinarily obscure by modern-day standards. A fascinating figure in every respect, Montaigne never ceases to entertain, even if his views on any given subject remain enigmatic and inconclusive. Self-consciously modelling himself on the great classical writers of the ancient past, he nonetheless achieved an originality of style and thought that belies any simple attempt to categorize him as a product of the Renaissance. He was, truly, both a man of his own age and one deeply indebted to the classical past. As such, the selective study of certain aspects of his *magnum opus* provides a fitting conclusion to this volume, raising as it does numerous questions on the fate of the Renaissance that continue to loom large in the work of modern-day scholars.

CHAPTER ONE

Renaissance and reform

BY ANNE LAURENCE

Objectives

When you have completed this chapter you should be able to:

- understand how the Renaissance reached Germany from Italy;
- appreciate the distinctively 'bookish' nature of the German Renaissance and its debt to humanism;
- understand how Martin Luther, under the influence of humanism, rejected the authority of the Roman Catholic church and, through his study of scripture, sought to develop a new approach to salvation;
- recognize how Luther's ideas were subsequently developed and altered by fellow reformers in the German-speaking lands;
- analyse the extent to which the Reformation in Germany constituted an acceptance or rejection of Renaissance values and ideas.

Introduction

> The culture of the North ... could not be a Renaissance in the sense of a rebirth of classical antiquity such as Italy experienced in the springtime following its cultural lag of two centuries behind the great achievements of medieval France, for the Germans were not Romans and did not have the artistic and architectural monuments, the learned notaries and *dictatores* [secretaries] who kept the memory of antiquity partly alive in even ordinary Italian minds. The culture of the North became rather a bookish culture more than a visual culture.
>
> (Spitz, 1975, p.372)

In the first three chapters of this book, we explore the concept of the Renaissance as it evolved in the German-speaking lands of central Europe. In particular, we shall focus attention on the thorny issue of the precise relationship between the Renaissance and that other great movement, the Protestant Reformation, which first took root in Germany in the early decades of the sixteenth century. Historians have long debated the nature of this relationship, some choosing to see the onset of religious reform as essentially antipathetic to Renaissance values, while others have preferred to envisage the two movements as largely continuous and mutually reinforcing. Here, we seek to illuminate this debate by looking at the contribution of humanism to the emergence of the Lutheran reform movement in Germany. The debt of Luther to humanist thinking is fully acknowledged, while at the same time we aim to contextualize the growth of a movement for reform within the church, by looking at the impact of Italian Renaissance values on an emerging German 'nationalism' with its own distinctive culture.

I have used the singular term 'Reformation' in preference to the more usual plural form, 'Reformations', because these three chapters are largely concerned with the process of Protestant reform that took place in Germany in the immediate aftermath of Martin Luther's dramatic renunciation of papal authority in 1517. It is arguable that there were further Protestant Reformations: that of Ulrich Zwingli in southern Germany and Switzerland in the 1520s; the '**Radical Reformation**' led by Thomas Müntzer and the Zwickau Prophets, which culminated in the **Anabaptist** rising in Münster in the 1530s; and that of the followers of John Calvin, whose message was to find a receptive audience throughout much of northern and eastern Europe in the second half of the sixteenth century. Moreover, in recent years, it has become common practice to include in the general term 'Reformations' the movement for reform in the Catholic church that culminated in the foundation by Ignatius Loyola (1491–1556) of the Society of Jesus, or Jesuits (1540), and the deliberations of the Council of Trent (1545–63) (see Chapter 2).

The growing tendency of historians to perceive much common ground between the various movements for Protestant and Catholic reform in sixteenth-century Europe largely reflects the decline of confessional history (that is, history written from the perspective of particular religious denominations) in academic circles. Reformation historians are keen to stress ways in which, despite obvious differences on doctrinal issues, the two great religious communities – Protestant and Catholic – shared a common concern with eradicating unbelief and superstition, promoting moral reform and raising educational standards among both the clergy and the laity. This new understanding is informed by a more sociological approach to the religion of this period, one that treats it as an integral element of the social, economic and cultural life of the time, as opposed to merely a reflection of contemporary theological and spiritual concerns.

Perhaps the most significant development in current historical studies of the Reformation and its relationship to the Renaissance is the sense in which scholars stress the interconnectedness of the two movements. The use of the commonplace phrase 'Renaissance and Reformation' to identify the period immediately succeeding the **Middle Ages** is a testament to this process. It was not always so, however. The founding father of Renaissance studies, Jacob Burckhardt (1818–97), not only ignored the various manifestations of the Renaissance outside Italy, but implicitly rejected the claims of those who sought to establish a connection between the values of Renaissance scholars and those of the German reformers. Although Burckhardt showed little concern for the process of religious reform in northern Europe – his interest in it was largely confined to the observation that the Reformation saved the institution of the papacy by forcing reform on the Catholic church (Burckhardt, 1990, p.294) – his cultural approach to the subject of religion and religious belief was certainly more in tune with modern approaches than those preferred by confessional historians. His remark that the 'relation of the various peoples of the earth to the supreme interests of life, to God, virtue and immortality, may be investigated up to a certain point, but can never be compared to one another with absolute strictness and certainty' (p.271) was a timely reminder not to apply nineteenth-century standards of censure to the morals of fifteenth-century Italy.

Exercise

Read Burckhardt, pp.271–306. This section is not an account of religious life in the Renaissance, but rather, in Burckhardt's own phrase, 'a string of marginal notes'. Consequently, we should not expect to find a coherent and well-documented history of religion, morality and spiritual authority. With this proviso in mind, what suggestions did Burckhardt make about the intersections between these three?

Discussion

Although Burckhardt referred to the general prevalence of irreligion in this period, it is clear from the first section (pp.272–3) that he was primarily interested in the morality of the humanists and in rebutting the criticism that they rendered themselves morally unfit. The subject of personal morality exercised Burckhardt considerably. Notice that he mentioned it in relation to politicians; to revenge and vendetta; to relations between the sexes; and to criminal violence.

He was insistent, however, that Italians were not individually culpable for their moral failings, which he was more inclined to see as the inescapable product of the age in which they lived. It is perhaps worth observing that such a view would seem to stand at variance with his deep-rooted attachment to the idea that the Renaissance saw the emergence of modern, individual man. Throughout this work, Burckhardt eagerly contrasted the communal, superstitious and excessively religious life of the Middle Ages with the secularity and freedom of the age of the Renaissance, as, for example, where he talked about the replacement of 'the Christian ideal of life' with that of 'the cult of historical greatness'. ❖

In raising such issues, Burckhardt was inevitably drawn into the question of the role played by Italians in voicing criticisms of the church in the period immediately prior to the Reformation. These, we are informed, never extended much further than opposition to the hierarchy of the Catholic church, which, with the friars, represented the greatest obstacle to the spread of what Burckhardt termed 'positive religious doctrines'. The question that is left largely unanswered is why the movement for spiritual reform in fifteenth-century Italy failed to achieve a reformation on the scale of that unleashed by Luther in Germany in the following century.

Reform before the Reformation

Burckhardt clearly saw the religious failings of the age in a much broader cultural context than we might expect of a church historian, a point accentuated by his later discussion of such issues as unbelief, paganism and magic. He also drew attention to the fact that the Roman Catholic church had frequently been subjected to orchestrated campaigns of criticism in the Middle Ages. On numerous occasions, would-be reformers had called for a return to the values of the early Christian or apostolic church, which many felt had been perverted by the accretions of later centuries. The establishment of two orders of friars, the Franciscans (1209) and the Dominicans (1220), represented one such moment of reform and temporarily checked the spread of heterodox movements that threatened to destroy the unity of the medieval church. By the late fourteenth and early fifteenth centuries, the growth of new 'heresies' – most notably the **Lollards** in England and the **Hussites** in **Bohemia** – was indicative of a new phase of religious discontent, which, to varying degrees, affected the peoples of Europe. Individuals and communities responded in a variety of ways, some seeking to inject new life into religious practices with the support of the ecclesiastical hierarchy, while others preferred to reject entirely the customs and beliefs of the medieval church.

One example of the former, cited by Burckhardt (1990, pp.301–6), was the charismatic preacher and Dominican friar, Girolamo Savonarola (1452–98), who was ultimately executed for preaching that the French invasion of Italy in 1494 was a sign of divine displeasure and a necessary prelude to the spiritual revival of the church. For a brief period, Savonarola gained the support of the ruling powers in Florence, who eagerly listened to his damning sermons advocating repentance and moral renewal:

> We must struggle against the evil ... which the lukewarm commit today and which those commit who know they are doing evil and want to do it ... I say to you that if Christ were to return down here again, he would again be crucified.

(Anthology, no. 57, p.286)

Savonarola was only one of a number of dissatisfied clerics who, from the fifteenth century onward, were concerned with the wickedness of the age and sought a return to a purer church and more virtuous society. Savonarola's particular reform proposals relied upon inspiring personal discipline through a strict regime of spiritual self-examination (see Anthology, no. 57). This was a more interior and individualistic form of religious practice than that envisaged by earlier reformers, one that owed something to the **late medieval revival of mysticism**. In time, elements of such practices would be integrated into the reformed Catholic church, most notably in the introspective and meditative practices proposed by the founder of the Jesuits, Ignatius Loyola, in his *Spiritual Exercises* (1548).

Ideas about personal moral and religious reform were not confined, however, to individuals. They also gave rise to communities of like-minded men and women, both lay and clerical. In the fourteenth century, the intellectual movement known as *Devotio Moderna* (*The Modern Devotion*), which originated in the Netherlands, stressed meditation, prayer and practical virtue, as well as mysticism. Adherents went on to found the Brethren of the Common Life, in an attempt to bridge the gap between secular and monastic ways of life. Members were encouraged to read the Bible in the vernacular and tended to be hostile to **scholasticism**, although they possessed no distinctive theology of their own. Perhaps the most significant aspect of the work of such groups was their desire to share more fully in the religious life of their respective communities, a process that we can also see at work in the growing popularity of lay **confraternities** in the towns and cities of fifteenth-century Europe.

These religious societies were particularly prominent in Italy. To take one example, in 1497 a prominent Genoese layman, Ettore Vernazza, founded the Genoese Oratory of Divine Love, a confraternity of devout laymen who subscribed to the idea of personal spiritual self-examination and renewal, which they hoped to achieve in part by the performance of pastoral work and acts of charity in their native city.

The Introduction to the Oratory's Rule sets out its main priorities (see Anthology, no. 58). It also urged strict secrecy and a rigorous programme of religious observance, with frequent confession and communion. In the early sixteenth century, a similar institution, the Roman Oratory of Divine Love, was founded in Rome, where it attracted the support of a number of powerful laymen and senior clerics. Although its work was halted by the **Sack of Rome** in 1527, when many of its members fled to Venice, it nonetheless played a crucial role in encouraging the Catholic church to adopt a more reformist role in the wake of the Lutheran Reformation.

Alongside a growing desire in late medieval European society for moral and spiritual renewal, there arose widespread criticism of the institution of the church. Particular complaint was reserved for the personnel of the church. The quality and performance of the clergy at every level, from parish priest to pope, was the subject of much debate. Clerics and monks were frequently mocked for their ignorance and avarice, while senior clergymen, including popes, were accused of a series of practices ranging from **simony** and **non-residence** to financial corruption and **nepotism**. How far such practices amounted to a popular rejection of the church on the eve of the Reformation, however, is open to question. Whereas in the past it was automatically assumed that the picture of spiritual and moral bankruptcy painted by opponents of the church such as Savonarola and Luther was widely shared by the population at large, recent studies have sought to demonstrate the continuing vitality of religious life at the local level (see, for example, Duffy, 1992). The evidence of such research reminds us, perhaps, that we should look more carefully at the motives of some of those who supported opposition to the established church in the years prior to the Reformation. Secular rulers, for example, who increasingly aspired to control lucrative ecclesiastical appointments, taxes and property in their realms, were eager to challenge claims of papal supremacy in such issues. One by-product of this mood of anti-papalism among the burgeoning nation-states of late medieval Europe was a growth in support for the theory of **conciliarism**. Conciliarists asserted that the power of the papacy was in fact subordinate to the authority of church councils – a convenient argument that secular rulers were able to invoke whenever they felt obliged to challenge the authority of papal interference in the internal affairs of their principalities.

For much of the late fourteenth and early fifteenth centuries, the institution of the papacy was largely powerless to refute such claims, weak and divided as it was by the **Great Schism**. However, by the early sixteenth century, the financial and political position of the papacy was much improved and encouraged successive popes to reassert earlier notions of papal supremacy. In 1512, riled by the attempt of the French king, Louis XII (1498–1515), to call a rival church council at Pisa, Pope Julius II (1503–13) responded to the conciliarists by convoking an alternative council in Rome, the Fifth Lateran Council (Figure 1.1). This body, which deliberated intermittently for the next five years, provided a rare opportunity for various critics of the papacy to voice their concerns about the current state of the church. The Council opened with an address from one of the most influential churchmen of the age, the prior general of the Augustinian friars, Giles of Viterbo (1469–1532).

Figure 1.1 Depiction of the eighth session of the Fifth Lateran Council, 1513, from I.B. De Gargiis, *Oratio in octava sessione Lateranensis Concilii ...*, Rome, Marcelo Silber, n.d. Reproduced in Minnich, N.H. (1993) *The Fifth Lateran Council (1512–17): Studies on its Membership, Diplomacy and Proposals for Reform*, Aldershot, Ashgate Publishing Ltd, frontispiece. Reproduced with permission of the author and publisher

Read the extract from Giles of Viterbo's opening address to the Fifth Lateran Council in 1512 (Anthology, no. 59). What kinds of reform did it imply were necessary for the future well-being of the church?

At the start of his address, Giles insinuated support for a programme of spiritual renewal similar to that advocated by Savonarola, as, for example, in his use of the crucial phrase 'men must be changed by religion, not religion by men'. Giles acknowledged the prevalence of ambition, greed, licence, contempt for the sacraments and irreligion in the contemporary church. He also indicated a willingness to engage in practical reform, as evidenced by his call 'to root out vice, to arouse virtue, to catch the foxes who ... destroy the holy vineyard'. Despite the fact that he was a close associate of Pope Julius II, Giles continually asserted the usefulness of councils in ensuring that the church did not deviate from a true Christian path: 'as no living thing can long survive without nourishment ... so man's soul and the Church cannot perform well without the attention of Councils'. ❖

We might also note in passing Giles's reference to contemporary divisions in the church, an allusion to the conflict between the pope and Louis XII of France (occasioned in the first instance by Louis's reaffirmation of the Pragmatic Sanction of Bourges in 1499, which established the principle of the semi-autonomous nature of the French church).

Giles was one of the most celebrated preachers of his time and this address was said to have moved many present to tears. The language he employed is particularly interesting given his reputation as a linguist and humanist scholar. In many respects it seems more indebted to mystical strains of Christian thinking than it does to Giles's training in conventional theology and humanist literature. His reference to the church as the bride of Christ is particularly telling. Elsewhere in the work he employs the Canticles, or Song of Solomon, a text widely cited by mystics in this period.

Giles, however, was no radical. Despite his undoubted learning (he was also an accomplished Hebraist, well versed in the occult lore of the Jewish **Cabala**), he eagerly defended religious faith from the assaults of the philosophers and upheld the authority of the pope against the arms of foreign princes. Significantly, his speech is peppered with military allusions, some of which may have been metaphorical ('our weapons ... are piety, devotion'), while others were probably intended to remind his audience of the threat posed to Italy by the recent defeat of the papal forces by the French at the battle of Ravenna. Moreover, as a friend and supporter of Julius II, he applauded the political aspirations of the papacy and praised the pope for rebuilding St Peter's, 'the most magnificent temple of the Lord ever seen by man'.

Despite Giles's call for the institution of a programme of moral reform in Christendom, the proceedings of the Fifth Lateran Council were largely taken up with more mundane business relating to institutional affairs. Pope Julius II was nonetheless on the defensive, and he feared that he would be held to account for his failure to implement the reforms that, before his election to the papacy, he had promised to undertake. Julius's awareness of the need to address such issues is evident in his opening speech to the Council in which he stated:

> Not only has the ecclesiastical discipline turned from its proper course, but every institution of human life has collapsed and a great upheaval of morals has occurred in every age group and social class. This being the case, we are able to hope that we will return, through this holy synod legitimately gathered in the Holy Spirit, to the norm, and from harmful ways to the rule. Evil customs will be eradicated, good ones planted, the seedlings of virtue will prevail, and the field of the Lord, having been cleansed of thorns and weeds, will produce richer fruit in proportion to the care and greater diligence spent in its cultivation.

> (Minnich, 1993, p.166)

Julius concluded by urging the Council to 'weed out completely the thorns and brambles from the field of the Lord; to lead morals back to a better state of virtue, and finally to decree an expedition against the enemies of the faith who are at variance among themselves' (Minnich, 1993, p.164). The Council sat until 1517, during which time it recognized the need for institutional reform in the church, while at the same time affirming papal authority. A gesture was made in the direction of more practical reforms in the decree of the Council that:

> No clerics ... shall be admitted to exercise that office [of preaching] unless they have first been carefully examined by their respective superiors and found competent and fit as regards morals and integrity, age, knowledge, uprightness, prudence and exemplariness of life ...

> We command all who are engaged in this work and who will be so engaged in the future that they preach and explain the truth of the Gospel and the Holy Scripture in accordance with the teaching of the doctors of the church.

> (Hillerbrand, 1964, p.423)

The initial phase of Catholic reform, in reaction to the same impulses and abuses that inspired Martin Luther, culminated in the decision of Pope Paul III (1534–49) to convene a commission to consider reform of the church, not just in the spirit of moral renewal but partly in response to the specific threat posed by the new heresy, Protestantism. The commission published its conclusions in 1537 as ***Consilium ... de emendanda ecclesia*** (*The Report ... for the Reform of the Church*) (Figure 1.2), a more comprehensive and radical programme than that recommended

CONSILIVM

DELECTORVM CARDI-
NALIVM ET ALIORVM
PRÆLATORVM,

De emendanda Ecclesia, S. D. N. D. PAVLO III. ipso iubente, conscriptum & exhibitum, Anno. 1538.

BEATISSIME pater, tantum abest vt verbis explicare possimus, cp magnas gratias Respub. Christiana Deo Opt. Max. agere debeat, cp te Pontificem hisce temporibus ac pastorem gregi suo præfecerit, eamcp qua habes mente dederit: vt minimè speremus, cogitatione eas quas Deo gratias debet, consequi posse. nam spiritus ille Dei, quo virtus cælorũ firmata est, vt ait Propheta, *Psal. 32. b* labantem, imò ferè collapsam, in præceps Ecclesiam Christi per te restaurare, & huic ruinæ manum, vt videmus, supponere decreuit. eamcp erigere ad pristinam sublimitatem, decoricp pristino restituere, certissimam diuinæ huius sententiæ coniecturam nos facere valemus, quibus sanctitas tua ad se vocatis mandauit, vt nullius aut commodi tui, aut cuiuspiam alterius habita rõne, tibi significaremus abusus illos, grauissimos videlicet morbos, quibus iampridem Ecclesia Dei laborat, ac præsertim hæc Romana curia, quibus effectum propè est, vt paulatim ac sensim ingrauescentibus pestiferis his morbis magnam hanc ruinam traxerit quam videmus. Et qm̃ sanctitas tua spiritu Dei erudita, qui (vt inquit Augustinus) loquitur in cordibus nullo verborum strepitu, probè nouerat, principium horum malorum inde fuisse, cp nulli Pontifices tui predecessores prurientes auribus, vt inquit apost. Paulus, coaceruauerunt sibi magistros ad desideria *2. Timo. 4.* sua non vt ab eis discerent, quid facere deberent, sed vt eorũ studio & caliditate inueniretur ratio, qua liceret id quod liberet. Inde effectum est, præterquàm cp principatum omnem sequitur adulatio, vt vmbra corpus, difficilimuscp semper fuit aditus veritatis ad aures principũ, cp confestim prodirent Doctores, qui docerent Pontificem esse dñm beneficiorum omnium: ac ideo cum dñs iure vendat id, quod suum est, necessario sequi, in Pontificem non posse cadere simoniam, ita cp voluntas Pontificis, qualiscuncp ea fuerit, sit regula qua eius operationes & actiones dirigantur: ex quo proculdubio effici, vt quicquid libeat, id etiã liceat. Ex hoc fonte, sancte pater, tancp ex equo Troiano, irrupere in Ecclesiam Dei tot abusus & tam grauissimi morbi, quibus nunc conspicimus eam ad desperatione ferè salutis laborasse, & manasse harum rerum famam ad infideles vscp. Credat sanctitas vestra scientibus, qui ob hanc præcipuè causam, Christianam religionem derident, adeò, vt per nos, per nos, inquimus, nomen *Rom. 2.* Christi blasphemetur inter gétes. Tu verò sanctissime pater, & verè san-

A

by the members of the Fifth Lateran Council (see Anthology, no. 60). The authors of the report (several of them members of the Roman Oratory of Divine Love) placed great emphasis on the need for the papacy to set an example to the rest of Christendom: 'For how can this Holy See set straight and correct the abuses of others, if abuses are tolerated in its own principal members?' (Anthology, no. 60, p.294).

Significantly, the report also touched on the subject of the 'great and dangerous abuse in the public schools, especially in Italy, where many professors of philosophy teach ungodly things' (Olin, 1969, p.194), a reference to the growing disquiet in Catholic circles relating to the impact of learning on orthodoxy. This was not simply motivated by the fear of Protestantism. Among the various recommendations of the report was that princes should be instructed to control the printing of books in their territories and that works such as the *Colloquies* by the influential Dutch humanist scholar, Desiderius Erasmus (*c.*1466–1536), should be banned.

Humanism and reform

In condemning Erasmus in the period after the Protestant Reformation, the Catholic church was promoting 'conservative' reform, in marked contrast to the encouragement that many leading clerics had afforded to the critical aims of earlier generations of humanist reformers. The role of humanism in preparing the ground for the Lutheran assault on the Catholic church is widely acknowledged today as a crucial factor in explaining the origins of the Reformation. Yet doubts remain as to the exact nature of the relationship between humanism and the Lutheran reform movement.

The most striking similarity between the two movements is evident in the way in which both advocated a return to original sources (*ad fontes*). The humanist desire to resurrect the wonders of ancient Greece and Rome through textual and linguistic study of original Greek and Latin manuscripts was closely paralleled by the reformers' desire to recreate the purity of the **apostolic church** by applying similar philological methods to the study of the New Testament. In the process, the work of scholars such as Erasmus, John Colet (1467–1519) and Jacques Lefèvre d'Etaples (*c.*1455–1536), all of whom applied the new humanist techniques to biblical scholarship, paved the way for the architects of Protestant reform. An important by-product of this process was a gradual shift in humanist circles away from a scholastic, or philosophically based, theology to a more 'pure' and practical one, based on a revised reading of the Bible and the early works of the **Church Fathers**. It is no coincidence that so many of the early reformers, Luther included, were enthusiastic proponents of linguistic studies, particularly Hebrew and Greek, which provided the key to unlocking the mysteries of divine revelation. Nor is it surprising that both humanists and reformers shared a common concern for promoting the virtues of education and seeking to widen access to the new learning. Education and piety were widely perceived as complementary rather than contradictory in this period.

Despite the fact that humanists and would-be reformers of the church shared much in common, historians have raised a number of concerns about the precise nature of the relationship between the two. In the first place, there would appear to be little consensus as to what is meant by the term 'humanism', given the wide variety of beliefs that so-called humanist scholars studied and promoted. Erasmus was not a 'typical humanist', because no such entity existed. Humanists came in many different hues and colours. Some specialized in the application of humanist techniques to the study of history and the natural sciences, while others were attracted to the rediscovery of ancient texts, the content of which frequently aroused the censure of the clerical authorities (see, for example, the discussion of hermeticism in Chapter 6). The lack of any discernible organization simply compounds the problem of attempting to identify any clear set of principles or practices that might be labelled as definitively 'humanist'. The term itself, we ought to remind ourselves, was a product of the nineteenth century and was not used by contemporary scholars in order to define their intellectual researches. Under the circumstances, we should not be too surprised to learn that scholars such as Paul Oskar Kristeller, writing in the 1960s and 1970s, have warned against too clear a demarcation between the 'progressive' concerns of humanists on the one hand, and the stultifying influence of scholastics on the other. Individual writers, Luther included, rarely displayed ideological purity in their choice of scholarly sources and methods – a timely reminder of the dangers implicit in imposing anachronistic categories upon the intellectuals of the past.

?

Two further problems arise with respect to the school of thought that presupposes a close causal connection between humanism and Lutheran reform. First, if it is true that humanist learning and methods equipped men with a new-found critical ability to question truths that had hitherto been regarded as sacrosanct, why did so many humanists ignore or reject the claims of the reformers? Erasmus's eventual repudiation of Luther was not an isolated instance of this trend, but was symptomatic of the response of many European humanists, who remained steadfastly loyal to Rome in the years after 1517. And secondly, how should we account for the relative failure of the Lutheran reform movement to make inroads into Italy, the home of Renaissance humanism, in contrast to its much greater success in the lands of northern Europe? Why was Germany the home of the Protestant Reformation? And are scholars correct in arguing that the Lutheran Reformation represented the 'Renaissance of the north'? In order to answer these questions, we need to focus our attention on the intellectual and religious situation in Germany, beginning with an examination of the reception of humanism in this part of Europe prior to 1517.

Humanism in pre-Reformation Germany

The debate surrounding the precise relationship between humanism and religious reform in Germany must include reference to the problematic nature of the term 'Germany' as used in the sixteenth century. Despite the fact that Germany, like Italy, did not acquire the status of a nation-state until the end of the nineteenth century, commentators in the sixteenth century nonetheless frequently invoked the phrase 'German nation' or 'German people' in a wide variety of contexts. What did they mean in so doing? Perhaps the first point to stress is that the existence of 'Germany' was largely defined by linguistic rather than political boundaries. When humanists such as Conrad Celtis (see below) called for the reform of German customs and culture, they were largely referring to those inhabitants of central Europe who shared a common heritage by virtue of their use of one of the many dialects of the German language. By this definition, Renaissance Germany was far larger than its modern counterpart, even after re-unification in the twentieth century, including, as it did, parts of the Low Countries, modern France and Switzerland, Bohemia and Luxemburg. Both at the time and since, commentators and historians have commonly equated the German-speaking lands with those ruled by the Holy Roman emperors (see Figure 1.3 overleaf). From the second half of the fifteenth century onwards, this meant, in effect, that embryonic notions of German nationhood were, more often than not, focused on the authority of the imperial dynasty of the Hapsburgs, whose feudal base lay in German-speaking Austria. It is perhaps unsurprising, then, that when humanists sought the reinvigoration of German letters and culture in this period, they frequently did so by appealing to the authority and example of the emperor, who they saw as the embodiment of the German people.

In reality, the ability of the emperor to provide anything other than the most superficial gloss to the aspirations of this nascent nationalism was severely circumscribed. Not only was the actual authority of the Hapsburgs limited by the constitutional and geographical complexities of the empire (it consisted of a vast

Figure 1.3 Map of the Holy Roman empire in 1519. Photo: from Hay, D. (1986) *The Age of the Renaissance*, London, Guild Publishing, p.142. Reproduced by permission of the publisher

patchwork of tiny principalities and imperial free cities, many of which were effectively self-governing), but the dynasty also had to acknowledge the existence of large numbers of subjects whose cultural, linguistic and political identities were defined by something other than Germanness. In short, the Holy Roman empire and early modern Germany was a multi-national, multi-cultural and multi-ethnic entity – a pan-European rather than a national phenomenon, which defies the modern categorization of the nation-state.

There is little doubt that the ongoing debate as to the role and place of Germany in modern Europe – something that has exercised the minds of intellectuals and politicians ever since the nineteenth century and the foundation of modern Germany – has had a direct impact upon historians studying the reception of the Renaissance in early modern Germany. German historians inspired by the revival of German nationalism, for example, have tended to characterize German humanism as a home-grown movement, the product of factors specific to the cultural and spiritual milieu of northern Europe. (One by-product of this approach was an early attempt to locate the genesis of northern humanism in the teachings of the Brethren of the Common Life, a distinctively northern religious body.) In more recent years, however, and perhaps as a reflection of greater European unity, historians have emphasized the international and pan-European character of humanist scholarship – a line of thinking that would appear peculiarly apposite when applied to discussion of the reception of humanism in the German-speaking lands of central and northern Europe.

Today, there is a broad consensus that acknowledges the fact that humanism in Germany was largely indebted to the direct influence of Italy, which first became manifest in the middle of the fifteenth century (Overfield, 1992, p.103). Cultural contacts between Italy and Germany flowed naturally from the close economic, religious and educational ties that characterized relations between the two in the late medieval period. With very few exceptions, most of Germany's leading humanists spent some part of their career either travelling or studying in Italy. There was also traffic in the other direction. The celebrated Italian humanist, Enea Silvio Piccolomini (1405–64) (Pope Pius II from 1458), served as secretary in the imperial chancellery in Vienna in the 1440s, and he was followed by numerous lesser lights of Italian humanism in the decades that followed. From the 1450s onwards, German cultural life was transformed by these links, most notably in the universities, where humanism was unofficially encouraged by a host of scholars and teachers working outside of the traditional curriculum.

The role of the universities in disseminating humanist values in Germany has frequently been commented upon as one of the most distinctive features of German humanism, in contrast to the way in which the cause of humanism was more commonly propagated elsewhere in Europe through the patronage of princes or wealthy patricians (Overfield, 1992, p.104). In the case of Germany, this was largely the result of the limited resources of the emperor and the numerous secular and ecclesiastical lords who dominated the empire, compounded by the relative absence of a large urban patrician class comparable to that found in Italian cities such as Florence. The early flowering of humanism within the burgeoning university sector in Germany (the fifteenth century witnessed a rapid increase in the number of German students studying in native universities, as well as the establishment of many new institutions) was to prove significant in a number of ways. In the first place, it led to the introduction of the study of the humanities (*studia humanitatis*) to university teaching, even if instruction in subjects such as history, oratory and poetry was often conducted outside the formal curriculum. Secondly, it encouraged the writing and printing of basic primers and texts for use in the classroom – a process that undoubtedly helped to spread widely the knowledge of classical Greek and Latin authors. And thirdly, and perhaps most important of all, it forced many German scholars to reassess the role of scholastic learning in the traditional syllabus, particularly with respect to the teaching of the most important element in the curriculum, theology.

By the end of the fifteenth century, then, the ground was well and truly laid for the broad reception of humanism in German society and education. For it to succeed fully, however, it was essential to persuade the powers that be, both within the universities and outside, of the merits of a full-blown programme of reform that would transform the cultural and intellectual life of the German people.

Figure 1.4 Hans Burgkmaier the Elder, Memorial woodcut of Conrad Celtis, 1507, 21.7 x 14.3 cm. This 'death portrait', or *Sterbebild*, by the Augsburg artist, Hans Burgkmaier, was commissioned by Celtis a year before his death in 1507. Celtis's immortal aspirations are clearly focused on his published works, on which his hands are resting. The inscription above his head proclaims 'outcome crowns one's achievements' and is taken from Ovid, *Heroides* 2:85. Photo: Staatliche Graphische Sammlung, Munich

One of the most dedicated and articulate exponents of such a programme was the poet, playwright and scholar, Conrad Celtis (1459–1508). The son of a peasant, Celtis studied at various German universities, whence he embarked on an itinerant career as poet and scholar. In 1487, he was rewarded by the Emperor Frederick III (1440–93) with the title of poet laureate, the first to be so honoured, and shortly thereafter he set off on a tour of Italy, where he encountered at first hand the eloquence and classical erudition of Italian humanists. On his return to Germany, and provoked by the aloofness and feigned superiority of the Italian scholars he had met, Celtis determined to set the record straight. Single-handedly, he embarked on an ambitious attempt to sell the merits of classical learning to his fellow countrymen, in the belief that Germany was destined to become a second Rome. In 1492, Celtis was provided with the perfect opportunity to propagandize on behalf of the cause, when he was appointed to the chair of poetry and rhetoric at the University of Ingolstadt.

Exercise

Read the extract from Celtis's inaugural address to the students, masters and local dignitaries of the University of Ingolstadt in 1492 (Anthology, no. 61). To what extent was Celtis's reform programme indebted to the example of Italy and Italian humanism?

Discussion

Celtis's response to Italy and its revival of classical culture was highly ambivalent. On the one hand, he acknowledged the superiority of the Italians in their 'love and study of letters' (he hailed one of their number as the saviour of the ancient university of Prague). But on the other, he consistently exhorted his German audience to emulate the ancient Greeks and Romans, who, he thought, were alone worthy of the greatest respect. A further source of antagonism to Italy is suggested by Celtis's criticism of leading German clerics, many of whom, he said, had been corrupted by 'Italian luxury'.

On balance, it was Celtis's patriotism, or sense of Germanness, that determined his reaction to the revival of letters in his own day. He was confident that once the German people had thrown off the yoke of their barbaric past, they would supersede the deeds of the Italians. He believed that Germany's destiny was to assume the mantle of imperial splendour formerly held by the Romans, and that this fate was inevitable once Germany's rulers abandoned foreign customs and employed advisers well versed in true philosophy and the liberal arts. ❖

Regardless of Celtis's pronounced ambivalence toward Italy and Italian scholarship, there can be little doubt of his own personal debt to humanism, which first reached Germany from across the Alps in the second half of the fifteenth century. His speech is laced with oratorical devices that owe everything to the Italian revival of rhetoric, as, for example, where he ironically stresses his own inadequacy as a Latinist and a speaker in order to advertise to his audience the importance of classical learning and eloquence. Elsewhere in the address he argues 'what does it profit us to know many things ... if we are prevented from speaking of them with dignity, eloquence and gravity, and if we are not able to transmit our thoughts to posterity?' (Spitz, 1972, p.17). In the process, Celtis implies in typically humanist fashion that the medium is as important as the message.

Celtis's speech is also redolent of Italian fifteenth-century humanism in the way in which it incorporates a thoroughly secular philosophical outlook with regard to man and nature. The morality of pagan authors poses no apparent problems for Celtis, the Christian humanist. Of the ancient philosophers, poets and orators, Celtis says 'they alone have prescribed for us the way to live well and happily and have set before us Nature ... as an example and mirror of life to be imitated'. There is no sense here of any incompatibility between the secular and pagan nature of classical culture and the demands of contemporary Christianity, despite the growing anxiety exhibited by some churchmen on this issue. Celtis, like so many other humanists of his generation, remained a faithful son of the established church, regardless of his passion for classical learning. In common with others, he was also not averse to criticizing specific ecclesiastics and corrupt practices, which he generally attributed to the corrosive effect of papal interference in the affairs of the German church. In another part of the address, Celtis hints at the papacy's exploitation of the German people and the drain on the public purse as a result of papal taxes. He was, however, no radical – for example he condemned the Hussites' 'heresy'.

The fusion of anti-papal sentiment and German patriotism in the work of men like Celtis is perhaps one reason why, by the end of the fifteenth century, humanists were beginning to make inroads into the courts of German princes, in addition to their presence in the universities of the empire. Many German princes were only too eager to emulate the achievement of the rulers of France and England in gaining access to the wealth of the church through the appropriation of important powers of appointment and taxation. German humanism thus fused with broader 'national' concerns to create a climate of opinion that was broadly hostile to continuing papal interference in the affairs of the German church.

A further factor in this process was the growth of interest in governmental and administrative circles in the humanist advocacy of the study of Roman law. The revival of classical jurisprudence probably began in central Europe in the fourteenth century under the influence of Johann von Neumarkt (1310–80), chancellor to the Emperor Charles IV (1355–78) and a correspondent of the Italian poet and scholar, Francesco Petrarch (1304–74). It was further stimulated by the intellectual contacts that arose as a result of the great church councils held at Constance and Basle in the early fifteenth century. The most important stimulus to humanist studies in Roman law was provided by the Emperor Maximilian (1493–1519), who appointed humanist-trained civil servants and advisers at the imperial court. By the early sixteenth century, their presence had spread to many of the larger courts of the prince-bishops and princes and they were even to be found in the more prosperous cities of the empire. The humanist lawyer, Conrad Peutinger (1464–1547), for example, combined the role of town clerk in the city of Augsburg (a city, incidentally, that did not possess a university) with that of counsellor to the Emperor Maximilian. Likewise, another humanist, the lawyer and celebrated Hebraist, Johannes Reuchlin (1455–1522), occupied the post of chancellor to the duke of Württemberg.

Interest in the study of Roman law and antiquarian research such as that carried out by Peutinger frequently coalesced with another typically humanist preoccupation, the study of history. Celtis, for example, whose oration at Ingolstadt in 1492 was studded with references to the historic destiny of the German people as the inheritors of the Roman empire, produced in 1500 an important edition, with commentary, of *Germania*, a work by the Roman historian Tacitus (*c.*55–120), which had just such a theme. This was designed to provide further support for Celtis's thesis. Histories of this kind, not surprisingly, accorded well with the practical political goals of many German princes, including the emperor, who wished to demonstrate the historic 'independence' and sovereignty of the German people. The proliferation of humanist histories of ancient and medieval Germany in the early sixteenth century, and the widespread patronage of their authors at the courts of Germany's ruling class, was not, therefore, coincidental. Nor was the growth of anti-papalism within Germany at this time unrelated to these developments. Not only were humanists the most vocal and articulate exponents of anti-papal diatribes, but more often than not they received the protection of powerful lay rulers, whose interests were clearly best served by a diminution of papal authority in their lands. But was this sufficient to generate and sustain a schism within the church? In order to answer this question, we shall need to look more closely at the origins of religious discontent in Germany in the period immediately prior to Luther's dramatic arrival on the scene in 1517.

The prelude to reform

Luther was clearly not the first German to voice criticisms and anxieties about the state of the Roman Catholic church in his homeland. Earlier discontents are sporadically evident, as, for example, in the aftermath of the Hussite revolution in neighbouring Bohemia, and were only partially addressed by the Councils of Constance and Basle in the early fifteenth century. In 1457, Martin Mair, chancellor to the Archbishop of Mainz, wrote to the recently elevated Cardinal Piccolomini, enumerating just a few of the complaints being voiced in Germany against the Roman curia.

Exercise

Read Mair's letter to Cardinal Piccolomini (Anthology, no. 62) and consider the wider implications of his remarks for the Catholic church in Germany.

Discussion

After identifying a whole litany of abuses that the German people perceived the curia to have committed (not dissimilar from those later enumerated and satirized by Erasmus), Mair referred crucially to the growing discontent of the German princes, who were speaking of throwing off the yoke of papal rule in order to regain ancient freedoms. In practice, this would leave German princes free to collect lucrative ecclesiastical revenues and to make clerical appointments in their territories, duties hitherto reserved to Rome or its agents. The language of the letter is highly nationalistic and reminiscent of that later invoked by Celtis in his address to the University of Ingolstadt. ❖

In traditional accounts of the origins of the German Reformation, documents such as this are frequently cited in order to demonstrate, implicitly at least, that there was an element of inevitability about the emergence of Protestantism in the sixteenth century. The role of Luther, routinely cast as the catalyst of reform, is discussed in the context of a series of long-term factors or preconditions (humanist criticisms of the church; anti-papal sentiments of the German nobility; popular **anti-clericalism** and opposition to a broad selection of clerical abuses including simony, non-residence and nepotism) which, taken together, proved irresistible. In recent years, however, new approaches to a number of these issues have suggested a very different picture of the state of the German (and European) church on the eve of the Reformation.

One of the more interesting and controversial aspects of this revisionism has been the increasing tendency of religious historians to suggest that, far from being irredeemably corrupt and unpopular, the pre-Reformation church was, in fact, in remarkably good health. In order to illustrate the point, numerous studies have pointed to the growth of lay involvement in the day-to-day affairs of the church, evident, for example, in the continuing popularity of pilgrimages and the establishment of confraternities devoted to the veneration of particular saints, the Virgin Mary, the **Sacred Host** or the **Rosary**. Shrines to the bleeding host were particularly popular in Germany and spawned important tourist industries in major centres such as Wilsnack (Muir, 1997, p.165). Even the monastic orders may not have been as indigent and unpopular as some contemporary, but many more recent, commentators have suggested. The Dominican, Jacob Sprenger (*c.*1436–95), for example, known more today as co-author of one of the most important demonological manuals of the period, the *Malleus maleficarum* (*The Hammer of Witches*, 1486), founded the brotherhood of the Rosary in Cologne in 1475. There may even have been a link between his promotion of popular piety and his work as an **Inquisitor** and witch hunter; witch-hunting was, after all, an activity that usually depended on the cooperation of large sections of the community (for witch-hunting and the *Malleus*, see Chapter 6).

Further evidence for the essential vitality of popular religion and lay participation in the affairs of the late medieval church can be found in the increase of lay endowments, either for masses for the dead in purpose-built chantry chapels, or for the appointment of new preachers. Moreover, the state of the clergy on the eve of the Reformation does not appear to be as bad as that suggested by some of its critics. For example, the proportion of priests in southern Germany who had attended university prior to ordination was around 50 per cent – a fair accomplishment in an age in which a university degree was not considered an indispensable qualification for membership of the priesthood. It is, nonetheless, the case that enthusiastic lay piety was not matched by a comparable movement of spiritual renewal among the clergy. The impact of late medieval mysticism, which had reinvigorated some of the religious orders, was on the wane by the end of the fifteenth century. Most monastic foundations seem to have been entering a period of stagnation rather than revival. An exception was the German branch of the order of Augustinian friars or hermits, which underwent reform around 1500, five years prior to the arrival of Luther.

Luther

Martin Luther (1483–1546), the son of a well-to-do copper miner, was born in the town of Eisleben. His family moved to Mansfeld shortly after Martin's birth, and he had a traditional education in the fundamentals of grammar, logic and rhetoric in his home town, before entering the school of the Brethren of the Common Life at Magdeburg in 1497. The Brethren, as a branch of the *Devotio Moderna*, possessed a reputation for educational innovation, and Luther was introduced to modern teaching methods, as well as to the lay order's aim of placing learning in the service of piety. However, the suggestion, once popular among Luther scholars, that the mature reformer owed much to the teachings of the Brethren is now largely discredited. The fact that Erasmus, too, was taught by the Brethren undoubtedly encouraged the suggestion of a link between reform and the order. Luther spent just one year under the instruction of the Brethren, and in later life rarely mentioned this brief phase in his educational development.

At the age of fourteen, Luther moved to Eisenach in Thuringian Saxony, where he spent the next four years preparing for entry to university. In 1501, he entered the University of Erfurt and studied the traditional curriculum based largely on the works of the Greek philosopher, Aristotle (384–322 BCE). Erfurt was no educational backwater. As one of the oldest and largest universities in Germany (it was founded in 1392), it had a good reputation as an innovative centre for the study of the liberal arts. It was here that Luther first encountered two of the most important influences upon his later thinking: humanism and **nominalism** (see below). In 1505, after his graduation as a Master of Arts, Luther resolved to remain in Erfurt to study for a higher, professional degree. Following his father's advice, he initially chose the law, in preference to either theology or medicine. Shortly after commencing his studies, however, he made the momentous decision to join the order of the Augustinian friars in Erfurt, a choice that he later claimed was dictated by a vow to St Anne, which he had taken during a thunderstorm.

Luther spent the next six years of his life teaching at the university and studying for a doctoral degree in theology. As well as pursuing his academic interests, he was involved intermittently during this period in the performance of a variety of duties on behalf of his order. In 1507, for example, he was ordained and began to preach regularly in Erfurt, and in 1508 he was dispatched to Wittenberg for a year in order to bolster the teaching of the theology faculty at the university there, which had recently been founded by Frederick the Wise, Elector of Saxony (1463–1525). In October 1511, he returned to Wittenberg, where he finally graduated as a Doctor of Theology, continuing his career as a university professor and preacher. Between 1513 and 1516, he lectured on the Psalms and Paul's Epistle to the Romans, and it was during this period that he began to formulate serious objections to various practices and beliefs in the church.

In Catholic doctrine, confession and the demonstration of contrition for sins required the performance of penitential acts in order to absolve the individual from the effects of those sins. True repentance mitigated the impact of sin upon the Christian, offering relief to the soul on its journey through purgatory to heaven. (Purgatory is held to be the state of suffering to which the souls of the dead who have failed to expiate all their sins are subjected.) In the early church, confession and penance had taken place in public. By the fifteenth century, however, they could be carried out in private and this consequently afforded plentiful opportunities for abuse. Penances, such as pilgrimages and visits to holy shrines, were increasingly commuted into payments of money. Out of such practices, a system of credits or 'indulgences' arose, which allowed the purchaser of the credits to earn merit in advance of the commission of sins, a practice that was not often accompanied by evidence of genuine contrition. For a number of years, Luther had expressed reservations about these and related practices, particularly as they impacted on one of the most important aspects of Christian theology, namely the source of man's salvation.

The circumstances that precipitated Luther into open conflict with the church were ostensibly concerned with the issue of the sale of indulgences. Although this was not a new practice in Germany, it was attaining notoriety in the vicinity of Wittenberg at this time due to the activities of the Dominican, Johann Tetzel (d.1519). Tetzel was preaching, among other things, that popes could remit the sin of guilt and that individuals could purchase remission for the sins of others who were held in purgatory. Tetzel himself was merely the agent of higher authorities, in this case his archbishop, Cardinal Albrecht of Mainz. Cardinal Albrecht was an ambitious and aristocratic young man, who had borrowed money to pay the papacy for allowing him to hold more than one office. He planned to use money from the sale of indulgences promoted by Tetzel to pay off his debt.

Luther was concerned to expose this fraud, but this did not stem from a personal vendetta, nor was it prompted by recent misgivings on the subject of indulgences. On the contrary, Luther had for a number of years, like many of his contemporaries, wrestled with the wider issues raised by the sale of indulgences. At this stage, though, Luther was still in the process of formulating his objections to such practices in the light of his intensive study of the scriptures and the early Church Fathers. He decided to seek an opportunity to debate these and related issues by nailing 95 'theses' to the door of the church in Wittenberg, which he did on 31 October 1517. This was not a premeditated attempt to reject centuries of orthodox teaching on the subject of salvation. Even the manner of his challenge was entirely in keeping with local tradition (notices of academic disputations were customarily posted in this way) and posed no immediate threat to the peace of the church. Two factors transformed this local dispute in a remote part of Christian Europe into a movement for universal reform. First, the sheer speed with which the news of Luther's stand against indulgences spread through the empire was to prove crucial in escalating the crisis. Against Luther's wishes, the theses were translated from Latin into German and published at Nuremberg. Later editions, all dating from 1517, were printed with Luther's approval at Nuremberg, Leipzig and Basle. Soon Luther's stand against indulgences was the talk of Europe and could no longer be confined to the limited academic audience of a university debating chamber. And secondly, Luther's own response, one characterized by a steadfast refusal to recant any of the positions he outlined in the theses, determined that affairs would soon spiral out of control.

By early 1518, Luther was ordered by Rome to rescind his observations, a command that had the full support of the superior of his religious order, Johannes von Staupitz (c.1468–1524), who was keen, as Luther's mentor and friend, to avoid a heresy trial. Luther's refusal was predicated upon his growing conviction that the evidence of scripture rather than the authority of popes and theologians was the only sure guide in spiritual matters. In 1518, he twice defended his theological objections to indulgences – at Heidelberg before the German Augustinians and at Augsburg before the leading Dominican theologian, Cardinal Cajetan (1468–1534) (Figure 1.5 overleaf) – but he was now in a vulnerable position, as he faced the threat of excommunication and an imperial ban for his obduracy. That he was able to continue to defy both pope and emperor was largely due to a combination of political circumstances at this critical juncture in the crisis and, above all, to the support and protection that he received from Frederick the Wise, Elector of Saxony, the patron of the University of Wittenberg. Emboldened, perhaps, by the support of the elector and the growing groundswell of opinion in his favour throughout much of Germany, in 1519 Luther delivered a fierce denunciation of the authority of the papacy, in a debate with yet another theologian, Johannes Eck (1486–1543), at Leipzig. In the meantime, he became increasingly involved in the publication of tracts critical of various aspects of the doctrine and practices of the church.

In 1520, the papacy finally responded by issuing a **bull** threatening Luther's excommunication, *Exsurge domine* (*Arise, O Lord*), to which Luther and his supporters in Wittenberg replied by burning the offending document, along with various books of canon law. Now, under the threat of an imperial ban, Luther faced the prospect of becoming an outlaw in his own land. In April 1521, he was given a final opportunity to recant when he was provided with a safe pass to attend the **Diet of Worms** by the new emperor, Charles V. It was here that he made his most famous stand against the papacy by declaring:

> Unless I am convinced by the testimony of the scriptures or by clear reason (for I do not trust in pope or councils alone, since it is well known that they have often erred and contradicted themselves), I am bound by the scriptures I have quoted and my conscience is captive to the word of God. I cannot and I will not retract anything, since it is neither safe nor right to go against conscience. I cannot do otherwise, here I stand, may God help me, amen.
>
> (Spitz, 1985, p.75)

One month later, he was placed under imperial ban, an outlaw liable to summary execution.

Luther's original criticism of indulgences in 1517 had developed by 1521 into an all-out assault upon the very foundations of authority in the Roman Catholic church. During the intervening period, he began to write and publish a prolific number of pamphlets and treatises, in which he developed his condemnation of the corrupt practices of the clergy into a wholesale critique of the theological teachings of the church. His earlier misgivings with regard to Catholic teaching on the nature and origins of human salvation began to mature into a rejection of the idea that man was saved by 'good works', and this culminated in his elaboration of the doctrine of justification by faith alone (solefideism). Moreover, as it became increasingly evident that the breach with Rome was beyond repair, Luther began to lay the foundation for a new form of worship, in works such as *The Babylonian Captivity of the Church*, otherwise known as *The Pagan Servitude of the Church* (1520), in which he elaborated his opposition to the sacraments of the Catholic church (see Anthology, no. 72 and below). As we shall see, these various developments in Luther's thought were interconnected; his discussion of the sacraments, particularly the **eucharist**, was a necessary consequence of his wider view of the nature of salvation. The final outcome, in the words of one of the foremost scholars of the religious history of this period, was the creation of two distinct churches and ways of life, which were ultimately 'incommunicable to each other' (Bossy, 1985, p.127).

Luther is, then, rightly regarded today as the father of Protestantism. But there remain many questions surrounding the contribution of Luther to the process of reform and the source of his theological opposition to the traditional beliefs and practices of the medieval church. Recent generations of Reformation historians, for example,

Figure 1.5 Woodcut of the meeting between Cardinal Cajetan and Martin Luther in 1518. Photo: Staats- und Stadtbibliothek, Augsburg

have increasingly drawn our attention to the role played by social, economic and political factors in the reception and spread of Lutheranism. The perception of Luther as a 'reluctant revolutionary' has also gathered pace in recent years. Increasingly, Luther is depicted as a man who was in many respects temperamentally ill-suited to the role of leader of a reform movement. One aspect of this reappraisal of Luther, which has important consequences for our view of the Reformation, is the extent to which scholars today seek to emphasize the long and often tortuous route by which the scholar of Wittenberg arrived at his radical new approach to issues such as salvation and the scriptures. Increasingly, we are being made aware that Luther's journey to spiritual enlightenment encompassed a lengthy process of scholarly introspection – beginning perhaps as early as 1509 – which was informed by a range of intellectual currents then fashionable in northern Europe, including humanism.

The failure of earlier historians to recognize this important aspect of Luther's development as a theologian and would-be reformer may stem in part from the emphasis that he himself placed in his autobiographical writings on sudden impulses or moments of enlightenment. In 1545, the year before his death, Luther described one such moment when, in a sudden inspiration, he instantly understood the mysteries of the scriptures (in particular, the passage in Romans 1.17: 'the righteous shall live by faith') and so laid the foundation for his doctrine of justification by faith. This new-found conviction has been assigned to various dates ranging from 1513 to 1519. By focusing on such dramatic events, there has been a tendency to underestimate the extent to which Luther was indebted to a wide range of sources, which he had spent years studying in order to address his growing doubts as to the nature of salvation and the relationship of God to man.

Exercise

Read the autobiographical fragment in which Luther referred to his conversion experience in the monastery at Wittenberg, where he recalled the process by which he claimed to have arrived at a new conception of salvation (Anthology, no. 63). What evidence is there in this extract to suggest that Luther's theological progress was slow and indebted to a range of authorities?

Discussion

Luther made it clear from the outset that his study of the scriptures, particularly the Pauline epistles, had occupied much of his time and energy. He also referred disparagingly to his immersion in the teachings of 'all the doctors' – a reference that might allude to the writings of the early Church Fathers as well as to the scholastic theologians of the Middle Ages. Although Luther's journey to spiritual enlightenment was obviously a slow one, it was punctuated by moments of inspiration and insight (such as that described here). There is a strong sense that, as his journey progressed, he experienced the growing realization that the Word of God, as revealed in the scriptures, was the prime source of spiritual salvation. ❖

This was not, then, a conversion experience in the sense of a sudden revelation from God. The road to spiritual enlightenment had been long and hard for Luther, but by 1519 at the latest, as this document suggests, Lutheranism had acquired two of its most important and distinctive theological insights: justification by faith alone and the primacy of scripture (*sola scriptura*). In line with the view, implicit in his attack on indulgences, that men could do nothing by their own actions to guarantee the justifying (saving) grace of God, Luther advanced the belief that grace was a gift of God, freely bestowed on those with sufficient faith in Christ. The Catholic doctrine of justification by works – one predicated on the assumption that salvation might be earned by worthy actions or personal endeavour (for example, through prayer, confession, penance, receipt of the eucharist, or charitable works) – was thus redundant in Luther's eyes, opposed as it was to the Word of God as revealed in the scriptures. In reaching this position, Luther would seem to have moved outside the realm of academic discourse that he had inhabited for so much of his life. In truth, however, he owed much to the cut and thrust of academic debate and intellectual controversy that characterized his age, not least in his debt to humanism which, as we have seen, had taken deep root in Germany by the beginning of the sixteenth century.

Luther and humanism

Luther probably first encountered humanism during his period of study at the University of Erfurt (1501–5). Here, Luther was introduced to the humanists' love of letters and classical literature (the Roman writers Plautus (*c*.250–184 BCE) and Virgil (70–19 BCE) were two particular favourites whom he continued to quote for the rest of his life). He also began a life-long interest in the study of classical languages, which continued at Wittenberg, where he underwent training in Hebrew and Greek. A particularly strong influence was his close friend and collaborator at Wittenberg, Philipp Melanchthon. As professor of Greek at Wittenberg (he was appointed in 1518), Melanchthon, the grand-nephew of the lawyer and Hebraist, Reuchlin, taught Luther the rudiments of the Greek language. Although Luther does not appear to have been attached to a definite circle of humanist scholars at Erfurt, he was fully acquainted with the cultural reform programme of the humanists, including Erasmus's satirical critique of the church. One of his fellow students at Erfurt, Crotus Rubeanus (*c*.1480–1539), remembered Luther as a 'budding humanist' (Oberman, 1989, p.124). Luther, in turn, must have followed the progress of his former colleague with some interest. In 1519, Rubeanus, in collaboration with the Lutheran convert, Ulrich von Hutten (1488–1523), published a work purporting to defend the scholarly research of the humanist Reuchlin into the Jewish Cabala. However, this work, *Letters of Obscure Men*, was nothing less than a passionate defence of humanism against the obscurantism of the scholastics, and it has frequently been cited by scholars since as evidence of the incompatibility of the two.

Certainly, in the case of Luther and the reception and spread of his work and ideas, there is a great deal of evidence to suggest that humanism performed a vital role in securing wide support for his stance. In addition to his personal debt to humanist methods of textual analysis, particularly with respect to biblical study, Luther also owed much to the support that other German humanists offered in his struggle with the Catholic church, culminating in what Lewis W. Spitz has referred to as 'a happy conjunction of the humanist program and Luther's reform efforts':

NB

> From 1517 to 1521 the humanists in many cities were the chief propagandists and carriers of his cause ... [They] sincerely believed that their ideal was being realised openly: the rejection of Aristotle and scholasticism and their replacement by the Scriptures and early fathers ... The fact that both the humanists and the reformers were concerned with hermeneutics [the study of interpretation, especially of the Scriptures] made them partners in serious scholarly conversation ... Luther shared certain central positions with the humanists ... His assertion [in 1519] ... that 'All men are equal in humanity, which is of all the highest and most admirable equality, from which men possess all dignity' was an early expression of his affinity with humanism.

> (Spitz, 1985, pp.82–3)

But not everyone is content to ascribe Luther's success to the support that he gained from humanist colleagues in the universities of Germany. In recent years, a number of historians have sought to stress the point that humanism and scholasticism were not fundamentally opposed to each other in the minds of German academics (Overfield, 1984). In Erfurt itself, both seem to have happily co-existed in the arts faculty, where the humanist director of studies, Nicholas Marschalk (d.1525), recommended the Aristotelian textbooks of the scholastic philosopher, Jodocus Trutfetter (*c*.1460–1519). Trutfetter was a leading light of the late medieval philosophical movement known as nominalism or the *via moderna* (*modern way*), which some scholars have seen as playing a seminal role in the development of the radical theology of the young Luther. Put simply, nominalists, in opposition to their scholastic colleagues known as **realists**, denied the existence of universal concepts such as 'mankind' and argued instead that all philosophical speculation should be tested by reference to experience, regardless of what traditional authorities might prescribe. Theologians as well as philosophers were subject to the same criteria: theological speculation must be tested by scriptural authority. In the case of Luther, his early subscription to nominalist thinking is evident in the way in which it allowed him to place the evidence of divine revelation and the Word of God above that derived from human reason. And in time it led him to reject entirely the whole corpus of medieval scholasticism based on the revival of Aristotle (Oberman, 1989, pp.116–23).

A further complicating factor in attempting to unravel the puzzle of the intellectual origins of Luther's thought is posed by his apparent attraction to, and interest in, late medieval mysticism. Early in his career as a theologian and a preacher, Luther had come across a small work entitled *A German Theology* by an unnamed German mystic, which he published in 1518. It is notable that Luther's preface to this work provides some evidence of his ambivalence towards both humanism and scholasticism (see Anthology, no. 64). However, it would be wrong to infer that Luther wished to disparage all forms of human learning in the education of good Christians. Although his new theology ultimately led him to reject any virtue in scholasticism (see below), he remained throughout his life committed to the wider humanist programme of educational reform.

Exercise

Read Luther's letter to the humanist poet, Eobanus Hessus, written in 1523 and his pamphlet addressed to urban authorities throughout Germany in 1524 (Anthology, nos 65 and 66).

1   What were the main features of Luther's suggested programme of educational reform?

2   What reasons did he offer for the pursuit of humanist aims in scholarship?

Discussion

1   In the private letter, Luther commended literary studies, in particular poetry and rhetoric, without which, he thought, theology was unteachable. In order to prepare men to receive divine truths, he believed they must first acquire skill in languages. In the pamphlet, Luther went a stage further, by praising the virtues of the 'sacred' languages, Greek and Hebrew, while at the same time minimizing reliance upon study of the Church Fathers and the commentaries or 'glosses' of subsequent generations of theologians. In addition to languages, he promoted the virtues of a broad secular curriculum, including study of history, music and mathematics, which was to be extended to girls as well as boys.

2   Luther's vision of a humanist educational programme incorporated two main aims. First, to create godly and virtuous Christians through knowledge of languages and the scriptures. And secondly, to effect a reform of society itself through the inculcation of civic virtues. In ancient Rome, the study of the liberal arts, he noted, had formed 'intelligent, wise and

competent men', who had contributed to the general well-being of the commonwealth. In imitating this model, Luther was in effect arguing for a more practical, goal-oriented educational system, which would produce a more harmonious and better governed society. ❖

Although Luther was not a humanist in the strict sense of the term (he did not, for example, develop a polished Latin style in his published work), he was nonetheless a fierce and powerful advocate of humanist reform in Germany. As the head of the new evangelical movement, and with the support of Elector Frederick, Luther transformed the University of Wittenberg into a model institution, the humanist-inspired curriculum of which was rapidly imitated throughout Germany and beyond. New chairs in Greek and Hebrew were established, and far less emphasis was placed upon scholastic methodology, particularly in relation to the study of theology (Nauert, 1995, pp.132–6). One of the chief aims of these reforms was to produce educated clergymen, who were increasingly expected to expound and interpret the gospel to the laity. Skill in the biblical languages acquired through humanist literary techniques was thus important in this training. Equally important, however, was the humanist emphasis on rhetoric, an essential attribute for a clergyman whose prime function now lay in preaching the Word rather than performing the various rituals of the Catholic church. In one sense, then, the Lutheran Reformation was indisputably a product of the Renaissance. But the relationship between Renaissance and reform was not a simple one-way process. In appropriating humanist values, reformers like Luther effected an equally significant transformation in the fortunes of the Renaissance. Whereas, prior to Luther, humanism was perceived by men like Erasmus as an end in itself, henceforth it was viewed by the proponents of reform as primarily a means to an end – the revelation of the divine will. Consequently:

> The true driving force of the Reformation did not come from Renaissance humanism but from Luther's striking insight into what he and his followers regarded as the true inner spirit of Christianity.

(Nauert, 1995, p.163)

Luther and spiritual reform

Humanist learning could not, though, bridge the gap between God and humanity. As a human artefact, it could not invoke divine grace, nor could it replace the scriptures as a guide to salvation. The real work of revelation and conversion was performed by the Holy Spirit, rather than by reason and book-learning. The importance of Luther's insights into the nature of salvation lay in the fact that they implied a spiritual reform of the individual in addition to the institutional reform of society. For the sake of simplicity, I make a distinction here between spiritual and institutional reform. In reality, of course, the two were never separate and distinct categories. The role of the clergy as instruments of spiritual regeneration, for example, was dependent to a large extent upon their own training and preparation within institutions such as universities. A similar fusion of spiritual and institutional concerns is evident in the case of Luther's response to indulgences.

Exercise

Following the presentation of the 95 theses in 1517, Luther published an explanation of his objections to indulgences. Read Article 32 from Luther's *Explanations of the 95 Theses* (Anthology, no. 67). On the evidence of this brief extract, how did Luther perceive the issue of indulgences as (a) an institutional matter and (b) a spiritual matter?

Discussion

(a) Luther claimed (not always convincingly!) that he did not believe all the charges laid at the door of indulgence preachers, but he was patently critical of the way in which such men abused their authority and seduced poor and ignorant Christians. He clearly implied that the role of the preacher in selling indulgences was a violation of the true vocation of the priest.

(b) Luther stated that parchment and indulgences could never confer salvation, nor any of the other qualities required of a believer, such as contrition, faith and grace. In particular, he pointed to the spiritual ignorance of the general populace, who heard what they wished to hear and consequently misinterpreted the force and meaning of their preachers' words. ❖

In this extract it is already possible to detect the central tenet of Luther's emerging view of the nature of salvation and the relationship between God and man. If salvation is only attainable through the free gift of God's righteousness, then the performance of works, the purchase of indulgences included, is immaterial to the fate of the individual soul.

It was this issue – salvation by grace as opposed to salvation by works – that ultimately led to the public refutation of Luther by the most important figure in the Catholic reform movement, Erasmus. Prior to 1517, and as late as 1520, there remained much common ground between the two men. Both were committed to the general need for a wide-ranging institutional reform of the Catholic church, and no one had done more than Erasmus to bring this view before a European public. Luther, in turn, was a great admirer of Erasmus's writings and swiftly adopted his Greek New Testament (1516) in preparing lectures at Wittenberg. Yet there was also a tension between the two, exacerbated after 1517 by Luther's tendency to use outrageous invective in arguing with his detractors. In short, Erasmus was placed on the horns of a dilemma. On the one hand, he was utterly opposed to the corruptions and abuses of the church, although he remained committed to the ideal of a single, universal church. On the other, he feared that Luther's defeat at the hands of his enemies would in all probability mean the defeat of his own, more moderate programme of church reform.

Until 1524, an uneasy silence prevailed between Luther and Erasmus. In that year, the deadlock was finally broken when Erasmus published *De libero arbitrio* (*On Free Will*), in which he objected to the implications of Luther's belief in salvation by grace on the grounds that it excluded the possibility of free choice. At the heart of Erasmus's objections to Lutheranism was his belief in the fundamental goodness of human nature and the capacity of man to play a role in his own salvation. Unlike Luther, who held that the performance of good works was symptomatic of man in the state of grace, Erasmus continued to affirm the traditional Catholic belief in the saving power of human actions and hence the necessity of free will. In 1525, Luther, who had until then been reluctant to commit himself on paper to a position that placed him at odds with Erasmus, finally replied in *De servo arbitrio* (*The Bondage of the Will*).

Exercise

Read the extract from Luther's reply to Erasmus (Anthology, no. 68). Comment on the sources that Luther cites in order to defend his belief in justification by faith alone.

Discussion

Luther's arguments are almost exclusively drawn from the New Testament, and in particular the works of St Paul (although he does allude in later chapters to the work of other evangelists). These prove beyond doubt for Luther that no man, no matter how proficient in good works (he begins with the example of Abraham), can be saved or justified except by the free gift of divine grace. Even submission to the law (a reference to the rules received from God by Moses as recorded in the Old Testament) fails to secure God's grace (since the law exists to punish wrong-doing rather than to effect salvation). All men are innately corrupt and sinful as a result of the Original Sin of Adam. It follows that they are utterly incapable of securing salvation through their own efforts.

Apart from his disparaging comments on 'the authority and writings of the ancient doctors' (he later singles out the third-century father

Origen, a particular favourite of Erasmus, for censure), the emphasis of Luther's argument is firmly rooted in his own biblical studies. He also demonstrates a familiarity with the tools of literary humanism. His appreciation of Paul's use of repetition as a rhetorical device and his refutation of the suggestion that Paul was using a trope rather than speaking literally betray Luther's debt to humanism. ❖

On the basis of his close reading of scripture, then, Luther was left in no doubt as to the source of salvation: 'no works ... count for anything in the sight of God ... For if the man himself is not righteous, neither are his works'. Salvation could not be earned or bought, regardless of man's free will. The significant issue for Luther was not man's freedom, but that of God. The truly righteous live by faith alone and those without faith are predestined to eternal damnation.

Luther and institutional reform

Luther, as we have seen, closely identified the spiritual failings of the Catholic church with its institutional corruption. In *An Appeal to the Ruling Class of German Nationality*, published in 1520 (see Anthology, no. 69), he set out his objections to the venal practices of the papacy. Even though Luther's excommunication was not a foregone conclusion at this stage, it is apparent that Luther himself was moving toward a complete repudiation of all papal authority in the church. Shortly afterwards, the papacy published a list containing 41 objections to Luther's preaching against the church, which later formed the basis for the bull of excommunication issued in January 1521. Luther, in turn, replied with a series of *Defences*, in which he set out his reasons for repudiating the authority of the pope, who he dismissively referred to as 'the bishop of Rome'.

Exercise

Read Article 25 from Luther's *Defence ... of all the Articles ... which were unjustly condemned by the Roman Bull* (Anthology, no. 70). To what extent did Luther's criticisms of the papacy exceed those detailed in the report of the Fifth Lateran Council (1512–17) and the *Consilium ... de emendanda ecclesia* (1537) (see above and Anthology, no. 60).

Discussion

Luther challenged not just the extent of papal authority but the very existence of the pope in his capacity as vicar of Christ, arguing that there was no scriptural warrant for such an office: 'there is not one single letter which states that St. Peter is above all the churches in the world'. At one point, he claimed indifference toward the existence of the papacy, but this did not prevent him from publicizing its capacity to do harm in Christendom, a product of the fact that the pope and his followers lived 'without faith or the gospel and the sacraments' and 'do not obey God in a single letter'.

Luther's criticisms went well beyond those of earlier and later critics from within the Catholic church and raised the spectre of a Christendom divided into permanently warring camps. ❖

As the conflict between Luther and the pope reached its climax in 1521, it was becoming increasingly obvious to Luther and his supporters that some form of alternative church structure and worship was necessary to replace that of the unreformed church. Luther's use of the term 'priesthood of all believers' to describe those who withdrew from the auspices of the Roman church may at first beguile us into thinking that Luther himself preferred some form of ecclesiastical democracy. This was far from the case. In many respects, the Wittenberg theologian was a profoundly conservative thinker. His belief that all men possessed a responsibility to interpret the scriptural message for themselves was not intended to imply that he favoured an unlettered ministry. Quite the contrary. The rigour of his educational reform programme, much of which was aimed at reforming the training undertaken by would-be ministers, is sufficient testimony to this fact.

Luther's conception of what kind of a church might take the place of that in which he was reared was nonetheless poorly developed and he left the implementation of proposed changes to others. As a letter written in 1521 to his close friend and associate Melanchthon suggests, Luther experienced real difficulty in discerning what should and should not be allowed in the reformed church (see Anthology, no. 71). By 1521, a revised form of communion was in wide use, but it was not until 1523 that Luther issued a new Latin service, and there was no German text until 1526. In all of these matters, Luther was essentially cautious and conservative, the most radical changes taking place at the instigation of others. However, he could not escape the consequences of his theology of the sacraments, which was spelled out most emphatically in 1520 in *The Babylonian Captivity*. The seven sacraments of the Roman Catholic church were baptism, communion or eucharist, confirmation, marriage, extreme unction, penance and holy orders. Only two (baptism and communion) eventually survived in the newly constituted Lutheran church,[1] of which communion long remained the most problematic and contentious.

Exercise

Read the extract from Luther's *Babylonian Captivity* (Anthology, no. 72). What are the chief points of difference between Luther and Roman Catholics on the subject of the eucharist?

---

[1] Luther initially believed that penance should also be retained see below, page 41.

First, Luther insists that **communion in both kinds** (that is, both the bread and the wine) should be given to the laity as well as to those in holy orders. He can find no scriptural defence for restricting the administration of the wine solely to the latter.

Secondly, Luther rejects the Catholic doctrine of transubstantiation, that is, the belief that the bread and the wine are transformed into the actual body and blood of Christ. In its place, he argues for consubstantiation, suggesting that the body and blood of Christ are present with the bread and the wine, but that no alteration in the substance of the latter occurs during the communion service.

Thirdly, he argues that the mass is not a sacrifice, but rather a testament or promise made by God through Christ of man's future salvation. As a promise, access to its merits can only be gained through faith and not works: 'For where there is the Word of the promising God, there must necessarily be the faith of the accepting man.' ❖

These three points were not unique or original to Luther; earlier reform movements such as those of the Lollards and the Hussites had adopted similar views. They were, however, a fundamental feature of Luther's theology of the sacraments and had great bearing upon the creation of a Protestant church. Most importantly, the Lutheran minister no longer performed a sacrifice when administering communion, but instead offered the bread and the wine for blessing in a service intended to resemble Christ's Last Supper as closely as possible.

In *The Babylonian Captivity*, Luther set out a great many points of difference with the Roman Catholic church, although he demonstrated familiar indecision on a number of issues. On the question of the rites and ceremonies to be observed during the mass, Luther was characteristically ambivalent. Although he clearly favoured a simple ceremony, free of excessive pomp, colour and embellishment, he remained opposed to enforcing a specific liturgy on the communion service. Later generations of reformers were not so readily reassured on these points. On the potentially more contentious issue of the general significance of the mass, it was not until 1523, when he wrote *The Adoration of the Sacrament*, that he answered several criticisms arising from his earlier pronouncements. Luther was especially at pains to clarify his position with regard to the need to honour the sacrament. In this work, he again set out the view that, although the bread and the wine were never actually transformed into the body and blood of Christ, and should not therefore be worshipped, they should nonetheless be honoured, because Christ was physically present with them. As Luther willingly acknowledged on a number of occasions (see, for example, Anthology, no. 72), the subtlety of such an explanation might transcend Aristotle and the scholastics ('What does it matter if philosophy cannot fathom this? The Holy Spirit is greater than Aristotle', p.325), but it was perfectly comprehensible to those with sufficient faith. In order to prove the point, he needed only to refer to the figure of Christ Himself, who was both God and man at the same time:

> it is not necessary for human nature to be transubstantiated and the divine nature contained under the accidents of the human nature. Both natures are simply there in their entirety ... Even though philosophy cannot grasp this, faith grasps it nonetheless.

(Anthology, no. 72, p.325)

Figure 1.6 Albrecht Dürer, *Mass of St Gregory*, 1511. Dürer's engraving provides striking evidence for the way in which the Catholic mass invoked the physical presence of Christ in the transubstantiated eucharist. Photo: from Cameron, E. (ed.) (1999) *Early Modern Europe*, Oxford, Oxford University Press, p.85. Graphische Sammlung Albertina, Vienna

Figure 1.7 *Luther Holding Pope Leo X on a Wheel while Melanchthon Turns the Handle and Elector John Frederick Looks On*, oil on paper, 32.5 x 22.5 cm. Photo: from Kirmeier, J. *et al.* (eds) (1997) *... wider Laster und Sünde. Augsburg Weg in der Reformation. Katalog zur Ausstellung in St Anna, Augsburg 26 April bis 10 August 1997*, Augsburg and Köln, Haus der Bayerischen Geschichte and DuMont, p.152

The one man who, more than anyone else, was responsible for turning Luther's vision into a practical programme from which a service book, catechism, liturgy and coherent theology might evolve was Melanchthon.

Melanchthon

Philipp Melanchthon (1497–1560) was born in south-west Germany and educated at the universities of Heidelberg (1509–12) and Tübingen (1512–18). In 1518, partly at the instigation of Luther, he arrived in Wittenberg to occupy the chair of Greek at the university.

Figure 1.8 Hans Holbein, *Philipp Melanchthon*, n.d. Photo: Niedersachsisches Slandesmuseum, Landesgalerie, Hannover

Initially, his interests lay in the humanist study of ancient texts, particularly those of Aristotle, whom he wished to restore from the accretions and misunderstandings of medieval scholars. But he maintained throughout his life an unwavering commitment to a broad humanist programme of educational reform, which, in large part, was to act as a model for reformed communities throughout Europe during the course of the sixteenth century.

Exercise

Read Melanchthon's inaugural address to the University of Wittenberg in 1518 (Anthology, no. 73). Identify the chief features of Melanchthon's proposed programme of curricular reform.

Discussion

The key to Melanchthon's vision of an educational golden age is the revival of the 'literary sciences', in particular Greek and Hebrew, as well as 'true sciences' and philosophy. Melanchthon hints that Aristotle himself, the father of philosophy, is likely to receive his proper due only when shorn of the 'intellectual immoderation' that generations of medieval scholastics had heaped upon his head. The demise of classical studies in the Middle Ages was accompanied, he says, by the growth of corruption in society and decay in the life of the church. He believes that biblical scholarship and theology will benefit from the training that humanist studies confer. ❖

Melanchthon's affinity with Luther is immediately apparent. Like Luther, he held the view that theology should be 'led by the Holy Spirit, but accompanied by humanist studies'. As such, the study of theology demanded the active engagement of scholars wrestling with the scriptures in their original language. Under Luther's influence, Melanchthon increasingly transferred his prodigious energy into the study of theology. While he continued to work on the ancient philosophers, he no longer cited them as authorities when discussing matters of faith such as salvation.

In his *Loci communes* (*Common Places*), first published in 1521 and frequently reprinted and enlarged thereafter, Melanchthon attempted to construct a coherent synthesis of Luther's theological writings and statements. In the process, he, like Luther, sought to authenticate the new theology by subjecting his findings to the authority of scripture as opposed to human reason. His aim, in his own words, was to demonstrate how doctrinal matters might be illuminated through the study of the Word rather than through the 'theological hallucinations of those who have offered us the subtleties of Aristotle instead of the teaching of Christ' (Reardon, 1995, p.114). Prior to the publication of *Loci communes*, Luther's followers possessed no readily accessible handbook of Lutheran teachings, and few were able to understand with any conviction the scriptural warrant for them. Between 1519 and 1521, Luther had produced a prodigious number of works on a bewildering variety of religious subjects, some highly erudite and others crude and propagandistic. All were produced in haste, often prompted by the demands of the moment and the need to go in to print in order to silence his detractors. Although they are as consistent as we might reasonably expect from a man in Luther's position (he was, for much of this period, living in fear of his life), they could not provide a programme for the kind of reform that his followers increasingly desired. In short, there was no such thing in these years as Lutheran*ism*. Melanchthon filled the vacuum, and in the process laid the foundations for the creation of a new church and doctrine modelled on the teachings of Luther.

Exercise

1   Compare the extract from Melanchthon's *Loci communes* (Anthology, no. 74) with Luther's ideas on grace and justification as expressed in *The Bondage of the Will* (Anthology, no. 68). How did Melanchthon help develop Luther's thinking on this subject?

2   Compare Melanchthon's view of the sacraments with those of Luther as expressed in *The Babylonian Captivity* (Anthology, no. 72).

Discussion   1   Luther expounded his ideas on grace in *The Bondage of the Will* (1525) by means of an analysis of St Paul's writings, in the course of which he argued that, if God had promised grace before He gave the law to Moses, grace could not conceivably derive from either works or observation of the law.

Perhaps the first thing to note about Melanchthon's discussion of these issues is the orderly method and simple language that he adopted throughout. Subject-matter was categorized under neat headings, and points were enumerated for ease of reading. The overall impression is more scholarly and systematic than that of Luther. In addition, Melanchthon's survey of sources and authorities is more comprehensive. Referring to the scholastics, Melanchthon refuted the arguments of 'the Thomists', a reference to the followers of the Italian theologian, Thomas Aquinas (1225–74). He also demonstrates wide-ranging knowledge of Hebrew, Greek and Latin, which he cites extensively, particularly in reference to etymological disputes over the meaning of certain words and phrases in the scriptures.

2   The chief point of difference between the two men lies in Melanchthon's reduction of the sacraments to two rather than the three that Luther initially favoured (Luther subsequently decided not to include penance).

Like Luther, Melanchthon held the view that even the two sacraments that carry scriptural authority cannot of themselves effect saving grace (justification) in man: 'faith alone justifies ... Signs do not justify'. Both believed that the promise of grace from God is acknowledged by those with faith in the taking of the sacrament, an act that buoys up or strengthens the communicant. The chief purpose of communion is to strengthen the faith and conscience of believers when they experience doubt. The sacrament is a sign of the receiving of grace through faith but does not of itself confer grace. Luther is saying much the same when he writes in *The Babylonian Captivity* (a work cited by Melanchthon in the extract): 'in every sacrament the sign as such is incomparably less than the thing signified'.

Both men believed that the laity should receive communion in both kinds and both subscribed to the view that it was possible for Christ to be physically present with the bread and the wine without the need for their transubstantiation.

Both believed that the sacrament was not a sacrifice of Christ's body (in the form of the bread and the wine) made to obtain salvation, but a re-enactment of the original sacrifice of Christ's body on the cross, which had made salvation accessible to individuals with the faith to accept it. If anything, Melanchthon was even more vehement in his opposition to the idea of communion as a sacrifice: 'All Masses are godless.' ❖

Figure 1.9 Lucas Cranach the Elder, *The Law and the Gospel*. Cranach's woodcut, with accompanying text, underlines a central theme of Protestant iconography. In particular, he contrasts the fate of those who live under the law (note Moses holding the Ten Commandments), where sin and wilfulness reign and are punished, with those in a state of grace, where faith is rewarded with peace and forgiveness. From Scribner, R.W. (1981) *For the Sake of Simple Folk: Popular Propaganda for the German Reformation*, Cambridge, Cambridge University Press, p.216. Photo: © The Trustees of the British Museum, London

Luther's continuing subscription to belief in the 'Real Presence' – the idea that Christ is physically present with the bread and the wine of the eucharist – is perhaps yet a further mark of his religious conservatism and unwillingness to break completely with the doctrines of the Roman Catholic church. Although widely accepted in many parts of Germany, Luther's teachings on the sacraments, especially communion, were to prove a constant source of debate within reformed circles. Under pressure from men like the Swiss theologian, Ulrich Zwingli, Luther was forced to defend his view of the role of the Lord's Supper in the Protestant communion – a development that ultimately led to a violent and irreparable breach in the ranks of the reform movement.

Zwingli

Ulrich Zwingli (1484–1531) was born at Wildhaus in Switzerland. He studied at the universities of Vienna (1498–1502) and Basle (1502–6) before he became a parish priest in Glarus in the diocese of Constance. His university education had exposed him at an early age

Figure 1.10 Hans Asper, *Huldrych Zwingli*, 1549, oil on wood, 62.4 x 51.2 cm. Photo: Schweizerisches Landesmuseum, Zurich to strong humanist influences, which he later applied to his study of the scriptures. As a young student, he studied Greek and Hebrew as well as Latin, and developed an early passion for classical literature. Not surprisingly, he soon became a keen advocate of **Erasmianism** and shared Erasmus's criticisms of the church. In 1518, he was appointed minister of the Grossmünster in the city of Zurich, a prestigious appointment that provided him with a centre for the dissemination of his own radical religious beliefs.

Zwingli's friendship and correspondence with Erasmus lasted from 1515 until 1523, ending in the latter year when Zwingli afforded protection to von Hutten, the German reformer and humanist and defender of Reuchlin (see above). Erasmus's influence on Zwingli's early intellectual development is indisputable. Not only did the Swiss reformer imbibe Erasmus's thoroughly **christocentric** theology, but he also shared Erasmus's disdain for scholasticism. By 1516, Zwingli was already convinced of the supremacy of scripture in theological debate and was evidently supportive of Luther's stance against the papacy during his disputation with Eck in Leipzig in 1519. Zwingli did not, however, express public support for the aims of the Reformation until the early 1520s, his early reading of Luther being largely conditioned by his attachment to Erasmian humanism rather than a desire for root-and-branch reform in the church. Later in life, he sought to rationalize his position by claiming that he had arrived at his 'reformational discoveries' independently of Luther. Whatever the truth of this claim, it would seem impossible to deny the influence of Luther upon Zwingli, although it is probable that Luther's actions rather than his evolving theology were the chief source of inspiration for the Swiss reformer.

Disputes over priority in cases such as this are, in the last resort, insoluble. The work and interests of both men clearly overlapped, although there were also significant differences in the style and content of their theological beliefs. Zwingli, for example, anticipated Luther in condemning the intercession of saints and the mediatory role of the priest, a logical consequence of his conviction in the singularity and centrality of God in the process of salvation. However, the greatest distance between the two men focused on the ongoing debate in reform circles over the nature of the eucharist. We do not know for sure whether Zwingli's position was a reaction against Luther's doctrine of the Real Presence, or whether he had in fact arrived at his own conclusions by a separate route. What is certain is that Zwingli was expressing reservations about the nature of the eucharist in 1522 and that his doubts on the subject were not fully resolved until 1526, when he first articulated his belief that communion was best understood as a commemoration of Christ's sacrifice on the cross. The eucharist was not, therefore, a re-enactment of that sacrifice, but a recognition of the symbolic significance of this unique moment in history.

Exercise

Read the extracts from Zwingli's *On the Lord's Supper* (1526) and *An Exposition of the Faith* (1531) (Anthology, nos 75 and 76). How does Zwingli's view of the eucharist differ from that of Lutherans and Roman Catholics?

Discussion

The major point of difference is that Zwingli, unlike both Lutherans and Catholics, rejects in its entirety any attempt to argue for the Real Presence of Christ with or in the bread and the wine. He believed that although Christ might be spiritually present, His spiritual essence was separate from His bodily form, which, following the crucifixion, was at God's right hand. Like his critics and opponents, Zwingli claimed the evidence of the scriptures as the authority for his radical stance. In order for the key phrase 'this is my body' to be consonant with other passages of scripture, Zwingli argued that the words must be understood metaphorically rather than literally. In spite of the fact that Zwingli emphasized the purely commemorative aspects of the eucharist, like Luther he believed that faith was strengthened by participation in communion. ❖

The dispute between Luther and Zwingli over the meaning of the eucharist was to have profound consequences for the fate of the Reformation. In 1529, at the behest of the landgrave, Philip of Hesse (1504–67), an early convert to the new evangelical faith, the two men met at Marburg in an attempt to reconcile their differences. Philip himself was eager to promote a united Protestant front in the face of renewed political hostility to the evangelical cause.[2] However, despite the fact that Luther and Zwingli were able to agree on a whole host of outstanding issues, they failed to convince each other of the correctness of their respective views on the Lord's Supper. Division over this issue was to blight all further efforts among the two reform camps – Lutheran and Zwinglian – to create a single church. In 1530, the two movements drew up their own separate confessions, or statements of doctrinal belief, and, despite the death of Zwingli in 1531, the die was cast. Increasingly, Protestant Germany and Switzerland were divided into two spheres of influence. Lutheranism, with its base at Wittenberg, dominated the new evangelical churches of northern and north-eastern Germany, while the influence of Zwingli was felt most strongly in the cities and territories of south-western Germany and the Swiss cantons – a pattern that we will

[2] The term 'Protestant' was coined just six months prior to the meeting at Marburg, when the minority of evangelical estates in the empire 'protested' against the decision of the majority to destroy the Reformation.

examine more closely in Chapter 2 in the case studies of Augsburg and Zwickau .

By the middle of the sixteenth century, both the Lutheran and Zwinglian confessions were on the defensive. The defeat of the German Protestant princes at the battle of Mühlberg in 1547 left Germany, temporarily at least, at the mercy of the Catholic emperor, Charles V. Luther was dead, and the leadership of the Protestant movement in Germany was in crisis. Large parts of Germany were undergoing reconversion to Catholicism – a process that was to gather speed with the onset of the Catholic Reformation or Counter-Reformation (see Chapter 2). Of critical significance to the survival of the evangelical movement in the second half of the sixteenth century was the renewed impetus that it found through the impact of the work and thought of the French reformer, John Calvin (1509–64), from his base in the small Swiss city of Geneva.

Calvin

Calvin, the son of a well-to-do ecclesiastical notary, was born in Noyon in Picardy, northern France, in 1509. Originally intended for the priesthood, Calvin was sent to the University of Paris at the age of twelve, where he soon encountered the evangelical humanism of Erasmus and the great French scholar, Lefèvre d'Etaples. His studies took a dramatic turn in 1528, when his father decided that he should become a lawyer instead of a priest. For the next five years, Calvin worked on a law degree at the universities of Bourges and Orléans, while at the same time continuing to pursue his love of classical literature and humanist learning. In 1532, he published an edition, with learned commentary, of *De clementia* (*On Clemency*) by the Roman philosopher Seneca (*c.*4 BCE–65 CE). A year later, his growing unease with traditional Catholicism led him to side openly with the nascent French reform movement, which was gathering pace in the University of Paris at this time. Fearing official persecution, he fled France and went into exile, where he was soon to be joined by a number of his fellow countrymen who were increasingly attracted to evangelical reform.

Between 1533 and 1536, Calvin wandered Europe, visiting a number of the leading centres of Protestantism. In the latter year, he was persuaded to remain in the city of Geneva, where he was to spend the next three years engaged in the work of a pastor and teacher. Geneva was a small city of some 10,000 people, which was technically under the control of the local bishop. However, by the time of Calvin's arrival the religious situation in the city was confused and uncertain.

Figure 1.11 Anonymous, Authenticated portrait of John Calvin. Photo: Bibliotheque Publique et Universitaire de Genève, Geneva

The influence of reformed religion had reached the city, which, since the 1520s, leading citizens had been seeking to free from episcopal control. Between 1536 and 1538, Calvin and his allies (mostly exiled Frenchmen) wrestled with the problem of effecting a thorough religious transformation in the lives of the citizens of Geneva. The greatest obstacle to reform was the town council, which steadfastly refused to cooperate with Calvin, who sought greater ministerial control over ecclesiastical discipline and the power of excommunication.

In 1538, Calvin was once again forced into exile, following a defeat at the hands of his opponents on the town council. He spent the next three years in Strasburg, where he continued to lecture and act as a pastor to an exiled French congregation, as well as falling under the spell of one of the foremost exponents of Protestantism, Martin Bucer (1491–1551). In 1541, at the invitation of the town council, Calvin returned to Geneva, where he remained for the rest of his life. Soon after his return, the council accepted Calvin's *Ecclesiastical Ordinances*, which contained his blueprint for the reform of Geneva. These regulations stipulated that the administration of the church should lie in the hands of four groups of officers: pastors, teachers, elders and deacons. In order to coordinate their activities, ultimate control would be placed with a consistory, made up of pastors and elders, who would have final responsibility for the reform of every aspect of the lives of the citizens of the city. Between 1541 and his death in 1564, Calvin sought to make Geneva into a model godly commonwealth. However, it was not until 1555 that he was in a sufficiently secure position to guarantee the success of his life-long mission to convert the people of Geneva to his new theology.

Two aspects of Calvin's life and work stand out in respect of the influence that they were to bring to bear on the progress and fate of the Reformation in early modern Europe. In the first place, Calvin left a rich legacy of writings and published works that later followers were able to synthesize into a coherent body of doctrine and belief. These in turn provided a powerful source of inspiration for later generations of reformers throughout northern and eastern Europe, and helped in the process to reinvigorate the reform movement following its brief decline in the middle decades of the sixteenth century. In particular, the influence of Calvinism was a critical factor in the creation of evangelical churches in the Netherlands, France and Scotland, as well as in the remoter regions of eastern Europe such as Hungary and Transylvania. It was also of critical importance in the Anglican church, established after the accession of Elizabeth I in 1558, although in England the impact of Calvinism was largely restricted to matters of doctrine rather than church governance.

At the heart of Calvin's reformed theology lay the idea of predestination, or more precisely *double* predestination, which he enunciated in his most famous work, *The Institutes of the Christian Religion* (1536).[3] The doctrine of predestination was originally elaborated by St Augustine (354–430), who claimed that God had predestined those who were to be saved (the elect), leaving the rest to a fate determined by their own sinful actions. Luther echoed these sentiments. Calvin, however, developed the idea of divine omnipotence that underlay such beliefs to its logical conclusion, by stressing that God consigned the sinful, or reprobate, to Hell, as well as choosing those reserved for Heaven. From a modern perspective, Calvinism seems both harsh and problematic. Why should God create mankind simply in order to consign certain people to a fate that they could not alter? Calvin responded to his critics by emphasizing the idea that no one could tell who was saved and who was not. His own

---

[3] The *Institutes* was in fact published in numerous, expanded editions, its purpose changing over time. The first edition is now largely seen as an attempt by Calvin to explore and clarify through writing his growing disenchantment with established religion. Later editions were intended more as textbooks or manuals for godly Christians and would-be ministers.

moderation is evident in the way in which he frequently argued for an assumption of election, that is, that if a person lived and acted as a Christian and partook of the sacraments, then he or she must be assumed to be one of the elect. These issues continued to divide Protestants, however, and were, if anything, given greater prominence by later generations of Calvin's followers, beginning with his intimate friend and colleague in Geneva, Théodore de Bèze (or Beza) (1519–1605).

The other issue that undermined Protestant unity in the second half of the sixteenth century was Calvin's position on the meaning of the sacrament of communion. While agreeing with Luther and Zwingli on the reduction of the sacraments to just two, he rejected the position of both men with respect to what was meant by Christ's words at the Last Supper. In essence, Calvin adopted a middle position between his illustrious predecessors. On the one hand, he denied Zwingli's view that participation in the communion service was a purely symbolic or commemorative act, arguing instead that those who received the host were 'fed with the substance of Christ'. On the other hand, he refuted Luther's retention of a physical presence in the host. In the place of both, he argued that Christ's presence was real, but confined to his spiritual rather than his bodily substance. Although such ideas may have prevented greater unity among the various Protestant churches of late sixteenth-century Europe, they were nonetheless to prove highly successful in attracting large numbers of men and women, princes as well as subjects, to the evangelical cause.

The second great legacy of Calvin's work and thought lay in the impetus that he gave to the role of education, including humanism, in the creation of godly citizens and good Christians. Increasingly, scholars are acknowledging the formative debt of Calvin's theology to his early encounter with humanism at the University of Paris. Here, in the 1520s, he became immersed in the French movement for Erasmian reform of the church and education, which had first taken root in the city under the guidance of Guillaume Budé (1467–1540) and patronage of Marguerite of Navarre (1492–1549), the sister of King Francis I (1515–47). The appeal of humanism to Calvin was not restricted to its emphasis on the 'three languages' (Latin, Greek and Hebrew) so beloved by the Erasmians. On the contrary, the young Calvin was a passionate admirer of all facets of classical culture and learning, which he continued to cite and invoke throughout his later career as a theologian and pastor. Above all, however, it has been claimed that it was 'the rhetorical culture of Renaissance humanism' that 'left a profound mark on every aspect of Calvin's mature thought' (Bouwsma, 1988, p.14).

The fruit of Calvin's humanist labours is perhaps most evident in that monument to sixteenth-century learning, the Geneva Academy, which he established in the city in 1559. Here, students were inducted into study of the classical languages and exposed to a humanist curriculum which was largely borrowed from that of the celebrated school at Strasburg founded by Johann Sturm (1507–89). Its chief purpose was to train future ministers and exiled missionaries, who might spread the word in their native lands, but the Academy was also intended to act as a training ground for civic leaders and godly magistrates. Humanism for Calvin, then, was not simply an adjunct of the educated minister; it existed to educate the whole man, regardless of vocation (Bouwsma, 1988, pp.113–27).

In time, the Geneva Academy would act as a model for reformed communities throughout Europe. Calvin and his successors hoped that such establishments might create not just godly subjects and citizens, but also godly communities in which immorality and vice were eradicated. The moral dimension to Calvin's thought, however, was often in conflict with certain aspects of Renaissance culture. As a result, he frequently expressed criticism of those classical authors, such as the Greek satirist, Lucian (*c*.115–*c*.180 CE), whom earlier generations of humanists had praised and imitated in their mockery of the practices of the Catholic church. Subsequent generations of his followers reiterated his attack on the blasphemous and unchristian writers of his own age – men like François Rabelais (*c*.1494–*c*.1553), who had been a prominent member of the circle of Erasmians admired by Calvin in Paris during the 1520s. Once again, we are reminded of the point – firmly made by historians like Peter Burke, writing in the twentieth century – that the relationship between Renaissance and reform was often highly complex and ambiguous. In the last resort, men like Luther, Melanchthon and Calvin sought some form of accommodation with the classical past. Compromise, not ideological purity, was the order of the day (Burke, 1998, pp.150–4).

The Protestant Reformation: a Renaissance of the north?

The Reformation has long fascinated scholars of the Renaissance for a number of reasons. Chief among these is the widely held view that the Reformation was the logical and inevitable consequence of the Renaissance. In this chapter, we have encountered a great deal of evidence that would appear to substantiate such a claim. The debt of individual reformers like Luther, Zwingli and Calvin to a humanist education is readily apparent. All three men were essentially the product of a broad cultural and educational movement, Erasmianism, which created an atmosphere conducive to the reception of reform ideas. At a more basic level, the humanist pledge to return to first sources, *ad fontes,* was imitated in the reform movement and the commitment of men like Erasmus and Luther to original biblical research. In other respects, too, the two movements shared a common goal. Humanists and reformers alike were devoted to the cause of education and educational reform. Both were committed to the twin principles that education should be practical and pious. In this way, not only were souls saved but society too stood to gain through the employment of well-trained men and women, who were increasingly able to fulfil their allotted roles in the social hierarchy. It is no coincidence that the two most influential educational reformers in Protestant Europe – Melanchthon and Sturm – were both committed to the values of a classical and humanist education. Nor should it surprise us to learn that Luther was a passionate advocate of the establishment of good public libraries in every German town as well as a proponent of universal education, for girls as well as for boys.

But there is also a sense in which the Reformation, and its values, may be seen as antipathetic to those of the Renaissance. The study of pagan authors was always a fraught occupation for the pious Christian, never more so than in the aftermath of the Lutheran schism. One of the main casualties of the Catholic response to reform was moderate Erasmianism. In the wake of the predictable assault by many conservative Catholics on the Erasmian tradition in the church, the criticism of the pagan influence of classical texts grew ever louder and more frequent. By the middle of the sixteenth century, both confessions were beginning to reassess the validity of much humanist literature, a process that frequently led to the prescription of certain authors and texts. It would be a mistake to conclude, however, that the onset of the Reformation spelled the end of the Renaissance. Religion and humanism were not incompatible:

> Separately, but also together, they opened up, or recovered, a vast Classical and Christian heritage, and launched an impressive onslaught on corruption and complacency. Often in a love-hate relationship ... they fed off one another rather than on one another.
>
> (Matheson, 1990, p.42)

Bibliography

BOSSY, J. (1985) *Christianity in the West 1400–1700*, Oxford, Oxford University Press.

BOUWSMA, W.J. (1988) *John Calvin: A Sixteenth-Century Portrait*, Oxford, Oxford University Press.

BURCKHARDT, J. (1990) *The Civilization of the Renaissance in Italy*, trans. S.G.C. Middlemore, Harmondsworth, Penguin; first published 1860.

BURKE, P. (1998), *The European Renaissance: Centres and Peripheries*, Oxford, Blackwell.

DUFFY, E. (1992) *The Stripping of the Altars: Traditional Religion in England 1400–1580*, New Haven and London, Yale University Press.

HILLERBRAND, H.J. (1964) *The Reformation in its Own Words*, London, SCM Press.

MATHESON, P. (1990) 'Humanism and reform movements' in A. Goodman and A. MacKay (eds) *The Impact of Humanism on Western Europe*, London and New York, Longman, pp.23–42.

MINNICH, N.H. (1993) 'Concepts of reform proposed at the Fifth Lateran Council' in *The Fifth Lateran Council 1512–17: Studies in its Membership, Diplomacy and Proposals for Reform*, Aldershot, Variorum, vol. IV, pp.163–251.

MUIR, E. (1997) *Ritual in Early Modern Europe*, Cambridge, Cambridge University Press.

NAUERT, C.G. (1995) *Humanism and the Culture of Renaissance Europe*, Cambridge, Cambridge University Press.

OBERMAN, H.A. (1989) *Luther: Man Between God and the Devil*, New Haven and London, Yale University Press.

OLIN, J.C. (1969) *The Catholic Reformation: Savonarola to Ignatius Loyola 1495–1540*, New York, Harper & Row.

OVERFIELD, J. (1984) *Humanism and Scholasticism in Late Medieval Germany*, Princeton, Princeton University Press.

OVERFIELD, J. (1992) 'Germany' in R. Porter and M. Teich (eds) *The Renaissance in National Context*, Cambridge, Cambridge University Press, pp.92–122.

REARDON, B.M. (1995) *Religious Thought in the Reformation*, 2nd edn, Harlow, Longman.

SPITZ, L.W. (1972) *The Northern Renaissance*, Englewood Cliffs, NJ, Prentice-Hall.

SPITZ, L.W. (1975) 'The course of German humanism' in H.A. Oberman and T.A. Brady (eds) *'Itinerarium Italicum': The Profile of the Italian Renaissance in the Mirror of its European Transformations. Dedicated to Paul Oskar Kristeller*, Leiden, E.J. Brill, pp.371–436.

SPITZ, L.W. (1985) *The Protestant Reformation 1517–1559*, New York, Harper & Row.

Anthology sources

Girolamo Savonarola, The Sermon on the Renovation of the Church (1495): *The Catholic Reformation: Savonarola to Ignatius Loyola: Reform in the Church 1495–1540*, ed. J.C. Olin, Harper & Row, New York, 1969, pp.13–14. (Anthology, no. 57)

The Introduction to the Rule of the Genoese Oratory of Divine Love (1497): *The Catholic Reformation: Savonarola to Ignatius Loyola: Reform in the Church 1495–1540*, ed. J.C. Olin, Harper & Row, New York, 1969, p.18. (Anthology, no. 58)

Giles of Viterbo, Address to the Fifth Lateran Council (1512): *The Catholic Reformation: Savonarola to Ignatius Loyola: Reform in the Church 1495–1540*, ed. J.C. Olin, Harper & Row, New York, 1969, pp.44–53. (Anthology, no. 59)

The *Consilium de emendanda ecclesia* (1537): *The Catholic Reformation: Savonarola to Ignatius Loyola: Reform in the Church 1495–1540*, ed. J.C. Olin, Harper & Row, New York, 1969, pp.187–91, 196–7. (Anthology, no. 60)

Conrad Celtis, Inaugural address to the University of Ingolstadt (1492): *The Northern Renaissance*, ed. L.W. Spitz, Prentice Hall, Englewood Cliffs, New Jersey, 1972, pp.15–23, 25–7. (Anthology, no. 61)

Martin Mair, Summary of a letter to Cardinal Enea Silvio Piccolomini (1457): G. Strauss (ed.), *Manifestations of Discontent in Germany on the Eve of the Reformation: A Collection of Documents*, Indiana University Press, Bloomington, 1971, pp.37–8. (Anthology, no. 62)

Martin Luther, Autobiographical fragment on his conversion (1545): K. Leach, *The German Reformation: Documents and Debates*, Macmillan, Basingstoke, 1991, pp.21–2, from G. Rupp and B. Drewery, *Luther: Documents of Modern History*, 1970, pp.5–6. (Anthology, no. 63)

Martin Luther, Preface to the complete edition of *A German Theology* (1518): *Luther's Works, vol. 31, The Career of the Reformer I*, ed. H.J. Grimm, Mühlenberg Press, Philadelphia, 1957, pp.75–6. (Anthology, no. 64)

Martin Luther, Letter to Eobanus Hessus (1523): *The Religious Renaissance of the German Humanists*, ed. L.W. Spitz, Harvard University Press, Cambridge, 1963, p.243. (Anthology, no. 65)

Martin Luther, *To the Councilmen of all Cities in Germany That They Establish and Maintain Christian Schools* (1524): *Luther's Works, vol.45, The Christian in Society II*, ed. W.J. Brandt, Mühlenberg Press, Philadelphia, 1962, pp.348–70. (Anthology, no. 66)

Martin Luther, Article 32 from his *Explanations of the 95 Theses* (1518): *Luther's Works, vol.31, The Career of the Reformer I*, ed. H.J. Grimm, Mühlenberg Press, Philadelphia, 1957, pp.79–83. (Anthology, no. 67)

Martin Luther, *The Bondage of the Will* (1525): *Luther's Works, vol.33, The Career of the Reformer III*, ed. P.S. Watson, Fortress Press, Philadelphia, 1972, pp.270–7. (Anthology, no. 68)

Martin Luther, *An Appeal to the Ruling Class of German Nationality as to the Amerlioration of the State of Christendom* (1520): *Martin Luther: Selections from his Writings*, ed. J. Dillenberger, Anchor Books, New York, 1961, pp.428–31. (Anthology, no. 69)

Martin Luther, Article 25 from *Defence and Explanation of all the Articles of Dr Martin Luther which were unjustly condemned by the Roman Bull* (1521): *Luther's Works, vol.32, The Career of the Reformer II*, ed. G. Forell, Mühlenberg Press, Philadelphia, 1958, pp.67–71. (Anthology, no. 70)

Martin Luther, Fragment of a letter to Philipp Melanchthon (1521): *Luther's Works, vol.48, Letters*, ed. G.G. Krodel, Fortress Press, Philadelphia, 1963, pp.277–82. (Anthology, no. 71)

Martin Luther, *The Babylonian Captivity of the Church* (1520): *Luther's Works, vol.36, Word and Sacrament II*, ed. A.R. Wentz, Mühlenberg Press, Philadelphia, 1959, pp.18–19, 21–3, 34–9, 51–2, 54. (Anthology, no. 72)

Philipp Melanchthon, Inaugural address to the University of Wittenberg (1518): *The Reformation in its own Words*, ed. H.J. Hillerbrand, SCM Press, London, 1964, pp.58–60. (Anthology, no. 73)

Philipp Melanchthon, *Loci communes* (1521): *Melanchthon and Bucer*, ed. W. Pauk, Library of Christian Classics, vol.19, SCM Press, London, 1969, pp.86–9, 133–6, 145–7. (Anthology, no. 74)

Ulrich Zwingli, *On the Lord's Supper* (1526): *Zwingli and Bullinger*, ed. G.W. Bromiley, Library of Christian Classics, vol. 24, SCM Press, London, 1953, pp.222–3. (Anthology, no. 75)

Ulrich Zwingli, *An Exposition of the Faith* (1531): *Zwingli and Bullinger*, ed. G.W. Bromiley, Library of Christian Classics, vol. 24, SCM Press, London, 1953, pp.254–65. (Anthology, no. 76)

CHAPTER TWO

The spread of reform

BY ANNE LAURENCE

Objectives

The objectives of this chapter are that you should:

- understand how the Reformation took different forms in different contexts in sixteenth-century Germany;
- assess the extent to which the Reformation in Germany was a predominantly urban phenomenon;
- recognize how reform ideas fused with social discontent to create popular movements that demanded wholesale change in the social and political order;
- appreciate the impact of the Protestant Reformation on Italy and Spain.

Introduction

As we saw in Chapter 1, the relationship between humanism and religious reform is an important factor to take into account when seeking to define the Renaissance. In this chapter, we aim to look at how the spread of reform in Germany was shaped by the receptivity of northern Europe to Renaissance values. Case studies of two cities – Augsburg and Zwickau – provide contrasting examples of this process in action. We also examine the role played by other factors in determining the reaction of sixteenth-century Germans to the religious upheavals of this period. One of the most important features of the German Reformation, in contrast to the Renaissance, was the extent to which it appealed to a broad spectrum of society, including the largely uneducated mass of the population. A consideration of the onset of the Radical Reformation, which culminated in the Peasants' War of 1524–6, provides a valuable opportunity to examine this process in action. The chapter concludes with a brief assessment of the impact of reform outside the borders of Germany, in particular in those lands that ultimately remained loyal to Roman Catholicism, Italy and Spain.

The study of reform

The ideas of Martin Luther, adapted and expounded by Philipp Melanchthon and challenged by Ulrich Zwingli, would have been of no more lasting significance than those expressed by Giles of Viterbo (Anthology, no. 59) had it not been for the fact that Luther's ideas were almost immediately implemented in his native Germany. The success of the Protestant Reformation ultimately brought to an end the universal authority claimed by the papacy in spiritual affairs. How, then, did Luther succeed in shattering the religious peace of Europe where others before him had failed?

One of the most extraordinary aspects of the Lutheran reform movement was the speed with which it took root in Germany. In 1545, a year before Luther's death, only Bavaria remained loyal to Roman Catholicism (Figure 2.1). However, while reform doctrine and the new liturgical practices associated with Protestantism were widely adopted, it is difficult to know to what extent the theological implications of the new faith were understood and assimilated by the population as a whole. Although reformed religion, on the face of it, captured much of Germany, in many places it co-existed with Roman Catholicism. In addition, many of those most enthusiastic for reform continued to express uncertainty about various aspects of the doctrinal changes that, on the surface, they appeared to endorse. Movement between the two camps was not uncommon. Nor was it always motivated, as some have suggested, by factors other than matters of faith. For these reasons alone, many Germans, both Protestant and Catholic, continued to believe for much of the sixteenth century that some form of religious rapprochement was possible between the two confessions.

The imperfect assimilation of reformed religion is often described in terms of a two-tier model in which the elite, educated, text-based culture of the early reform leaders is contrasted with the popular, oral culture of the vast majority of the population. In this model, the text-based debates are thought to have appealed to intellectuals such as humanist scholars and university students, who were capable of understanding the academic points at issue between the religious protagonists. In contrast, the reformers' insistence on the authority of scripture and Lutheran notions such as the **priesthood of all believers** are seen as critical factors in converting urban artisans and rural peasants to the new faith. Under the influence of charismatic preachers such as Thomas Müntzer and the Zwickau Prophets (see below), the anti-intellectual implications of Luther's spiritual programme propagated new strains of reformed religion (usually referred to by the catch-all phrase, 'Radical Reformation'). The

Figure 2.1 Map showing the spread of Protestantism during the latter part of the sixteenth century. Adapted from Greengrass, M.A. (1998) *The Longman Companion to the European Reformation c.1500–1618*, London and New York, Longman, pp.376–7

mystical and apocalyptic pronouncements of the leaders of this radical wing of the Reformation engendered deep divisions in the ranks of the reformers. Luther himself, a social and political conservative, was deeply averse to the political extremism of those who appropriated his theology for radical ends. Other reform leaders were often more sympathetic to the plight of the poor, who flocked to support the peasant armies in the mid 1520s. Indeed, some of these leaders, such as Müntzer and Andreas Bodenstein von Karlstadt (*c.*1480–1541), were highly educated, and their role in the Radical Reform movement is indicative of the problematic nature of the simple two-tier model outlined above.

The appropriateness of this two-tier model has been further undermined by much recent research, which suggests that the process by which reform ideas were spread was probably more haphazard and incomplete than had formerly been supposed. This reassessment is based largely on the result of a number of detailed local and regional studies, which have shown how reformed religion was unevenly assimilated in sixteenth-century Germany, as well as demonstrating how its reception was dependent upon a variety of contingent factors.

A central issue in much of this recent research is the extent to which historians of the German Reformation have tended to envisage the adoption of the new faith as initially an urban phenomenon. To some extent, this reflected the strong focus on urban studies, driven by the search for the origins of capitalism, that characterized the work of Marxist historians, especially in the post-war German Democratic Republic (East Germany). According to the Marxist school, the Reformation was seen first and foremost as arising from a socio-economic response to the inadequacies of feudalism, which acquired ideological support in the form of the new Protestant faith. For Marxist historians, the Reformation was the inevitable product of deep-rooted social and economic changes, which, prior to 1517, were particularly evident in the prosperous towns and cities of northern Europe. Even historians antipathetic to Marxism were largely conditioned to envisage some form of causal relationship between the onset of capitalism, urbanism and religious change. Here, the work of the sociologist Max Weber (1864–1920), and his pioneering study, *The Protestant Ethic and the Spirit of Capitalism* (1905), have proved particularly influential. Weber argued, among other things, that Protestantism fostered distinctive attitudes that encouraged the accumulation of capital, a major precondition for modern capitalism. Weber, too, laid great stress on the role of towns and cities in the promotion of reformed religion.

Weber's thesis, despite its ground-breaking attempt to integrate sociology and history, has attracted widespread criticism. His application of sociology to an understanding of the role of Protestantism in the formation of the modern world has nonetheless continued to inform the work of scholars eager to identify the social roots of the new faith. In America, especially, historians of the Reformation have tended to avoid ideological debates over the origins of the Reformation in favour of a more pragmatic approach, which has focused on detailed urban case studies of the reception of reform ideas. One product of this new research is a greater awareness of the problems inherent in any approach that tends to exaggerate the division of German society into two neat categories, urban and rural. Increasingly, historians of Reformation Germany speak of an interplay between town and country. They also identify the importance of lay intervention in encouraging or discouraging the adoption of reform practices, particularly preaching, in German towns and villages.

Let us now look at how the Reformation arrived and was received in two German cities: Augsburg and Zwickau.

Augsburg

Augsburg was a free imperial city located in the region of Swabia in southern Germany. Political authority was largely in the hands of a small group of patrician families, who dominated the two councils that oversaw the government of the city. In theory, this ruling elite was answerable only to the emperor, and not to powerful local princes such as the neighbouring dukes of Bavaria.[1] Augsburg was a prosperous city with a rapidly expanding population in the early sixteenth century (its population may have doubled from 20,000 to 40,000 between 1500 and 1540). The city's prosperity was based on its booming textile industry, as well as its role as a vital centre of commerce and banking in southern Germany. It was, however, first and foremost an important regional economic centre, providing employment to people from the surrounding countryside, as well as a market for local produce and goods. During the course of the sixteenth century, it also became the centre for a flourishing printing industry, specializing in religious pamphlets and illustrated books.

Figure 2.2 View of Augsburg. Stadtarchiv, Augsburg

[1] In the late sixteenth century, the Bavarians were the main supporters of Catholic reform, in opposition to Protestantism, in Germany.

In addition to its regional and 'national' roles, Augsburg lay at the heart of an international network of commerce and trade. Its merchants traded the length and breadth of Europe, the wealth created by such trade assisting the city's development as one of the most important banking centres north of the Alps. Such activities laid the foundations for one of the most distinctive features of the city – the emergence in the late fifteenth century of two great families of merchant-princes: the Fuggers and the Welsers. As their wealth and connections grew (the Fuggers, for example, were one of the wealthiest families in Europe and acted as bankers to the emperor), so they began to eclipse some of the older families who had traditionally dominated the government of the city. Remarkably, however, the Fuggers were not admitted into the ranks of the governing elite until 1538, after, that is, their ennoblement by the emperor.

Unusually for a city of its size (it was the third largest in Germany), Augsburg possessed no university. There was, however, no lack of intellectual life and cultural activity in the city. As a centre for printing, it attracted large numbers of scholars, many of whom were exponents of humanism. Included in the ranks of the latter was the lawyer and town clerk, Conrad Peutinger, a friend of Conrad Celtis and a great advocate of humanist learning. Among other endeavours, Peutinger was responsible for amassing a collection of antique sculpted stones and inscriptions found in the neighbourhood of Augsburg. This research was subsequently published, partly to answer those critics – mainly Italian – who persisted in stereotyping the German people as uncivilized and 'barbaric' (Figure 2.3). As a humanist of international renown, Peutinger's response to the Reformation in Augsburg is perhaps indicative of the ambivalence expressed by others of similar background. Peutinger was an Erasmian through and through, and supported a number of the early reforms advocated by the Lutherans. These included the marriage of clergy, the administration of communion in both kinds, and the use of the vernacular in the liturgy. However, he never officially converted to Protestantism and was ultimately forced to resign his post as town clerk in 1534, when the city sanctioned the new faith (Ozment, 1975, p.127).

A further source of support for learning and the arts came from the wealthy patrician families, such as the Fuggers, whose international connections facilitated cultural as well as economic exchange (see Chapter 3). However, with one or two notable exceptions, the Fugger family remained steadfastly loyal to the Roman Catholic faith and, during the second half of the sixteenth century, constituted one of the major patrons of the Catholic Reformation (or Counter-Reformation) in the city. During the same period, various members of

Figure 2.3 Conrad Peutinger, Title page of the *Inscriptiones vetustae roman.* (*Ancient Roman Inscriptions*), Augsburg, 1520. From Hay, D. (1986) *The Age of the Renaissance*, London, Guild Publishing, p.135. The title page shows the rape and suicide of Lucretia and depicts seven Roman emperors. Among those who supplied Peutinger with inscriptions were the Fuggers and Paumgartners, two of the leading merchant families of Augsburg. Photo: Landesmuseum Mainz, Mainz

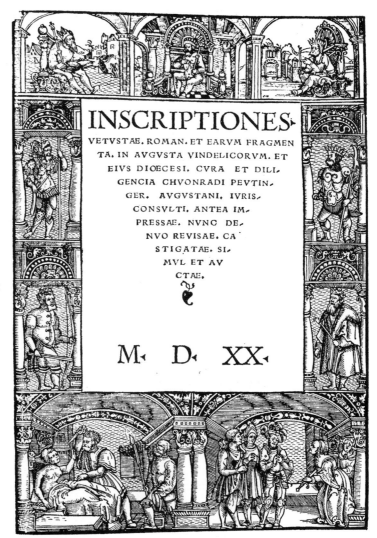

the family also supported a range of scientific endeavours, including alchemical research, which largely stemmed from the Fuggers' extensive interests in the mining industry of central Europe.

The religious life of Augsburg on the eve of the Reformation reflected the city's growing economic and political significance. It was the seat of a bishopric (subsequently removed to Dillingen in 1537 following a series of conflicts with the new Protestant governors of the city) and there were six parish churches, as well as a cathedral. There were a number of religious houses for both men and women: Dominicans, Franciscans, Augustinians, Benedictines and Carmelites, of whom the Dominicans proved most resistant to reform. Some indication of the growing prosperity of the city and its leading inhabitants is evident in the extensive programme of church building that took place in the city in the late fifteenth century. The church of St Ulrich and St Afra was built between 1467 and 1500 and that of St Anna between 1472 and 1510. The former attracted worshippers and pilgrims from outside the city who came to venerate the relics of the two saints. In addition, the church of the Holy Cross, which housed a miraculous bleeding host, was one of the most important pilgrimage sites in late medieval Germany.

Historians have noted that throughout Europe, in the late fifteenth century, there was a growing religious fervour among the laity, who were able to display their piety and commitment to the church in a number of ways. One such was involvement in charitable works. The laicization of charity – that is, the increased responsibility of the laity for the administration of charity – was not, as earlier generations of historians have assumed, solely the consequence of the Protestant Reformation. During the later Middle Ages, both individuals and organized groups of laymen (confraternities) were active in a variety of charitable works, which probably fulfilled political as well as spiritual imperatives. The rapid growth of cities like Augsburg swelled the ranks of the urban poor and created a range of public order problems. It was probably in response to such concerns that the Fuggers established a complex of almshouses, the Fuggerei, in Augsburg in 1519 (Figures 2.4 and 2.5).

Figure 2.4 View of the Fuggerei in 1626. The brothers Ulrich (1441–1510), Georg (1453–1506) and Jakob II Fugger (1459–1525), grandsons of Hans Fugger, who was the founding member of the Fugger dynasty, bought a plot of land in the city on which they built a village of 110 small terraced houses, arranged in streets on a grid plan. Residents, who had to be Catholic, were charged a nominal rent and had to pray for the souls of the Fugger family. Photo: from Seybold, H. (1953) *Augsburg: A Small Book about a Great City*, Augsburg, Brigg Verlag GmbH, p.27

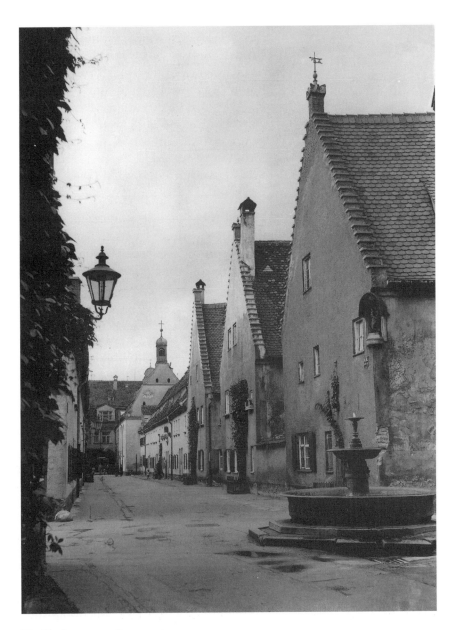

Figure 2.5 View of the Fuggerei in 1953. Photo: Bildarchiv Foto Marburg, Marburg

Religious reform

At the same time as the Fuggers were attempting to alleviate the condition of the poor in the city, other citizens in Augsburg were expressing the need to reform the Catholic church. Initially, the bishop and the city council were sympathetic to moderate, Erasmian reform: both, for example, attempted to improve the quality of preaching in the city's churches. They were resisted, however, by the cathedral **chapter**, which controlled the appointment and payment of clergy. Lutheran reform ideas were first heard in the city in October 1518, when Luther appeared in person at Augsburg to defend himself before the papal legate, Cardinal Cajetan (the two met in the Fuggers' house). Soon after Luther's departure, support for his ideas began to grow in the city, although their spread was restricted by the loyalty of the wealthier and more powerful families, including the Fuggers, to Roman Catholicism. Unlike other parts of Germany, where reform was largely encouraged and implemented by the local prince or civic authorities, in Augsburg the adoption of reformed ideas was restricted in the first instance to intellectuals and artisans, who were attracted, to varying degrees, to the spiritual and political messages of Lutheranism.

However, Luther's appearance in Augsburg in 1518 was not the only route by which reformed ideas percolated into the city. Critical to the success of the new faith was the role played by the printing industry in Augsburg, which rapidly disseminated pro-Lutheran literature printed elsewhere, as well as encouraging the production of reform pamphlets by local citizens and artisans. A good example of this process in action is provided by the case of a weaver, Ulz Rychssner. In 1524, inspired by hearing sermons imbued with the humanist spirit of reform, Rychssner published his own attack on the papacy in the form of a pamphlet, *Selections from the Chronicle of the Popes*, which sought to demonstrate that the pope's authority was a human invention without scriptural warrant. This was not Rychssner's first venture into publishing. He had earlier written a reply to the cathedral preacher in which he rejected auricular confession (Figure 2.6). This work, written in the form of a dialogue, also contained a defence of the Lutheran sacraments (communion, baptism and penance).[2] Its significance, however, perhaps lies in the light that it sheds on the various influences affecting the reception of reform in Augsburg at this time. Rychssner was clearly well read, his own works showing the influence of both Luther and Zwingli, as well as reflecting the general criticisms expressed by moderate Erasmians towards corruption in the church. He was also disinclined to support radical change. Like other lay pamphleteers, he sought to discourage violent demonstrations or resistance to secular authority in the city, although he was arrested and imprisoned in 1524 following a rowdy incident in the Franciscan church.

During the course of the 1520s, then, reform doctrines and practices were assimilated and expounded by the citizenry. But the process was neither smooth nor consistent. The city was increasingly divided into warring camps – Catholics, Lutherans, Zwinglians and radicals – all of

[2] Although Luther originally subscribed to the continuation of these three sacraments from among the seven stipulated by the Catholic church, he subsequently dropped penance; for his early ambivalence on this issue, see Anthology, no. 72.

Ain hübsch Gespräch biechlein / von aynem
Pfaffen vnd ainem Weber / die züsamen kumen seind
auff der straß was sy für red / frag / vñ antwort / gegen
ainander gebraucht haben / des Euangeliums vnd an-
derer sachen halben:

Vtz Rychsner Weber: 1524.

Figure 2.6 Frontispiece of Ulz Rychssner, *A Dialogue between a Priest and a Weaver*, 1524. Photo: from Russell, P.A. (1986) *Lay Theology in the Reformation: Popular Pamphleteers in Southwest Germany 1521–1525*, Cambridge, Cambridge University Press, p.134. Reproduced by kind permission of the publisher

whom possessed natural constituencies among sections of the city's population. Those loyal to the Catholic faith tended to look to the bishop and the Benedictines, as well as to the Fuggers, for leadership. Lutherans and Zwinglians were found in equal measure among the members of the city's ruling elite who dominated the city council, as well as among the artisanal class represented by the city's guilds. Finally, sympathy for the cause of the Radical Reform movement (discussed in more detail below), tended to emanate from the poorer sections of the community who, not surprisingly, were attracted by the egalitarian and utopian message of the radicals. For much of this period, co-existence among the factions was tolerated.

However, an uneasy alliance prevailed between the ecclesiastical and secular authorities in Augsburg and friction was never far from the surface. One of the main areas of tension concerned the control and appointment of new clergy. In particular, the secular authorities wished to exercise greater control over the religious life of the city by acquiring the right of appointment to the city's churches. For example, as early as 1521, the bishop had forced the resignation of the humanist and pro-Lutheran minister, Urbanus Rhegius (1489–1541), who held the post of cathedral preacher. However, in 1524, at the invitation of the city council, he returned to the city to fill the post of preacher at the church of St Anna.

Reform and confrontation

The arrival of reformed doctrines in Augsburg coincided with the growing polarization of the city's population into rich and poor. The great merchant families such as the Fuggers and the Welsers found themselves increasingly at odds with the growing number of impoverished artisans, who felt themselves excluded and alienated from the government of the city. In 1512, violent protests against the city council were orchestrated by poor day labourers and guildsmen. With the coming of the Reformation to Augsburg, religious protest afforded a further opportunity for this group to express its discontent. Between 1524 and 1525, a series of incidents occurred in the city that suggests a growing tendency for economic and political grievances to become conflated with religious ones. In 1524, for example, the radical preacher Johann Schilling was ejected from the city, an act that provoked a riot involving a crowd of more than 1,800 people. In this and subsequent events, objects of Catholic devotion were destroyed and churches attacked and vandalized. In one incident, cow's blood was smeared on a crucifix and Catholic service books destroyed. This and related episodes raised for the council the spectre of a new alliance between lesser guild members and the city's poor, two groups who appeared, for the first time, to engage in opposition to the government of the city by the wealthier guild members and merchant classes. Religious issues were becoming fused with social protest. This was an alarming development since it implied the destruction of the common bond that had previously existed between all guild members, regardless of individual wealth and status.

However, despite such events, the city council continued throughout the 1520s to remain sympathetic to the cause of religious reform. During this period, Roman Catholicism was on the defensive in the city, although it continued to function due to the support that it received from the bishop and influential families such as the Fuggers. Some attempt was made to suppress the more inflammatory and controversial aspects of the Catholic religion, such as miraculous cults and the veneration of relics. There was also a body of opinion in the city that continued to adhere to the belief that some form of reconciliation between the various religious factions was possible, a position broadly in line with that of Peutinger (see above). In 1530, an opportunity arose for the moderate wing of the Lutheran party in Augsburg to promote this conciliatory approach, when an imperial diet was convened in the city, and charged with, among other things, resolving the differences between Protestants and Catholics in the empire.

At this meeting of the imperial electors and other representatives of the cities, states and prince-bishoprics that made up the Holy Roman empire, the Lutherans submitted a statement of their views, the so-called Augsburg Confession, which they believed might form the basis for a compromise with the Catholics. In the hope that the Catholic church might call a council to initiate reform along Lutheran lines, the spokesmen for the Lutherans sought to minimize points of difference between their position and that of their Catholic opponents, but all to no avail. However, the meeting at Augsburg did allow outsiders to experience, and comment upon, the religious situation in the city.

Exercise

Read the report of the Venetian ambassador in Augsburg at the time of the diet in the Anthology (no. 77).

1 How did the writer depict the relative strengths of the various religious factions in the city?

2 Bearing in mind that the author of the report was almost certainly Catholic, what did he identify as particularly noteworthy in the conduct of the Protestant population?

Discussion

1 The writer implied that the Catholics were very much in the minority, eclipsed as they were by the followers of Zwingli, the strongest element in the city, and the Lutherans.

2 The writer identified the popularity of preaching, which, he remarked, was accompanied by little ceremonial. He referred to the communal psalm-singing and the sense of devotion it generated. He also noted the liberal payment of alms by the congregation, and the central role of education, with the teaching of classical languages in Protestant schools. ❖

The writer of this report captured the religious life of the city at a very specific point in history: after the victory of the Zwinglian faction over the Lutherans and before the imposition of major restrictions on Catholic worship. In 1534, however, following the collapse of the 'peace talks' initiated at Augsburg, the Zwinglian-dominated city council increased the pressure on Catholics by limiting the celebration of the mass to specific locations in the city. Three years later, Catholicism was banned altogether and the bishop left his palace in the city to set up an alternative administration in the nearby city of Dillingen.

Exercise

Read the first part of 'Art of idol? Religious sculpture' by Jeffrey Chipps Smith in the Reader (no. 18, pp.212–14).

1   What were the visible signs of reform in Augsburg in the 1530s?

2   How did these reflect the importance of visual imagery in the life of the citizens of Augsburg?

Discussion

1   Prior to 1537, when Lutherans, Zwinglians and Catholics were all able to worship in the city, some damage to Catholic churches had taken place. Images had been destroyed or defaced, and to protect those remaining, many had been placed in safe storage. This process gathered pace after 1537 when the city council abolished Catholicism in the city. Church fixtures and ecclesiastical art, including clerical epitaphs, were either destroyed or removed for preservation, although we might note the fact that the Protestant iconoclasts left untouched memorials to laymen. The internal appearance of the Catholic cathedral and churches was much altered. The abolition of Catholic services required a new form of church furnishings in line with Protestant thinking (this is discussed in more detail in Chapter 3).

2   The destruction of church property and art, much of it sanctioned by the Protestant city council, was not the product of unlicensed vandalism. The selective nature of the process is suggestive of the very real significance that the citizens of sixteenth-century Augsburg attached to the use of sacred objects and imagery in religious worship. The dispute between the Protestant, Marx Ehem, and the Catholic, Anton Fugger, provides a further example of the way in which attitudes to ecclesiastical imagery polarized attitudes in the community. Augsburg was a divided city whose internal conflicts were frequently played out in the forum of its public churches. The material culture of the city was as likely to promote division and discord as were the heated debates over theological issues. The exiled bishop's letter to the Emperor Charles V, in which he claimed that Protestants were replacing Christian statues with 'heathen idols', typifies this process. ❖

During the late 1540s, the Protestant ascendancy in Augsburg suffered a reverse at the hands of a resurgent Catholicism. Under the powerful influence of the new bishop of Augsburg, Otto Truchsess von Waldburg (1543–73), Catholic authority was reasserted in the city. The process of Catholic renewal gained added momentum after the victory of the Emperor Charles V (Figure 2.7) over the Protestant forces at the Battle of Mühlberg in 1547. Fearful of its imperial overlord, the Augsburg city council restored Catholic services in the city and reimbursed Catholics for the destruction of their ecclesiastical property. New works were commissioned to replace those that had been destroyed, most notably a great altarpiece for the high altar in the cathedral. The Dominican church, which had remained more or less untouched, was embellished, a sign of growing confidence in the Catholic community. Chipps Smith makes the point that the new works were often self-consciously old-fashioned in style in order to emphasize the antiquity and authority of the Roman

Figure 2.7 Titian, Equestrian portrait of Charles V at the Battle of Mühlberg in 1547, 1548, oil on canvas, 332 x 279 cm. Prado, Madrid. Photo: Bridgeman Art Library, London

Catholic faith (Reader, no. 18). But he also points out that for much of the second half of the sixteenth century the leaders of the various religious denominations were eager to maintain some form of peaceful co-existence. Under the leadership of Bishop Otto, the religious atmosphere in Augsburg was for the most part consensual and Protestants were allowed to continue to worship and educate their children according to their particular confessions. At the same time, the process of Catholic reform gathered pace in the city, and a renewed emphasis on preaching, education and moral reform undoubtedly led to the reconversion of many Protestants to the Catholic faith.

The fact that Augsburg was chosen as the venue for numerous imperial diets in the sixteenth century owes something perhaps to its reputation as a city in which controversial issues could be debated in an atmosphere of relative calm and freedom. In 1555, it once again played host to an imperial diet, the outcome of which was to lay the foundations for religious peace in the empire for the next 60 years. The Peace of Augsburg, as it is generally known, was founded on the idea that the religion of a particular imperial territory should reflect that of its ruler – a formula summed up in the phrase *cuius regio, eius religio* ('your region determines your religion'). Although it did guarantee a general peace in much of the empire, the Peace of Augsburg was fatally flawed, however, by the fact that it acknowledged only one form of Protestantism – Lutheranism – at a time when the influence of the French theologian, John Calvin, was steadily infiltrating many parts of the empire.

Zwickau

While Augsburg was a free imperial city, Zwickau was merely the largest of a number of small provincial cities located in Saxony, in eastern Germany. Saxony itself was predominantly rural, and the division between rural and urban life was far less distinct than it was in other parts of Germany. The rural economy was divided between smallholdings occupied by tax-paying peasants and noble estates worked by **serfs** or semi-free peasants. Saxony also contained some of the largest silver mines in Europe, which became increasingly profitable in the sixteenth century due to technological improvements in the extraction of silver from argentiferous copper ore.

In 1485, the principality of Saxony was divided into two parts (although the precise boundaries remained somewhat vague), each ruled by separate branches of the Wettin family. The elector of Saxony governed the territory known as Ernestine Saxony (or electoral

Figure 2.8 View of Zwickau. Photo: Bildarchiv Foto Marburg, Marburg

Saxony), while the duke of Saxony ruled the part known as Albertine Saxony (or ducal Saxony). Electoral Saxony was ruled by Frederick the Wise (1465–1525), whose support for Luther was a critical factor in the early stages of the German Reformation. On the face of it, Frederick was an unlikely candidate for Luther's foremost protector. He was a conventionally pious figure, whose commitment to Roman Catholicism was never in question prior to 1517 (nor indeed for some time after). Among his proudest possessions was one of the most valuable collections of relics in Germany, which were housed in the castle church in Wittenberg. As a result, Wittenberg became one of the major sites of pilgrimage in this part of Europe, providing valuable opportunities for indulgence sellers to peddle their wares. But there was another side to Frederick, which undoubtedly endeared him to Luther and the nascent reform movement. The elector was a great patron of the arts and learning who assembled, at his court in Wittenberg, some of the leading artists and intellectuals of his day. Among the painters who worked for him were Albrecht Dürer and Lucas Cranach the Elder, as well as the Venetian, Jacopo de' Barbari, who wrote to the elector seeking his support for the recognition of art as the eighth **liberal art**. His most significant and long-lasting achievement, however, was the foundation of the new University of Wittenberg in 1502. The teaching was originally designed on traditional lines, but in 1518 the elector provided the funds for a thorough overhaul of the university's curriculum. Humanist studies in

Figure 2.9 Mine, woodcut, from Georgius Agricola, *De re metallica*, 1556. Reproduced from the English translation by H.C. Hoover and L.H. Hoover, New York, Dover Publications, Inc., 1950, p.104

rhetoric, poetry and the three classical languages (Latin, Greek and Hebrew) were endowed with chairs. Scholasticism and the study of Aristotle were relegated to a minor role. Frederick even wrote in person to the leading German humanist, Johannes Reuchlin, asking for his advice in finding men suitably qualified to teach Greek and Hebrew. (Reuchlin responded by proposing his own great-nephew, Philipp Melanchthon, who was to play a crucial role in propagating the Lutheran Reformation in Germany.)

To some extent, Frederick's promotion of relics, art and learning formed part of a wider political strategy aimed at raising the profile of electoral Saxony in the cauldron of central European politics. Among his rivals were members of his own family who ruled neighbouring territories. Chief of these was his cousin, Duke George of Albertine Saxony (1471–1539), a devout and loyal Catholic, who, in line with other German princes, was eager to retain strict control over the Saxon church.

The city of Zwickau was one of the largest in electoral Saxony, with a population of around 7,500. Not only did it have a university, but in

1519 a school for the teaching of Greek was set up here by a *sodalitas* or humanist brotherhood. The school was transformed into an institution with the backing of the municipal authorities, who had been won over to the cause of 'good letters' (Mandrou, 1973, p.62).

In common with other cities in this region, Zwickau was a prosperous community that was experiencing important social and economic changes. Perhaps the most significant of these in the long term was the gradual decline of the traditional guild system whereby individual trades were responsible for overseeing all aspects of their members' work. Wages, working conditions, admission to trades, weights and measures and trading standards were all managed by craft guilds which, in conjunction with city councils, sought to preserve the privileges of guild members. In Zwickau, the changes were most evident in the city's well-developed textile industry, where increasingly competition was eroding the traditional guild system. One consequence was growing differentiation between skilled and unskilled labour and an attempt by **journeymen** to defend themselves from unscrupulous masters who sought to undermine traditional working practices and cut wages. Throughout Germany, this created tension and conflict between masters and their employees, which frequently erupted into organized strikes. In 1516, for example, there were strikes of blacksmiths in neighbouring Annaberg, and five years later, in Zwickau itself, bakers and millworkers went on strike. The whole nature of late medieval industrial relations began to change as journeymen formed alliances with fellow journeymen in other trades in order to protest against the introduction of new working methods and the destruction of traditional practices.

Such issues were central to the concerns of government in this period, none more so than for the city and town councils, which traditionally maintained close links with guilds. In Zwickau, as elsewhere in Germany, the council and guilds shared joint responsibility for a variety of matters, including the regulation of trade, public order and health. The council itself was a self-perpetuating oligarchy, consisting of twelve councilmen who were responsible for electing their own successors. Once appointed, and with the approval of the elector, they held office for life. In line with other Saxon cities in this period, Zwickau's ruling elite was careful to cultivate close links with the electoral administration in Wittenberg, a strategy that was largely based on a mutual alliance of interests.[3] Accordingly, the elector possessed his own military administrator in the city.

---

[3] '[Saxon] cities tended to prefer the most distant overlord, powerful enough to protect them, yet far enough away to let them thrive according to their own customs' (Ozment, 1975, p.33).

One of the greatest problems facing the city council of Zwickau was the influx of rural poor, who were attracted to the city by the opportunity to work in the increasingly deregulated woollen industry. Traditionally, poor relief was a matter for individual consciences – an obligation on the part of devout Catholics who, in giving alms and caring for the sick and destitute, were procuring their own salvation by good works. Almsgiving was a normal part of late medieval life. However, by the late fifteenth century, it was common for city councils to channel private donations into charitable institutions, such as hospitals (not just places for the sick, but more usually refuges for the destitute). Some confraternities were based on craft guilds, and these were increasingly active in providing corporate forms of charitable relief, particularly for their own members.

After the Reformation, the need for the city authorities to play a more active role in charitable provision for the poor and the sick became acute. This was partly the result of economic factors outside the control of the community (for example, inflation and growing poverty), but also a consequence of the abolition of the Catholic lay confraternities. It was, moreover, exacerbated by the decline in the moral imperative for individuals to give alms – a direct consequence of Protestant teaching on this subject. The authorities' response to the problem in Zwickau was a pragmatic one, inspired largely by anxiety about the danger of public disorder if nothing was done to care for the growing number of homeless citizens begging in the streets of the city. Income from **ecclesiastical benefices** was transferred to a community chest and the council attempted, without much success, to enforce almsgiving. These communal funds were also used to pay the pastor and teachers at the city's grammar school. One undoubted consequence of the Reformation in Zwickau, therefore, was a tendency for the council to assume greater authority in the supervision of the social, economic and moral lives of the city's inhabitants.

Reform and local protest

Prior to the Reformation, Zwickau society was seething with unrest and barely repressed conflict. The city was overcrowded and the gap between rich and poor was growing ever more threatening. Not surprisingly, relations between the city's governors and the populace at large were rapidly deteriorating. In particular, the opposition of the guilds to what they saw as the usurpation of authority in the city by a new, wealthy elite caused dangerous divisions to appear in the ranks of the citizenry.

Between 1509 and 1510, the council imposed restrictions on brewing and introduced a form of licensing in the city; it already controlled

Figure 2.10 Lucas Cranach the Elder, *Women Hunting Monks*, 1537, pen and ink drawing. A similar incident occurred in Zwickau in 1524. Germanisches Nationalmuseum, Nuremberg

the price of grain through its monopoly of the mills. In 1510, the council attempted to extend its economic control in the city by placing impositions on the sale and distribution of salt. In 1516, the guilds reacted by refusing to swear the oath of allegiance to the new council. At the same time, they presented a list of 21 grievances, detailing their objections to the council's high-handedness in imposing the new restrictions, particularly those on brewing. Further strikes followed, in which a group of artisans also presented a list of its grievances to the council. In the event, the council's concessions were insignificant, since it was able to call on the support of the elector in its struggle with the townspeople. Temporarily, at least, the alliance between the elector and the governors of Zwickau was beneficial to the interests of the latter. But this could not be guaranteed in every situation. On a series of other matters, particularly those pertaining to the religious life of the city, the elector, town council and guilds often took opposing views and aligned themselves in various combinations.

Like Augsburg, Zwickau had its own harbingers of the Reformation, men who felt distinctly uneasy about certain aspects of the Catholic faith. One such was the humanist preacher at the church of St Mary's, Johannes Wildenauer Egranus (d.1535), who supported Luther's stand against indulgences and argued that there was no scriptural warrant for the Catholic doctrine of the three marriages of St Anne, the mother of the Virgin.[4] In 1517, the Franciscan friars in the city mounted a strenuous attack on Egranus. Egranus, however, was supported by the city council which, concerned to keep the power of the Franciscans in check, raised his stipend and built him a new house. The Franciscans in the mean time were warned to desist from further attacks.

However, Zwickau's main claim to fame in the annals of the Reformation lies in the fact that it was the place where Thomas Müntzer first began to practise a brand of radical, apocalyptic preaching, which culminated in his death, alongside that of some of his followers, following the battle of Frankenhausen in 1525. Although Müntzer's stay in Zwickau was brief, others in the city were prepared to preserve and develop his message of spiritual renewal, particularly the supporters of three local men known as the Zwickau Prophets.

Müntzer

Thomas Müntzer (c.1489–1525) arrived in Zwickau in May 1520. He was apparently recommended to the city by Luther himself, and was appointed minister to St Mary's on a temporary basis to provide cover for the incumbent, Egranus. Unfortunately, we know little of Müntzer's immediate background, nor much of the content of the early sermons that he preached at Zwickau. What is clear, however, is

[4] 'St Anne was the patron saint of people in distress in thunderstorms as well as the patroness of miners. The cult of St Anne had spread across central Germany before Luther's time [...]. At the church of St Mary in Eisenach, where Luther's friend Johannes Braun was vicar, a special liturgy was sung for St Anne. Anne was the Virgin Mary's mother, but she was venerated for more than that because through the doctrine of the Immaculate Conception [...] Anne, too, participated in the miracle of the incarnation of Christ. As a reformer Luther later rejected the "doctrine of Anne" completely: "It also applies to St Anne, whose feast is being celebrated today, that I cannot find a word about her in the Bible. I believe that God left this unmentioned so that we would not seek out new holy places, as we are now doing, running to and fro and thus losing sight of the true Saviour, Jesus Christ" ' (Oberman, 1989, p.93). Luther had himself invoked St Anne in 1505 when he was caught in a thunderstorm.

Figure 2.11 *Thomas Müntzer*. Bildarchiv Preussischer Kulturbesitz, Berlin

that he rapidly departed from the moderate Lutheranism of Egranus (who later returned to the Catholic fold) and soon began to preach a more radical message, which led to divisions within the city. Following Egranus's return to Zwickau in October 1520, relations between the two evangelical preachers rapidly deteriorated. Müntzer was moved to the parish church of St Katherine's, but he continued to attack his colleague in a series of fiery sermons in which he castigated Egranus for his advocacy of 'an easy, inexperienced, externally officiated Christianity' that owed more to book learning than it did to the spiritual message of the gospels (Ozment, 1973, pp.61–7; quote at p.66).

The differences between the two men came to a head in early 1521 when their dispute threatened to disrupt the peace of the city. The council itself was divided in its support for the two men, and despite its attempt to conceal this split, electoral pressure was brought to bear to resolve the situation. Accordingly, the bishop summoned Egranus and Müntzer to appear before the church court at Zeitz (neither would seem to have appeared in person) and the town council invited an associate of Luther, Nicholas Hausmann, to fill the post of town preacher in place of Egranus. Meanwhile, the religious temperature continued to rise in Zwickau. Müntzer's apocalyptic preaching grew more radical in tone as he began to incite his supporters to violence in order to bring about the long-awaited revival of true religion and social egalitarianism. Not surprisingly, he was perceived by many in authority as a radical subversive whose preaching threatened social chaos. Among other incidents, a Catholic priest who attempted to hear Müntzer preach was stoned by members of his congregation. Not long after, further pressure was brought to bear on the council to remove Müntzer from the city. In April 1521, the elector's agent in Zwickau demanded that the council eject Müntzer, and shortly after this he left for Prague, where he hoped to spread his radical new version of the Reformation.

At the point of his departure, Müntzer clearly retained a loyal following in the city, which included, unexpectedly perhaps, some drawn from the ranks of the more prosperous citizens, as well as large sections of the town's poor and dispossessed. Indeed, he was given the honour of an escort, although as soon as he had left, 56 of his followers were promptly arrested and imprisoned overnight.

Exercise

Read the letter from Egranus to Luther, written in May 1521, shortly after Müntzer's departure from Zwickau (Anthology, no. 78). What reasons does Egranus give for objecting to Müntzer's presence in the city?

Discussion

Despite the theological differences between the two men, Egranus's complaint against Müntzer is more concerned with his flawed character and capacity for sowing discord than it is with the content of his preaching. Egranus specifically refers to Müntzer's followers as debtors, lawbreakers and 'persons given to revolt', a motley crowd who scream against 'every person of rank, every preacher and priest'. For Egranus, it is not so much Müntzer's theology that is reprehensible as the social implications of his 'revelations'. ❖

Egranus was vague about the content of Müntzer's preaching, saying simply that it did not possess the authority of scripture but was supported merely by 'revelations'. Hence he taught schism and heresy. It would be easy to concur with Egranus and to dismiss Müntzer's apocalyptic teachings as the pronouncements of a social revolutionary, committed to a war against the rich and powerful. Some Marxist historians would doubtless uphold this interpretation. There is, however, another side to Müntzer's evangelical preaching, which owes much to the same humanist training and background that men like Luther and Egranus had experienced in their formative years. Among his many attributes, Müntzer:

> knew some Greek and Hebrew, read Plato and Quintilian, taught pupils the elements of Latin grammar and syntax, and above all buried himself in the study of the Church Fathers ... He became convinced that in its liturgy and discipline the pure virgin Church of the Apostles

had been replaced by a wretched hag, corrupt and corrupting. He translated the mass into German before Luther, and the *Order and Explanation* of his German Order of Service shows a broad and contextualist understanding of the development and variety of Christian traditions in East and West.

(Matheson, 1990, p.39)

Müntzer was an educated man who, ironically, used his learning to disparage and subvert the authority of texts, even scripture, in the quest for spiritual enlightenment. According to Müntzer, all people must be free to interpret the message of the Bible in their own way, subject to the guidance of God's Holy Spirit. Consequently, there was no need for an authorized ministry of trained and learned pastors, whose job it was to administer and interpret the Word of God. In Müntzer's radical theology, the Word of God was written in the hearts of individual believers. God spoke directly to man, not through books or other human inventions. In many respects, this was the logical corollary of Luther's own subscription to the idea of a 'priesthood of all believers'. And yet, as Luther was soon to understand, it carried with it grave risks. Müntzer was not alone in concluding that book learning and organized religion was a fraud, perpetrated by those in authority in order to keep the common people under control. The popular appeal of Müntzer's preaching lived on, long after his departure from Zwickau in 1521, not least among a small group of men and women who now transferred their allegiance to another group of radical preachers in the city, the so-called Zwickau Prophets.

The Zwickau Prophets

Although Müntzer's influence over certain members of the city council seems to have evaporated on his departure from Zwickau, he left behind a loyal following among some of the townspeople. In August 1521, Hausmann, the new town preacher, recorded his anxiety about the prevalence of false beliefs, both radical and Catholic, in the city. A few months later, reports of a secret brotherhood were widely dispersed. The leaders of this group were three men – Nicholas Storch, a weaver, Thomas Dreschel, a smith, and Marcus Stübner, an ex-student of Melanchthon at Wittenberg – who were self-proclaimed prophets of God. All three claimed direct communication with God, as well as asserting that revealed truths, or revelations, were more authoritative than the evidence of the scriptures. Those suspected of membership of this brotherhood were called before the council, but its three leaders escaped to Wittenberg, where they were met and questioned by Melanchthon. Three months later, in March 1522, Luther, currently in hiding in the Elector of Saxony's castle at

Wartburg, commented on them in a letter to his friend and colleague, Hausmann, in Zwickau.

Exercise

Read the letter from Melanchthon to Elector Frederick the Wise (27 December 1521) and that from Luther to Hausmann (17 March 1522) (Anthology, nos. 79 and 80). Compare the reactions of Melanchthon and Luther to the Zwickau Prophets.

Discussion

Melanchthon, who met the men in person, professed himself deeply moved by the experience and by their claim to hear God speaking directly to them. He was convinced of their sincerity, but, in a telling statement that betrays Melanchthon's deference to Luther, sought the great man's reassurance.

Luther, in contrast, based his judgement on what he had heard from others. He was clearly not impressed. He believed that the prophets were nothing less than charlatans, agents of the devil, who, if allowed, would do untold damage to the cause of reform. As a man of profoundly conservative social views, Luther objected strenuously to the imposition of religious reform from below, by 'popular decree or force'. He was equally scathing of those who continued to practise the Catholic faith. Significantly, however, he argued that genuine change could only be brought about by the peaceful preaching of the Word of God; violence or physical force was to be avoided at all costs. Once exposed to the teaching of the gospel by godly ministers, he believed, the people would come to a new understanding of faith and so reject intuitively the corrupt practices and institutions of the Catholic church. ❖

Religious reform or social transformation?

The expulsion of Müntzer and the suppression of the Zwickau Prophets may well have owed more to the fear of public disorder in the city than to a full understanding of the theology that underlay their beliefs. Nonetheless, after 1522, the way was clear for the reception of moderate Lutheranism in Zwickau, which followed Wittenberg as the second city in Saxony to adopt wholeheartedly the new faith. As the preaching of Müntzer and the Zwickau Prophets graphically demonstrates, Luther himself exerted little control over the way in which his evangelical message was spread and received by the people of Germany. In a short space of time, however, he soon came to realize that if inflammatory incidents were to be avoided, he would need to rely heavily on the support of the secular authorities in propagating the Word. Consequently, he worked closely to cultivate the support of men like Elector Frederick the Wise, and his brother and successor, John the Constant (1468–1532) (who was also Duke of Saxony). The latter was a particularly useful ally of Luther's since, unlike his predecessor, he was committed to the Lutheran reform programme and helped to create a hierarchical structure of church governance in Saxony.

Exercise

Read 'Progress towards reform' by Susan Karant-Nunn in the Reader (no. 19). To what extent was the progress of religious reform in Zwickau tied to secular concerns?

Discussion

Karant-Nunn believes that the creation of a Lutheran church in Zwickau provided a valuable opportunity for the council to extend its jurisdiction in the city. The council's temporal ambitions coincided, in the main, with the spiritual ambitions of the Lutheran town preacher, and principal advocate of religious reform, Hausmann. Both, for example, sought to eradicate the institutions of the Roman Catholic church and to establish, in their place, a reformed ministry. Hausmann, like Luther, believed that religious reform should progress with the support of the secular authorities, or magistracy, and that conflict with them should be avoided at all costs.

The council's involvement in religious affairs, however, was not always free of conflict. Disagreements between the council, Hausmann and the elector were never far from the surface. It is also apparent that the town's institutions did not permit a clear division between secular and ecclesiastical concerns. The council, for example, took the lead in inviting Luther to Zwickau and gave him licence to preach in the Franciscan friary. The Franciscans were a major source of friction, and the council attempted to install its own nominee to run the friary, ostensibly on the grounds of public order. The council's decision to divert the funds of the Calend Fraternity to poor relief was equally divisive. Moreover, when the council used the riot at the Cistercian monastery as an excuse to close it down and appropriate the land and buildings of the order, it found itself in direct conflict with the elector.

The council increasingly saw ecclesiastical revenues – for example, taxes on clerical properties and incomes from benefices – as a source of income for the city. Benefices were a valuable source of income for which the council would not be answerable to taxpayers (although heirs of benefactors objected to what they saw as the confiscation of family property). Initially, the revenues were used in part to fund activities for which the council had recently assumed responsibility. (For example, the council had to provide for displaced Catholic clergy who refused to subscribe to the new doctrines.) In the longer term, however, the revenues would fall to the exclusive use of the council.

The council decided to establish a community chest to fund charitable relief and education. (This was a very important

As Luther said it should be

development in these early years of Protestant rule in Zwickau.) After the Reformation, governance of the church and the administration of charity was largely centralized in the hands of the secular authorities, the council assuming direct control over all aspects of provision for the poor. ❖

The effects of the Reformation on the government of the city of Zwickau were far-reaching. The council, largely dominated by Lutherans, gained unlimited control over clerical appointments and the various institutions formerly administered by Catholic religious bodies. In particular, schooling and poor relief became the responsibility of the municipal authorities. One interesting side-effect of these changes was a reduction in the custom of private charity or almsgiving. Lutheranism, then, was widely adopted in the city, although it proved impossible to eradicate completely adherence to the Catholic faith. There were also pockets of religious radicalism in the city, the legacy of Müntzer and the Zwickau Prophets, but, as a proportion of the city population as a whole, those involved were few in number.

The appearance of the city itself must also have changed in these years. The Reformation did not lead to an end to public confrontations on the streets of Zwickau (mostly economic in origin), but it did see a marked decline in the number of religious festivals, processions and displays. Another reform that must have impacted upon the street life of the city was the prohibition on begging, by priests, monks and nuns, as well as by poor laypeople. Change was also evident in the city's churches. After 1524, communion was administered in both kinds to the laity and preaching became a much more prominent feature of church services.

The most visible effect of the Reformation upon the public life of the city, however, was probably evident in the marked decline in the number of secular priests (that is, priests who were not members of monastic orders) and **regular clergy**. The closure of the Cistercian monastery and Dominican friary must have radically altered the composition of the city. We do not know the precise impact of the Reformation in this respect upon Zwickau, but it must have been considerable and immediately visible to contemporaries. In the north German town of Rostock, for example, the clerical population shrank from over two hundred to just thirteen (Ozment, 1993, p.26).

The Peasants' War

An important aspect of the successful reception of the Reformation in urban Germany was the way in which the message of the reformers appealed to a wide cross-section of the population, particularly those who felt buffeted by the winds of social, economic and political change. The reason why so many citizens and guild members were attracted to the new faith is highly elusive. Few, in all probability, were converted because of their understanding and appreciation of the doctrinal complexities of Protestantism. The vast majority, perhaps, were attracted to Lutheranism because of its simple message of spiritual consolation in the face of external threats and new challenges to the old social order:

> When the citizens of a German town or a Swiss village, habituated to certain local customs and privileges, found themselves facing incorporation into the territory of a local prince and subject to his laws, Protestant sermonizing about the spiritual freedom and equality of Christians had an immediate, sympathetic ring and understandably gained captive audiences.

(Ozment, 1993, p.20)

What was true for the city was equally applicable to the countryside, where social unrest in the early sixteenth century was endemic. The rights and traditional liberties of the German peasantry were increasingly threatened in this period by the encroachments of secular and ecclesiastical landlords. The freedom of the peasantry, for example, to access forest land was curtailed, as was their ability to move from one estate to another. In 1524, rural unrest erupted in a series of provincial rebellions, which began on the Swiss border and rapidly spread to much of southern Germany. Groups of peasants banded together to form associations and many set out their grievances in printed pamphlets. One such was that based on the Swabian town of Memmingen. Here, artisans from the town and peasants from the surrounding countryside joined together to form a local association, dedicated to removing a whole range of abuses and injustices. Protest marches were convened and strikes organized. The protestors also refused to pay tithes (an annual levy of one tenth of a household's income for the support of the local church). The peasants appealed to the town council of Memmingen, which agreed to negotiate with them, and they drew up a charter of grievances, known as 'The Twelve Articles'.

Exercise

Read the articles written by the peasants of Swabia (Anthology, no. 81). What evidence do you detect in this document for the influence of reformed religious thinking on the protest of the peasants?

Discussion

Religion, in the sense of the need to call on God as a witness to the truth of the peasants' claims, is very much in evidence throughout the document. There are biblical references in the margin designed to show that the points in the body of the pamphlet conform to scripture. Similar references appear in the preamble, in the articles themselves and in the conclusion.

Moreover, the preamble is saturated with the language of the Bible, particularly in its reference to those 'Antichrists' who intimate that the peasants' demands are subversive and ungodly. The peasants say that, on the contrary, they deny any desire to overthrow constituted authority, but insist instead on 'a Christian justification for ... disobedience'.

We need to be careful here, though, to draw a distinction between a general desire to call on God as a witness to the righteousness of their cause (a feature of many peasant rebellions prior to the Reformation), and more concrete evidence of the influence of reformed ideas. The latter is suggested by the frequent references in the preamble to the authority of the 'Word of God'. It is also evident in the specific details of the articles.

Article 1, for example, shows evidence of the influence of reform in its espousal of the principle that the community should nominate its own pastor as well as monitor his performance (parish clergy in the Roman Catholic church were normally subject to the discipline of the local bishop). The chief task of the minister – preaching the gospel 'without any human additions to doctrines and commandments' – was fully in accordance with Lutheran practice. And grace rather than works was seen as the source of salvation. This theme is continued in Article 2, in which the peasants seek reform of the system of tithe payments in accordance with their communal and evangelical programme.

The peasants systematically invoke God to support a broad programme of political and social reform, linking evangelical principles with community participation in government (as, for example, in Article 4, where the 'Word of God' is again invoked in defence of catching game and fish). ❖

The articles drawn up by the peasants of Swabia were printed in March 1525 and soon became the model for many other sets of articles drawn up by peasants in neighbouring parts of Germany. Some commentators have seen the articles as essentially moderate in scope and ambition (nowhere, for example, do the peasants reject the authority of magistrates or landlords). Others have seen them as radical in tone since they declare the Word of God to be the only true test of legitimacy. While negotiations were taking place in Memmingen between the town council and rebel petitioners, peasants from other parts of Swabia began to assemble in the town and to meet in a 'peasant parliament'. Here, they agreed to form a

Christian Union and issued their own articles of association, known as 'The Federal Ordinance'.

Exercise

Compare the demands of 'The Federal Ordinance' (Anthology, no. 82) with those of 'The Twelve Articles' (Anthology, no. 81). In what way do they differ?

Discussion

Unlike 'The Twelve Articles', 'The Federal Ordinance' did not constitute a reform programme. Rather, it was intended to form a plan of action for a group of people who possessed a common general purpose, although with different local demands and aims. Hence, certain details such as those relating to military preparation (Article 4) and the preservation of the Union (Article 10) were quite specific, but demands about justice, preachers and other issues were left deliberately vague.

'The Federal Ordinance' does, however, resemble 'The Twelve Articles' in one important respect, namely its constant invocation of the Word of God to justify the acts of the rebels. ❖

We might wish to add that neither of the documents is particularly Lutheran or Zwinglian in tone. Both cite the Word of God extensively in order to justify their aims and demands. And both demand a preaching ministry answerable to the local parish or community. But there is little here to suggest that the teachings of Luther and Zwingli have made anything more than a superficial impact upon the minds of the rural and urban poor. Paul Russell, in his study of lay religion in south-western Germany during the Peasants' War, suggests that this may well have been the case. He argues that the peasants were motivated more by an appeal to the Bible, popular millenarianism (a belief in the imminent destruction of the world, as prophesied in the Book of Revelation) and anti-clericalism than they were by the writings of the great leaders of the reform movement (Russell, 1986). Other historians, however, have pointed to the influence of Lutheran propaganda on the masses, much of which depicted the pope as the Antichrist. And some have pointed to the strong influence in Swabia of the Zwinglian Reformation and the city of Zurich, one of the first cities to adopt the institutions of a reformed church.

Whatever the source of the peasants' demands, the actions of those in southern Germany rapidly spread to other parts of the empire. By the middle of 1525, Saxony itself was affected by peasant insurrection and Luther was forced to rebut the claims of those who firmly laid the blame for the Peasants' War on his shoulders. In fact, Luther was profoundly opposed to the peasants' disobedience, his disapproval of their demands matched by his excoriating assault on the self-proclaimed leaders of the revolt, such as the 'renegade' Lutheran,

Figure 2.12 *The Origins of the Pope*, 1545. From Scribner, R.W. (1987) *Popular Culture and Popular Movements in Reformation Germany*, London and Ronceverte, The Hambledon Press, p.279

ORTVS ET ORIGO PAPAE.

Hie wird geborn der Widerchrift/
Megera fein Seugamme ift/
Alecto fein Kindermeidlin/
Tifiphone die gengelt jn.

Mart. Luther D.
IX.   1545.

Müntzer. Indeed, Luther's bitter and violent repudiation of the peasants exceeded that of many of his more moderate colleagues. (Melanchthon, for example, was sympathetic to some of the peasants' claims, although he denied, with Luther, any suggestion that rebellion was justified by scripture.)

Exercise

Read the letter from Luther to John Rühel, written on 4 May 1525 (Anthology, no. 83). How did Luther characterize the opposition of the peasants?

Discussion

Luther saw the peasants as simply disobedient to lay authority. Not only did they rebel against their lawful rulers, but they compounded their sin by invoking divine authority for their actions. He particularly objected to the fact that they invoked the word of scripture in order to create a new social and political order in this world. ❖

Although the conflict between the peasants and their lords is always referred to as the Peasants' War, it did include urban artisans, as we saw in the case of 'The Twelve Articles'. The artisans of Erfurt in Saxony produced their own version of 'The Twelve Articles' and Luther was invited to comment on these by the town council of Erfurt.

Exercise

Read the articles drawn up by the peasants and artisans of Erfurt in May 1525 (Luther's objections to specific clauses appear in italics) (Anthology, no. 84). What characterizes these demands as distinctively urban?

Discussion

There are frequent references to the conduct of town government and a demand for greater public scrutiny of the actions of the town council. Its members are also to be made more accountable for the performance of their duties. While 'The Twelve Articles' dealt with land ownership and tenancies, the articles of Erfurt are more concerned with loans, interest rates, taxation, prices and religious endowments. All in all, this is a more 'sophisticated' document than that composed by the Swabian peasants, one that demonstrates the extent to which commerce and capital dominated urban life in this period. It even advocates a reform of the city's university (Article 23) – a move that may have been motivated by a deep-seated respect for learning, but might equally have emanated from the rebels' understanding of the economic significance of the university in the life of the town. ❖

Luther's response to the demands of the Erfurt petitioners is typical of his generally hostile attitude towards those who sought to use evangelical reform as an agent of social and political change. Luther opposed the rebels on two grounds. First, he understood only too well that if his reform movement was to succeed then it would need the backing of those in authority, from town magistrates to princely rulers. And secondly, and more importantly one suspects for Luther, obedience to secular authority carried the warrant of scripture. It is hardly surprising, therefore, that Luther sided wholeheartedly with the magistrates and town council of Erfurt against the rebels. Nonetheless, his implacable opposition to protest and resistance of this kind did not endear him to some of his early supporters. One such was Hermann Mühlpfort, mayor of Zwickau, who hosted Luther's visit to the city in 1522 and was instrumental in the appointment of Luther's friend and colleague, Hausmann, as town preacher (see Reader, no. 19). By the middle of 1525, Mühlpfort would appear to have had second thoughts about Luther, following his intervention in the Peasants' War.

Read the letter from Hermann Mühlpfort to Stephen Roth, dated 4 June 1525 (Anthology, no. 85). Why did Mühlpfort object to Luther's stance with regard to the peasants?

Mühlpfort's view seems to be that the villains of the piece were not the peasants, but the nobility. Luther's opposition to the peasants appeared to further empower the nobility to exploit the poor and thus give the latter continued reason to rebel. Mühlpfort was far from supporting the peasant cause. He nonetheless believed that the chief responsibility for preventing noble exploitation of the poor lay with the great territorial princes, who ought to exercise their power in defence of the weak and oppressed. He seems to have been genuinely concerned for the plight of the poor (poverty was a daily concern for the governors of Zwickau), and felt that Luther was insufficiently sympathetic to the causes and consequences of poverty. There is also a slight hint at the end of the letter that Luther's actions, and the bloody suppression of the rebels, may have weakened popular support for the Reformation. ❖

The progress of reform: success or failure?

As the case studies above have shown, the German Reformation, unlike the Renaissance, was not exclusively an urban or court-based phenomenon restricted to the ranks of an educated minority. In Germany, rich and poor, learned and unlearned, and town and country dwellers played their part in the reception and dissemination of reformed practices and beliefs. The response of these various groups was not, however, uniform and consistent throughout the German-speaking lands. In seeking to determine why men and women in the sixteenth century were attracted to the cause of religious reform, we are immediately struck by interesting parallels with the Renaissance, and the way in which it was adopted, adapted and, in certain cases, rejected. The example of the rural insurgents in the Peasants' War is a case in point. Although their response was clearly indebted to some extent to the language of religious reform, and its appeal to the authority of scripture, it was highly unlikely that the vast majority of those who took part in the conflict had anything other than a fleeting acquaintance with the more detailed programme of the reform movement. However, the same may well be true of many of those in the towns and cities, where the Reformation first took root. Popular anti-clericalism, often motivated by jealousy of the economic privileges of the church, was probably just as likely to encourage conversion to the Protestant faith as was a deep-seated understanding of, and concurrence with, the theological niceties of reformed doctrine.

As a result of the recent interest in local studies of the German Reformation, historians have become increasingly aware of the apparent failure of the Protestant reform movement to effect a full and rigorous transformation of popular culture in the sixteenth century. There are, it has been argued, many ways in which this failure is apparent. It is evident, for example, in the case of Augsburg, where the initial support for reform, which could be found at every level of society, was not accompanied by an overnight shift to Protestantism. Indeed, support for the Reformation in the city peaked around the middle of the century. Thereafter, a resurgent Catholicism led to the reconversion of large numbers of Protestants – a process repeated in a number of cities throughout Germany in the second half of the sixteenth century.

Another example of the failure of the Reformation to achieve its goals is the way in which ordinary parishioners did not manage to live up to the expectations of their reformed leaders. Men like Luther, and later Calvin, were convinced that the spread of evangelism would effect a fundamental change in the moral and spiritual condition of the people. In order to ensure success in this respect, various measures were adopted. Reformed communities actively promoted lay understanding of the scriptures through an increased emphasis on preaching and catechizing the young. Educational reform was widely encouraged in Protestant circles. New schools were founded and literacy rates improved dramatically. Most important of all, reform leaders of every persuasion sought to effect a new alliance with sympathetic magistrates in the towns and villages of Protestant Germany in order to ensure that the full force of the law was brought to bear on those who continued to resist the message of the gospel and to pollute the commonwealth through their immorality. Yet, despite all these changes, precious little was achieved in the actual transformation of the lives, beliefs and customs of the vast majority of those who lived under Protestant rule (see, for example, Strauss, 1978).

To label the Reformation a 'failure', however, is perhaps unfair, reflecting as it does the hopelessly unrealistic ambitions of men like Luther and Zwingli, who wished to change the world in a single generation. Viewed from the perspective of the present, much was effected, not least in the towns and cities of Germany, where the Reformation first received sustenance and support. The urban nature of the Reformation remains one of its most distinctive features. It was in urban areas, for example, that the full implications of reformed theology were most thoroughly adopted and debated. And it was here that the first experiments in the creation of a Protestant-inspired new order were conducted – ranging from the various ordinances of Lutheran and Zwinglian town councils to the utopian dreams of men like the Zwickau Prophets, which resulted in the events that occurred at **Münster** in 1535.

There were a number of reasons why towns and cities were the natural focus of reformers and their ambitious programmes. Not only did urban regions contain large numbers of ordinary men and women whose economic and social position inclined them to listen favourably to the message of Christian consolation preached by men like Luther, but they were also centres of intellectual and learned debate. Germany's towns and cities played a critical role in fostering the growth of a native humanist movement. This, as we have seen, was an essential ingredient of the German Reformation. We should not be surprised, therefore, to find support for humanism in a city like Augsburg, whose wealthiest citizens were among the first in Germany to adopt Italian styles in the visual arts. What is noticeable, however, is the extent to which humanist values and ideas permeated many of the smaller towns and cities of central Europe in this period, and thus helped to lay the ground for future religious reform. In Zwickau, for example, the role of the moderate humanist preacher, Egranus, was clearly important in this respect. More surprising, perhaps, is the debt of those like Müntzer and Stübner (one of the Zwickau Prophets) to early contact with humanism.[5]

Large towns and cities also possessed the significant advantage for reformers of containing access to printing presses, which enabled them to spread their evangelical message further afield. It also allowed Protestant propagandists to tailor their publications for particular audiences: learned, theological tracts for an educated elite and illustrated broadsheets for the illiterate masses. Above all, urban centres contained wealthy patrons who, more often than not, were able to provide financial as well as moral support for reform-minded clergy and intellectuals. In much the same way as artists and writers looked to princely benefactors in the courts and cities of Italy to promote the arts, so religious reformers drew stimulation and material sustenance from their urban surroundings.

Historians are, then, still debating the full extent of the impact of reform upon the lives of sixteenth-century Germans. The jury, as they say, remains out. Although much was undoubtedly achieved –

---

[5] Interestingly, when the Zwickau Prophets visited Wittenberg in 1521, the weaver Storch sought for converts among the workers of the city, while the educated Stübner focused his energies upon the university professors (Ozment, 1973, p.64).

particularly in those urban centres that acted as the natural focus for discontent in this period – we must nonetheless acknowledge the limits of Protestant success. In the process, it is equally important to recognize that the failure of Protestantism was not exclusively the fault of its own leadership or the body of ideas to which the reformers subscribed. By the middle decades of the sixteenth century, the evangelical churches were forced to confront a new threat to their tenuous hold on the religious minds of their communities in the form of a Catholic revival, known variously as the Counter-Reformation or Catholic Reformation.

Reform outside Germany: counter-reform or Catholic reform?

The movement known as the Counter-Reformation or Catholic Reformation is usually identified with the attempt by the Catholic hierarchy to implement wholesale reform of the church in response to the successful establishment of Protestantism in northern Europe in the early sixteenth century. Between 1545 and 1563, a general council met in three sessions at Trent, in northern Italy, and issued a series of decrees that were intended to reinvigorate traditional Catholic practices and beliefs. New religious orders, such as the Jesuits were expected to carry forward the Catholic reform programme and to reclaim Protestants for the Catholic faith. In the mean time, a new emphasis was placed upon the spiritual welfare of the laity; old practices were reformed, new cults and saints emerged. The description of this process as a 'Counter-Reformation' is, however, highly misleading. Catholic reform was not simply a reactionary movement, characterized and shaped by the need to oppose or 'counter' Protestantism. It was also a movement of positive reform, whose roots pre-date Luther's attack on indulgences and the pope.

We have already seen how widespread was the movement for spiritual renewal and institutional reform of the church in northern Europe prior to 1517 (see Chapter 1). The onset of the Reformation in Germany did not bring to an end Catholic attempts to reform the church from within. In Italy itself, many high-ranking clerics continued to argue for a programme of renewal and reform, culminating in 1537 in the publication of the report of a select group of senior churchmen, who publicly acknowledged the failings of the church and its leadership (see Anthology, no. 60). Its signatories included Gian Matteo Giberti (1495–1543), a man of impeccable humanist credentials and the first Italian bishop to attempt to put into practice the new reformist creed. In his diocese of Verona, to which he fled from Rome in 1528, he instituted a range of pastoral reforms, which were aimed at improving the quality of the parish clergy as well as increasing lay involvement in the day-to-day affairs of the church. Much of this was achieved through traditional means, such as 'visitations' or diocesan inspections, which had largely fallen into disuse. More innovatory was his attempt to achieve greater uniformity between parishes by concentrating religious activity outside the towns in larger parish churches. Masses in private houses were prohibited and the use of churches for non-devotional activity was discouraged and circumscribed.

Greater lay participation was fostered by the foundation of new confraternities in parishes. At the same time, potentially dissident figures such as lay **hermits**, around whom local devotional practices grew up, were discouraged. The relative absence of religious orders in the rural parts of the diocese was counteracted by the support that Giberti gave to the establishment of new confraternities devoted to the eucharist. Later in the century, confraternities based on **Marian cults** and the cult of the Rosary were established. Together, they provided a new focus for lay devotion and piety, as well as allowing the ecclesiastical hierarchy to exert a firmer hold on religious activities undertaken in the name of the church in the diocese.

The case of Giberti, popularly lauded as the first 'model bishop' of the Catholic Reformation, is indicative of the extent to which reformist trends continued to prosper in the Catholic church despite opposition to the Lutheran Reformation in Germany. Significantly, Giberti was an early advocate of Erasmus who, on receipt of a copy of Erasmus's *De libero arbitrio*, described its author as the best antidote to Lutheranism. But the question arises: since Erasmus's writings and influence travelled across the Alps, did those of Luther do the same?

Protestants, or proto-Protestants, can in fact be found in sixteenth-century Italy and Spain, the two regions of Europe most hostile to reformed ideas. But they never established a firm base. If further evidence of the importance of magisterial support for the spread of Protestantism was needed, the cases of Italy and Spain demonstrate how, in the absence of political support, reform could not progress beyond a small minority of dissidents.

Italy

In many respects, the efforts of bishop Giberti to impose reform on his rural flock were not much different in kind from earlier attempts in Italy to bring order and spiritual refreshment to the Catholic laity. Charismatic preachers such as Girolamo Savonarola (see Chapter 1) were essentially motivated by the same urge to promote a more active and lively faith among ordinary Christians. In the case of Savonarola, his memory and ideas were kept alive well into the sixteenth century by a group of followers known as the **Piagnoni**, who could often count upon the support of men of rank and intellectual stature (Gianfrancesco Pico della Mirandola, who you will encounter in Chapter 6, was one of their most steadfast patrons) (Polizzotto, 1994).

Erasmian humanism and anti-clericalism were also influential in governing circles and among Italian intellectuals. It is not surprising, therefore, that Italy harboured numerous heterodox religious communities who were familiar both with the writings of Luther (first translated into Italian in 1518) and the work of other reformers. Particularly popular in these circles were the works of the Spanish-born Erasmian reformer, Juan de Valdés (1509–41), who was forced to leave Spain in 1530 and spent the rest of his life in exile in Naples. In typically Erasmian fashion, Valdés sought to synthesize the traditional Catholic position on justification by works with the Lutheran view of justification by faith. Valdés remained a Catholic until his death in 1541.

Many of Valdés's Italian followers, however, were less inclined to stay within the boundaries of orthodoxy. One of his closest associates, Bernardino Ochino (1487–1564), formerly superior of the Capuchin order, fled from Italy in 1542, and after many travels ended up in Moravia among a group of Italian Anabaptist exiles. Peter Martyr (1500–62), a friend of Ochino and an associate of Valdés, converted to Protestantism, as did another member of the group, Peter Paul Vergerio (1497/8–1565). Vergerio's conversion was particularly dramatic since it occurred as a result of a meeting with Protestant leaders in 1541, during which he was responsible for demonstrating the error of the Protestant position. He finally fled Italy in 1549 and settled among a group of Italian Lutherans based in Germany.

Support for Protestantism in Italy was patchy. Some north Italian cities such as Lucca, Siena and Modena possessed small Lutheran communities that were protected, to some extent, by the support of the patrician and governing classes. Occasionally, Italian princes afforded limited protection to well-connected Protestant refugees. This was the case at Ferrara, where Renée, the daughter of Louis XII of France, and wife of Hercule (or Ercole) II d'Este, provided a safe haven for French Protestants (she was a patron, among others, of Calvin, who visited her in Ferrara in 1536). In general, however, Lutheranism was not a major concern of the authorities in Italy. Even in cities such as Lucca and Venice, where the influence of the new 'heresy' was most apparent, the numbers of those investigated and prosecuted for their heterodox views was very small. The records of the local **Inquisition** suggest that as few as 0.5 per cent of the populations of these cities were examined for their espousal of Lutheran views.

The process whereby such ideas reached their urban audiences included not only the printed word, but also popular preaching. This was the method used by earlier reformers such as Savonarola, whose public preaching in Florence drew vast audiences. Protestants, however, had to tread more carefully, and their meetings, or conventicles, usually took place in private away from the glare of the authorities. Nonetheless, in the 1530s and 1540s, underground networks of Protestant sympathizers could be found in many Italian cities, many of them strengthened by association with groups of Catholic reformers, known as *spirituali*, who received their inspiration from prominent figures such as the Cardinals Contarini, Pole and Morone.[6]

In the long term, the **eirenic** aspirations of Lutherans and Catholic sympathizers foundered on the growing opposition in the established church to the Erasmian-style programme of the *spirituali*. Various measures adopted by the ecclesiastical hierarchy aided this process. From 1542, the work of the revitalized Italian Inquisition proved increasingly effective in undermining grass-roots support for Protestant reform, and, in 1559, the establishment of the **Index** placed the writings of even moderate reformers like Erasmus on a list of proscribed authors.

The most important defeat for the proponents of reform, however, came at the hands of the Council of Trent which, in its first session (1545–8), rejected the Protestant view of salvation and reaffirmed the traditional view of the church that grace was the result of good works. At the same time, other doctrinal differences between Catholics and Protestants were given renewed emphasis: the Vulgate was confirmed as the only authorized version of the Bible; communion in both kinds was forbidden; and the monopoly right of priests to expound and interpret the scriptures was reasserted. Importantly, such conservatism was moderated by a growing acknowledgement among the churchmen

[6] Gasparo Contarini (1483–1542) was one of the foremost advocates in Italy of church reform. A firm believer in the values of both civic and biblical humanism, he was sympathetic to Luther's general theology, and led the attempt of the Catholic church to seek some form of compromise with the German Lutherans. The Englishman Reginald Pole (1500–58) was, like Contarini, a signatory of the Report advocating reform of the Catholic church in 1537. His attempt to promote biblical humanism in place of the traditional emphasis on scholasticism in the training of churchmen was defeated at the Council of Trent in 1546. Giovanni Morone (1509–80) was another leading advocate of Catholic reform, whose roots lay in the pre-Reformation Oratory movement (see Chapter 1).

who met at Trent of the need to institute some changes in the church that would bring about an improvement in the quality of pastoral provision as well as redress some of the more flagrant abuses and corrupt practices of church officials.

By 1560, such measures, combined with growing pressure on lay authorities to support the **Tridentine** decrees, saw the effective demise of embryonic Protestantism in Italy. Most Protestant sympathizers or converts chose exile or conformity (Hercule d'Este expelled the Protestants from his dominions, and even sent his wife back to France). Some remained, organized in clandestine cells or conventicles. By the second half of the sixteenth century, the majority of those who opted to remain looked to Calvin and Geneva, rather than the Lutheran communities of Germany, for support. French and Swiss publishers continued to produce Italian translations of Calvin's works well into the 1560s, despite the prohibition of such works by the Index. However, the audience for these works was almost certainly limited by this period to artisans. The most distinctive feature of the early reform movement in Italy – its fusion with the ideals of the Catholic Erasmians – was largely a thing of the past. Although numerically insignificant, the movement, temporarily at least, had exerted an important influence upon the development of religious reform in Italy and was, as a result, more than just a 'failed extension of the new doctrines propounded by the great Swiss and German reformers' (Firpo, 1996, p.363).

Spain

On balance, Spain would appear to have been more impervious than Italy to the ideas of Luther and the Protestant reformers. In some respects, this probably reflected Spain's relative isolation from the main currents of European religious and intellectual belief prior to the sixteenth century. In Spain, the subversive influence of heterodoxy owed more to native traditions provided by the presence of substantial numbers of Jews (until 1492) and Muslims (until 1499) than to Protestantism. After the forcible conversion of these two groups, Catholic orthodoxy, rather than reform, was the major preoccupation of the rulers of the Iberian peninsula. Nonetheless, during the course of the 1520s, the winds of religious change were felt in Spain as the ideas of both Erasmus and Luther were introduced into the country.

Despite the fact that Spain was to turn decisively towards Catholic orthodoxy in the second half of the sixteenth century, it did, briefly, promise to create an atmosphere conducive to religious reform. As in much of the rest of Europe, the pre-Reformation church in Spain was the subject of criticism and debate. Its prelates, mostly drawn from the aristocracy, were more interested in secular than ecclesiastical affairs. The Spanish monastic orders were prone to the same kinds of criticism as those levelled at their brethren elsewhere in Europe, and the country's parish priests were largely unlearned and ignorant.

Partly in response to these shortcomings, a native group of reformers – the *Alumbrado* or illuminist movement – had developed in the late fifteenth century. This movement was particularly popular among the urban artisan class and those of *converso* ancestry (that is, those who came from a background of Jewish conversion to Catholicism). The beliefs of individual adherents of the new sect are difficult to define with any precision, but they tended to subscribe to an emotional, mystical faith, which emphasized personal spiritual renewal above respect for the formalities and ceremonies of established religion. On occasions, this home-grown movement fused with another reformist element within the Spanish church, one that was largely the product of the growing influence of the writings of Erasmus among a group of senior Spanish churchmen and intellectuals. The leading figure in this group was Cardinal Francisco Ximénez de Cisneros (1436–1517), archbishop of Toledo. Cisneros's most significant achievement was the foundation of the University of Alcalá in 1508, which, under his leadership, was destined to become the main centre of Erasmianism and humanist scholarship in Spain. Among its many achievements was the famous six-volume polyglot Bible, known as the **Complutensian Bible** (compiled 1514–17; published 1522), which was a monument to the success of Spanish biblical humanist studies. This contained the text of the Vulgate Latin accompanied by the scriptures in their original languages, which were set alongside for ease of comparison and interpretation. Because of the continued presence of a sizeable *conversi* population in Spain in the sixteenth century, Hebrew scholarship was more advanced here than in any other part of Europe (three *conversi* were in fact responsible for the Hebrew text of the Complutensian Old Testament). Alcalá was, then, an important centre for the reception and discussion of reformist ideas and was responsible for introducing many of the finest minds in Spain to the new currents of thought. Among those who were educated here were the Erasmian scholar Alfonso de Valdés (1500–32), whose published attacks on clerical abuses and papal conduct were directly influenced by contact both with the great Dutch humanist and with Juan Gil (*c*.1500–55), the cathedral preacher of Seville and founder of a Lutheran cell in that city (Spach, 1995).

The final boost to Spanish Erasmianism and reform was provided by the arrival of the learned and cosmopolitan court of the young Hapsburg prince, Charles, in 1516, following his succession to the

Spanish throne as Charles I (1516–58).[7] During the 1520s, Erasmus was widely read in Spain and reform remained a viable option as long as Charles's patronage of humanist-minded statesmen and ecclesiastics provided a counter-balance to more conservative elements in the Spanish church. Charles's final departure for Germany in 1529 was a hard body-blow for the Erasmians that was immediately followed in the 1530s by a crackdown on the reformers, including the moderate Erasmians. Many fled into exile in the face of the threat posed by the **Spanish Inquisition**.[8] For those who remained, further draconian measures were introduced in the late 1550s, following the succession of Philip II (1558–98). *Autos de fé*, culminating in the public execution by burning of heretics, were widely implemented, the Index was rigidly enforced and purges of Spanish universities were instituted in order to root out potential dissidents. Finally, in 1559, Philip II issued a decree forbidding his subjects to study in foreign universities. By the 1560s, Spain found itself cut off from the mainstream of European intellectual and religious thought. Thereafter, the dominant influence in Spanish educational circles was to be provided by the Jesuits, who zealously defended Catholic orthodoxy as laid down by the Council of Trent.

There remains some doubt as to the extent to which Lutheranism ever fully permeated Spanish religious life in the sixteenth century. Although most agree that Spain was fertile territory for reform, the evidence for a native Lutheran movement is ambiguous. There is some evidence to suggest, for example, that Spaniards present in the entourage of the Emperor Charles V at the Diet of Worms in 1521 demonstrated more than a passing interest in the ideas of Luther. And Inquisitorial records frequently allude to discussion of Lutheranism in Spain from the 1520s onwards. However, only 39 cases of Lutheranism were officially tried in Spain before 1558. The problem is also complicated by the fact that many of those who brought prosecutions against 'heretics' frequently elided Lutheranism with other strains of religious heterodoxy such as illuminism and Erasmianism. Even worse, some of those who were themselves accused of holding Protestant opinions often tried to avoid punishment by naming others, including high-ranking officials in church and state.

---

[7] Charles was the ruler of the Netherlands when he inherited the title of King of Spain following the death of his maternal grandfather, Ferdinand, in 1516. In 1519, he inherited the title of Holy Roman emperor from his paternal grandfather, Maximilian I.

[8] The Spanish Inquisition was originally established in 1479 in order to expedite the forced conversion of the Jewish and Morisco populations of Spain, but by the second half of the sixteenth century it was destined to play a crucial role in stamping out all forms of religious dissent.

The Hellenist, Juan de Vergara, for example, was denounced as a Lutheran by Francisca Hernández, the leader of a mystical sect at Valladolid, at her trial in 1530 (Kamen, 1997, p.88).

The case of Juan Gil is perhaps indicative of the kinds of problem involved in attempting to rediscover the impact of Lutheranism on sixteenth-century Spain. As preacher in the cathedral of Seville for over 20 years, Gil stood accused before the Inquisition in 1552 as a heretic and leader of a Lutheran conventicle in the city. Although he escaped execution, he was posthumously convicted of having held and preached the Lutheran heresy. In 1560, sentence was finally carried out. His remains were exhumed and burned, alongside the bodies of fifteen other recently convicted heretics from the city of Seville. How far Gil was a Protestant in the true sense of the word remains open to question. He most certainly believed in the merits of religious reform and many of his ideas and opinions bear close comparison with those of men like Luther and Melanchthon. Among other things, he denied the power of the pope to excommunicate, that it was necessary to attend mass and the need to confess to a priest. His views on salvation were also consonant with orthodox Lutheranism. He argued, for example, that faith was the only means to salvation and that reliance upon confession, penitence and the other sacraments was inefficacious without sincere belief. He also preached a social gospel, stressing the importance of works, not as a means to salvation, but rather as the product and evidence of true faith. Many of these ideas, however, could have derived from Gil's reading of Spanish Erasmians, rather than the works of Lutherans (Spach, 1995).

As in Italy, so too in Spain, 'Protestantism' was most frequently found in towns and cities, where the intellectual stimulus and breadth of understanding of the new trends in European religious thought were more likely to find a congenial home. In both countries, however, the failure of Protestantism to take deep root was closely associated with the fragile and discontinuous support shown for such ideas by those in authority, or with access to political influence. The departure of Charles V to Germany in 1529 effectively sealed the fate of the reform movement in Spain.

Conclusion

The examples of Italy and Spain provide further evidence of the contrasting ways in which the various regions and countries of Europe received and experienced the process of reformation in the sixteenth century. Local factors and conditions were crucial in this respect. Just as the Renaissance was not uniformly adopted throughout Europe, so too notions of religious reform were appropriated and shaped in a number of different and conflicting ways. As a result, socio-economic explanations for the proliferation of Protestant communities in northern Europe simply do not work when superimposed on the regions of southern Europe. One important outcome of this was the creation of a new religious map of Europe, characterized by a permanent division between a Protestant north and a Catholic south.

The failure of Protestant and Erasmian reform in Italy and Spain, and the success of the Tridentine movement for reform of the Catholic church, also impacted upon the fate of the Renaissance in sixteenth-century Europe. The backlash in Italy and Spain against the Erasmians was reflected in a general assault on humanist learning. It led not only to the proscription of many pagan authors, but also to the banning of much contemporary literature that drew its inspiration from classical sources. Among those works placed on the Spanish Index were the *Decameron* of Boccaccio, various works by Erasmus and the *Essays* of Montaigne. The Catholic Reformation, however, did not stand opposed to all facets of Renaissance learning. In some respects, it was of critical importance in ensuring their propagation. One of the most important agents for the dissemination of the Renaissance were the new schools and colleges that the Jesuits founded in Catholic Europe in the second half of the sixteenth century. The curricula of these new foundations, like those established by Protestants such as Melanchthon, were 'explicitly concerned with the *studia humanitatis*' (Burke, 1998, p.156).

In the period since Jacob Burckhardt first dismissed the Reformation as a matter of little consequence to the cultural development of Europe in the sixteenth century, historians have attempted to demonstrate its overwhelming importance, both in Catholic and Protestant Europe. The role of humanism in the formation and reception of reformed ideas is now beyond dispute. There remains, however, another aspect of Renaissance culture that was deeply affected by the religious changes of the sixteenth century. Let us now turn in Chapter 3 to look at the impact of the Reformation upon the visual arts and music in this period.

Fred the Wise
protector of Luther
Wittenberg University

Bibliography

BURKE, P. (1998) *The European Renaissance: Centres and Peripheries*, Oxford, Blackwell.

FIRPO, M. (1996) 'The Italian Reformation and Juan de Valdés', *Sixteenth Century Journal*, vol. 27, pp.353–64.

KAMEN, H. (1997) *The Spanish Inquisition: An Historical Revision*, London, Weidenfeld & Nicolson.

MATHESON, P. (1990) 'Humanism and reform movements' in A. Goodman and A. MacKay (eds) *The Impact of Humanism on Western Europe*, London and New York, Longman, pp.23–42.

MANDROU, R. (1973) *From Humanism to Science, 1480–1800*, Harmondsworth, Penguin Books.

OBERMAN, H.(1989) *Luther: Man Between God and the Devil*, New Haven and London, Yale University Press.

OZMENT, S.E. (1973) *Mysticism and Dissent: Religious Ideology and Social Protest in the Sixteenth Century*, New Haven and London, Yale University Press.

OZMENT, S.E. (1975) *The Reformation in the Cities: The Appeal of Protestantism to Sixteenth-Century Germany and Switzerland*, New Haven and London, Yale University Press.

OZMENT, S.E. (1993) *Protestants: The Birth of a Revolution*, London, Fontana Press.

POLIZZOTTO, L. (1994) *The Elect Nation: The Savonarolan Movement in Florence 1494–1545*, Oxford, Clarendon Press.

RUSSELL, P.A. (1986) *Lay Theology in the Reformation: Popular Pamphleteers in Southwest Germany 1521–1525*, Cambridge, Cambridge University Press.

SPACH, R.C. (1995) 'Juan Gil and sixteenth-century Spanish Protestantism', *Sixteenth Century Journal*, vol. 26, pp.857–79.

STRAUSS, G. (1978) *Luther's House of Learning: Indoctrination of the Young in the German Reformation*, Baltimore, Johns Hopkins University Press.

Anthology and Reader sources

Jeffrey Chipps-Smith, Art or idol? Religious sculpture: *German Sculpture of the Later Renaissance, c.1520–1580*, Princeton University Press, Princeton, New Jersey, 1994, pp.39–41, 111–16. (Reader, no. 18)

Venetian diplomatic report, Description of the religious situation in Augsburg: *The Reformation in its Own Words*, ed. H.J. Hillerbrand, SCM Press, Harper & Row, London, 1964, pp.402–3. (Anthology, no. 77)

Johannes Wildenauer Egranus, Letter to Martin Luther (1521): *Zwickau in Transition 1500–47: The Reformation as an Agent of Change*, ed. S. Karant-Nunn, Ohio State University Press, Columbus, 1987, p.103. (Anthology, no. 78)

Philipp Melanchthon, Letter to Elector Frederick the Wise of Saxony (1521): *Melanchthon in English: A Memorial to William Hammer*, ed. L.C. Green and C.D. Froelich, Center for Reformation Research, St Louis, Sixteenth Century Bibliography 22, 1982, p.1. (Anthology, no. 79)

Martin Luther, Letter to Nicholas Hausmann (1522): *Luther: Evidence and Commentary*, ed. I.D. Kingston Siggins, Oliver & Boyd, Edinburgh, 1972, pp.105–6. (Anthology, no. 80)

Susan Karant-Nunn, Progress toward reform: *Zwickau in Transition 1500–47: The Reformation as an Agent of Social Change*, Ohio State University Press, Columbus, 1987, pp.121–5, 127–36. (Reader, no. 19)

Sebastian Lötzer, The Twelve Articles of the Peasants of Swabia (1525): *The German Peasants' War: A History in Documents*, ed. T. Scott and R.W. Scribner, Humanities Press International, Atlantic Highlands, New Jersey, 1991, pp.253–7. (Anthology, no. 81)

The Federal Ordinance (1525): *The German Peasants' War: A History in Documents*, ed. T. Scott and R.W. Scribner, Humanities Press International, Atlantic Highlands, New Jersey, 1991, pp.130–32. (Anthology, no. 82)

Martin Luther, Letter to John Rühel (1525): *Luther's Works 49, Letters II*, ed. G.G. Krodel, Fortress Press, Philadelphia, 1972, p.109. (Anthology, no. 83)

The Erfurt 'Peasant Articles' (1525): *The German Peasants' War: A History in Documents*, ed. T. Scott and R.W. Scribner, Humanities Press International, Atlantic Highlands, New Jersey, 1991, pp.174–6. (Anthology, no. 84)

Hermann Mühlpfort, Mayor of Zwickau, Letter to Stephen Roth at Wittenberg (1525): *The German Peasants' War: A History in Documents*, ed. T. Scott and R.W. Scribner, Humanities Press International, Atlantic Highlands, New Jersey, 1991, pp.322–4. (Anthology, no. 85)

CHAPTER THREE

The representation of reform

BY ANNE LAURENCE, DAVID MATEER AND NICK WEBB

Objectives

When you have completed this chapter you should be able to:

- evaluate the impact of Protestantism on ritual, music and art in sixteenth-century Germany;

- appreciate the factors that influenced the Protestant debate about the use of imagery;

- assess the extent to which the Italian Renaissance contributed to the representation of reform in Germany.

Reform and ritual

> The kingdom of God is a kingdom of hearing, not of seeing.
>
> (Martin Luther, quoted in Belting, 1994, p.465)

As we saw in Chapter 1, Martin Luther's primary concern in the early stages of the Reformation was with spiritual reform and the propagation of the message that salvation was effected by grace rather than by works. This understanding was to be instilled into Christians primarily by means of the word of scripture rather than through the ceremonies, institutions, traditions or officials of the church. Early on, and certainly by the time he wrote *The Babylonian Captivity* in 1520, Luther had rejected the seven sacraments of the Catholic church. Initially, he argued that there were only three (baptism, communion and penance). Later, he adopted the view that there were properly only two: baptism and communion.

Exercise

Look again at what Luther had to say about the nature of communion, and its administration, in *The Babylonian Captivity* (Anthology, no. 72). What are the implications, in terms of the liturgy, of Luther's objections to the Catholic eucharist?

Discussion

Luther argued strongly for the administration of both the elements (the bread and the wine) to the laity, and asserted that these are not transubstantiated, or transformed, into the body and blood of Christ by the priest. Communion was not therefore a sacrifice, but rather a promise of the forgiveness of sins made by God and confirmed by the death of His son, Jesus Christ.

In translating these beliefs into practice, Luther argued that it was necessary to concentrate exclusively on those practices that Christ first instituted at the Last Supper, and not to be misled or distracted by subsequent human accretions to the communion service: 'we must be particularly careful to put aside whatever has been added to its original simple institution by the zeal and devotion of men: such things as vestments, ornaments, chants, prayers, organs, candles, and the whole pageantry of outward things'. ❖

Doctrinal issues thus clearly impinged upon the physical arrangements for the administration of the sacraments. In the Catholic church, the priest played a central role in acting as a mediator between man and God. The special authority and power of the priest, which derived in part from his ordination at the hands of a bishop, were reflected in the fact that he alone was able to consume both the body and blood of Christ at the eucharist. It was also manifest in the growing tendency in the late medieval church for the priest to orchestrate a whole series of gestures and rituals that were intended to underline the miraculous nature of the Catholic mass and the supernatural authority that God had invested in the priesthood. Throughout much of this ceremony, the laity were little more than awestruck bystanders, whose role in the liturgical drama that unfolded before their eyes was essentially passive:

> Whereas a priest was expected to have an intellectual understanding of the doctrine of transubstantiation and of the scriptural basis for the mass, nothing of the sort was expected of the laity who were instructed, rather, on how to assume their proper role in the ritual drama ... The task of the laity was simply to envision Christ elevated on the cross whenever they saw the raised host. They were to adore, not think.

> (Muir, 1997, p.164)

At the culmination of this service, lay communicants were expected to receive the bread, in the form of a specially baked wafer, in a kneeling position – in homage, as it were, to the resurrected Christ whose body they were about to consume. At this point, great care had to be taken to ensure that no crumbs or spillages took place, since the wafer had now been transformed into the actual body of Christ. Luther's rejection of the doctrine of transubstantiation implied a very different approach to the administration of the sacraments, which now included wine as well as bread. Rather than concentrate on the rituals surrounding the presentation of the elements, Luther wished to see far greater emphasis placed upon the words used by the priest in the communion service in order to explain the precise meaning of the Last Supper: 'the sign ... is incomparably less than the thing signified' (Anthology, no. 72, p.324).

Luther's reference to setting aside vestments, ornaments, etc. was not intended as an injunction to do away with them, but rather as a prelude to a review of their place in the communion service in order to retain those that were beneficial to faith. Later in the same work, Luther wrote: 'the more closely our mass resembles that first mass of all, which Christ performed at the Last Supper, the more Christian it will be' (Anthology, no. 72, p.327). For Luther, this meant the creation of a service at which men and women came together to hear the word of God, rather than witness the re-enactment of a sacrifice. The minister must 'sound in our ears the word, or testament, in a loud, clear voice, and in the language of the people' (Wentz, 1959, p.54). It is the Word of God that instils faith, and leads to justification, not the ceremonies that act as an adjunct, or 'sign', of saving grace.

Despite the fact that Luther's injunctions and reservations with regard to the mass were clearly formed by 1520, he said little at the time about what, exactly, should replace the Catholic service. At first, Luther himself was content to leave such decisions to individual congregations and secular authorities, provided that the formula conformed to the Word of God. Whatever was good, useful or edifying in ceremony or religious art should be preserved, unless it was forbidden by scripture. Luther had no objection either to local variations, although he believed that it was probably helpful for churches in the same region to adopt similar practices. In 1521, Philipp Melanchthon and others took communion in both kinds in Wittenberg, and other congregations abandoned the Catholic mass, adopting a variety of forms in its place.

By 1523, Luther had published a form of Latin mass to be used by reformed churches, although it did not appear in German until 1526. In his correspondence with the preacher at Zwickau, Nicholas Hausmann, Luther set out some of his priorities. In 1523, he advised Hausmann to abolish private masses and announced his intention of revising the canon (the part of the service containing the words of consecration). 'But', he wrote, 'I do not see why I should revise the rest of the ritual, together with the vestments, altars and holy vessels, since they can be used in a godly way and since one cannot live in the church of the Lord without ceremonies' (Luther to Hausmann, October 1523, quoted in Krodel, 1972, pp.55–6).

Luther's thoughts on this subject were prompted in part by the challenge to his more conservative position in the writings of his former colleague at Wittenberg, Andreas Bodenstein von Karlstadt. Karlstadt, who had been expelled from Saxony for his advocacy of a range of radical theological beliefs (he was also sympathetic to Thomas Müntzer), opposed Luther's view of the sacraments, adopting instead the ideas of the Swiss reformer, Ulrich Zwingli (see Chapter 1). Fearful of the consequences of Karlstadt's preaching, and the possibility of disorder and violent confrontation that might ensue, Luther was thus forced to confront the issue of a uniform Lutheran approach to the liturgy and ceremonial practices of the new church. Conscious of the need to provide more effective guidance to congregations, Luther nonetheless backed away from prescriptive measures that might alienate his supporters (see Anthology, no. 86).

Figure 3.1 Albrecht Dürer, *The Last Supper*, 1510, woodcut. Kupferstichkabinett, Staatliche Museen zu Berlin, Berlin

How, then, did Luther's new eucharistic theology affect the conduct of services in the evangelical churches? Useful insights on this subject can be gleaned from representations of the Last Supper in Protestant art. Traditional Catholic imagery relied heavily on depictions of the wafer and the paschal lamb. The wafer or host signified the body of Christ. The paschal lamb, the traditional sacrifice of the Jewish Passover, represented the occasion for the biblical Last Supper and reinforced the Catholic view of the eucharist as a sacrificial event. Both these elements figure prominently in a woodcut by Albrecht Dürer, dating from 1510 (Figure 3.1).

In a later woodcut (Figure 3.2), Dürer, an early convert to Protestantism, shows prominently a large goblet of wine, a clear reference to the reformed practice of taking communion in both kinds. In addition, the platter, which in older images was shown holding the lamb, is here empty, indicating the Protestant rejection of the belief in the mass as a sacrifice. In some respects, this is a traditional image of the Last Supper, with Christ depicted cradling the head of St John. But it was largely innovatory. Judas is missing

Figure 3.2 Albrecht Dürer, *The Last Supper*, 1523, woodcut. Photo: Germanisches Nationalmuseum, Nuremburg

from the scene; nobody, except Christ, is shown with a nimbus; and, unlike medieval depictions of the Last Supper and those found in popular printed broadsheets, Christ is shown the same size as the disciples.

Dürer's representation, however, tells us only part of the story, for Luther found himself stepping back from some of the implications of his theology, lest by proceeding too far and too fast he precipitated disorder. His gradualist approach was based firmly on the idea that unnecessary ceremonies and institutions would wither away as they became redundant. In addition, such a process would prevent violence being done to popular sentiment, for, once people's hearts were liberated from old beliefs, Luther confidently expected that liturgical reform would naturally follow. In 1525, Luther wrote in a reply to Karlstadt that 'there is to be neither commanding nor forbidding' (Bergendoff, 1958, p.130). In the same letter, Luther noted that at Wittenberg mass was celebrated without the chasuble (the sleeveless vestment worn by the priest at the celebration of the mass) and without the elevation of the host, in a plain and simple way. This was in contrast to the practice adopted in the parish church, where such traditions were continued, alongside other customs such as positioning the communion table altarwise.

Exercise

In terms of Luther's theology, what were the implications of the continuing use of special clothing (vestments), the elevation of the host (often to the accompaniment of the sound of a bell after consecration) and the positioning of the communion table with its back to the wall (altarwise)?

Discussion

Special clothing distinguished the priest from the rest of the congregation. Contrary to Lutheran ideas, it implied that the priest was distinct from the laity by virtue of his ordination. A divine aura surrounded the priest, whose role in the communion service as the intermediary between God and man reinforced the fundamental distinction between the priesthood and the laity.

The elevation of the host was associated with the idea that some form of sacrifice was being practised. It was held up so that the congregation might bow down before it and show adoration. The image of the priest standing with arms raised was reminiscent of Christ's crucifixion on the cross. Accordingly, the practice was in stark contrast to Luther's understanding of communion as the distribution of a testament and the acceptance of a promise.

The altar was specifically understood to represent a table upon which a sacrifice took place. Because of its position against a wall or altarpiece, anything that the priest did or said while standing over the altar had to occur with his back to the congregation. In Lutheran eyes, this was not compatible with his office as a minister of the word whose voice needed to be clearly audible to the whole congregation. ❖

In Catholic ritual, vestments were explicitly prescribed to distinguish the celebrant (the priest) from those to whom he ministered the sacrament, because he was the channel by which the elements were transubstantiated into the body and blood of Christ. The ability to perform such a 'miracle' was an endowment of the priest's office, bestowed on him as a result of consecration (one of the seven sacraments in the Catholic church). Consecration into the priesthood took place by the laying on of hands by a bishop, who claimed this right by virtue of his own consecration at the hands of a bishop, and so on, in an apostolic succession that ultimately extended to St Peter, the first bishop of Rome. Priests thus carried with them a quality that set them apart from the laity, a fact recognized in their celibacy and the many regulations that governed their way of life.

Such a view of the priesthood was in marked contrast to that of Protestants like Luther. According to him, the role of the minister in the mass was focused on the need to preach the word to members of the congregation in order to remind them of the significance (literally, that which was signified) of the sacrament of communion. This role, in effect, could be carried out by anyone. It did not require divine authorization, as Christ's Real Presence in the host was not effected by the words or actions of the priest. Ministers, then, were no different from the laity; both were members of a single community of the faithful, which increasingly refused to recognize the sacerdotal nature of the priesthood. This was reflected in countless ways. Whereas the Catholic priest addressed the congregation in prayer as 'you', Lutheran ministers preferred to use the pronoun 'us'. There was, however, one aspect of communion that continued to pose problems for Luther. The reformer believed that those who were unrepentant should be *excommunicated* (excluded from the Lord's table), but he was somewhat vague as to how this was to be implemented and who should administer the punishment.

Other aspects of the traditional Catholic liturgy served to underline the central role of the mass and the priest in everyday religious life. Vestments and the furnishings used to cover the altar were becoming increasingly ornate and expensive. The supply and care of these articles and precious objects also provided a multiplicity of tasks in which the laity could take part. In particular, the maintenance of priestly clothing, altarcloths, processional banners, and clothing and jewellery for small images of the Virgin and the saints that were carried in parades on feast days, provided work for women.

Figure 3.3 Sixteenth-century German monstrance. The monstrance was often made of precious metals and decorated with jewels. The transparent container in the middle of the monstrance allowed the laity to view the host. Photo: Bildarchiv Foto Marburg, Marburg

In the late medieval Catholic church, the host had become an object of special veneration in Christian communities. It was frequently paraded through the streets on special occasions, such as the Feast of Corpus Christi (held eleven days after Pentecost), and a special device known as a monstrance was devised for its public display (Figure 3.3). The Feast of Corpus Christi, originally established in the thirteenth century, soon became one of the most popular religious festivals in the Christian calendar (Figure 3.4). On this day, art, ritual and drama combined to create a range of festivities focusing on the supernatural authority that was thought to radiate from the host. In many places, it provided an occasion for public displays of civic pride and political solidarity, manifest in the processions organized by craft guilds and religious confraternities. Elsewhere, it became an opportunity for ordinary Christians to express their own brand of popular piety, actively and passively, in the performance of mystery plays, pageants, *tableaux vivants* and religious parades, in which they carried the

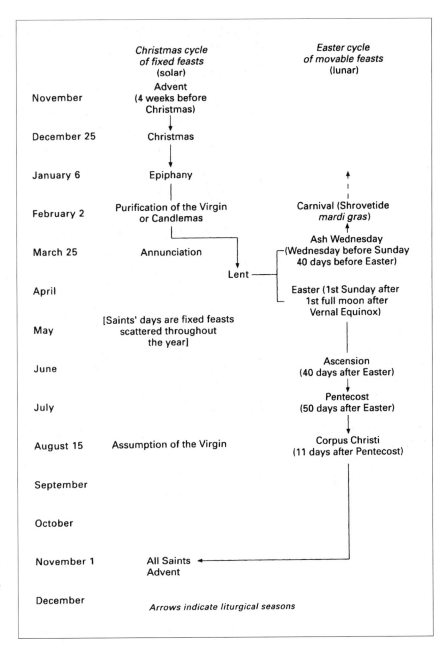

Figure 3.4 The Christian ritual calendar. From Muir, E. (1997) *Ritual in Early Modern Europe*, Cambridge, Cambridge University Press, p.59

statues and relics of saints. Play cycles and pageants re-enacted scenes from the Bible and particular episodes or scenes, performed by members of the laity in the vernacular, were often associated with occupational guilds or confraternities. These ceremonies owed nothing to the Renaissance, but were characteristic of the popular culture of late medieval communities. Above all, they were occasions for the expression of communal solidarity or the affirmation of group identity in the larger community. And, like other forms of popular celebration, they frequently led to brawls and public hostility between rival groups and factions.

Among later reformers, festive occasions such as these, centred on the miracle of transubstantiation, were frequently the object of scorn and censure. Most were eventually abolished in the Protestant countries of northern Europe. However, during the early stages of the Reformation, there was little unanimity among the reformers as to how to proceed against such ritual and ceremony. Luther himself, as we have seen, was ambivalent with regard to much of the ritual that surrounded the mass. And although he objected to the adoration, or elevation, of the host, he refused to abolish it because of the support that it might seem to offer to his radical opponents. Thus, he wrote in 1525:

> Although I had intended also to abolish the elevation, now I will not do it, to defy for a while the fanatic spirit [of Karlstadt], since he would forbid it and consider it a sin and make us depart from our liberty.

> (Bergendoff, 1958, pp.133–4)

Reform of practices such as the elevation of the host, which exaggerated the sacrificial nature of the Catholic mass, was thus slow to develop in early Lutheran churches. In time, however, changes were implemented. Many churches introduced a table in front of the altar so that the minister might officiate and speak while facing the congregation. Moreover, the use of elaborate and controversial gestures, especially those that might be construed as emulating the crucified Christ, were phased out. Luther's essential conservatism, though, was never far from the surface. Ministers continued to use Latin in church services. Indeed, Luther specifically recommended its use in those places where the congregation could be expected to understand the Latin formula. Elsewhere, however, the demand for services in the vernacular grew rapidly and was in large part met by Luther's new German mass of 1526 (see below).

Unlike Luther, Zwingli was much more inclined to embrace radical change in an attempt to reform the ritual practices and ceremonies of the Catholic church. In 1525, he published *Action oder Bruch des Nachtmals Gedechtnus oder Dancksagung Christi*, which set out the form of the Zwinglian communion, the prayers and gestures of the minister, and the conduct and responses of the congregation. Significantly, the work was in German, not Latin. The illustration on the title page shows Christ with a nimbus round his head, but not significantly larger than any of the apostles among whom he sits at a round table (Figure 3.5). On the table in front of Christ and the

Action oder Bruch des Nachtmals /Gedechtnus /

oder Sancksagung Christi/ wie sy vff Osteren zů Zürich angehebt wirt/ jm jar als man zalt

M· D· XXV·

Christus (Matth.xj.
Kummend zů mir alle die arbeytend vnd beladen sind/ vnd ich wil üch rüw geben.

Figure 3.5 Title page of *Action oder Bruch des Nachtmals Gedechtnus oder Dancksagung Christi*, 1525. Photo: Zentralbibliothek, Zurich

apostles lie pieces of bread, rather than the thin eucharistic wafers that the Lutherans had retained. There are also two drinking vessels instead of a single chalice.

However, some of the imagery is little different from that found in contemporary Catholic and Lutheran depictions of the Last Supper. The paschal lamb, Christ's cradling of the head of St John, and Peter shown with a knife were all traditional elements of such imagery. The woodcut was clearly intended to give guidance to the people of Zurich as to the changes that had been made with regard to the administration of communion, removing it from the realm of the miraculous to the everyday. But it was not intended as an accurate depiction of the reformed communion service, as the following account suggests:

> The people of Zurich did not enact the images' arrangement of figures and objects. The Zurich pious were not seated, gathered round the simple tables that had replaced the altars in the Zurich churches, but stood in the nave of the church, men to the right, women to the left, the 'others' in the vault or choir. At the beginning of the communion that was held in Zurich on Easter, 1525, following the sermon, the minister turned to the congregation and opened the communion service with a short prayer. He then read Paul's narrative of the Last Supper from 1 Cor[inthians] 11:20–29. The congregation next offered thanksgiving, the lines of which were spoken alternately by the men and the women. The minister read the narrative from John 6:47–63. The congregation recited the Apostles' Creed, again alternating lines between men and women. The minister and the congregation offered prayers. And then the bread and the wine were distributed ...
>
> The congregation did not come forward to the table to receive the wine and bread. The bread, first, was brought to them. Each was to tear a 'bite or mouthful' from the loaf. After all had eaten of the bread, each received the cup from the server. After all had eaten or drunk, they closed with a Psalm (113) of praise. The Zwinglian 'evening meal', while simpler than the medieval mass, was still structured temporally, spatially, and socially; it retained certain divisions, between genders, and spatial distance, between the congregation and the table.
>
> (Wandel, 1993, p.35)

The representation of the Last Supper in this woodcut was therefore intended to symbolize the role of communion in the Zwinglian church. It is the commemorative aspect of the ceremony that is highlighted here. Christ, for example, is not depicted performing a miracle, nor is he, in his posture, prefiguring the crucifixion. He is one with the community of apostles. The apostles themselves bear no symbols of sainthood. Christ's spiritual presence in the celebration of the eucharist is alluded to by the use of the nimbus, a sign of his divinity. But his physical absence from the bread and the wine is reinforced by his representation as an ordinary man, in much the same way as the bread is the same as that eaten every day of the week by the citizens of Zurich. Although the form of the woodcut is crude, it nonetheless conveys complex and sophisticated ideas that supplement the words of the accompanying text (in this case, an account of how the eucharist was to be administered).

As the example of these simple images demonstrates, the emerging Protestant churches sought to develop a distinctive visual language to differentiate themselves from their Catholic opponents. This did not lead to an outright dismissal of ritual and ceremony, but rather the adaptation of traditional religious practices, which, as we shall see, were as likely to be shaped by native sources as they were to derive from the influences of 'foreign' Renaissance beliefs. Protestant alterations in the way communion was administered suggest that not only was the altar bound to become a less prominent piece of furniture, but also that much of the decorative furnishings that surrounded it would need to change. In particular, the attention of the reformers was likely to focus on the altarpiece, the elaborate backdrop to the altar, which was traditionally made from painted or carved wood.

Altarpieces: Catholic and Protestant

During the late fifteenth and early sixteenth centuries, Catholic altarpieces represented a major opportunity for craftsmen and painters to demonstrate their artistic virtuosity. In subject-matter and composition, they also reflected, in a highly visible way, important aspects of Catholic worship and belief.

One of the finest examples of this art form is the Isenheim altarpiece (Plates 1–4), painted between 1512 and 1516 by Matthias Grünewald (1470–1528) for the church of the Antonine monastery in Isenheim in Alsace (then part of the Holy Roman empire). The members of the Antonine order were devoted to the care of the sick. The altarpiece itself was designed to cover a sculpted shrine that had been carved about 50 years earlier. The painted panels of the altarpiece form a series of doors, which were opened to reveal the shrine on specific occasions such as feast days, according to the Catholic liturgical calendar (see Figure 3.4). In terms of the subject-matter of the panels, the altarpiece is typically Catholic. Saints, martyrs (with their emblems) and scenes from the Life of the Virgin and Christ form the focus of the commission. The medical context of the altarpiece (the Antonine complex contained a hospital) is suggested in various ways. Images of pain and suffering are omnipresent. One of the figures suffers from the disease popularly known as 'St Anthony's fire',[1] and is depicted in close proximity to the saint, who was widely believed to intercede and cure those so afflicted. There are also depictions of

[1] St Anthony's fire or erysipelas, which is caused by ergotism (poisoned rye), was first diagnosed as such in 1597. It has many different symptoms (Hayum, 1989).

herbs (Plate 4). The prominence of St Anthony, a desert hermit and the founder of monasticism, underscores the theme of suffering and healing (he appears on three panels, and is the central figure of the sculpture; Plates 2 and 4); he was celebrated for his battle against overwhelming physical pain and spiritual temptation. The figure of St Sebastian reiterates the theme of physical suffering and healing (Plate 2). He was widely invoked for his power to protect against the plague. The concept of the human and the divine is united in the intense suffering of the crucified Christ, the image of the saving power of the eucharist evident in the positioning of the chalice and the lamb at the foot of the cross (Plate 2). The altarpiece stood behind the main altar across the east end of the church, but was shielded from the nave by a screen. Consequently, it was visible only to the monks seated in the choir, and served primarily as an object of spiritual devotion and prayer for those engaged in the work of healing. The laity were firmly excluded from such exercises.

The Isenheim altarpiece makes an interesting contrast with that constructed for the funerary chapel of the Fugger family, the Fuggerkapelle (Fugger chapel) in St Anna's church in Augsburg (Figure 3.6), which dates from roughly the same period (1509–18).

Figure 3.6 The Fugger chapel in St Anna's church, Augsburg, 1510–12, interior as restored. From Kirmeier, J. et al. (eds) (1997) ... wider Laster und Sunde. Augsburg Weg in der Reformation. Katalog zur Ausstellung in St Anna, Augsburg, 26 April bis 10 August 1997, Augsburg and Köln, Haus der Bayerischen Geschichte and DuMont, p.70

The new high altar in the Fugger chapel was situated at the east
end of St Anna's church and was surrounded by relief panels
commemorating various members of the Fugger family (see
Chapter 2). The skull of Jakob II Fugger, who commissioned the
chapel, is shown borne aloft by Roman soldiers (Figure 3.7); Georg
Fugger is depicted with Samson and the jawbone of an ass (Figure 3.8).
A third panel shows Ulrich Fugger in a scene of Christ's resurrection,
accompanied by *putti* and sleeping German soldiers, sculpted to
appear in typical Roman fashion as barbarians (Figure 3.9). Beneath
each of the latter two scenes lies a recumbent and shrouded corpse,
depicted with skulls, satyrs and sea creatures. In a fourth panel, two
Roman soldiers hold up a wreath with a lily, the badge of the Fugger
family. Other decoration in the chapel continued the theme of

Figure 3.7 Epitaph of
Jakob II Fugger. Photo:
Bildarchiv Foto Marburg,
Marburg

117

Figure 3.8 Epitaph of Georg Fugger. Photo: Bildarchiv Foto Marburg, Marburg

combining sacred and profane subject-matter. Above the reliefs, for example, there was a gallery for the organ, with wings painted by the local artist, Jörg Breu the Elder (d.1536). These show Christ and Mary ascending to heaven, the invention of music, and Pythagoras demonstrating weight and tone. The combination of Christian motifs with details taken from classical sculpture represents one of the first, and finest, examples of the importation of a modified Italianate or Renaissance style to Germany.

The altarpiece itself consisted of a sculpture of Christ supported by an angel, accompanied by the Virgin Mary and St John, in three-quarter life-size (Figure 3.6). Beneath these, and directly above the altar, three relief sculptures portrayed scenes from the life and death of Christ (Christ on the way to Calvary; the Deposition; and the Descent into Hell).

Figure 3.9 Epitaph of Ulrich Fugger. Photo: Bildarchiv Foto Marburg, Marburg

The altarpiece seems to have remained in place until 1581, when it was moved to the chapel of St Mark in the Fuggerei (see Chapter 2). Prior to this period, however, its function was largely dictated by the various changes in religious confession in Augsburg following the arrival of the Reformation in the city in the early 1520s. For the first few years of its existence, it served as a backdrop to Catholic services in the church. During the mid 1520s, however, following the appointment of the reformer, Urbanus Rhegius, to St Anna's (1524), it became the subject of dispute. Initially, the reformers wished to see the chapel separated from the chancel of the main church by a bronze screen. Following objections by the powerful patrons of the chapel, the Fuggers, a balustrade, decorated with *putti* and **Tuscan** columns, was erected. The chapel continued to function as a private Catholic place of worship.

Why might the altarpiece in Augsburg have been less objectionable to the Lutherans than that at Isenheim?

The Isenheim altarpiece relied heavily on images of saints, who, in traditional Catholic practice, were commonly thought to intercede for the sick and secure miraculous recovery from a range of illnesses. Such beliefs were anathema to Protestants, who rejected, out of hand, the power of Catholic mediators, be they priests, saints or the Virgin Mary, to perform supernatural cures. God alone possessed such power. Another aspect of the Isenheim altarpiece that was likely to offend the Lutherans relates to the way in which its separation from the main body of the church reinforced the idea of a radical division between the laity and the clergy, and enhanced the quasi-magical authority of the latter.

The Augsburg altarpiece, on the other hand, was set in a chapel that was intended for public as well as private worship. Despite the objections of some reformers to the interior decoration of the chapel, the altarpiece itself did not contain imagery that was intrinsically offensive to Protestants. Its depiction of biblical scenes taken from the life and death of Christ was perfectly acceptable to them, as were the inclusion of standard figures found in representations of the crucifixion, such as the Virgin Mary and St John the Evangelist. ❖

These two works clearly drew on very different traditions. The Isenheim altarpiece contains many references to suffering and mysticism, notions that informed much popular German Catholicism in this period (see, for example, Luther's debt to such thinking in Anthology, no. 64). Moreover, in terms of style, it was essentially a work of late medieval, **Gothic** art. There is little evidence here of a concern for perspective or classical composition, although the written inscriptions and division of the panels into a series of smaller works may owe something to the influence of printing. In contrast, the Augsburg altarpiece was intended to form part of a much larger and more ambitious architectural scheme, designed to advertise both the private and communal benevolence of one of Augsburg's leading families. In constructing the funerary chapel, with its lavish interior decoration, but simple and restrained altarpiece, the Fuggers sought to commemorate themselves after death as well as to display their wealth and taste. In doing so, they drew on the visual vocabulary of the Italian Renaissance (see below) rather than native, Gothic traditions.

Luther's own views about altars and their setting, like so much else, were never clear or consistent. He did not object in principle,

Figure 3.10 *The Last Supper*, depicting the reformer Johann Hess as Christ, 1537, originally in the city hall in Breslau, now in the Herder-Institut, Marburg. From Fleischer, M.P. 'Humanism and reformation in Silesia: imprints of Italy – Celtis, Erasmus, Luther, and Melanchthon' in M.P. Fleischer (ed.) (1992) *The Harvest of Humanism in Central Europe: Essays in Honor of Lewis W Spitz*, St Louis, Concordia Publishing House, p.77. Herder-Institut, Marburg

however, to the use of altarpieces. Once the initial danger of the destruction of such furnishings at the hands of iconoclasts had subsided (see below), a number of new altarpieces were commissioned for Lutheran churches, usually by lay patrons or municipal councils. In 1530, Luther declared that if there were to be decorations on or near the altar, the Last Supper was an appropriate subject. Thereafter, it commonly appeared on the new Protestant altarpieces that were commissioned from the later 1530s, in stark contrast to Catholic practice where it rarely featured in German churches (Christensen, 1979).

One of the finest examples of a Protestant altarpiece is that commissioned for the city church in Wittenberg, which was painted by Lucas Cranach the Elder (1472–1553) in 1549 (Plate 5). It depicts a scene from the Last Supper in which the figures of reformers, including Luther, are shown in the guise of the disciples taking communion in both kinds from Christ. In 1537, the Silesian city of Breslau (modern-day Wrocław in Poland) advertised its adherence to the new faith by commissioning a painting of the Last Supper for the council chamber in the city hall (Figure 3.10). It depicts the city's first reform minister, Johann Hess (1490–1547), as Christ surrounded by members of the town council in the guise of the disciples (Fleischer, 1992, p.77).[2]

The propagandistic role of such works of art is self-evident. What is less clear is how the reformers were able to justify the use of such images, which, to many of their opponents, must have bordered on the idolatrous.

The debate about images: iconoclasm and iconophobia

The Protestant ambivalence towards the use of images in religious worship is linked to the strict observance of part of the first of the Ten Commandments: 'Thou shalt not make unto thee any graven images or any likeness of any thing that is in heaven above, or that is in the earth beneath, or that is in the water under the earth. Thou shalt not bow down thyself to them, nor serve them' (Exodus 20.4–5). Hence, Protestantism is commonly associated in many people's minds with the *absence* of images, as a consequence of their violent removal from churches and public acts of destruction (iconoclasm), as well as of a general antipathy to all religious imagery and representations (iconophobia).

As with so much else in late medieval Christianity, the Reformation debate over the proper place of religious imagery in the church was not new. In the century prior to the Reformation, many Catholics, including senior ecclesiastics, were beginning to reassess the role that images played in everyday religious observance and practice (Christian, 1981; Zika, 1988). During this period:

> the scope of a visible and sensible religious experience was being more diligently circumscribed and supervised. Religious visions were increasingly met with scepticism and rituals involving sacred objects were carefully scrutinised for their orthodoxy and kept firmly within clerical control.

> (Zika, 1991, p.154)

One of the most eloquent and outspoken critics of this aspect of late medieval religion was the great Christian humanist, Erasmus, whose views on this subject, as in so much else, were to presage those of later Protestant reformers. In his *Paraclesis*, or introduction to the New

---

[2] There is some doubt as to the provenance of this ascription. It has also been suggested that the figure of Christ depicts the Breslau merchant, Jacob Boner, a staunch supporter of the Reformation in the city.

Testament, Erasmus contested the value of physical images, preferring instead to redirect the attention of the pious to the inward contemplation of the word of God:

> If anyone displays the tunic of Christ, to what corner of the earth shall we not hasten so that we may kiss it? Yet were you to bring forth His entire wardrobe, it would not manifest Christ more clearly and truly than the Gospel writings. We embellish a wooden or stone statue with gems and gold for the love of Christ. Why not, rather, mark with gold and gems and with ornaments of greater value than these, if such there be, these writings which bring Christ to us so much more effectively than any paltry image? The latter represents only the form of the body – if indeed it represents anything of Him – but these writings bring you the living image of His holy mind and the speaking, healing, dying, rising Christ himself, and thus they render Him so fully present that you would see less if you gazed upon Him with your very eyes.

> (Olin, 1965, p.106)

The debate over images in Protestant circles raised a whole series of issues, many of which went well beyond a purely religious concern for the dangers of idolatry. For example, the question of the legitimacy of religious imagery was linked to a metaphysical issue: the power commonly ascribed to images and religious icons in the late medieval world. Images were not perceived simply as passive, material objects that merely represented reality. On the contrary, they were widely believed to possess spiritual or supernatural powers, which resided in them by virtue of their intimate relationship to the thing that they signified, and which might, under certain circumstances, affect the condition of the onlooker. Thus, spectators commonly believed that by gazing on an image of the Virgin Mary, the crucifix or the host they might receive all manner of benefits, partaking of the special qualities inherent in the image. At the root of such beliefs lay an idea that is fundamentally at odds with the modern, 'scientific' understanding of the nature and function of sight. The extromission theory of sight, which received universal assent in this period, posited the view that the process of vision involved the object acting upon the eye, and not vice versa. 'The object was active and powerful, the eye passive and receptive' (Muir, 1997, p.193).[3]

[3] This theory of vision was finally debunked in the early seventeenth century by the work of the astronomer and mathematician, Johannes Kepler (1571–1630). A classic account of the extromission theory can be found in the work of Leonardo da Vinci: 'Just as a stone flung into the water becomes the centre and cause of many circles ... so any object placed in the luminous atmosphere diffuses itself in circles, and fills the surrounding air with infinite images of itself' (Lindberg, 1976, p.161).

catholics

images

protestants

object

have an impact on

why it was important / did it.

The importance of these ideas is evident in the way in which Protestant reformers sought to clarify their objections to images or 'idols' in the sixteenth century. What separated radicals like Karlstadt and Zwingli from Luther was not any perceived difference over the potential power of images to distract or deceive, but rather the extent to which they undermined the preeminence of the Word. Thus, Luther was happy to concede that images might fulfil a useful, didactic purpose in their proper place. Statues and other images were neither good nor bad; what was at issue was the state of the believer's heart. If people continued to believe that grace could be earned through the provision or worship of images, then such acts were sinful. Equally, however, no merit could be earned by the removal or destruction of images. In contrast to Luther, Karlstadt and Zwingli based their opposition to religious imagery on a more fundamental premise that took as its starting-point the idea of a complete separation between the material and spiritual realms. Just as Zwingli denied the physical presence of Christ in the eucharist, so too he flatly rejected any suggestion that material objects such as statues might function as containers or agents of supernatural power in the world of man. This view was firmly wedded to his broader theological outlook, which postulated a radical disjuncture between the physical world of man and the spiritual realm of God.

This assault on the potency of religious images lay at the heart of the orderly removal of all idols and images from the churches of Zurich in the summer of 1524. But the removal of images also represented part of a programme of social reform in which Zwingli and his supporters were keen to point out that money spent on images might be better spent on relieving the suffering of the sick and the deserving poor. In this context, 'voracious idols' that 'devoured' poor Christians deserved their fate and iconoclasm was fully justified (Wandel, 1989; Wandel, 1995). In Zwingli's Zurich:

> Iconoclastic reformers destroyed oil lamps that required continual feeding, forbade expensive candles, and removed crucifixes to sell the wood as lumber, the proceeds of which became alms for the poor. Rather than the consequence of an irrational destructive urge, iconoclasm can be seen as a vast social project that reoriented Christian work toward solving the practical problems of the community. Charity became the pious alternative for image veneration.
>
> (Muir, 1997, p.194)

Issues of order and authority inevitably arose whenever images were destroyed or removed from churches. At Strasburg and Zurich, for example, one of the chief considerations of the local magistrates who demanded the removal of images in 1524 was that such actions should be carried out in a lawful and orderly fashion. The fear of insurrection and popular disorder – that attacks on images might spill over into wider protests against the ecclesiastical and political authorities – was a constant factor in the minds of those who authorized iconoclasm.

The issue of property rights was also never far from the surface of such deliberations. In 1529, the Augsburg patrician Sigmund Welser defended his involvement in the destruction of images in the Franciscan church by claiming that the items that he destroyed were his personal property and thus his to do with as he pleased (Cuneo, 1996, p.15). Respect for property rights was widespread, and was shared by many of the peasants and artisans who rose in 1525 and who often included provision for ecclesiastical property in their reform demands. Thus, the insurgents in Erfurt were careful to protect lay endowments of altars and legacies by stipulating: 'Where these are already established, the clergy should no longer receive them, but the heirs and the descendants of those who founded them.' Where the latter could no longer be traced, such endowments were to be placed in a community chest (Anthology, no. 84, p.351). These concerns, more often than not, were shared by large sections of the population, including those involved in open insurrection against the secular authorities. None of the major reformers, either, countenanced the violent removal or destruction of images.

There can be little doubt that the debate about religious imagery was influenced by a variety of factors. Theological opposition to idolatry merged with social, economic and political considerations to create a widespread antipathy in Protestant circles to any form of decorative ecclesiastical imagery. But the end result was the same. In large parts of reformed Europe, the walls of churches were whitewashed and all traces of idolatrous worship removed from the sight of Christian eyes. The sensual and visual nature of medieval Catholicism gave way to a 'bookish' culture based on the power of the spoken and written word. Henceforth 'believing could no longer be identified with seeing' (Zika, 1991, p.155).

Luther and the debate

In the initial stages of the Reformation, Luther's views on the place of images in religious worship were not unlike those he expressed in 1523 on the subject of ceremony and vestments, which he considered acceptable if 'used in a godly way' (Luther to Hausmann, October 1523). Luther undoubtedly understood the power of images. He believed that Bibles should contain pictures because 'ordinary people are taught more easily by analogies and illustrations than by difficult and subtle discussions; they would rather look at a well drawn picture than a well written book' (Christensen, 1992, p.9).

He also understood the significance of public acts of destruction, as, for example, in 1520, when he threw the papal bull threatening excommunication on to the bonfire of books of canon law and scholastic philosophy erected by the students of Wittenberg. This was an act of iconoclasm, culminating in the destruction of documents that he believed embodied the false church and contained false religion. In the following year, he argued that the Bishop of Rome (i.e. the pope) was neither the vicar of Christ nor head of the church. 'This is another of the key teachings which abolish the holy gospel and replace Christ with an idol in Christendom', he wrote, using the term 'idol' in its metaphorical sense: the pope was a false god or object of devotion (Anthology, no. 70, p.318).

However, Luther regarded real images, such as statues, as insignificant, matters of external worship, to which later reformers would give the title of *adiaphora* (matters indifferent). He believed that images, like much else in the old church, would eventually disappear from places of public worship, as more and more men and women became aware of their inefficacy. Images of the Virgin Mary, for example, would become superfluous as popular support for the cult of the Virgin was extinguished by the preaching of the gospel. Once Christians achieved a proper understanding of faith and grace, Luther believed, all external aids to worship and prayer would become redundant.

The riots that took place in Wittenberg in January 1522 forced Luther to take a hard line against those who opposed ceremonies and ornaments in worship and sought the destruction of images in churches. Following the arrival of the Zwickau Prophets in the city in the previous month, images were destroyed in two churches: in the Augustinian monastery, where the friars were led by Gabriel Zwilling, and in the parish church, where the destruction was carried out by townspeople. The town council subsequently approved the changes (although not the means by which these had been achieved) and authorized further removal of images in order to avoid wider disorder. It was at this time that Luther's former supporter, Karlstadt, published his treatise on the removal of images. Luther himself was absent from Wittenberg, but he rapidly aligned himself with the more conservative faction among the city reformers. In sermons that he gave at Lent 1522, he argued that although images were not desirable, nor were they sufficiently objectionable to the point that violence and disorder were justified in their removal. Shortly after, the city council ordered the restitution of images to the city's churches, but only if this could be achieved without resurrecting further opposition to their existence.

It was the subsequent activities of Müntzer and Karlstadt that consolidated Luther's position on the question of images. In 1523, Müntzer had arrived in the Saxon town of Allstedt, where he preached his radical doctrine of the primacy of the indwelling spirit, and set about instituting his own German liturgy. In the process, he openly attacked Luther for his lax and lukewarm approach to reform. Luther objected vehemently to the revolutionary social implications of Müntzer's preaching, and he also disliked the implicit violence of Müntzer's religious beliefs. In response, Luther wrote a *Letter to the Princes of Saxony concerning the Rebellious Spirit* (1524), in which he argued that the destruction of altars and images proposed by Müntzer and his followers was unjustified on biblical grounds. In response to the radicals' claim that their actions were authorized by God's command to Moses and his people to destroy the altars and images, Luther retorted: 'At that time the Jews had a particular command of God enjoining them to destroy altars and images. We in our time do not have such a command' (Bergendoff, 1958, p.55). He added, in a somewhat sarcastic tone, that if the radicals were so keen to follow the Mosaic code, then they should get themselves circumcised and practise every other aspect of Old Testament Judaism.[4]

In the meantime, acts of iconoclasm were occurring elsewhere in Germany, partly as a result of the preaching of men like Müntzer and Karlstadt. The latter, who was expelled as a trouble-maker from Saxony in 1524, reappeared in Strasburg, where his arrival provoked general unrest. A letter of Luther's in reply to the local ministers confirms the spread of iconoclasm: 'Dr Karlstadt has started disturbance among you with his fanaticism in the matter of the sacraments, images and baptism' (Bergendoff, 1958, p.67). Later the same year, he returned to the subject in an attempt to counter the growing influence of Karlstadt.

Exercise

Read the extract from Luther's treatise on images (Anthology, no. 87). On what grounds does Luther defend the use of images?

Discussion

Luther is essentially arguing for images and pictures on the grounds that they assist 'remembrance and better understanding'. By implication, those who stand to benefit most from them are those who are unable to read. But he is adamant that such illustrations must conform to biblical stories and not depict 'shameless worldly

---

[4] In adopting this position, Luther was probably drawing on his humanist training, which habituated Renaissance writers to think of the past as a world apart from their own; see Book 1 in the series, Chapter 3, pp.94–105.

things', a reference, perhaps, to Renaissance paintings and images of classical and pagan subjects. ❖

Throughout the ensuing debate, Luther remained wedded to the view that the retention or removal of images was ultimately a matter for individual congregations, in accordance with his belief that there was to be 'freedom of choice in everything that God has not clearly taught in the New Testament'. Agreement to remove images was thus acceptable 'so long as this takes place without rioting and uproar and is done by the proper authorities' (Bergendoff, 1958, pp.85, 127).

Luther's moderation on the issue of images was reflected in his growing conservatism with regard to the observation of the traditional Christian calendar (see Figure 3.4). In 1528, for example, he argued for the retention of some holy days, in addition to Sundays, 'because it is not possible to instruct the people in all of Scripture in one day'. Teaching the word of God should be 'distributed over certain seasons, just as the schools might arrange to read Virgil on one day, Cicero on another' (Bergendoff, 1958, p.309). The holidays that he proposed keeping were those associated with Christ's life (Christmas, Circumcision, Epiphany, Easter, Ascension and Pentecost), and not those relating to the commemoration of saints. Moreover, although he wanted to retain Holy Week, he was eager to disavow a number of the more controversial practices, such as the covering of the altar and the veiling of pictures, which were traditionally observed at this time of year in the medieval church. Elaborate processions were also proscribed. Holy Week was to proceed like any other week, with the difference that daily services would be held to allow the minister to expound the history and meaning of Christ's Passion.

The abolition of saints' days implied the rejection of the role of the saints as intercessors, and consequently the need for images of them in churches, which traditionally provided a focus for supplicants. Yet to abolish such feasts was to remove an extremely important element of lay participation in the life of the church. For many ordinary people, religious observance had little to do with understanding the theological niceties of transubstantiation and everything to do with daily activities, such as tending shrines and taking part in communal practices like processions and mystery plays, which were often associated with particular saints. Participation in such events was popular in the widest sense of the term. It involved everyone from the top to the bottom of society and provided an important affirmation of communal and group solidarity, which might take many forms (civic, parochial, guild or confraternity) in the late medieval period. Saints' statues and crucifixes, or images of the Virgin Mary, frequently played a central role in these festivities. They were widely admired as objects of great beauty and power, and, in certain cases, acquired the status of miraculous icons to which pilgrims flocked in huge numbers in order to receive relief from physical pain or spiritual suffering. The debate surrounding their abolition, then, impinged on every aspect of popular Christianity and, not surprisingly, evoked heated opinions that went way beyond a general concern for the significance of imagery in religious worship.

Sixteenth-century Europeans found it desperately difficult to dispense entirely with ritual forms of behaviour. Even Müntzer and his radical associates, for whom the process of reform was celebrated in the sound of breaking glass, unconsciously invoked ritualistic behaviour in the very act of desecration. Violence against statues and other forms of ecclesiastical furnishings was rarely mindless or arbitrary. More often than not, the damage to such images focused on the ritual decapitation of heads or the cutting off of limbs in a way that was intended to imitate the forms of punishment routinely imposed on real criminals (Merback, 1999, p.285). In 1537, for example, many of the statues in the cloisters of Augsburg cathedral were decapitated in an outburst of iconoclastic violence. In a similar fashion, iconoclastic behaviour often mimicked elements of ritual found in popular culture. In 1524, for instance, an image of St Francis was adorned with asses' ears and set on the town fountain in Zwickau (Scribner, 1987, p.116). Such ritualistic behaviour, it has been argued, helped to purify the community by mocking those elements deemed deviant or unchristian. Iconoclasm itself therefore constituted a form of ritual response to the religious crisis initiated by Luther in 1517. Ironically, it served to remind those who led the reform movement, Luther included, that images and ritual could not be dispensed with entirely in the struggle against religious superstition and the forces of the papal Antichrist – a point underlined by the frequent resort of Protestant propagandists to printed engravings and images that borrowed heavily from popular culture.

Reform and portraiture: Luther as 'hero'

As the debate between the two confessions gathered pace in the sixteenth century, both sides were quick to exploit the medium of the printed woodcut as a weapon in the ensuing war of words. In the process, a large body of literature evolved, often illustrated with crude illustrations drawing on popular culture, which was designed to reinforce the message of the preachers (Figure 3.11). An image of a Catholic martyr tortured by infidels, for example, might be reproduced to show a Protestant being tortured by Catholics.

Figure 3.11 *The Origins of the Pope*, 1545. From Scribner, R.W. (1987) *Popular Culture and Popular Movements in Reformation Germany*, London and Ronceverte, The Hambledon Press, p.282

An important feature of the Lutheran adoption of the visual image was the extent to which it focused attention on the figure of Luther himself, whose portrait, as a result, became one of the most widely recognized of the era. Not only did he frequently appear, as we have seen, in altarpieces, but he was also regularly portrayed in a range of pamphlets that were intended for popular consumption. In many cases, these images reflected a traditional concern in late medieval and Renaissance art to portray patrons within the context of key moments in the life of Christ. Many early woodcuts of Luther, for example, show him in the company of his own protector and patron, John Frederick, Elector of Saxony (1503–54) (Figures 3.12 and 3.13).[5]

[5] John Frederick succeeded John the Constant (brother of Frederick the Wise) as Elector of Saxony and Luther's protector.

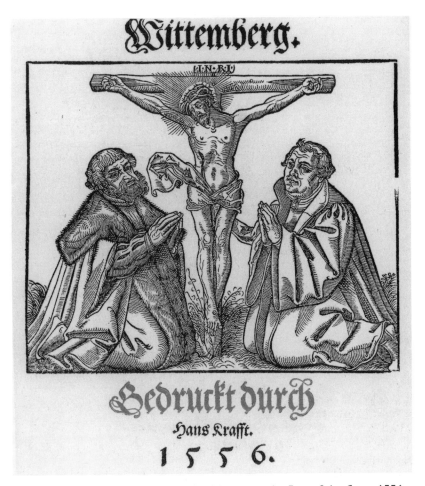

Figure 3.12 *Luther and the Elector of Saxony at the Foot of the Cross*, 1556.
Photo: © Herzog August Bibliothek Wolfenbüttel

The image of the 'saintly figure', a familiar icon in Catholic circles, was thus appropriated by the reformers to create a new 'hero' of Protestantism in the guise of the saintly Luther. Woodcuts of Luther regularly depict the reformer alongside the image of a dove (a traditional symbol of divine inspiration) or surrounded by a nimbus or halo (the sign of sainthood). It is not clear whether Luther approved of such images, but they were exceedingly popular among his early supporters. In 1521, the papal nuncio at the Diet of Worms reported pictures on sale showing Luther with a halo. Other early representations of Luther commonly depict him in the garb of a monk or a doctor of the church (Figures 3.14 and 3.15). At first sight, this might appear paradoxical. Luther was, after all, one of the chief architects of the downfall of the monastic orders in Germany. Such images, however, alongside those that drew on the visual vocabulary of the medieval saint, demonstrate once again the gradual nature of the early Reformation and the reluctance of many of its leaders and supporters to break fully with the past. In other respects, however, the familiar image of Luther, both then and now, owes much to the Renaissance revival of portraiture and the Burckhardtian 'discovery of the individual' (see Chapter 2 in Book 1 in the series).

The tendency of so much of this art to project an image of the reformer as 'hero' is profoundly paradoxical. The Renaissance idea of the individual, as described by Jacob Burckhardt, must surely be at odds with Lutheranism, in which the roles of individual actors (be they saints, popes or priests) is of no consequence in comparison to the impersonal authority of the word of God and the workings of faith in the hearts of believers. Burckhardt believed that humanists, through their familiarity with antiquity, had chosen to substitute the cult of historical greatness for the Christian ideal of life (1990, p.272). Luther's image, however, is one of the most potent symbols of the sixteenth century. So how can this be? Are we witnessing here Luther

Figure 3.13 *Luther and the Elector of Saxony Witnessing Christ's Baptism.* © The Trustees of the British Museum, London

Figure 3.14 *Luther in Doctoral Robes*, 1519, woodcut. Photo: Germanisches Nationalmuseum, Nuremberg

Figure 3.15 *Luther in a Monk's Cowl*, 1520, woodcut. Photo: © Herzog August Bibliothek Wolfenbüttel

raised to the status of a 'hero' by a public familiar with the cult of historical greatness? Or, is Luther's iconic status the product of an earlier model of individual endeavour focused on the figure of the medieval saint?

Read 'Luther myth: a popular historiography of the reformer' by Bob Scribner in the Reader (no. 20). To what extent is it fair to see the development of the Luther myth in terms of the Burckhardtian cult of individual greatness?

Scribner believes that the 'myth' of Luther the hero drew explicitly on medieval imagery associated with the worship of saints. It was also indebted to earlier traditions of religious dissent, such as that of the Hussites, in which popular prophecy, dreams and miracles played an important part. German folk traditions were particularly receptive to this kind of thought, creating as they did an appetite for stories in which great individuals performed superhuman deeds. Although all these traditions helped to create a potent image of Luther as the heroic individual, such an image was primarily the product of a popular folk culture and owed little to classical models of the hero. ❖

Significantly, the artist chiefly responsible for popularizing the image of the great reformer, both in 'official' portraits and popular woodcuts, was the Wittenberg painter, Lucas Cranach the Elder, one of the few German-born artists thoroughly familiar with Italianate art (see Plate 5 and below).

During the early sixteenth century, portraiture found a ready reception in Germany, not just among the nobility, but also among the ranks of the wealthy urban patricians and merchants, such as the Fuggers of Augsburg. Painted and engraved portraits as well as portrait medals were widely commissioned to celebrate ancestral pride and personal achievement. These in turn were often distributed as gifts to friends, patrons and customers. The celebrated German humanist and patron of Dürer, Willibald Pirckheimer (1470–1530), sent an engraved portrait (Figure 3.16) and portrait medal of himself to his friend Erasmus who placed these in his study at Basle.

Figure 3.16 Albrecht Dürer, *Willibald Pirckheimer*, 1524, engraving, second state, 19 x 12.2 cm. Educated in Italy, Pirckheimer was a patrician merchant-banker and city counsellor in Nuremburg, who translated scores of Greek works into Latin and German. He was a friend and patron of Celtis and Dürer, was acquainted with Luther and corresponded with Zwingli. He did not, however, leave the Catholic church. Photo: The Metropolitan Museum of Art, New York. Fletcher Fund, 1919. (19.73.119)

Figure 3.17 Albrecht Dürer, *The Martyrdom of the Ten Thousand Christians*, 1508. Private Collection. Photo: Bridgeman Art Library, London

Pirckheimer (or perhaps Celtis) was also depicted with Dürer in a decorated altarpiece by the artist dating from 1508 (Figure 3.17).

A by-product of the growing interest in portraiture in early sixteenth-century German art was the 'death portrait' or *Sterbebild*. The prototype was that designed by Hans Burgkmaier for Celtis in 1507 (see Chapter 1 and Figure 1.4). In typical humanist fashion, the Latin inscriptions on the engraving allude to Celtis's classical wisdom and are largely devoid of pious sentiment. Later images of Erasmus, Luther, Melanchthon and lesser lights of the reform movement by artists such as Dürer and

Figure 3.18 Printed memorial sheet for the Reverend George Müller, 1607, woodcut, Augsburg. Taking advantage of the new medium of print, engraved images of Protestant laymen and clergy were frequently published to commemorate the lives of the worthy. Photo: Germanisches Nationalmuseum, Nuremburg

Melchior Lorck (1526/7–after 1588) adapted this genre, frequently replacing classical tags with those drawn from the writings of Luther or the Bible.

The idea was developed yet further in the Lutheran funerary epitaph or monument, which frequently contained a likeness of the deceased (Christensen, 1972). The epitaphs of Protestant burghers and clergymen provided another opportunity for reform-minded artists to demonstrate how *pictura* (art) might complement the Lutheran emphasis upon *eloquentia* (the word) (Figure 3.18). Once again, Luther's close friend and colleague, Lucas Cranach the Elder, was largely responsible for popularizing this particular art form in Germany.

Music and the culture of reform

Another art form, music, has also attracted the interest of cultural historians of the Reformation. Contrary to what one might expect, Luther was a passionate advocate of music, who accorded it a central role in the newly reformed church. In the preface to his German mass of 1526, he happily conceded that 'if it would help matters along I would have all the bells pealing, and all the organs playing, and have everything that can make a sound' (Leupold, 1965, p.62). Luther's love of music extended to performance and recital. Not only did he possess some skill on the lute and the flute, but he is also reported to have sung the alto part in performances of polyphonic music at his home. He was also a competent enough musician to compose melodies and at least one short four-voice piece.[6] Moreover, his writings are filled with discerning observations about the music of his contemporaries and the effects of music on the listener. Among his favourite composers were Ludwig Senfl (*c*.1486–*c*.1543) and Josquin Desprez (for whom, see Chapter 4 in Book 1 and Chapter 2 in Book 2 in the series). Of the latter, Luther wrote: 'Josquin is a master of the notes, which must express what he desires; on the other hand, other composers must do what the notes dictate' (Buszin, 1946, p.91). On another occasion he wrote:

> God has his Gospel preached also through the medium of music; this may be seen from the compositions of Josquin, all of whose works are cheerful, gentle, mild and lovely; they are neither forced nor coerced ... by rigid rules, but, on the contrary, are like the song of the finch.
>
> (Buszin, 1946, p.91)

Luther proclaimed, as did no other religious leader of his century, the value of music in church life. Unlike Zwingli or Calvin, who either excluded music from the sanctuary altogether or drastically curtailed its use, Luther enthusiastically embraced the art as an integral part of liturgical worship. Zwingli and Calvin were suspicious of music because it had a power of its own, which, in their view, could undermine the primacy of the Word of God. It was also subject to abuse. Instead of praising God in edifying hymns it was often used to celebrate the less worthy aspects of human nature in bawdy songs. Luther was aware of the scruples of those who feared church music on moral grounds; he had, after all, read the Church Fathers, who had much to say on the subject. St Augustine, for instance, although devoted to music, nonetheless feared the pleasure he experienced in

---

[6] Zwingli too was an accomplished musician. Ironically, Zwingli, who effectively banished music from church services in Zurich, has been described as 'the most musically gifted of the Protestant reformers'. Among those instruments he played were the lute, harp, viola, flute, reedpipe, cornet, trumpet, dulcimer and foresthorn (Ozment, 1993, p.27).

listening to it. As he wrote in the *Confessions,* 'when it happens to me to be more moved by the singing than by what is sung, I confess myself to have sinned criminally' (1912, vol. ii, p.168). Luther, however, was at pains to play down the saint's misgivings:

> Music is a beautiful and lovely gift of God which has often moved and inspired me to preach with joy. St Augustine was afflicted with scruples of conscience whenever he discovered that he had derived pleasure from music and had been made happy thereby; he was of the opinion that such joy is unrighteous and sinful. He was a pious man; however, if he were living today, he would hold with us.
>
> (Buszin, 1946, p.89)

Luther's first liturgy, the *Formula missae et communionis pro Ecclesia Wittembergensi* (*Form of Mass and Communion for the Wittenberg Church*) of 1523, was a mixture of conservative and radical ideas. The five parts of the **Ordinary** – with appropriate seasonal hymns – still formed the kernel of this evangelical mass, which was sung to plainsong. The use of Latin was retained too, for Luther was aware of its educational and international importance. From a theological point of view, however, the *Formula missae* was revolutionary. Luther interpreted the mass not as a propitiatory sacrifice offered to God by the priest on behalf of the congregation, but rather as God's gift of grace and forgiveness to all Christians. It is also in the *Formula missae* that we detect the first signs of Luther's innovative conception of music's place in the mass.

Exercise

Read the following extract, which is a translation of part of Luther's prefatory matter to his *Formula missae.* What does it tell us about the reformer's ideas concerning the role of music in church? To what extent do these reflect his theological position, and what factors prevented their immediate implementation?

> I also wish that we had as many songs as possible in the vernacular, which the people could sing during Mass after the chanting [in Latin] of the Gradual and also after the Sanctus and Agnus Dei. For who doubts that originally all the people sang those parts which now only the choir sings or responds to while the bishop is consecrating the host? In fact, the singing of these congregational songs may be so arranged by the bishop that they are sung immediately after the Latin chants have been sung, or interchangeably, in Latin on one Sunday, in the vernacular on the next, until the time comes that the whole Mass is sung in the vernacular. But we need poets: as yet we have none who are able to prepare for us pious and spiritual songs (as St Paul called them) which deserve being used in the church of God. In the meantime, one may sing after communion 'Let God be blest, be

praised'. Another good hymn is 'Now let us pray to the Holy Ghost' and also 'A child so worthy'. For few are found that are written in a proper devotional style. I mention this to encourage any German poets to compose evangelical hymns for us.

(quoted in Weiss and Taruskin, 1984, pp.103–4)

Discussion

Luther wished to make attendance at church a participatory, active experience, in keeping with his vision of the church as a community of the faithful. Functions that had hitherto been the domain of the choir were now to be shared by the entire congregation. No longer would the act of praising God be the preserve of a skilled minority. A new musical dimension was therefore to be added to the traditional music of the mass, namely, simple songs in the vernacular sung in unison by the people. (Thus was born a genre that was to have far-reaching consequences for Protestant church music: the unaccompanied congregational hymn known as the Lutheran chorale.) Music was now invested with a function that was more than just decorative, one that gave concrete expression to a fundamental theological precept. However, it is equally clear from this extract that the idea could be put into practice only in a very limited way, because of a lack of suitable verse and composers (poets). ❖

Luther's vision of a revised role for music presented a problem: he required a repertory of sacred songs in German that was simple and tuneful enough for the common people to sing, and he required it instantly. However, the demand for suitable material far exceeded the supply. Luther and his musical advisers therefore turned to three existing repertories, whose melodies and texts – either translated, paraphrased or completely rewritten – were taken over wholesale and incorporated into the Protestant liturgy. These were:

(a) certain memorable chants of the Catholic church. A good example of this process is the Latin hymn 'A solis ortus cardine' ('From dawn's far horizon'), which became the chorale 'Christum wir sollen loben schon' ('Let us now praise Christ');

(b) non-liturgical, spiritual songs in the vernacular, most of which dated from before the Reformation. Thus, the twelfth-century Easter song 'Christ ist erstanden' ('Christ is risen') was crafted into the chorale 'Christ lag in Todesbanden' ('Christ lay in bonds of death');

(c) popular pieces of secular music adapted to devotional words. According to what is undoubtedly Luther's most frequently quoted remark about music, he could not see why the devil should have all the best tunes. An example of this 'parody' technique is Heinrich Isaac's popular song 'Innsbruck, ich muss dich lassen'

('Innsbruck, I now must leave thee'), which was converted to Lutheran use as 'O Welt, ich muss dich lassen' ('O world, I now must leave thee').

The advantage of these three repertories was that they contained music with which Luther's congregation were already familiar. To them, we should add a fourth:

(d) new melodies that were composed for poems specially written for inclusion in the reformed services. One of the most famous chorales of this type is 'Ein feste Burg ist unser Gott' ('A mighty fortress is our God'), the words and music of which are attributed to Luther himself.

Towards the end of 1523, broadsheets containing German hymns, complete with melodies, were circulating in Wittenberg. These spread rapidly, and in the following year three collections appeared – the *Achtliederbuch* (literally, *Book of Eight Songs*) and two volumes with the title *Enchiridion* (*Manual*). In 1524, Luther asked Johann Walter, a singer in the chapel of Frederick the Wise of Saxony, to compose choral settings of the Wittenberg hymns, which by then numbered about 40. Thus was created the first great compendium of Lutheran church music, the *Geystliches gesangk Buchleyn* (*Little Book of Spiritual Songs*). This was not a unison hymnbook designed for congregational use, for in Walter's settings the chorale melody in the tenor was decorated with additional parts in the soprano, alto and bass. Rather, it was intended for use by school and church choirs. Luther wrote in the preface:

> I and several others have brought together certain spiritual songs with a view to spreading abroad and setting in motion the Holy Gospel ... These songs are set for four voices [some of the compositions are in fact written for three, others for five, voices]. I desire this particularly in the interest of the young, who should read and must receive an education in music as well as in the other arts if we are to wean them away from carnal and lascivious songs and interest them in what is good and wholesome. I am not of the opinion that because of the Gospel all arts should be rejected violently and vanish, as is desired by the heterodox, but I wish that all arts, particularly music, be employed in the service of Him who has given and created them.
>
> (quoted in Strunk, 1952, p.342)

Music, for Luther, had educational as well as liturgical functions. This work was to be used in the schools of Wittenberg as part of the pupils' musical education. Once the compositions had been learned, they were sung by the choir in the church services as the representative of the congregation. The choir therefore taught the people how to sing the new hymns. In 1525, a congregational hymnal – for use of the laity rather than the choir – was published at Wittenberg; its texts and melodies were given in exactly the same order as in Walter's earlier collection.

Although Luther's revision of the Latin mass was far-reaching, for some it did not go far enough. Already, by 1524, reformers in Strasburg were celebrating the mass in German. Luther quickly followed suit, and in 1526 he published his *Deutsche Messe und Ordnung Gottesdiensts* (*German Mass and Order of God's Service*). Even more than the introduction of chorales in worship, this vernacular liturgy was a practical demonstration of the Lutheran principle of the universal priesthood of all believers, for in rendering the text of the mass understandable to the whole congregation, it allowed all present to participate in divine service. However, although the new service was 'arranged for the sake of the unlearned folk' (*Deutsche Messe und Ordnung Gottesdiensts*, 1526, preface), it is clear that Luther did not intend it to replace the *Formula missae*. On the contrary, he envisaged the co-existence of both forms. The *Deutsche Messe* was designed mainly for congregations in small towns and villages that were unfamiliar with Latin. The *Formula missae*, meanwhile, would continue to be used in the cathedrals and churches of larger towns and cities, where there were Latin schools and universities. Yet, even in the latter, parts of the vernacular liturgy were adopted, and Lutheran Germany quickly developed a tradition of worship that was bilingual.

Walter worked with Luther on the *Deutsche Messe* and assisted him in creating plainchant appropriate for use in the German language. The close association between words and notes was extremely important to Luther. In 1525, in the pamphlet *Wider die himmlischen Propheten* (*Against Heavenly Prophets*), he wrote that 'both text and notes, accent, time and melodic direction ought to grow out of the true mother tongue and its inflection' (Pelikan and Lehmann, 1955, p.141). Walter confirmed the reformer's fastidiousness and skill in word-setting when, in the 1560s, he recalled their collaboration:

> And it can be seen from the German Sanctus how he arranged all the notes to the text with the right accent and concent in masterly fashion. I, at the time, was tempted to ask His Reverence from where he had these pieces and this knowledge: whereupon the dear man laughed at my simplicity. He told me that ... all music should be arranged that its notes are in harmony with the text.
>
> (cited in the *New Grove Dictionary of Music and Musicians*, 1980, entry for 'Luther, Martin')

We have traced the early course of liturgical reform in Germany, examined the role of music in the evangelical service and suggested reasons for the importance that Luther attached to it. However, the extracts that I have cited do not fully convey the richness and diversity of Luther's thinking on the subject of music and its various benefits. The following exercise is intended to enable you to form a fuller picture of Luther's debt to music.

Exercise

Read the following translated excerpts from Luther's works. What do they tell us about the reformer's love of music?

1

God has created man for the express purpose of praising and extolling God. However, when man's natural ability is whetted and polished to the extent that it becomes an art, then do we note with great surprise the great and perfect wisdom of God in music, which is after all His product and His gift.

(Foreword to Georg Rhau, *Symphoniae jucundae*, 1538)

2

St Paul ... insists that Christians appear before God with psalms and spiritual songs which emanate from the heart, in order that through these the Word of God and Christian doctrine may be preached, taught, and put into practice.

(Preface to Johann Walter, *Geystliches gesangk Buchleyn*, 1524)

3

For we know that to the Devil music is something altogether hateful and unbearable. I am not ashamed to confess publicly that next to theology there is no art which is the equal of music, for she alone, after theology, can do what otherwise only theology can accomplish, namely, quiet and cheer up the soul of man.

(Letter to Ludwig Senfl, dated 4 October 1530)

4

I have always loved music. Those who have mastered this art are made of good stuff – they are fit for the task. It is necessary, indeed, that music be taught in the schools. A teacher must be able to sing, otherwise I will not so much as look at him. Also we should not ordain young men into the ministry unless they have become well acquainted with music in the schools. We should always make it a point to habituate youth to enjoy the art of music, for it produces fine and skilful people.

(Buzin, 1946, p.85)

Discussion

1 Man was given the gift of music so that he could fulfil the role for which he was created, namely, to glorify God. Music, therefore, is essential to God's purpose.

2   Luther here sees music as a means of propagating God's word. It could therefore be said to possess missionary powers. The extract is also reminiscent of his earlier comment, that Josquin's music was 'like the song of the finch' (see above).

3   Music, it is claimed, can alter our mental state. It is endowed with an ethical purpose. Music stands next to theology (high praise indeed!), since both can make us better people. (These thoughts are echoed in Luther's unfinished treatise on music (1530) in which he states that 'music induces one to forget all wrath, unchastity, arrogance and other vices', Barker, 1969, p.175.)

4   Here, the pedagogical value of music is emphasized. To Luther, a knowledge of the art was of the utmost importance in the education of the young. He declares that a schoolmaster must know how to sing. He even holds the view that no one should be ordained without practical experience of music. Thus, it became customary in the Lutheran church, until the eighteenth century, for musicians to study theology and for prospective pastors to study and practise music. ❖

Music therefore constituted an important element in the cultural life of the Lutheran world.

Reformation and Renaissance visual culture

Reform culture was an amalgam of old and new traditions and art forms. The influence of local, native and popular traditions is widely acknowledged as a major determinant of the visual appearance of the Reformations in Germany. The continuing use of Gothic artistic styles is a case in point. Less certain is the relationship between the Reformations and the development of Italianate Renaissance art in Germany.

Renaissance visual culture[7] may have spread slowly and fitfully to Germany, but it certainly took root there during the course of the late fifteenth and early sixteenth centuries. Italian artists had been deeply affected in the fifteenth century by the naturalism of the northern Renaissance. The adoption of *all'antica* style art in Germany was initially piecemeal and involved varying degrees of classicizing rather than the faithful imitation of the form and subject-matter of classical art. Similarly, there were varying degrees of compromise with pre-existing

---

[7]   In the context of this study, this term is intended to incorporate not only painting, sculpture and architecture but also jewellery, furniture, tapestries, interior decoration and other objects made from precious metals and stones.

styles according to region and use. In art and architecture, the relative unfamiliarity of German artists or patrons with Italy was reflected in the more frequent quotation of individual motifs rather than complete designs *all'antica*.

From the late fifteenth century, a number of factors led to a growing interest in Italian Renaissance art among German artists. In the first place, several artists, particularly from southern German cities such as Nuremburg and Augsburg, began to travel across the Alps in the footsteps of German humanists and scholars, who, from the middle of the fifteenth century, were regular visitors to Italy and its universities. Many returned to Germany inspired by their engagement with classical sculpture and Italian art. By the middle of the sixteenth century, Italy had become the customary destination of German artists who, following the completion of their apprenticeship, spent their *Wanderjahre* (wandering years) studying and travelling in the Italian peninsula.

A second factor in this process of reception was the tendency of some German artists, under humanist influence, to reappraise the intellectual status of their work, prompted by the superior claims made for the Italian artistic genius. Artists who followed this route frequently collaborated with German humanists in the creation of *all'antica* style art, which, it was felt, placed the visual arts and their learned practitioners on a par with the liberal arts taught in the German universities. Scholar and poets such as Peutinger, Celtis and Pirckheimer worked closely with native-born artists like Dürer and Burgkmaier to create elaborate designs and allegorical inventions for books and paintings. The intellectual and moral qualities found in such works consequently elevated the artist above the rank of a mere craftsman[8] (see e.g. Kaufmann, 1995, pp.72–3, 108–9; Hope and McGrath, 1996, pp.168, 171, 173, 174–5, 179–82).

Thirdly, during the course of the sixteenth century the collection of prints and drawings became a fashionable and ultimately systematic activity in patrician and princely circles – a process that assisted the understanding and identification of individual artistic styles and genre labelling according to conventional categories such as portraits, landscapes and *historia* (narrative painting). In particular, the popularity of woodcuts and engravings helped to disseminate knowledge of Italian visual culture in Germany. This could take two forms. Printed images

[8] Such ideas had been in circulation since the mid fifteenth century, and owed much to the manuscript treatise *De pictura* (*On Painting*) of Leon Battista Alberti (see below). They were also introduced to Germany by artists such as Jacopo de' Barbari (see below), who, in about 1502, offered his services to Frederick the Wise of Saxony in a letter espousing the 'excellency of painting' as the eighth liberal art (Belting, 1994, p.552).

could either reproduce original works of art (paintings and sculpture, for example), or, alternatively, create new images in their own right. A good opportunity for the latter was afforded by the illustrations to humanist texts in which the artists produced an independent and complementary interpretation of the text (thus establishing a constructive tension between word and image).

Fourthly and finally, interest in Italian Renaissance art was stimulated in Germany by growing political and economic ties between the two regions, most notably following the marriage of the Hapsburg emperor, Maximilian I, to Bianca Maria Sforza, the niece of Ludovico il Moro, the duke of Milan, in 1494. This alliance, and Maximilian's subsequent immersion in north Italian politics, prompted a vogue for Italian culture at the imperial court, exemplified in the appointment of Italian artists such as the Venetian, Jacopo de' Barbari (d.*c.*1515), as court painter at Innsbruck. An important consequence of imperial patronage of Italianate art and its practitioners was the lead that it gave to lesser princes in Germany to follow the example of their overlord. The example of Frederick the Wise, Elector of Saxony, has already been cited in this respect (see above). The appreciation of Italian Renaissance art also extended to some of the great patrician families of Germany, whose business ties, both with the emperor and Italy, encouraged 'burgher' patronage of the new art forms and styles.

The most celebrated example of this process can be found in the wholesale adoption of Renaissance visual imagery by the Fuggers of Augsburg. The Fugger family fortunes had begun to rise in the fifteenth century. By the end of the century, they had established themselves as one of the major banking houses in Europe, with financial connections to the papacy and, all importantly, as bankers to the emperor. Much of their wealth was expended on lavish projects of artistic consumption, such as the renovation of the Fugger chapel, undertaken in the 1510s (see above). Indeed, in some respects, wealthy patrons such as the Fuggers can be said to have outdone their more illustrious clients in their patronage of certain Renaissance art forms. The Fugger chapel has been described as one of the first examples of the successful introduction to Germany of classical sculpture and architecture (Kaufmann, 1995, p.113), but the Fuggers were also the first to incorporate the new styles into vernacular building. In 1515, Jakob II Fugger built a house and business premises (the Fuggerhaus or Fugger house) on Maximilianstrasse, the main thoroughfare of Augsburg, which had a Tuscan entrance hall and a courtyard constructed in the Italian manner, with a fountain, loggia with ornate **spandrels**, and frescoes by Jörg Breu the Elder (Figure 3.19).

Figure 3.19 Loggia in the Damenhof courtyard at the Fugger house, Augsburg. Photo: Bildarchiv Foto Marburg, Marburg

Figure 3.20 Interior of the library (known as the Badstuben) of the Fugger house, c.1570. Photo: Bildarchiv Foto Marburg, Marburg

During the course of the sixteenth century, the interior of the Fugger house underwent yet further Renaissance embellishment. In particular, around 1570, two rooms were designed and decorated according to the latest Renaissance fashion. Roman busts, stucco work and frescoes were added, clearly inspired by the Domus Aurea (Golden House) of the Emperor Nero, which had been rediscovered earlier in the century in Rome (Figure 3.20). The work is by the Dutch artist, Frederik Sustris (1540–99), who had spent much of his life in northern Italy. His first German commission was for Hans Jakob Fugger (1516–75), although much of his subsequent career was spent at the court of the Catholic dukes of Bavaria in Munich.

Albrecht Dürer: 'a painter for Germany'

One of the first German artists to exploit all of these developments was the Nuremburg painter and print-maker, Albrecht Dürer (1471–1528). The son of a Hungarian goldsmith, Dürer was trained in the late Gothic workshop of the Nuremburg artist, Michael Wolgemut, where he soon came into contact with humanist circles in the city. During the early 1490s, he worked for various printers in Basle, designing woodcuts for popular books such as Sebastian Brant's *Narenschiff* (*Ship of Fools*),[9] and illustrations for an edition of the Roman poet, Terence, that was never published. He subsequently visited Italy twice: in 1494–5 and 1505–6. Some time around 1500, following his return to Nuremburg, Dürer met de' Barbari, who stimulated his interest in the rational and systematic study of the human figure. His subsequent search for the principles of human proportion, and the ideal of beauty that underlay them, became a major preoccupation for Dürer. Both his artistic research and production explored aspects of the human form, although his thoughts on this specific subject were not finally published until after his death in 1528, in the treatise, *Four Books of Human Proportion*.

Dürer's enthusiasm for Italian art pre-dated his first trip to Italy. It clearly influenced his own artistic practice, as evidenced by the way in which he carefully copied the Bacchanal scene from a print by the Mantuan master, Andrea Mantegna (1430/1–1506) (Figures 3.21 and 3.22). Here, Dürer has repeated Mantegna's composition. The portly nude in the middle depicts Silenus, the drunken companion of Bacchus, the god of wine. He is being held up by satyrs and other nude figures, while behind them is a vine thicket. There are many technical similarities between the two images, such as the silhouetting

---

[9] Although the German, Sebastian Brant (1457–1521), was not a humanist, his popular satire, *The Ship of Fools*, echoed many of the concerns of contemporary humanist scholarship, particularly in its central motif of the fool (cf. Erasmus's *Praise of Folly*).

Figure 3.21 Andrea Mantegna, *Bacchanal with Silenus*, *c.*1490, engraving, 33.5 x 45.4 cm. © The Trustees of the British Museum, London

Figure 3.22 Albrecht Dürer (after Mantegna), *Bacchanal with Silenus*, 1494, engraving, pen and brown and sepia ink. Photo: Graphische Sammlung Albertina, Vienna

of the main figures, despite the fact that Dürer uses pen and ink
(Mantegna's original is an engraved print). The form of Dürer's copy,
though, does allow for a greater degree of artistic virtuosity, as, for
example, in the more detailed description of the grapes. Other copies
by Dürer of similar works are less meticulous, but they demonstrate
repeatedly his concern to learn the formal aspects of the Italian style
through imitation.

While Dürer assimilated much of what Italian art had to offer, he was
not an uncritical observer of the contemporary vogue for classically
inspired art. Thus, while he appreciated the varied figure-group
compositions recommended by the Italian theorist, Leon Battista
Alberti (1404–72), he found Italian narrative painting repetitive and
uninspiring. Among his paintings, only one mythological picture has
been identified, the majority are devotional images or portraits. In
addition, much of his work, it has been argued, owed as much to
native, Gothic traditions, as it did to the Italian Renaissance. His
realistic depiction of nature, his interest in human character and
physiognomy, and his repertoire of decorative ornament were as
much a product of his German training as they were shaped by his
early attachment to Italy. Indeed, the Italian artist and early art critic,
Giorgio Vasari (1511–74), who owned two works by Dürer, preferred
to stress his Gothic influence on Italian art, rather than claim him as
a convert to the Renaissance style. He believed, for example, that
Dürer's distorted treatment of the human figure verged on the
fantastical because the German artist had never seen the classical
statues of Tuscany or Rome with his own eyes.

Nonetheless, in Germany itself he was heralded by his humanist
friends and learned associates as the equal of any Italian. Dürer not
only aspired to the status of the intellectual artist; in the opinion of
well-known humanists – men like Erasmus and Pirckheimer – he
succeeded, and in the process helped to raise the public estimation of
others of his profession in early sixteenth-century Germany. In this
respect, Dürer's two visits to Italy left an indelible mark on the
ambitious artist. In 1506, he wrote from Venice to his friend
Pirckheimer: 'Here I am a gentleman, at home only a parasite' (cited
in Koerner, 1993, p.37). Following his return to Germany shortly
afterwards, Dürer made it part of his life's work to rectify this
perception of the artist, in both his artistic and his literary output
(Figure 3.23).

Dürer did, in fact, plan a comprehensive manual of art practice that
was intended to incorporate the ideas of Italian theorists such as
Alberti. While this project was never realized, his published treatises
on perspective, proportion, measurement and applied design were

Figure 3.23 Albrecht Dürer, *Self-portrait*, 1500, oil on panel, 67 x 49 cm. Alte Pinakothek Bayerische Staatsgemäldesammlungen, Munich

widely read and helped to establish his reputation as an intellectual artist in the Italian mould. His influence thus extended to humanist-trained scholars as well as to fellow artists, many of whom trained or worked with him in his Nuremburg workshop. Of these, perhaps the most celebrated was Hans Baldung Grien (1484–1545), who, unusually for a German artist, was socially well connected, the son of a university-educated lawyer. Baldung, who was apprenticed to Dürer from about 1503 to 1507, subsequently set up his own studio in Strasburg, where he propagated his highly unique response to Dürer's fascination with the human body. To some extent Baldung's depiction of the nude would contrast with an ideal based on classical sculpture, especially in his 'Gothick' prints and paintings of witches.[10] (See also Figure 6.9, which depicts a witches' sabbath.)

Dürer, like Baldung, was deeply affected by the religious upheavals of his day and was eventually converted to the moderate, Lutheran cause. Some of his later commissions reflect these growing convictions, most notably his depiction of the *Four Apostles* (1526), which he donated to the Nuremburg city council. Beneath the apostles are quotations from their writings (in Luther's German translation of the Bible), warning against false prophets and other perils of the age. For an artist who relied for much of his living on ecclesiastical commissions, the Reformation undoubtedly posed a serious obstacle to continuing employment. As it happened, his earlier religious prints remained popular with Catholics, even after he threw in his lot with Luther, but he was nonetheless forced to justify his occupation in the face of growing opposition to religious imagery in Protestant circles.

Exercise

Read the following extract from Dürer's *Painter's Manual* (1525), dedicated to his friend Pirckheimer. On what grounds does Dürer defend the art of painting from those who characterize it as a form of idolatry?

> At the present time the art of painting is viewed with disdain in certain quarters, and is said to serve idolatry. A Christian will no more be led to superstition by a painting or a portrait than a devout man to commit murder because he carries a weapon by his side. It must be an ignorant man who would worship a painting, a piece of wood, or a block of stone. Therefore, a well-made artistic, and straightforward painting gives pleasure rather than vexation. The books of the ancients show the degree of honor and respect in which the Greeks and Romans held the arts, in spite of the fact that they were lost or lay in hiding for a thousand years. Only during the last two hundred years they were again brought to light by the Italians.

(Belting, 1994, p.553)

Discussion

Dürer defends the morality of painting on two grounds. In the first place, he echoes the view of Luther and the moderate reformers (including many Erasmians), by arguing that an image or inanimate object, in itself, is neither good nor bad. By implication, people alone can invest art with harmful properties. Secondly, he reverts, in typically humanist fashion, to arguments drawn from antiquity. Because the Greeks and Romans held the arts in high regard, so should his contemporaries, who are fortunate to live in an age in which the virtues of classical art are once more apparent. ❖

---

[10] Baldung's fascination with the visual depiction of witches and witchcraft is discussed more fully in Hults (1987) and Koerner (1993), especially chapter 15.

Hans Holbein the Younger

An artist who followed a similar path to Dürer was Hans Holbein the Younger (1497/8–1543), the son of an Augsburg painter. In 1515, he left Augsburg for Basle, where he seems to have become firmly established. Much of his early work consists of murals, religious paintings and portraits. Exterior wall painting frequently included displays of **sgraffito** (incised stucco) decorated with *all'antica* motifs and classical subject-matter. A case in point is the façade of the townhouse of the wealthy merchant, Jakob von Hertenstein (*c*.1460–1527), which Holbein adorned with allegorical figures, fighting *putti*, moral tales from ancient history and a triumphal procession modelled on Mantegna's *Triumphs of Caesar* (see Cole, 1995, p.157, plate 116), all set within a painted architectural frame with classical pilasters and entablature (Figure 3.24).[11] The interior decorative scheme was more topical, containing a depiction of the recent battle

Figure 3.24 A. Landerer (after Hans Holbein the Younger), *Reconstruction of the Decorative Scheme for the House of Jakob von Hertenstein*, Constance, *c*.1824. Photo: Öffentliche Kunstsammlung, Kupferstich-kabinett, Basle. Inv. 1871.1a

[11] Holbein also painted a number of portraits for this important family, including those of Jakob and Benedikt. The latter, dated 1517, has a frieze behind the portrait depicting a triumphal procession, which, like the paintings in the Hertenstein townhouse, contains further allusions to Mantegna's series on the *Triumphs of Caesar* (Bätschmann and Griener, 1997, p.24). Jakob von Hertenstein represented the canton of Lucerne in the Swiss diet (the parliament of the Swiss confederation) and was, briefly, a protégé of the Emperor Maximilian.

The Closed Position

St Sebastian

Crucifixion

St Anthony

Lamentation

Stage 1

The Middle Position

Annunciation

Angelic Concert

Madonna and Child

Resurrection

Lamentation

Stage 2

The Shrine

Meeting of St Anthony with St Paul

St Augustine

St Anthony

St Jerome

Temptation of St Anthony

← Framework →

Christ and the Twelve Apostles

Stage 3

Plate I Plan of Isenheim altarpiece showing:
Stage 1: the altarpiece closed (see Plate 2)
Stage 2: the altarpiece half open (see Plate 3)
Stage 3: the altarpiece fully open (see Plate 4)

Plate 2 View of the Isenheim altarpiece, closed, showing left to right, *St Sebastian*, *Crucifixion*, *St Anthony*; and below, *Lamentation*. Unterlinden Museum, Colmar, Alsace. Photo: Bridgeman Art Library, London

Plate 3 From left: Annunciation, Angelic Concert, Madonna and Child and Resurrection, as they would appear with the Isenheim altarpiece half open. Unterlinden Museum, Colmar, Alsace. Photo: Bridgeman Art Library, London

Plate 4 From left: painted panel of the *Meeting of St Anthony with St Paul*, sculptures of St Augustine, St Anthony and St Jerome, painted panel of the *Temptation of St Anthony*; and below, sculpture of Christ and the Twelve Apostles, as they would appear with the Isenheim altarpiece fully open. Unterlinden Museum, Colmar, Alsace. Photo: Bridgeman Art Library, London

Plate 5 Lucas Cranach the Elder, *The Last Supper*, 1549, altarpiece. Wittenberg city church. Photo: Constantin Beyer, Weimar

Plate 6 Lucas Cranach the Elder, *Venus Restraining Cupid*, 1509, oil on canvas, 213 x 102 cm. Hermitage, St Petersburg. Cranach's depiction of a classical subject, the nude, is starkly at odds with contemporary Italian treatments of the same theme. Note in particular the sensuous quality of Cranach's work which largely derives from the artist's use of sinuous line at the expense of detailed observation of the actual parts of the body. Photo: Bridgeman Art Library, London

PELLE · CVPIDINEOS · TOTO
NE · TVA · POSSIDEAT

CONAMINE · LVXVS
PECTORA · CECA·A·T·

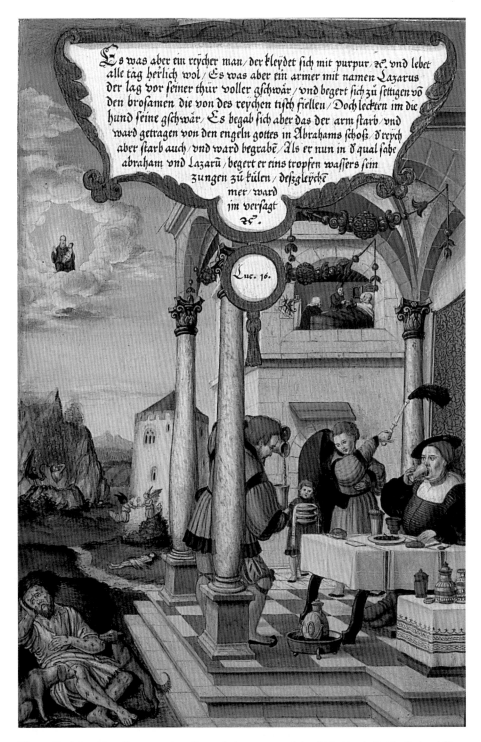

Es was aber ein reycher man / der kleydet sich mit purpur / ꝛc. vnd lebet alle tag herrlich wol / Es was aber ein armer mit namen Lazarus der lag vor seiner thür voller gschwär / vnd begert sich zü settigen vō den brosamen die von des reychen tisch fiellen / Doch leckten im die hund seine gschwär / Es begab sich aber das der arm starb / vnd ward getragen von den engeln gottes in Abrahams schoß / d' reych aber starb auch / vnd ward begrabē / Als er nun in d' qual sahe abraham vnd Lazarū / begert er eins tropfen wassers sein zungen zü külen / deßgleych̄ mer / ward jm versagt ꝛc.

Luc. 16.

Plate 7 Matthias Gernung (or Gerou), *Lazarus and the Rich Man's Table* (Luke 16), sixteenth century, oil on panel, section of wing panel from the Mompelgarter altarpiece, 41 x 28 cm. Kunsthistorisches Museum, Vienna, Austria. Photo: Bridgeman Art Library, London

Plate 8 Jacob Cornelisz van Oostsanen, *Saul and the Witch of Endor*, panel, 87.5 × 125 cm. Rijksmuseum, Amsterdam. Despite the biblical theme of the picture (based on Saul's visit to the Witch of Endor, 1 Samuel 28.7–24), the work owes much to contemporary lore on witchcraft. Note in particular the owls which shelter underneath the witch's garb, reminiscent of the idea that witches might take the form of the classical *strix*, or owl.

of Marignano (1515) in Italy, where Hertenstein's son was wounded. In this particular case, the family's Italian connections may have fostered their taste for an *all'antica* ensemble. On other occasions, Holbein executed exemplary subjects drawn from classical sources and based on humanist designs on civic buildings, such as those devised for the town hall of Nuremburg by the Erasmian humanist and historian, Beatus Rhenanus (1485–1547) (Rowlands, 1985, pp.220–1).

In 1526, Holbein travelled to England with an introduction from Erasmus to the famous English humanist, Thomas More (1478–1535). He eventually rose to the position of sergeant-painter, or court painter, to Henry VIII (1509–47), and became the official portraitist to the English court. During this period, he would appear to have tempered his personal religious leanings toward Lutheranism (a capital offence in England, despite Henry's breach with Rome in the 1530s) and to have focused instead on portrait painting, at which he excelled.

Unlike Dürer, who was absorbed with theoretical issues relating to the practice of his art, Holbein was largely satisfied to indulge his patrons' taste for colour and realistic detail, aspects of contemporary art that owed more to Holbein's native Gothic traditions than they did to the Italian Renaissance. Nevertheless, there is little doubt that he was thoroughly familiar with Italian art and the *all'antica* style, while preferring to focus on more recent Italian innovations in painting such as the use of perspective.[12] This is evident, for example, in the double portrait of Jean de Dinteville and Georges de Selve, entitled *The Ambassadors*, which Holbein painted in 1533 (Figure 3.25). Here, concern for observational realism is as important as the virtuoso demonstration of perspectival accuracy that informs the skull **anamorphosis** in the centre foreground. In the process, Holbein seeks to accommodate the actual experience of seeing with theories of perspective that allow objects to recede into the distance (cf. the work of Leonardo da Vinci in the Anthology, no. 31ii). In respect to subject-matter, the picture is largely devoid of direct references to antiquity. The objects on the table represent the liberal arts, although they also include a German Lutheran hymnal,[13] a reference to the

[12] There is no sure evidence that Holbein ever visited Italy, although the indirect evidence of his paintings, and their detailed understanding of composition, symmetry and decorative detail, has inclined some scholars to the view that he must have seen Italian art at first hand; see, for example, Bätschmann and Griener (1997), pp.147–8. For a more sceptical view, see Rowlands (1985), pp.29–30. Both agree, however, that if Holbein visited Italy it was probably around the time he was working in Lucerne in 1517.

[13] It is, in fact, the hymnal that was set to music by Johann Walter and published at Wittenburg in 1524; see above.

Figure 3.25 Hans Holbein the Younger, *Jean de Dinteville and Georges de Selve* (*The Ambassadors*), 1533, oil on panel, 207 × 210 cm. National Gallery, London. © The National Gallery, London

diplomatic attempt by de Selve to reunite the Lutherans with the Catholic church. The skull is a *memento mori*, a symbolic reminder of death, which featured frequently in northern art in this period.

Working in a country experiencing religious upheaval,[14] Holbein's tendency to avoid excessive imitation of overtly Italianate styles and classical subject-matter may reflect both the reformist tendencies and cultural conservatism of his patrons. Holbein was widely admired in England for his skill in catching a natural likeness and use of symbolic imagery, a characteristic feature of much northern, 'Gothic' art in the fifteenth century. The association in the eyes of many northern, Protestant patrons of an *all'antica* artistic treatment with the distinctly 'foreign' and 'idolatrous' culture of Catholic Italy reinforced the

[14] Holbein's precise religious position is something of a mystery. In the early 1520s, he executed a number of woodcuts to illustrate Lutheran pamphlets published in Basle. Sympathetic to the general tenor of the moderate reform movement, particularly its Erasmianism, he nonetheless refused to be drawn on the question of his own personal religious faith. In England, where he was employed primarily as a portrait painter, he was largely able to avoid the problem faced by many of his fellow artists in Germany, whose livelihoods frequently depended on religious commissions.

tendency of artists like Holbein to paint portraits in the traditional northern style. Only in the second half of the sixteenth century, and then mainly in Catholic regions of Europe such as Bavaria and Austria, were Italianate Renaissance styles wholeheartedly adopted in northern painting. A rather different pattern of reception, however, is evident in the case of sculpture and architecture (von der Osten and Vey, 1969, especially pp.223–30).

Sculpture and architecture in sixteenth-century Germany

In much the same way as historians of German art have debated the appropriateness of the term 'Renaissance' when applied to the painting of this period, so too have scholars questioned the extent to which Italy influenced German sculpture and architecture in the sixteenth century. In sculpture, there is little evidence of any extensive imitation of Italian models. Two of the most important figures in German sculpture, Tilmann Riemenschneider (1460–1531) and Veit Stoss (c.1438–1533), were Gothic artists, skilled in both stone and wood, whose work was largely unaffected by the Renaissance. Where strong Renaissance influences were felt, they were mostly restricted to one or two centres of production, such as Augsburg or Nuremburg, where a more sophisticated and Italophile audience existed. At Augsburg, for example, the sculpted interior decoration of the Fugger chapel owed much to classical designs and precedents based on drawings by Dürer, which were executed by the local sculptor, Hans Daucher (c.1486–1538) (Rowlands, 1985, pp.28–9).

The most important centre of Renaissance-style sculpture in Germany was Nuremburg, where the Vischer family encouraged the importation of Italianate forms and motifs in the early sixteenth century. Unusually for German artists, the brothers Hermann and Peter Vischer travelled to Siena and Rome in the 1510s, where they encountered Italian art at first hand. On their return to Nuremburg, they sought to imitate elements of what they had seen in a variety of ways, most notably in the new shrine to St Sebald in the church of that name in their native city. Peter Vischer the Younger (1487–1528) subsequently revived the use of classical motifs and designs in statues, medals and medallions made in bronze and brass (Figure 3.26). Medals and plaquettes produced by the Vischer workshop included reference to mythological subjects, such as Orpheus and Eurydice (Kaufmann, 1995, pp.109–11).

A good example of this type of artistic virtuosity, which demanded a thorough grounding in Renaissance principles, can be found in the work of the Nuremburg sculptor and member of the Vischer

Figure 3.26 Peter Vischer the Younger, Inkstand with an allegory of Fortune, *c*.1515–20, brass cast from wax and wood models, Nuremburg. Peter Burke (1998, p.188) comments that this was an appropriate furnishing for a humanist's study. Photo: Ashmolean Museum, Oxford

workshop, Peter Flötner (1485/90–1546). The *Apollo Fountain*, of 1532, was commissioned for the shooting yard of the local archery club (Figure 3.27). The work consists of two parts: a statue of the naked Apollo and an ornate pedestal with *putti*, sea monsters, imaginary heads and classical architectural motifs. The pose of the figure is modelled on an engraving of Apollo and Diana by de' Barbari made around 1504 (Figure 3.28), while the decoration on the pedestal may derive from Italian sculptures that Flötner saw in Padua during his trip to Italy in 1529–30. In his design, Flötner has smoothed the contours of the figure, slightly elongated the limbs and trimmed the hair. The pose, with the weight on one foot, may be a paraphrase of the recently discovered antique sculpture, the *Apollo Belvedere*, which formed part of the Vatican collection in Rome.

In producing this work, Flötner was clearly working within an established genre. The ornamental fountain, whether situated in public or private spaces (gardens, courtyards, etc.), was a hallmark of Renaissance fashion in cities such as Nuremburg and Augsburg (famous for its Hercules fountain), notwithstanding the fact that both cities were governed by Protestant councils. On seeing a model of the Nuremburg statue, an Italian cardinal commissioned a similar fountain for his own garden from the German artist – a sure sign that Flötner had achieved an authentic *all'antica* style in his work. Other work by Flötner, however, strongly suggests that he, in line with other German sculptors and artists of this period, was not a pure exponent of the new Italianate style. On the contrary, hybridity would appear to be the most accurate way to describe how artists like Flötner, Holbein and even Dürer incorporated traditional, Gothic-style native art with

Figure 3.27 Peter Flötner, *Apollo Fountain*, 1532, bronze, 100 cm high. Germanisches Nationalmuseum, Nuremburg

Figure 3.28 Jacopo de' Barbari, *Apollo and Diana*, 1504–5, engraving, 16 x 10 cm. Ashmolean Museum, Oxford

the new trends from across the Alps – a case in point being Flötner's collaboration with German, Polish and Italian artists in the design of the altarpiece for the Sigismund chapel in Cracow in Poland (1531–8).

Just as German painters had to look elsewhere for commissions following the drastic reduction in demand for religious images after the Reformation, so too sculptors like Flötner were forced to diversify their repertoire in the search for new patrons. Metal and relief casting offered one new source of employment. Flötner was also responsible for designing small-scale objects, such as mirrors, plates, flasks and goblets, often in precious metals like silver and gold. Such commissions were particularly popular in expanding commercial centres such as Nuremburg, where skilled craftsmen and artists like Flötner catered to the increasingly sophisticated tastes of their patrician customers (Chipps Smith, 1983, especially pp.198–244).

The search for a pure Italianate Renaissance style in German architecture is equally elusive. Individual buildings often display classicizing columns and *all'antica* decorative motifs, but whole new buildings were rarely constructed in accordance with the precepts of Italian Renaissance architecture (Figure 3.29). Accordingly, the

Figure 3.29 Rathaus, Leipzig. The Rathaus, or town hall, was built between 1556 and 1564, and contains a number of features that derive from Italian Renaissance forms and motifs. Note in particular the use of decorative S-shaped scrolls on the side of the gables and the Doric columns flanking the entrance. Photo: Herbert Lachmann, 1970. © Bildarchiv Preussischer Kulturbesitz, Berlin judgement of most historians of sixteenth-century German architecture has tended to the view that it consisted of 'little more than a system of classical ornament applied to essentially late Gothic structures' (Overfield, 1992, p.94). The main sources for German architects and patrons who sought to utilize and imitate Italianate architectural practices were the German editions of classical and Italian manuals that were in wide circulation in Germany by the middle of the sixteenth century. A German edition of Vitruvius's *De architectura* (*On Architecture*), for example, was published in 1548, and was soon followed by German translations of contemporary Italian architectural theorists such as Sebastiano Serlio (1475–1554).[15] Works such as these provided German patrons and builders with a general understanding of contemporary architectural fashions in Italy, but they were not the only, nor even the major, source of inspiration. Municipal building in eastern Germany, for example, was strongly influenced by Renaissance architectural ideals and practices in Buda (Hungary) and Cracow (Poland). Similarly, in south-west and north-west Germany, French and Netherlandish craftsmen mediated the importation of a 'pure' Renaissance style.

As a result, even those few buildings wholly constructed in sixteenth-century Germany in accordance with Renaissance principles were rarely the product of direct contact with Italy. A case in point is the castle and chapel of Augustusburg, near Chemnitz in eastern Germany, which was built by the Protestant Elector of Saxony, August, between 1569 and 1573 (Figure 3.30). The general design of the castle was supplied by a German military engineer, Hieronymus Lotter (*c.*1497–1580), who was also responsible for the work on Leipzig town hall (Figure 3.29). Following his dismissal, responsibility for overseeing the completion of the work passed to another German architect, with experience in France and Italy, who was probably responsible for the appearance of the chapel. As one of the first Protestant chapels built from new, its design and decoration are of particular interest for historians of the Reformation. Double, alternating plain and fluted **Doric** columns extend up the two-storey wall of the chapel, while banded coffering arches are placed round the barrel ceiling (Figure 3.30). The centrepiece of the chapel is occupied by an elaborate altarpiece – the work of Lucas Cranach the Younger (1515–86) – set in a contemporary classicizing frame (Figure 3.31).

The hybrid appearance of so much German Renaissance architecture owed much to the various routes whereby Italianate influence entered Germany. During the second half of the sixteenth century, a particularly powerful influence on German domestic, civic and

[15] Serlio's *Five Books of Architecture* were published in Italy between 1537 and 1547.

Figure 3.30 Erhard van der Meer and others, Augustusburg Schloss, chapel, 1569–73, interior.
Photo: Bildarchiv Preussischer Kulturbesitz, Berlin

Figure 3.31 Lucas Cranach the Younger, Altar, Augustusburg Schloss chapel. Photo: Staatlicher Schlossbetrieb, Augustusburg

Figure 3.32 Pieter van der Borcht, *Stadthuis*, or town hall, Antwerp, 1581. The façade included a triumphal arch, elaborate central pediment and obelisk. It also contained an inscription 'SPQA' (The Senate and the People of Antwerp) that was deliberately intended to invoke the idea of Antwerp as a second Rome (Burke, 1998, p.117). Photo: Stadsarchief Antwerpen, Belgium

court architecture was that which emanated from the Netherlands. Several Netherlandish manuals that sought to reinterpret Italian Renaissance architectural motifs were especially popular in northern Europe at this time. These helped to popularize a range of innovations such as the cantilevered eave gallery found on the façade of Antwerp town hall, a building that owed much to a reinterpretation of the designs of the Italian Serlio (Figure 3.32).

The integrity of the German Renaissance: the Munich Antiquarium

One of the paradoxes of the German Renaissance is that despite the general absence of 'pure' Italianate styles in the German visual arts, the country nonetheless contained one of the finest examples of that style anywhere in sixteenth-century Europe. In 1569, the Catholic duke Wilhelm V of Bavaria commissioned the construction of an art gallery for his palace in Munich (Figure 3.33). The duke possessed a fine collection of classical busts, purchased from the Fuggers of Augsburg in 1566, and built the gallery in order to accommodate his new purchase. The designer was the duke's artistic adviser, the Mantuan antique dealer, Jacopo Strada (1515–88), who modelled his plan on that of a room designed by Giulio Romano for the ducal palace at Mantua, the Palazzo Te.[16] The design of the Antiquarium

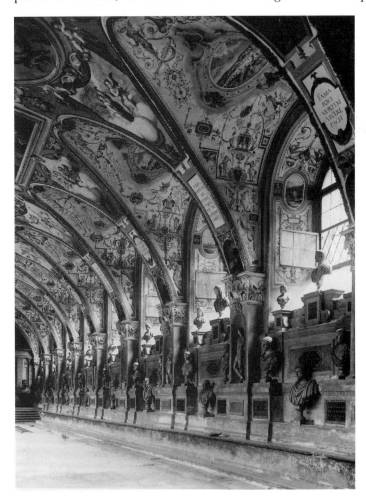

Figure 3.33 (1) Jacopo Strada and Wilhelm Egckl, (2) Frederik Sustris, Piero Candido il Padovano and Hans Thomaner, Antiquarium, Munich, Stadresidenz, (1) 1569–71, (2) 1586–1600, interior looking east. Photo: Bildarchiv Foto Marburg, Marburg

[16] Giulio's work at Mantua is discussed more fully in Chapter 1 in Book 2 in the series. A cousin of the ruling family in Munich had earlier built a Renaissance-style palace at Landshut in Bavaria (1536–43), which incorporated many of the features of the Palazzo Te at Mantua.

may also owe something to the statue corridors in the Uffizi Palace, Florence, begun by Vasari in 1560. Among the interior decorators who worked on the Munich scheme were a Florentine and a Dutchman who had trained in Florence. These included the artist, Sustris, who added the later decorations to the Fugger house at Augsburg.

The Antiquarium itself was a large-scale and highly elaborate example of an emerging type of space – a *Kunstkammer* (art room) – that was designed specifically to house works of art. In many respects, it evolved out of the practice of Italian princes and collectors of displaying books, precious objects and works of art in *studioli*, places for study and contemplation. The phenomenon was quintessentially Renaissance in kind. Several classical writers, for example, mentioned the Roman custom of displaying portrait busts of their ancestors as a sign of their noble status. In the Renaissance, a correlation between the form and function of an art work indicated an awareness of a classical concept that lay at the heart of Renaissance culture, the notion of decorum. In art-historical terms, the application of this idea required that certain forms of art, and their subject-matter, should only be seen in certain contexts. Paintings depicting nudity and scenes of a sexual nature were not, for example, considered appropriate for public spaces but were acceptable in private displays. In the case of portrait busts that were intended to signify nobility, the idea of decorum dictated that the image should manifest the qualities of proportion, restraint and calmness.

Exercise

Look at Figure 3.33. In what ways does the appearance of the Antiquarium reflect its function as a gallery for antique statues and portrait busts? How, in other words, can it be said to be 'decorous'?

Discussion

Clearly, the Antiquarium is not a museum in the modern sense of the word. The objects on display are not arranged for ease of inspection. Nor is the interior decoration of the room muted, as one might expect, so as to avoid distracting the viewer from focusing on the exhibits. Here, rather, the exhibits complement the interior decoration to form one large artistic composition.

The solid framework of vaulted arches corresponds with the niche settings of the casts of the taller, three-quarter-length statues, which form a rhythmical sequence. Between these there is a long row of portrait busts placed at various heights in an orderly and symmetrical fashion. The carefully gauged window light adds to the sense of gravity and decorum. Indeed, the lowered floor and restrained lighting of the ensemble suggest the sombre atmosphere of a mausoleum rather than a museum, although this effect is slightly relieved by the **grotesque** decoration on the ceiling. The mood of the room and its contents is fully in keeping with the classical appreciation of the funereal bust portrait and the demands of classical decorum. ❖

The Antiquarium, closely modelled on that at Mantua, was built beneath the duke's library, and represented an important statement of the learned and cultivated taste of its owner (there are also personifications of the liberal arts set in the **lunettes**). The room was intended as a shrine to the 'spirit' of antiquity. The overall seriousness and balance of the various classical components – each representing a different aspect of the *all'antica* style – would have suggested a sensitive awareness of the demands of decorum. As an expression of the principle of 'art for art's sake' (i.e. that the primary function of art is aesthetic), the Antiquarium represents one of the finest examples of the reception of Italian Renaissance ideals in sixteenth-century Europe.

Some German artists and patrons did attempt to appropriate Italian Renaissance culture in its entirety, but such attempts were exceptional and largely confined to the princely courts, whether Protestant or Catholic. Hybridity, in the sense of a mixture of local and 'foreign' styles, was largely the order of the day. Only in painting was the Italian influence potentially more extensive, and this was greatly reduced after the collapse of the mainstay market for religious pictures in Protestant areas after 1530 when the full impact of the Reformation began to take effect. Thereafter, words rather than images more commonly typified the German response to the Renaissance.

Bibliography

BARKER, J.W. (1969) 'Sociological influences upon the emergence of Lutheran music', *Miscellanea Musicologica*, vol. 4, pp.157–98.

BÄTSCHMANN, O. and GRIENER, P. (1997) *Hans Holbein*, London, Reaktion Books.

BELTING, H. (1994) *Likeness and Presence: A History of the Image in the Era before Art*, trans. E. Jephcott, Chicago and London, University of Chicago Press.

BERGENDOFF, C. (ed.) (1958) *Luther's Works, vol.40, Church and Ministry II*, Philadelphia, Mühlenberg Press.

BURCKHARDT, J. (1990) *The Civilization of the Renaissance in Italy*, trans. S.G.C. Middlemore, Harmondsworth, Penguin; first published 1860.

BURKE, P. (1998) *The European Renaissance: Centres and Peripheries*, Oxford, Blackwell.

BUSZIN, W.E. (1946) 'Luther on music', *Musical Quarterly*, vol. 32, pp.80–97.

CHIPPS SMITH, J. (1983) *Nuremburg: A Renaissance City, 1500–1618*, Austin, Texas, University of Texas Press.

CHRISTENSEN, C.C. (1972) 'The significance of the epitaph monument in early Lutheran ecclesiastical art (*ca.*1540–1600): some social and iconographical considerations' in L.P. Buck and J.W. Zophy (eds) *The Social History of the Reformation*, Columbus, Ohio State University Press, pp.297–314.

CHRISTENSEN, C.C. (1979) *Art and the Reformation in Germany*, Athens, Ohio, Ohio University Press.

CHRISTENSEN, C.C. (1992) *Princes and Propaganda: Electoral Saxon Art of the Reformation*, Sixteenth Century Essays and Studies, vol. 20, Kirksville, Missouri, Sixteenth Century Journal Publishers.

CHRISTIAN JR, W.A. (1981) *Local Religion in Sixteenth-Century Spain*, Princeton, Princeton University Press.

COLE, A. (1995) *Art of the Italian Renaissance Courts: Virtue and Magnificence*, London, Weidenfeld & Nicolson.

CUNEO, P.F. (1996) 'Propriety, property and politics: Jörg Breu the Elder and issues of iconoclasm in Reformation Augsburg', *German History*, vol. 14, pp.1–20.

FLEISCHER, M.P. (1992) 'Humanism and reformation in Silesia: imprints of Italy – Celtis, Erasmus, Luther, and Melanchthon' in M.P. Fleischer (ed.) *The Harvest of Humanism in Central Europe: Essays in Honor of Lewis W Spitz*, St Louis, Concordia, pp.27–107.

HAYUM, A. (1989) *The Isenheim Altarpiece: God's Medicine and the Painter's Vision*, Princeton, Princeton University Press.

HOPE, C. and MCGRATH, E.(1996) 'Artists and humanists' in J. Kraye (ed.) *The Cambridge Companion to Renaissance Humanism*, Cambridge, Cambridge University Press, pp.161–88.

HULTS, L.C. (1987) 'Baldung and the witches of Freiburg: the evidence of images', *Journal of Interdisciplinary History*, vol. 18, pp.249–76.

KAUFMANN, T. DAC. (1995) *Court, Cloister and City: The Art and Culture of Central Europe, 1450–1800*, London, Weidenfeld & Nicolson.

KOERNER, J.L. (1993) *The Moment of Self-Portraiture in German Renaissance Art*, Chicago, University of Chicago Press.

KRODEL, G.G. (ed.) (1972) *Luther's Works, vol.49, Letters II*, Philadelphia, Fortress Press.

LEUPOLD, U.S. (ed.) (1965) *Luther's Works, vol.53, Liturgy and Hymns*, Philadelphia, Fortress Press.

LINDBERG, D.D. (1976) *Theories of Vision from Al-Kindi to Kepler*, Chicago, University of Chicago Press.

MERBACK, M. (1999) *The Thief, The Cross and The Wheel: Pain and the Spectacle of Punishment in Medieval and Renaissance Europe*, London, Reaktion Books.

MUIR, E. (1997) *Ritual in Early Modern Europe*, Cambridge, Cambridge University Press.

NEW GROVE DICTIONARY OF MUSIC AND MUSICIANS (1980) London, Macmillan.

OLIN, J.C. (1965) *Desiderius Erasmus. Christian Humanism and the Reformation: Selected Writings*, New York, Harper & Row.

OSTEN, G. VON DER and VEY, H.(1969) *Painting and Sculpture in Germany and the Netherlands 1500 to 1600*, The Pelican History of Art, Harmondsworth, Penguin.

OVERFIELD, J. (1992) 'Germany' in R. Porter and M. Teich (eds) *The Renaissance in National Context*, Cambridge, Cambridge University Press, pp.92–122.

OZMENT, S. (1993) *Protestants: The Birth of a Revolution*, London, Fontana Press.

PELIKAN, J. and LEHMANN, H.T. (eds) (1955) *Luther's Works, vol.40*, Philadelphia, Mühlenberg Press.

ROWLANDS, J. (1985) *Holbein: The Paintings of Hans Holbein the Younger*, Oxford, Phaidon.

ST AUGUSTINE (1912) *Confessions*, Loeb Classical Library, 2 vols, Cambridge, MA, Harvard University Press.

SCRIBNER, R.W. (1987) *Popular Culture and Popular Movements in Reformation Germany*, London and Ronceverte, The Hambledon Press.

STRUNK, O. (1952) *Source Readings in Musical History*, London, Faber & Faber.

WANDEL, L.P. (1989) 'The reform of the images: new visualizations of the Christian community at Zürich', *Archiv für Reformationgeschichte*, vol. 80, pp.105–24.

WANDEL, L.P. (1993) 'Envisioning God: image and liturgy in Reformation Zurich', *Sixteenth Century Journal*, vol. 24, pp.21–40.

WANDEL, L.P. (1995) *Voracious Idols and Violent Hands: Iconoclasm in Reformation Zürich*, Cambridge, Cambridge University Press.

WEISS, P. and TARUSKIN, R. (1984) *Music in the Western World: A History in Documents*, London, Collier Macmillan.

WENTZ, A.R. (ed.) (1959) *Luther's Works, vol.36, Word and Sacrament II*, Philadelphia, Mühlenberg Press.

ZIKA, C. (1988) 'Hosts, processions and pilgrimages: controlling the sacred in fifteenth-century Germany', *Past and Present*, vol. 118, pp.25–64.

ZIKA, C. (1991) 'The devil's hoodwink: seeing and believing in the world of sixteenth-century witchcraft' in C. Zika (ed.) *No Gods Except Me: Orthodoxy and Religious Practice in Europe, 1200–1600*, Parkville, Victoria, University of Melbourne Department of History, pp.153–98.

Anthology and Reader sources

Martin Luther, from *The Babylonian Captivity of the Church* (1520): *Luther's Works, vol. 36, Word and Sacrament II*, ed. A. R. Wentz, Mühlenberg Press, Philadelphia, 1959, pp.18–19, 21–3, 34–9, 51–2, 54. (Anthology, no. 72)

Martin Luther, Letter to Nicholas Hausmann, town preacher at Zwickau (1524): *Luther's Works, vol.49, Letters II*, ed. G. G. Krodel, Fortress Press, Philadelphia, 1972, p.90. (Anthology, no. 86)

Martin Luther, Preface to the complete edition of *A German Theology* (1518): *Luther's Works, vol. 31, The Career of the Reformer I*, ed. H. J. Grimm, Mühlenberg Press, Philadelphia, 1957, pp.75–6. (Anthology, no. 64)

Martin Luther, from *Against the Heavenly Prophets in the Matter of Images and Sacraments* (1525): *Luther's Works, vol.40, Church and Ministry II*, ed. C. Bergendoff, Mühlenberg Press, Philadelphia, 1958, p.99. (Anthology, no. 87)

Robert W. Scribner, Luther myth: a popular historiography of the reformer: *Popular Culture and Popular Movements in Reformation Germany*, Hambledon Press, London and Ronceverte, 1987, chapter 14, pp.301–3, 306–22. (Reader, no. 20)

Leonardo da Vinci, Extracts from his *Notebooks* (ii) Perspective: *Leonardo on Painting*, ed. and trans. M. Kemp and M. Walker, Yale University Press, New Haven and London, 1989. (Anthology, no. 31)

CHAPTER FOUR

Lazarillo de Tormes

BY KEITH WHITLOCK

Objectives

The objectives of this chapter are that you should:

- study *Lazarillo de Tormes* as a Renaissance humanist text;

- examine the background to its printing, diffusion and anonymity;

- explore the tensions inherent in the book between author, narrator and translator;

- consider the book within the context of anti-Spanish propaganda;

- consider the book in terms of its impact on English Renaissance drama and on the evolution and practice of prose fiction.

Introduction

In this chapter we study a short, sixteenth-century Spanish prose narrative,[1] *Lazarillo de Tormes*, first published in 1554. Originally written in Castilian during the reign of Charles V (Charles I of Spain 1516–56; Holy Roman Emperor Charles V 1519–58; referred to hereafter in this chapter as Charles V), it soon became a Europe-wide best-seller. In some respects *Lazarillo de Tormes* is uniquely Spanish, but in others, as I hope to show, the book confirms, qualifies and challenges Burckhardt's 'portrait of an age' (1990, p.5).

The English translation on which the chapter is based is by David Rowland of Anglesey, from a surviving edition of 1586 (Whitlock, 2000).[2] While there are numerous other translations (the Penguin Classics *Two Spanish Picaresque Novels* (Alpert, 1977), for example, first published in 1969, has never been out of print), my preference for

---

[1] It is usual practice among critics and scholars to refer to the text as a novel. The work is very short and some scholars have had recourse to terms like 'proto-novel', 'anti-romance', or more simply 'book' or 'narrative'. Whichever term we adopt we have to be ready to defend our choice. You will find that in general I use the words 'book' or 'text' because they are neutral and do not impose a sort of closure on discussion. Some of the qualifications and questions that a generic term like 'novel' raises will be found in the following discussion, which includes some reference to the evolution of prose fiction.

[2] All quotations from and references to the text of *Lazarillo de Tormes* are from Whitlock, 2000. This edition has been edited to bring spelling and punctuation in line with present-day conventions, and paragraphing has been recast to accord better with standard Spanish editions and the sense of the narrative.

Rowland arises from the vigour of the Tudor English text, and its closeness in time to the original. Modern critical editions commonly draw on Rowland's rendering for their annotation.

In historical literary surveys it is common for *Lazarillo de Tormes* to be studied as a key text in the evolution of western prose fiction and **Spanish realism**. Our approach, however, has a different emphasis. In the first place we hope to show that it might be read as a contribution to the debate surrounding the impact of the Renaissance on Spain in the sixteenth century. Following Burckhardt, many scholars, particularly those from Protestant northern Europe, eagerly approved his view of Spain as a cultural backwater and its people as little better than barbarians. More recent studies, however, have stressed, among other things, the vital, if short-lived, role of humanism in Spanish cultural and religious life in this period. *Lazarillo de Tormes*, it is now argued, was a product of this environment, its central characters and themes a thinly veiled humanist critique of church and society in sixteenth-century Spain. Secondly we take up the theme of 'reception' by looking at how a text such as *Lazarillo de Tormes* was interpreted in Protestant England in the late sixteenth and early seventeenth centuries, and its relationship to contemporary works of an anti-Spanish nature in English Renaissance drama. The Protestant demonization of the Spanish was destined to play an important role in shaping the responses of northern Europeans to Spain for centuries to come. Here, we illustrate how Burckhardt's own version of the 'black legend' was indebted to this tradition.

Exercise

If you have not already done so, read through the text of *Lazarillo de Tormes* (Whitlock, 2000). ❖

Background

Printing and diffusion

Lazarillo de Tormes is shrouded in unresolved mysteries. It first appeared publicly in 1554, published as far as we know in four places: Burgos, Alcalá de Henares (a town near Madrid with a recently founded humanist university), Medina del Campo and Antwerp (then the main city of the Spanish Netherlands). All four editions are dated 1554, but there must have been an archetype, not necessarily printed, to which 'Burgos' (of all the editions this is the least polished and stylistically the most vigorous) is probably nearest (see Figure 4.1). 'Alcalá' bears the date 26 February, but since it calls itself a second impression, that date may have been copied from an earlier one and the additions (generally not regarded as by the author) may have been added later in the year (see Figure 4.2 overleaf). 'Medina' bears the date 1 March. 'Antwerp', it has been argued, was printed later in the year. Rowland's translation is based on the Antwerp text and the second edition of the French translation published by the printer Jean Saugrain in Paris in 1561. The first French edition had come out in 1560 in Lyons, then a centre of French Protestant activity. Rowland may also have used the first edition. There is unresolved scholarly debate over when the book was first written: internal evidence could support arguments for a date of composition as early as the 1520s or 1530s, but the weight of critical opinion now seems to favour a date closer to the first year of publication.

Figure 4.1 Title page of the 1554 Burgos edition of *Lazarillo de Tormes*. From Bjornson, 1979, p.23

The book is an early example of a Europe-wide best-seller because of the speed with which it was published and translated into all the major western European languages. There are many possible reasons for its enormous and immediate popularity, apart from the merit of being written in a vigorous and entertaining style. Certainly there was interest in the ways of rogues and beggars throughout Europe, and the book spawned a generation of **picaresque** novels. Similarly there was the long-standing popularity from medieval times of jest (or joke) books, a tradition that the work obviously taps. Lazarillo's revenge on his first master, the blind beggar, occurs in books of merry tales.

Figure 4.2 Title page of the 26 February 1554 Alcalá de Henares edition of *Lazarillo de Tormes*. © The Trustees of the British Library, London

Shakespeare possibly referred to the same incident in *Much Ado About Nothing* (2.1.206–7) and for this reason has been suspected of reading jest books. In all probability he did, but we must bear in mind that in *Love's Labours Lost* the central comic figure of Don Adriano de Armado has so close a comic resemblance to Lazarillo's third master, the proud and penniless squire, that there must be an equal presumption that Shakespeare had read Rowland's translation or heard a close account of it.

This observation raises another probable reason for the book's huge popularity: its contents were a propaganda gift to powers hostile to Spain, like France and England. The surviving edition of Rowland's translation dates from 1586, when relations between England and Spain had broken down. The two countries subsequently drifted into war, resulting in the failure of the Spanish Armada in 1588. Rowland's translation was regularly reprinted at moments of Anglo-Spanish crises during the following 90 years. Indeed a version of the book was even issued in the United States at the time of the Spanish-American war of 1898. *Lazarillo de Tormes* is also notably anti-clerical and a propaganda gift to Protestants attacking the Roman church. The censorship of the book in sixteenth-century Spain mirrors the loss of religious freedom in that country: the Inquisitor, Fernando de Valdés, placed it on the Index of forbidden books in 1559 and a version expurgated of the Fourth and Fifth Treatises and other anti-clerical material was published in 1573. The 'Medina del Campo' edition was recently discovered walled up in an old house in Barcarrota, Extremadura. With it were a Hebrew text, a book of Erasmus, a book on palmistry and a manuscript of an obscene text. All were on the Index. Erasmus's works were widely read and studied in Spain at the beginning of the sixteenth century but even the mention of his name was dangerous at the end.

Exercise

Read the following passage from Elizabeth L. Eisenstein's *The Printing Revolution in Early Modern Europe,* and consider what might have attracted Abell Jeffes as stationer (i.e. publisher and bookseller) to an English translation of *Lazarillo de Tormes.*

> In the course of the sixteenth century, vernacular Bibles that had been turned out on a somewhat haphazard basis in diverse regions were withheld from Catholics and made compulsory for Protestants. An incentive to learn to read was thus eliminated among lay Catholics and officially enjoined upon Protestants. Book markets were likely to expand at different rates thereafter. Bible printing, once authorized, often became a special privilege, so that its decline in Catholic centres had a direct impact on a relatively small group of printers. The entire industry, however, suffered a glancing blow from the suppression of the large potential market represented by a Catholic lay Bible-reading

public. Furthermore, vernacular Bibles were by no means the only best sellers that were barred to Catholic readers after the Council of Trent. Erasmus had made a fortune for his printers before Luther outstripped him. Both, along with many other popular authors, were placed on the Index. Being listed as forbidden served as a form of publicity and may have spurred sales. It was, however, more hazardous for Catholic printers than for Protestant ones to profit thereby.

Given the existence of profit-seeking printers outside the reach of Rome, Catholic censorship boomeranged in ways that could not be foreseen. The Index provided free publicity for titles listed thereon. Lists of passages to be expurgated directed readers to 'book, chapter, and line' where anti-Roman passages could be found, thus relieving Protestant propagandists of the need to make their own search for anti-Catholic citations drawn from eminent authors and respected works. Early copies of all the original Indexes found their way as soon as they were produced to Leiden, Amsterdam and Utrecht and were promptly utilized by the enterprising Dutch publisher as guides. Indeed, there was much to be gained and little to be lost for the Protestant printer who developed his list for forthcoming books with an eye on the latest issue of the Index. Decisions made by Catholic censors thus inadvertently deflected Protestant publication policies in the direction of foreign heterodox, libertine, and innovative trends. This deflecting action is worth pausing over. It suggests why printers have to be treated as independent agents when trying to correlate Catholic-Protestant divisions with other developments. It was the profit-seeking printer and not the Protestant divine who published Aretino, Bruno, Sarpi, Machiavelli, Rabelais, and all the other authors who were on Catholic lists. When the intervening agent is left out of account, it becomes difficult to explain why such a secular, freethinking, and hedonist literary culture should have flourished in regions where pious Protestants were in control.

(1993, pp.173–7)

| Discussion | One could infer from Eisenstein that *Lazarillo de Tormes* enjoyed publicity, perhaps notoriety, because it had been placed on the Index in 1559. This may have been a spur to sales in a society where a lay Bible-reading public was growing. Antwerp, where Rowland's Spanish copy had been published in 1555, contained many Protestants and was a distribution point for disseminating polemical materials by virtue of its financial and commercial importance. |

Abell Jeffes' 'logo' on the English translation (see Figure 4.3) carries the words 'Prase the Lorde with Harpe and Songe', and the bell, presumably a play on Jeffes' first name, Abell, is further suggestive of the ringing out of Protestant Christian news. ❖

Figure 4.3 Title page and verso of the 1586 Abell Jeffes edition of *Lazarillo de Tormes*. Photo: Bodleian Library, University of Oxford, 8 C 24 Th.Seld (3)

Authorship

The authorship of *Lazarillo de Tormes* has remained one of the best-kept secrets of European literary history. The initial act of publishing in four locations may simply reflect the book's immediate popularity rather than provide evidence of intention to evade authorial identification. Anonymity has not precluded a great deal of guesswork. There are two front contenders for authorship according to scholars who have investigated the matter. The first is Diego Hurtado de Mendoza (1504–75), who was named in this connection in 1607–8. A Spanish aristocrat and soldier, he lived in Italy during the 1520s and studied at the universities of Rome and Siena. He also served as Spanish ambassador to Venice, where he learned Greek and was painted by Titian. He owned a large library of Renaissance books. He is known to have been in Rome during the papal elections of 1550, and his literary style and anti-clericalism are judged to match

175

the text's. Secondly there is Juan de Ortega, a Hieronymite friar, elected general of his order in 1552. Both men suffered reverses in fortune which could have prevented their admitting authorship. My preference is for Juan de Ortega. He studied at the University of Salamanca and entered the Hieronymite monastery in the nearby town of Alba de Tormes. The church of the village of Tejares, where Lazarillo was born, belonged to that monastery. The text's first location is Salamanca (see Figure 4.4). The Roman bridge of course remains to this day, with its bull (I suggest it is a pre-Roman boar), against which the blind man dashed Lazarillo's head, recently raised on a plinth (see Figure 4.5).

Figure 4.4 Townscape of Salamanca. Photo: Spanish Tourist Office, London

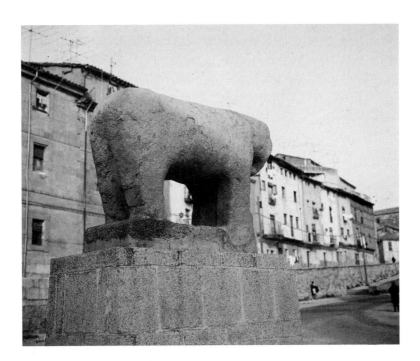

Figure 4.5 The bull, Salamanca. Photo: Institut Amatller d'Art Hispanic, Barcelona

Salamanca University shared scholarly and intellectual pre-eminence with other major centres of learning in Europe such as Paris, Bologna, Oxford and Cambridge. Notwithstanding that Catherine of Aragon's confessor came from there, the University of Salamanca pronounced her marriage to Henry VIII unlawful. At this university Francisco de Vitoria (*c.*1485–1546), who held the chair of theology (1526–46), developed the first modern arguments about international law and just wars. A superb university Renaissance library, lecture rooms, double cathedral and remarkable civil and ecclesiastical architecture survive today as evidence of intellectual life, independence of thought and cultural vigour.

Scholarly support for the possibility that Juan de Ortega wrote the book has arisen partly because in 1605 a member of his order reported that he was indeed the author. In addition, there are a number of circumstantial factors: the surname Ortega (meaning 'stinging nettle') suggests a 'new Christian', or *converso*, presumably of Jewish or Muslim ancestry, like the famous humanist and friend of Erasmus, Juan Luis Vives (1492–1540). A supposed authorship cannot be the focus of analysis of a literary work, but there is textual support for the view that the book's social critique is strongly influenced by an authorship reaching across an ethnic divide. We know that Juan de Ortega was a cultured man, noted for a reformist spirit. His election as general of the Hieronymite order proved too much for conservatives, who engineered his fall from grace and banishment to Valencia as a common friar. He was recalled, however, to complete arrangements he had already begun for Charles V's retirement to the Hieronymite monastery at Yuste.

Use of a vernacular

By the sixteenth century the vernacular Castilian used by our anonymous author had, like Tuscan in Italy, become a standard national speech against several competitors. Castilian became the dominant tongue through the military and political pre-eminence of Castile, which drove a wedge through the Iberian peninsula and ultimately, after unification with Aragon, destroyed the last Moorish stronghold in Granada. Humanists played a key role in standardizing major modern tongues like Italian, German, French, English and Spanish, their grammar and vocabulary. A vernacular obviously had a greater potential audience than Latin, and could reach all levels of society when read aloud. Like Dante's *Divina commedia* (*Divine Comedy*) in Italy, *Lazarillo de Tormes* and numerous other Spanish 'Golden Age' texts, through their popularity and canonization, helped to stabilize and standardize a language which is today a major world language. Renaissance humanists saw literature as having a civilizing role, or in the opening words of *Lazarillo de Tormes:*

> I am of opinion that things so worthy of memory, peradventure never heard of before nor seen, ought by all reason to come abroad to the sight of many, and not be buried in the endless pit of oblivion.

> (Prologue, p.2)

Lazarillo: humanist parody?

Exercise

Reread the first paragraph of the First Treatise and pause a moment over Lazarillo's name, his manner of birth, his parentage and his father's crime and punishment. Consider too the language of the passage and in particular allusions to religious or biblical themes. ❖

This remarkable first paragraph of the First Treatise has become a precursor of numerous others in the history of western prose fiction: like Pip in Charles Dickens's *Great Expectations*, Lazarillo tells us his name and how he came by it. Lázaro (the diminutive form is Lazarillo) was born not in an oxstall like Jesus but in a watermill. His parents' surnames were of the very commonest, the Spanish equivalent of Smith and Jones. The form of Lazarillo's surname, with a 'de', has chivalric resonances, like the champions of romances that Don Quixote later tried to emulate, such as Launcelot du Lac, Amadís de Gaula, Palmerín de Inglaterrra and, we may note, David Rowland of Anglesey (it is possible that 'David Rowland of Anglesey' is a sort of joke). Lazarillo gives first his high-sounding surname, claiming that he was born '*dentro del rio*' (within the river), and afterwards a much more banal description of his birth. The Spanish word used to describe Lazarillo's mother giving birth is more commonly reserved for animals: there was no lying in; Lazarillo's mother 'dropped' him among the sacks, doubtless in the manner of the rats and mice that commonly infest such places.

The name Lázaro, or as we say, Lazarus, did occur as the name of a proverbial simpleton in Spain at this time, but it is also the name of the biblical beggar who lay suffering at the rich man's gates, his sores licked by dogs:

> There was a certain rich man, which was clothed in purple and fine linen, and fared sumptuously every day:
>
> And there was a certain beggar named Lazarus, which was laid at his gate, full of sores,
>
> And desiring to be fed with the crumbs which fell from the rich man's table: moreover the dogs came and licked his sores.
>
> And it came to pass, that the beggar died, and was carried by the angels into Abraham's bosom: the rich man also died, and was buried;
>
> And in hell he lifted up his eyes, being in torments, and seeth Abraham afar off, and Lazarus in his bosom.
>
> And he cried and said, Father Abraham, have mercy on me, and send Lazarus, that he may dip the tip of his finger in water, and cool my tongue; for I am tormented in this flame.
>
> But Abraham said, Son, remember that thou in thy life time receivest thy good things, and likewise Lazarus evil things: but now he is comforted, and thou art tormented.
>
> (Luke 16.19–25)[3]

At this time lepers, or social outcasts, were treated in hospitals dedicated to Saint Lazarus. It was this figure, rather than Lazarus of Bethany (whom Jesus brought back to life from the dead (John 2.1–4)), who became an archetype for human destitution and degradation. With Pauper (poor man) he was polarized against Dives (rich man) in morality plays and homiletic stories that in turn had their roots in the preaching of the medieval church (see Plate 7). Some critics, however, argue that the other Lazarus may also fall within the book's meaning: whereas Lazarus dies physically but is reborn into a spiritual life,

---

[3] I have deliberately quoted from the King James Bible, the Authorized version of 1611, because this, itself a product of the English Renaissance and Christian humanism, is based on earlier English translations like those of William Tyndale and Miles Coverdale, contemporaries of *Lazarillo de Tormes*, and because its prose style is reminiscent of Rowland's.

Lazarillo dies spiritually but enters into a life of material well being. Such a heavy structural irony, like the numerous sacramental ironies and biblical allusions in the book, assumes considerable knowledge of the scriptures on the part of the reader.

Lazarillo's father, a miller, stole flour. A recurrent motif of the book is bread and starvation, terms which can be seen as metaphors for spiritual as well as material deprivation. The Spanish text refers to the miller as bleeding, rather than stealing from, the sacks. This could be thieves' slang or comic writing, but equally could refer to the bread and wine of Holy Communion and theological disputes over whether the bread and wine are the body and blood of Christ, the issue of transubstantiation. On being charged, Lazarillo's father responded like John the Baptist: 'And he confessed, and denied not; but confessed, I am not the Christ' (John 1.20). Lazarillo describes his father's fate quoting Christ's Sermon on the Mount, which includes the Beatitudes. In full these are as follows:

> Blessed are the poor in spirit: for theirs is the kingdom of heaven.
> Blessed are they that mourn: for they shall be comforted.
> Blessed are the meek: for they shall inherit the earth.
> Blessed are they which do hunger and thirst after righteousness: for they shall be filled.
> Blessed are the merciful: for they shall obtain mercy.
> Blessed are the pure in heart: for they shall see God.
> Blessed are the peacemakers: for they shall be called the children of God.
> Blessed are they which are persecuted for righteousness' sake: for theirs is the kingdom of heaven.
>
> (Matthew 5.3–10)

Although our text quotes the final verse of this biblical passage, it is easy to believe that the author had in mind the whole, surely one of the best-known Christian appeals on behalf of the marginalized and down-trodden. The grammar of both the Spanish and the English indicates not hope but certainty that Lazarillo's father is in heaven.

The first paragraph ends by recording that the erstwhile miller, as punishment, was forced to take part in a war against the Moors, or Muslims, as a muleteer. In fact the Spanish text uses not the romance word but the Arabic word for a watermill, and the word for muleteer is also Arabic. Millers and muleteers were often of Moorish origin; muleteering in particular was one of their favoured professions. We should bear in mind that at the time *Lazarillo de Tormes* was written Granada, the last Moorish stronghold in the peninsula, had already fallen in 1492, and war was continuing on the other side of the Mediterranean in North Africa. Perhaps Lazarillo's father had died in the unsuccessful action at Los Gelves (Jerba) in 1510 or 1520. The fortunes of Moors who remained in the peninsula declined: promises of religious toleration were broken; many were forcibly relocated; armed rebellion in the Alpujarras was suppressed in the 1560s; and by the second decade of the seventeenth century mass expulsions were completed.

The opening paragraph is on a knife-edge between knock-about comedy and a moral challenge that, in pointedly quoting key Christian teaching, comes close to blasphemy. If we may make such a distinction, the author appears to intend that we should understand a perversion of Christian values, but the narrator seems to misunderstand through ignorance or in order to make a blasphemous joke. Surely this is a humanist attempt to Christianize society, and the book is itself an affirmation of the equality of a vernacular tongue with the classical languages.

Exercise   Reread the next paragraphs of the First Treatise, which deal with the fortunes and fate of Lazarillo's stepfather. ❖

Lazarillo's mother, now a destitute widow, continues to try to hold the family together. In keeping with the pervasive irony of the text, she decides, in the words of a Spanish saying, 'to lean against good folks in order to become one of them' or, as Rowland translates, 'determined to inhabit among such as were virtuous and honest, to be of that number' (p.57), a translation reminiscent of another Spanish saying, 'tell me who you go round with and I will tell you who you are'. The same Spanish refrain, with its suggestion of immoral earnings, is repeated in the Seventh Treatise. She cooks for university students in Salamanca, washes clothes for the stable hands of a military–religious order that draws income from a parish in Salamanca dedicated to Saint Mary Magdalene, a fallen woman rehabilitated by Jesus (see Luke 7 and 8 and John 8), and uses the stables to practise as a prostitute. A blackamoor slave, doubtless originally Muslim, and ironically named Zaide (the Arabic *sayyid* means 'lord', as we find in *El Cid*), becomes the breadwinner and completes the family. Then comes the moment of recognition for the child of the liaison, that his father is black, the colour of the bogeyman of childish terror, and his mother white! Zaide's laughing rejoinder that the half-caste is the son of a whore produces an aside given to Lazarillo as adult narrator: 'there are many such in the world, which do abhor and flee from others because they cannot see what shape they have themselves' (p.59). Like several similar remarks, this is possibly an authorial intervention to warn the over-judgemental reader.

Zaide also steals to provide his adopted family with basic necessities, and is punished with whipping and basting. The narrator or author again intervenes, observing ironically that we should not be surprised that a priest or friar steals from the poor or from his convent when love moves a poor slave to steal too, implying that thieving is more to be expected in clerics than in a destitute slave. This is one of the passages expurgated in the Spanish edition of 1573. Rowland, following the French translation, mutes the directness of the Spanish, a point to which we will return later. The Spanish text is bitterly sarcastic: Zaide, denied all rights including a family, acted out of basic human instincts and love; the church, we are to understand, betrayed those who in Christian charity should have been relieved. Morally, life must take precedence over property.

Of course, devout Christians had for centuries denounced and satirized abuses in the priesthood and religious and secular administration. The book is not a homily, however, but a first-person narrative, a literary form that by its nature forces the reader to enter into a distinct consciousness or view of the world.

Throughout these first few paragraphs of the First Treatise we may identify the Sermon on the Mount and an attack on society's perversion of Christian and humane values. The most marginalized of family units collapses, and Lazarillo is handed over to a blind beggar, the first of a succession of masters.

Figure 4.6 Lazarillo's journey. Map: Allen Bjornson, from Bjornson, 1979, Figure 5

Now reread the Second Treatise and consider how style and subject matter extend issues raised in the First Treatise. ❖

Lazarillo goes from the frying pan into the fire, voluntarily entering the service of a priest, a man in holy orders, who is a cruel and pathological miser. There are classical references – to Alexander the Great and Penelope for example – but the entire episode is dominated by sacramental ironies and biblical allusions. The liturgy is surely mocked when a priest gives bones to a starving boy with the words 'Take down this to thee, and rejoice, seeing that thou hast the world at will. I am sure the Pope himself hath now no better life than thou hast' (p.85). This last remark could be interpreted both as an example of priestly hypocrisy and as an Erasmian swipe at papal pomp. The role of bread in the Christian liturgy and as a metaphor for religious communion and spiritual renewal must be understood. The priest denies the key to this paradise, and the climax of the story, the snake that never was, surely alludes to the Garden of Eden myth in Genesis 2 and 3. The entire episode reads like a satirical extension of the Dives/Lazarus, rich-man/poor-man motif. The priest, who should relieve the poor and suffering, behaves like Dives, begrudging Lazarillo even the crumbs from his bread coffer. The Spanish, by the way, uses the word '*arca*' for chest, thereby reminding the original readers of the Ark of the Covenant (the wooden coffer containing the tablets of the law, kept in the holiest place of the tabernacle) as well as a piece of church furniture.

The episode, and especially the scope of its allusions, reads like a parodic commentary on Matthew 12:

[David] entered into the house of God, and did eat the shew bread,[4] which was not lawful for him to eat ...

(verse 4)

He that is not with me is against me;

(verse 30)

All manner of sin and blasphemy shall be forgiven unto men; but the blasphemy against the Holy Ghost shall not be forgiven unto men.

(verse 31)

O generation of vipers, how can ye being evil, speak good things?

(verse 34)

[4] The shew bread was the twelve loaves that were placed every Sabbath 'before the Lord' on a table beside the altar of incense. At the end of the week they were eaten by the priests alone.

It is not the consecrated priest but a lay figure who saves Lazarillo's life, an old woman who recites popular charms, thereby confirming Matthew verse 50:

> For whoever shall do the will of my father which is in heaven, the same is my brother, and sister, and mother.

The priest rejects Lazarillo, crossing himself as if Lazarillo were possessed of the devil, recalling verse 26:

> And if Satan cast out Satan, he is divided against himself: how shall then his kingdom stand?

The priest directly contradicts the work of Jesus:

> Then was brought unto him [Jesus] one possessed with a devil, blind, and dumb: and he healed him ...

(verse 22)

Rowland himself picks up the religious parody by repeating the original's reference to Jonah, on which Matthew 12 could scarcely be more explicit:

> For as Jonas was three days and three nights in the whale's belly: so shall the son of man be three days and three nights in the heart of the earth.

(verse 40)

The Second Treatise, ostensibly knock-about comedy of the broadest kind, assumes a darker tone when its allusions to Matthew 12 are allowed full force. We do not have to restrict the book's message to the bodily misfortunes of its protagonist and narrator, Lazarillo. The book's structure is so unstable that a remarkably complex range of moral and religious possibilities are in play.

Exercise

Read Henry Kamen's article 'Excluding the Reformation' (Reader, no. 21) and consider how far the book's narrative form and content may have been shaped and influenced by contemporary religious debates and divisions.

Discussion

My first reaction is that I am not in the least surprised at the book's anonymity! Further, in a Spanish atmosphere of suspicion and at a time when Erasmianism could easily be treated as crypto-Protestant and anti-Catholic, any writer in Spain wishing to challenge conservative orthodoxy in favour of an interior and private religious practice required all available resources of irony, disguise and allusion. The form and religious content of the book seem substantially determined by the wider Spanish society. Kamen's account of the diffusion of new religious thinking – through the court and entourage of Charles V, and intellectual and social elites –

and of the resistance of scholastic theology, which eventually won the day in Spain, provides a convincing contemporary setting for the book's creation: it is a sophisticated social critique, under a popular disguise, written in a vernacular, not in Latin, for maximum diffusion. As Kamen notes, Latin was not widely spoken in Spain; and certainly our Lazarillo could not have known it. ❖

The book was placed on Valdés' 1559 Index along with the works of Erasmus, and Rowland's translation, influenced in part by the French translations, offers further evidence that the book was sensitive to the religious disputes of that time. His marginal gloss on the chance arrival of the tinker, 'Lázaro was a good Christian, believing that all goodness came from God' (p.89), has Lutheran resonances of which Gresham, the dedicatee of Rowland's translation and ardently Protestant, may well have approved. Rowland was also uncomfortable (as the footnotes to Whitlock make clear) with the anti-clerical venom of several passages. In this he followed the Saugrain (publisher of the second (1561) French translation), adopting a euphemistic practice that surely suggests that both English and French translators saw the text as embedded in religious controversy and did not wish gratuitously to offend a book purchasing public, Catholic or Protestant.

Exercise

What evidence is there to suggest that in translating the work Rowland may have altered the meaning of the original? In other words, in what ways could Rowland's text be said to show evidence of a translator's censorship?

Discussion

A respect for religious appearances does seem to have exercised a check on Rowland's freedom in translation. The first instance is in the First Treatise. Rowland's translation reads:

> Let us never therefore marvel more at those which steal from the poor, nor yet at them which convey from the houses they serve, to present therewith whom they love in hope to attain thereby their desired pleasure, seeing that love was able to encourage this poor bondman or slave to do thus much as I have said, or rather more, which by evident trial was afterwards proved true.

(pp.59–60)

As the footnote in Whitlock points out:

> This is one of several instances where Rowland softens ant-clerical material in the original Spanish. A more literal translation would be: 'Let us not be surprised at a priest or friar, because the one steals from the poor, and the other from a monastery for the benefit of his female followers and whatever, seeing that a poor slave gave into love and stole.'

(p.59)

The French translations which Rowland also consulted and followed were similarly restrained, muting the severity of anti-clerical material. Rowland, for example, fully grasps the sacramental ironies of bread and wine in the Second Treatise but his translation is sensitive and mutes the full ironic force of the Spanish original, perhaps because he was Protestant. Indeed, Rowland seems to have taken the tale as a genuine autobiography, which it is not, and as a 'documentary' on Spain, rather than as a literary work involving selection, exaggeration, allusiveness, parody, burlesque and so on. ❖

Lazarillo and the humanist critique of poverty

Exercise

Read the article 'Renaissance poverty and Lazarillo's family: the birth of the picaresque genre' by Javier Herrero (Reader, no. 23). ❖

As Herrero describes, there was a humanist response to the 'staggering social disease' of poverty in sixteenth-century Europe: More, Vives and Erasmus produced proposals that sought to challenge common assumptions about it, and *Lazarillo de Tormes* was artistically an attempt in part to confront it.

Elsewhere Herrero writes:

> Against fame and courtly love, the Erasmians preached hard work and marriage; the simplicity of a pious life, with the inevitable hardships of work, but with its rewards, and the sweetness of conjugal and family love were the new ideals which descended upon Southern Europe from the new devotion which blossomed in the North, especially in the Low Countries. There can be little doubt that the author of the *Lazarillo* shares them.

(1978, p.315)

In commenting on the economic decay and collapse that occurred in Spain during the second half of the sixteenth century, Herrero quotes a commentator of 1626:

> Those who travel through the fertile fields of Spain, see them covered with nettles and thorns, because there is no one to till them. Most Spaniards have been reduced to idleness ... and it is something worth seeing that all the streets of Madrid are full of lay-abouts and tramps, playing all day at cards, waiting for the time to go to the convents to eat.

(p.316; translated K. Whitlock, 2000)

There are then contrasting views on interpreting an ambiguous text like *Lazarillo de Tormes*. One strand of critical opinion regards it as essentially a reworking of medieval materials, as a sort of comic and irreligious entertainment, and denies any critique of economic collapse; other critics locate the text firmly in the religious ferment of that time and as a biting critique of a society shortly to experience economic collapse. The Spanish Exchequer experienced several bankruptcies in the late sixteenth and seventeenth centuries. Alan Deyermond's view that 'Spain's economic and political decline was half a century away in the future when *Lazarillo de Tormes* was published' (1993, p.16) will not stand against the evidence, which is that the years 1511–57 saw inflation, recession and financial crisis in government. During this time the tax burden fell largely on the poor:

> Sixteenth-century Spain was an unsettled place to live in. The texts of the period leave us with the impression of a people always on the move, fleeing from disaster or allured by the promise of riches. Soldiers on their way to the wars, emigrants to the Indies, Castilians and Galicians to the more prosperous south, hangers-on drifting after the court, French immigrants attracted by the promise of high wages, all were to be found on the Spanish roads. The problem of destitution or, as we should say, unemployment, grew more and more acute. Five times between 1523 and 1534 the Cortes complained of the host of beggars and vagrants who were over-running Castile.
>
> (Grice-Hutchinson, 1978, p.131)

Gresham, to whom Rowland dedicated his translation, must have been fully aware of these financial realities. He went to Seville to raise a large loan and had almost daily contact with the major European banking houses.

Autobiography: truth or fiction?

A cursory reading of the book identifies features of humanism: the classical and biblical quotations and references; the parody of learned terms and structure – the sections are 'treatises', not chapters as in the Penguin translation; the anti-clerical satire on members of the church; the studied dissonance of scholarly and vernacular forms of speech; and the confessional and autobiographical structure that holds the work's narrative together. The standard humanist vehicle of moral philosophy was the treatise, and there was a broad humanist campaign to rescue moral philosophy from scholasticism.

The book is of course written in the first person; indeed the very first word is 'I'. It is then a sort of fictional autobiography or letter addressed to someone called 'Your Reverence' or 'Your Worship', whom we may infer to be a member of the church hierarchy in Toledo. The relationship appears to be one of naïve layman and ecclesiastical superior. The organization of the book into Prologue and treatises could have been a late imposition but suggests a formal academic text perhaps intended to carry the presentation of a profound, abstract and searching moral or philosophical topic.

Exercise

Read again both the Prologue and the Seventh Treatise and consider the form of the narrative, the role and identity of the narrator, and any evidence for humanist literary practices.

Discussion

In the Prologue there are appeals to classical authority, appeals that are perhaps rather commonplace and pretentious – Pliny says, Tully (i.e. Cicero) says – typical of humanist display, quoting authorities in order to reinforce arguments. This practice clashes with the book's content, a sequence of adventures, ostensibly raw life experience itself. The narrator rejects Horace's famous dictum about epic poetry, that it starts in the middle ('*in medias res*'), serving notice that he will record presumably the 'epic' of his life, from its chronological beginning. There is then a comical but straight-faced demolition of learned and literary conventions. We are in the presence of a subversive text, but subversive in a peculiarly modern sense: since the work's authorship is completely unresolved, the reader must rely on a first-person narrator to take him or her through a sequence of sordid adventures.

The narrator is the only witness; but is that witness reliable? Does Lazarillo retain the reader's sympathy throughout? Is the narrator a consistent piece of fiction or broken between child and adult? Is the narrator gullible or a worldly wise entertainer? Is the reader not led into a literary game – a fiction drawing on a tradition of confessional literature, or even a deposition for an inquisitor, in the form of comic parody? The effect is to destabilize the reader's certainties. Are events to be treated as comical or serious? Speaking personally I find the book morally disturbing because there is no judgemental or guiding narrative voice to shape my reactions. In my view the sophisticated author intended his writing to have this effect because he chose to suppress the sort of narrative framework which could have supplied the reader with certainty. The reader is thus forced to arrive at his or her own moral position.

Lazarillo justifies the writing of the book on the classical grounds that it may prove instructive, may bring fame and may give pleasure. There is a clerical vocabulary – 'preach', 'confess', 'holy' – and classical allusions are conveyed in a Spanish so colloquial that the narrator calls it 'coarse'. Indeed there is an apology – doubtless tongue-in-cheek – for the inadequacy of the written expression.

Lazarillo ends his Prologue contrasting those who inherit fine estates with those, like himself, who even when fortune has been hostile, with effort and resourcefulness, nonetheless reach safe anchorage. This metaphor is picked up in the final sentence of the Seventh Treatise: 'I was then in my prosperity and at the height of good fortune' (p.167). 'Prosperity' originally could also mean good weather and fair sailing, though only a trained Latinist is likely to have known this. The Prologue and Seventh Treatise are also linked by reference to the wheel of fortune, according to which, as it revolves, we are at either the top or bottom. The political term 'revolution' obviously derives from this metaphor. Fortune and God seem synonymous. Lazarillo appears to insinuate that merit depends not on birth and inherited wealth but, in Dante's words, on 'personal excellence' (see Burckhardt, pp.230–1). As we set the last treatise against the Prologue, we meet the most astonishing bathos: the height of good fortune is to be a complaisant cuckold to an immoral and corrupt arch priest, 'Your Reverence's' subordinate. The simulated ignorance (if that is what it is) of the narrator is so perfectly held that we must infer that 'Your Reverence' will agree: Lazarillo has indeed reached safe harbour and good fortune, a success story in which the church is complicit. Lazarillo is like the husband Allwit in Thomas Middleton's *A Chaste Maid in Cheapside* (first performance 1613) who actually connives at his wife's adultery because he thereby guarantees himself a comfortable life. This 'ménage à trois' is 'the matter' on which apparently the first-person narrator has been charged to report, and links the Prologue to the Seventh Treatise. Honour, a pervasive theme of Spanish Golden Age drama (roughly 1560–1680), is claimed by Lazarillo for himself and his wife.

Should we take the opening of the Prologue at face value? It seems likely the real author expects us to be amused by the narrator's self-importance (e.g. the '*yo*' (I) is redundant, and '*cosas tan señaladas*' (things so worthy of memory) etc. is patently absurd). In the first part of the Prologue Lazarillo hopes for a wide audience for his work; in the remainder, however, he reveals that he was required only to explain '*el caso*' (the matter) but has taken it on himself to tell his whole life story, and sees it as 'proof' that the lowliest can rise. This complex narrative irony, the work's 'modernity', was largely missed by those (like Rowland?) who took the story literally, and by many later writers who imitated its (auto)biographical, episodic form and delineation of character. ❖

The book has more coherence than its episodic nature may suggest. It is a story of human survival and an exposé of a corrupt society whose moral policemen are party to the corruption. If we are to believe the narrator, a senior churchman required him to write 'the matter' down. Is the book anti-Catholic? The manner in which *Lazarillo de Tormes* was censored and expurgated in Spain suggests that it was judged irreligious. However this issue requires further reflection. Perhaps a marvellously 'spoof' autobiography smuggles in a plea for a meaningful spiritual life of the sort that an Erasmian and humanist would have favoured.

Now we begin an analysis of the rest of the text, beginning with the Third Treatise, in which the author extends his criticism of Spanish society to the aristocracy.

Lazarillo as social commentary

In the Third Treatise we encounter the penniless squire, doubtless chosen to enlarge the social commentary of the book and to extend discussion to the lowest level of the nobility, a near destitute member of the gentry. Our analysis of the Third Treatise in this section will examine a humanist representation of a Spanish social type.

Figure 4.7 Rouargue, townscape of Toledo, 1862, engraving. Mary Evans Picture Library, London

Exercise

Reread the Third Treatise. Note particularly where Lazarillo meets his third master, and what features of this master he singles out for attention. ❖

Lazarillo meets the master of the Third Treatise in 'this noble city of Toledo' or '*esta insigne ciudad de Toledo*', a very Latinate Spanish way of saying 'in this distinguished ancient and illustrious city of Toledo'. The city had been the **Visigothic** capital of Spain before the Moorish invasion and its recapture from the Moors in 1085 was of great significance. To this day five churches there preserve the pre-invasion liturgical rite, called the Mozarabic. Toledo's archbishop, usually a cardinal too, is Spain's primate, first churchman, and his revenues were once judged second only to the pope's. Toledo enjoyed renown for its swords, the best quality in Europe.

For long the capital city was where the court resided, and the court did not move permanently to Madrid until 1561. The late General Franco delayed his attack on Madrid in order to relieve the siege of Toledo in the Spanish Civil War, it has been said, because of that city's symbolic importance. An analysis of the Spanish aristocracy is then well located in Toledo, since many Castilian aristocratic families claimed pre-Moorish ancestry, to be 'Old Christians', to be blue-blooded, that is white-skinned and therefore able to show blue veins.

The material poverty of a squire, the lowest echelon of the aristocracy, was proverbial in Spain in this period. Our squire is in virtually unfurnished accommodation. He has a way of walking suggestive of pride, traditionally a nobleman's gait, not a merchant's or a Jew's. He is learned in the arts of courtship in the manner of the fourteenth-century Galician troubadour Macías, a proverbial model for faithful lovers, and more skilled than Ovid, who wrote of the *Art of Loving*, but he cannot afford even the poorest prostitute by the river side. Our anonymous author must have been aware that according to a popular Spanish ballad, the last Visigothic king of Spain, Roderigo, seduced La Cava, daughter of his governor of Ceuta Julian, by the river Tagus at Toledo, an event which folk tradition blamed for the Moorish invasion in 711. The linking idea would seem to be that of a collapsed aristocracy or social élite. The squire is scrupulous about etiquette, the forms of address appropriate to his rank; back home he has corrected a journeyman for addressing him with the words 'May God preserve your worship' instead of the appropriate 'I kiss your worship's hands'. He has abandoned his dilapidated property rather than doff his cap to a better-off neighbour. He exhibits a fastidiousness in eating and commends Lazarillo for daintiness:

It is a virtue to live soberly, therefore I commend thee much. Hogs fill themselves, and wise men eat discreetly what is only sufficient for them.

(p.109)

The theme of bread and destitution continues. Religion is ever present: Lazarillo attributes finding this master to God's intervention; the squire hears Mass and the Canonical hours sung every day, in Protestant eyes religious practices or good works unlikely to secure salvation. The Third Treatise is dominated by the adjectives 'dark' and 'gloomy', such that Lazarillo, to the amusement of his master, misunderstanding the laments of the followers of a funeral cortège, believes the destination of the coffin is his master's lodging, not the usual burial ground. Biblical allusions appear to be more to the Old Testament than the New, notably to Job and Deuteronomy; for example Lazarillo quotes Job 5:

[God] Which doeth great things and unsearchable; marvellous things without number ...

Behold, happy is the man whom God correcteth: therefore despise not thou the chastening of the Almighty:

For he maketh sore, and bindeth up: he woundeth, and his hands make whole.

(verses 9, 17, 18)

The squire takes on a servant whom he cannot feed. His caste forbids him profitable employment; he represents the economic collapse of a military caste and **rentier** mentality. He depends on his servant to feed him by his begging. He is so disabled socially that far from holding together a family, like Lazarillo's father and stepfather, he cannot procure a harlot's services in the open air. The house of this master may indeed be construed as a grave. He embodies social entropy. His religious devotion is an activity of empty forms. His only accoutrements of value are his cloak and sword, emblems of honour in later Spanish Golden Age drama.

The friar, the pardoner and Luther

Exercise

Read again the single paragraph of the Fourth Treatise and the whole of the Fifth. Why do you think the Fourth is so suddenly cut short, and the **pardoner's** practices in the Fifth presented in full? ❖

I cannot claim to offer authoritative answers but the following are offered as plausible explanations. The views of friars and pardoners presented here were prevalent throughout late medieval western Christendom. The English poet Geoffrey Chaucer (?1340–1400) had anticipated them over one and a half centuries before. Chaucer, let it be said, had visited Italy and brought Italian subject matter and poetic forms to English literature. In the General Prologue to the *Canterbury Tales* he gives vignettes of both a friar and a pardoner. His friar, like Lazarillo's, was a convivial womanizing rogue, a drunk who knew barmen and landlords:

Bet than a lazar or a beggestere;	*Better than a diseased man or beggar,*
For unto swich a worthy man as he	*for to such a distinguished man as he,*
Accorded nat, as by his facultee,	*it was not appropriate, if his profession be borne in mind,*
To have with sike lazars aqueyntaunce.	*to have anything to do with the sick and destitute.*

(ll. 241–4)

The 'lazar' of the passage means of course a poor, diseased man, possibly a leper, and etymologically the word shares the same root as Lazarus or Lázaro. Chaucer is repeating a conventional complaint. Perhaps then the narrator of *Lazarillo de Tormes* saw no reason to repeat what was widely known to his readers. There might, however, have been other reasons.

We do not know, of course, amongst whom this narrative may have circulated before it found its way into print, and as we have seen, its author could himself have been a friar. Perhaps our anonymous author exercised caution or alternatively assumed that his readers knew so much of such cases that to write further would be redundant. However, short though the Treatise is, there are links thematically to the rest of the book: Lazarillo's fourth master was a member of the Order of Mercy, which was chiefly engaged in the redemption of Christian captives from the Muslims in North Africa. Otherwise the anti-clerical satire is conventional: another priest without vocation who hated church services and monastic life. Some critics have, however, also inferred that this Friar was bisexual, and a pederast, and hence the final sentence of the paragraph: Lazarillo by implication was his catamite, the full story being suppressed.

Pardoners of course were not members of the priesthood – not in holy orders. Chaucer's pardoner too had all the resource and skills of his Spanish counterpart:

His wallet lay before hym in his lappe,	*His wallet lay before him on his lap,*
Bretful of pardon, comen from Rome al hoot.	*brimful of pardons, just come all hot from Rome.*

(ll. 686–7)

In the Prologue to his tale, Chaucer's pardoner boasts of his skills in the pulpit, his capacity to deceive ordinary churchgoers and rob them. Indeed, his criminality and immorality (the text also suggests sexual perversion) are presented so openly to the other pilgrims that the revelations which the pardoner makes in the Prologue and conclusion of his tale seem more Chaucer's than the narrator's. We might infer from reading Burckhardt's 'Religion in daily life' (pp.289–306) that the satire in *Lazarillo de Tormes* has Italian parallels. The tricks and deceptions are the same (see especially pp.292–3). Again there is a Spanish detail of thematic importance: our Spanish pardoner is of the 'Santa Cruzada', or 'Holy Crusade', and sold indulgences granting full remission of sins to raise money for and ransom those who fought or were captured in the campaigns against Muslims in North Africa and elsewhere. Their activities brought profits to the state but serious abuses were repeatedly condemned in the Castilian '*cortes*' (parliament), and in 1524 Charles V issued a decree to prevent pardoners from forcing their indulgences on the people. For Burckhardt 'spiritual police' (p.292) were not compatible with 'genuine religion' (p.313). This observation, admittedly from the hands of a nineteenth-century cultural historian immersed in the Protestant culture of northern Europe, invites a question on *Lazarillo de Tormes:* how far does the book demonstrate a sympathy for Lutheran Protestantism? This is hotly disputed, as you will see in the next reading, in which Thomas Hanrahan, a Jesuit, examines the theology of the book, treatise by treatise.

Exercise

Read the article '*Lazarillo de Tormes*: Erasmian satire or Protestant reform?' by Thomas Hanrahan (Reader, no. 22).

Discussion

Hanrahan, while acknowledging the presence in Spain of native movements critical of the practices and institutions of the church (e.g. Erasmians, *alumbrados*), prefers to see the author of *Lazarillo de Tormes* as primarily inspired by the early writings of Martin Luther and the Lutherans. Not only does *Lazarillo* include a full-scale attack on the whole notion of a separate clerical caste in society, but, Hanrahan argues, its ironic comments on the sacraments and the nature of salvation demonstrate its fidelity to the more radical Protestant cause. Indeed, Hanrahan goes so far as to suggest that the bitter and uncompromising language of the book is sufficient to date it to the early period of the Lutheran onslaught on the Catholic church in the 1520s. Other critics (for example Cruz, 1999) believe it is likely that the book was written around 1551, close to its publication date, when the Council of Trent was taken up with the reform of the clergy. The defaced portrait of Erasmus (see Figure 4.8) may reflect the violence of the debate. ❖

Figure 4.8 Defaced portrait of Erasmus, from a copy of Sebastian Munster's *Cosmographia*, Basle, 1550. Photo: Biblioteca Nacional, Madrid

The tambourine-painter, the chaplain and prosperity

To conclude our close scrutiny of the text, read again the Sixth Treatise and revisit the Seventh. Make a note of any points that strengthen the book's coherence and thematic ideas. ❖

Brief though the Sixth Treatise is, its very spareness is telling. Lazarillo apparently makes a foray into the real economy, assisting a painter of tambourines. The nature of Lazarillo's work is explicit in the Spanish, though muted in Rowland's translation: it is to grind the tambourine-painter's colours. In an engaging article called 'A case of functional obscurity' George Shipley (1982) suggests that this apparently innocent narrative detail may well be playful disguise. Lazarillo is apprentice to a master tambourine-painter who practises skilled craftwork which at that time is still in the hands of Moors. Lazarillo's father might have been a Moor; his stepfather certainly was one. Perhaps then he briefly took refuge in his caste. These then, in sum, could be the implications of this narrative incident.

Spanish, however, is very rich in proverbs and refrains, and these include many about tambourines and grinding. A tambourine has fun-loving associations, of music, rhythm and dance, and not surprisingly we find refrains like 'There's no marriage without a tambourine', and the scurrilous 'A fuck without a fart is like a marriage without a tambourine'. Even at the present day there still survive among the Moors of Morocco communal satirical poetry competitions, impromptu, to the rhythms of tambourines. The topics satirized may range widely across family rivalries, business greed, sexual philandering and so on.

The tambourine then is redolent of the pleasures of song and dance, festivity and sex. Shipley cites copious examples in medieval and Renaissance Spanish texts of just such nuances, in some of which a tambourine stands for a woman's genitalia. Grinding, of course, takes us into similar semantic territory, especially when we recall that the sort of grinding that Lazarillo did was with pestle and mortar. Again, there is sound contemporary evidence in refrains for an association of milling and love-making: 'when my dark girl turns her eyes, it's a sign that the mill is not grinding sand', and 'grain in the hopper of the mill, who comes first, grinds first'.

Of course, as Shipley acknowledges, there could be a cross-reference to the opening of the First Treatise, and perhaps in the Seventh the adult Lazarillo is but a 'miller' for an Archdeacon who 'grinds' his wife!

As Shipley correctly observes, such explanations are important in understanding *Lazarillo de Tormes*:

> it seems normal to suppose that objects and activities prominent in daily life about town would achieve, in the course of centuries of familiar presence, considerable prominence in the imaginative experience of townspeople.

(1982, p.242)

He adds:

> why should not mills have some of that capacity for structuring imaginative experience in collectively satisfying ways that we find in other fragments of reality that also impinge daily on the consciousness of many members of the group: bread and wine, say, and flowing water and dusty roads?

(p.242)

Indeed, perhaps the economy, ambiguity and the witty multiple allusiveness were intended sources of pleasure for early readers of the book. Readers were coached by the text in habit and attitude of mind, and by the Sixth Treatise duly rewarded. The book then offers 'insistent ironic play among competing conventions' (p.249). Discovered meanings are far richer then a single surface meaning. Perhaps the tambourine-painter was a skilled womanizer who drew Lazarillo into his activities.

Shipley asks finally 'Why does Lázaro bother to mention at all an episode that is dull on its surface and distasteful underneath?' And answers:

> Lázaro must write because he has been ordered to write; he must write well because he is being threatened by the authority of 'Vuestra Merced' [Your Reverence], by the 'malas lenguas' [evil tongues] that bruit about true and false reports concerning his cuckoldry. He chooses to write entertainingly, to convert his liabilities into credits, his infamy into a notoriety that can pass for fame.
>
> (p.253)

One is reminded of the bawd, Pompey, in *Measure for Measure* 2.1 (performed 1604), who seeks to deflect a magistrate's interrogation by comical reference to a dish of prunes, a deliberate attempt to change the agenda. Rowland's translation of the Sixth Treatise suggests reticence, as if he felt distaste for the original.

Lazarillo's next master is a chaplain of the church who, in a manner of speaking, sub-contracts him as a water-seller. The concession that allows Lazarillo to keep Saturday takings has led some critics to infer that the chaplain was a converted Jew, and to point out that Toledo Cathedral in 1547 laid down severe '*estatutos de impieza*', that is statutes of clean blood, to exclude New Christians. Ethnic cleansing is nothing new. The expression 'received me for his own' (p.157) can bear several interpretations, Christian, racial and sexual. The reader is challenged to ponder the vocation of the chaplain and the importance of the metaphor of water: the carrying of water marks genuine employment, whereas, as we shall see, the crying of wines in the Seventh Treatise coincides with hypocrisy and corruption. There is a cross-reference to the Prologue, where Cicero's remark 'Honour nourishes the arts' is followed by the image of a soldier mounting a ladder. We learn in the Sixth Treatise that the chaplain enables Lazarillo to mount the first social rung and that he thereby achieves '*buena vida*' (p.156), as opposed to '*triste vida*', that is good life, both in quality and honour, against a sad life. Lazarillo then dresses himself in secondhand clothes, what he calls '*hábito de hombre de bien*' (p.158), that is, the dress of a respectable man and a man of means – and gives up work. '*Hombre de bien*' or man of substance, gentleman, parallels the French expression of Montaigne, '*un honneste homme*' (see Chapter 8). Lazarillo follows his third master, the squire, and retains a secondhand sword from the same place of manufacture. There is irony in his imitating the dress of a squire whose false appearance he has exposed.

The constable, the civil service and illuminist vocabulary

Immediately after the chaplain, Lazarillo briefly serves a constable, the lowest officer in the organization of justice and the only untarnished master. The physical insecurity proves too much and he abandons him. He then becomes a civil servant – town-crier – held at that time to be the lowest of employments. There are linguistic resonances about Lazarillo's description of this choice of career that are especially noteworthy. He says in Rowland's translation that 'God by his grace lightened my mind' (p.161), in Spanish '*alumbrarme*' (p.160). The same verb was used in the First Treatise: after the blind man has bashed Lazarillo's head against the stone bull and taught him underworld slang, he blasphemously remarks, 'Neither gold nor silver can I give thee, howbeit, I do mean to teach thee the way to live' (p.63). The narrator/Lazarillo, using the verb '*alumbrar*', comments in Rowland's translation: 'It was he that gave me sight and taught me how to know the world' (p.63), and in the Second Treatise at the point when Lazarillo has a second key made he says he is '*alumbrado por el Espíritu Santo*', that is, in Rowland's words, 'by inspiration of the Holy Ghost'(p.89).

Lazarillo may refer here to the movement known as the '*alumbrados*', also sometimes called by historians 'illuminists'(see Reader, no. 21), whose members were guided by the light of God. It was suppressed as heretical. God and pious allusions are pervasive in the book, and it may be unwise to latch on to this metaphor. There is, however, startling irony in using the language of a movement intended to foster an inner spiritual life to characterize the process of acquiring the worldly wisdom of a blind beggar, getting a key made in order to steal bread, and joining the civil service. Lazarillo says that nobody prospers without a government job, and that through it he lives at the service of God and 'Your Reverence'.

Anti-Spanish propaganda

Protestants, ignoring the fact that this piece of caricature arose originally as a humanist critique in Spain itself, fastened on *Lazarillo de Tormes* with glee. It became a propaganda gift. In his dedication to the English translation Rowland, elaborating on the French version, wrote:

besides much mirth, here is also a true description of the nature and disposition of sundry Spaniards. So that by reading hereof, such as have not travelled Spain may as well discern much of the manners and customs of that country as those that have there long time continued.

(p.48)

Rowland's running heading ('A Spaniard's life') and marginal glosses (he borrowed and adapted fourteen from the French and added twenty of his own) insistently rub in the propaganda purpose, as can be seen in these examples from the Third Treatise:

There is not such provision of meat in Spain as in England.

Poor Lázaro did bear his master's dinner and his own in his bosom for fear of losing it.

In Spain many drink nothing but water, and some that may, have wine, but the squire drank it for want of better.

(pp.107, 109, 111)

The recurrent motif of bread and hunger is exploited. Of all Lazarillo's masters, it is the third, the destitute country gentleman who best lends himself to searching satire:

he taketh his sword and kisseth the pommel, and as he was putting it in his girdle, said unto me:

'My boy, if thou knewest what a blade this is, thou wouldest marvel, there is no gold that can buy it of me, for of as many as *Antonio* made, he could never give such temper to any as he gave this.'

Then drawing it out of the scabbard he tested the edge with his fingers, saying,

'Seest thou it? I dare undertake to cut asunder with it a whole fleece of wool.'

I answered him softly to myself, saying 'And I with my teeth though they be not of such hard metal, a loaf of bread weighing four pound.'

(p.113)

Of course, figures like Lazarillo's third master the squire gravitated naturally to Spain's wars and armies, especially in the Low Countries and Italy. Doubtless many in the Spanish forces swore and postured as if gentlemen born back home.

Exercise

Read the extract below, an example of Europe-wide pamphleteering printed in London in 1599 and thought to be a translation from Dutch or German. Note the aspects of a Spanish gentleman that are singled out here for satire, and their echoing of Lazarillo's squire. (This passage confirms a widespread practice of that time, of using Spanish and Italian forms of address almost interchangeably. There are abundant examples in pre-Civil War English drama, perhaps because Spaniards dominated so much of the Italian peninsula, or possibly because of a popular assimilation of Mediterranean Latin peoples in northern European eyes.)

> But *Signor* is a Cavalliero, he must be reverenced, *Guarda su Signoria* [the Lord preserve your worship], he must be soothed and flattered ... Moreover, you ought to know he is a *Hidalgo* [a son of something], although he have no patents [letters patent conferring title, nobility or property] thereof, even whose name and race, doth terrify the Moors ...
>
> This is a *Signior's* diet at another's cost, but alas if you find him at his owne Table, you may see it stately furnished with a *Sardinia* [sardine], or a crust of bread, a pot of *Aqua* [water], and perhaps a bone, yet abroad, if there be a Wolf at the Table, *Signor* is one ...
>
> Signor being in the street, or any other public place, his first gestures are to bend the head, turn the eye, and Peacock-like to behold himself: if nothing be amiss, his gait is like one who treads the measures ... [dances]. His Trade in Spain perhaps was to sew hand-baskets, or to blow glasses in the furnaces, scarce trusted to guard a flock of Cabritos [young goats]. And here he will bear the name of a Hidalgo or don ... he frieth in Love's searching flames like a fiery furnace.[5]
>
> (Jones, 1966, pp.xxiii–iv) ❖

Spaniards are portrayed as displaced military adventurers, projecting destitution, parasitism, pride, violence and lust. These themes, sometimes comic, at other times serious and tragic, became staples of late Elizabethan and Jacobean plays.

Protestant countries like England have, historically, nursed the so-called 'black legend' of the Spaniards. Hence English Renaissance drama is full of plots centred upon Spain and Italy, many exuding blood and thunder. Of this subject matter and characterization Shakespeare's texts are more restrained examples, yet the antipathy doubtless shared by his London theatre audience, staunchly Protestant, is plain to see. *Othello* opens with two Spanish adventurers in Italy, Roderigo and Iago, the one bearing the name of the last

---

[5] Jones's excellent introduction quotes a Spanish proverb: '*La comida de hidalgo poca vianda y mantel largo*' (the Spanish gentlemen's meal, little meat and a lot of table cloth).

Visigothic king whose military failure let the Moors into Spain in 711, the other named after Spain's patron saint, whose nickname was 'Kill Moors', plotting to destroy another culturally displaced person, a Moorish general. It is dramatically consistent that Othello, entrapped by Iago's machinations, kills himself with 'a sword of Spain the ice brook's temper' (5.2.254). Other English Renaissance dramatists like John Marston, Thomas Dekker, John Ford and Thomas Middleton created both comic and violent characters for the London stage in order to foment hispanophobia. Middleton's *A Game at Chesse* (published in 1624), attacking the projected Spanish marriage of Prince Charles[6] with a Spanish princess, was the first long-run stage hit of the London theatre. The Spanish ambassador protested to King James, who closed the play in August 1623. London rejoiced when the marriage project proved a fiasco. The most brilliant of the anti-Spanish dramatists was Ben Jonson, as we shall see.

Francis Beaumont's *The Woman Hater* (?1606, registered 1607), subtitled *The Hungry Courtier,* reworks similar material. The scene is set in Milan and the hungry courtier is variously called Lazarello and Lazarillo. His hunger presents a peculiarly Epicurean twist; he rejects plain fare and pursues around town the cooked head of a fish called '*umbrana*':

> *Duke.* Lazarello? what is he?
>
> *Arrigo.* A courtier my Lord, and one that I wonder your grace knowes not: for he hath followed your Court, and your last predecessors, from place to place any time this seven year, as faithfully as your Spits and your Dripping-pans have done, almost as greasely.

> (1.1.43–58)

The material destitution of an enemy was an effective propaganda tool to demonize and ridicule the Spanish. Our squire wore national dress. Spaniards wore national dress until Spanish Bourbon reforms of the 1760s stopped the practice by passing a law, a measure which provoked street riots in Madrid. In consequence, after the Treaty of Westminster of August 1604 established peace between England and Spain, Spaniards were easily identified and were often the object of direct abuse and physical assault in the streets of Jacobean London:

> Foreigners are ill regarded not to say detested in London, so sensible people dress in the English fashion, or that of France, which is adopted by nearly the whole court, and thus mishaps are avoided or passed over in silence. The Spaniards alone maintain the prerogative

[6] The eldest son of King James I of England (James VI of Scotland), who succeeded to the throne in 1625. The proposed marriage of Charles to the Spanish Infanta in 1623 was hugely unpopular in England.

of wearing their own costume, so they are easily recognised and mortally hated. Some of our party saw a wicked woman in a rage with an individual supposed to belong to the Spanish embassy. She urged the crowd to mob him, setting the example by belabouring him herself with a cabbage stalk and calling him a Spanish rogue, and although in very brave array his garments were foully smeared with a sort of soft and stinking mud, which abounds here at all seasons, so that the place better deserves to be called Lorda (filth) than Londra (London). Had not the don saved himself in a shop they would assuredly have torn his eyes out, so hateful are the airs here assumed by the Spanish whom the people of England consider harpies, which makes me think that they are less well known elsewhere.

The author of these words, the Venetian ambassador's chaplain Busino, goes on to describe part of the lord mayor's pageant as follows:

Other large and handsome stages followed, one of which, I was told, represented the religion of the Indians; the sun shining aloft in the midst of other figures. On another stage was a fine castle; while a third bore a beautiful ship, supposed to be just returned from the Indies with its crew and cargo. Other stages bore symbols of commerce, or the nations which trade with India. Among the figures represented was a Spaniard, wonderfully true to life, who imitated the gestures of that nation perfectly. He wore small black moustachios and a hat and cape in the Spanish fashion with a ruff round his neck and others about his wrists, nine inches deep. He kept kissing his hands, right and left, but especially to the Spanish Ambassador, who was a short distance from us, in such wise as to elicit roars of laughter from the multitude.

(HMSO, 1858, pp.60–1, 62)

Now consider for a moment these accounts of Orazio Busino in the light of Lazarillo's description of his squire. Busino of course is highly partisan, delighting in the public discomfort and humiliation of the representatives of a state, Spain, whom Venice feared. Indeed, the Venetian diplomatic mission in London sought to lobby James's support against Spanish military expansion. Which features of a Spanish national archetype does he single out for amusement back home in Venice? Clearly dress and gestures, a cultivated dignity and nicety, the cape, the closely trimmed moustaches and the overworked affectation of the kisses.

Frequently in the drama of this period personages who had Spanish names were the villains or fools. If a stage Spaniard wore national dress then his range of behaviour must have been substantially determined by audience expectations. Of the major dramatists, no one exploited this audience expectation more explicitly than Ben Jonson: in this extract from *The Alchemist* (1610) consider Face's excitement at catching what he thinks is a wealthy Spaniard in the London streets.

> A noble Count, Don of Spain, my dear
>
> A doughty Don is taken with my Dol;
>
>   ... Sweet Dol,
> You must go tune your virginal, no losing
> O' the least time
>
>   ... His great
> Verdugo-ship has not a jot of language;
> So much the easier to be cozened, my Dolly.
>
>   (3.3.10, 39, 66–8, 70–2)

'*Verdugo*' is Spanish for hangman or executioner. Jonson caricatures the Spaniard as a noble killing machine who goes after whores but is too proud to learn English.

His eventual entry (in reality he is an Englishman, Surly, in disguise) milks precisely the same comic famishment as we find in Lazarillo's third master:

> Slud he does look too fat to be a Spaniard ...
>
> You shall be emptied Don: pumped and drawn
> Dry, as they say.
>
>   (4.3.28, 44–5)

Jonson repeats the stock joke that Spaniards eat little, and are skinny and lascivious, but his vocabulary suggests that Dol will prove more than a sexual match and will transmit venereal disease.

Consider, however, the following passage from the same play. What is Jonson's judgement on Spanish culture?

> *Face.* Ask from your courtier, to your inns-of-court man,
> To your mere milliner: they will tell you all,
> Your *Spanish* jennet is the best horse. Your *Spanish*
> Stoop[7] is the best garb.[8] Your *Spanish* beard
> Is the best cut. Your *Spanish* ruffs are the best
> Wear. Your *Spanish* pavan the best dance.
> Your *Spanish* titillation in a glove
> The best perfume. And for your *Spanish* pike,
> And *Spanish* blade, let your poor captain speak.
>
>   (4.4.7–15; Jonson's italics)

[7] Dignified bow or act of condescension.

[8] Fashion.

Spanish culture is here clearly identified, albeit grudgingly, as dominant at the Stuart court of James I. Jonson had fought against the Spanish in the Netherlands in the early 1590s. As a former **recusant** Jonson had more sympathy with Catholicism than the majority of his audience, though his plays dramatize the prevalent fears of Protestant Londoners of Catholicism in general and the Spanish in particular as the dominant Catholic power.

In Jonson's late play *The New Inn* effete chivalry is embodied in an hispanophile character, Sir Glorious Tipto, who ends up drunk below stairs.

Within the English-speaking world nothing may illustrate the rootedness of hispanophobia better than the English term of abuse, '*dago*', still used by some indiscriminately of Mediterranean people. The patron saint of Spain, at least until 1814, was James The Less, Santiago, hence the battle cry of Burckhardt's hated troops, '*Santiago y cierra España!*' (Saint James and close Spain, i.e. with the enemy). English troops met the battle cry in the Netherlands in the 1580s and 1590s.

The coalesced form of the name, *Santiago*, with its fossilized dental ('t') in the middle, spawned a new line because, we must infer, it was popularly if irregularly construed as *San tiago* or *San Diego*. *Diego* is the usual Spanish form of James, *Iago* alone being a very uncommon first name in Spain. The preferred first name form is *Santiago*. In English pronunciation, *Diego* was rendered Deigo or Dego, and stood for a Spaniard as more recently Fritz has stood for a German. What strikes you about the hispanophobia of the following passage by the London playwright Thomas Dekker?

> *Bret.* Philip is a Spaniard, and what is a Spaniard?
>
> *Clo.* A Spaniard is no Englishman that I know.
>
> *Bret.* Right, a Spaniard is a Camocho, a Callimanco, nay which is worse, a Dondego, and what is a Dondego?
>
> *Clo.* A Dondego is a kind of Spanish Stockfish, or poor John.
>
> *Bret.* No, Dondego is a desperate Viliago, a very Castilian, God blesse us.

> (*The Famous History of Sir Thomas Wyatt*, 4.2.50 – 4; quarto first published 1607)

What I find striking is that hispanophobia is integral to the rabidly hostile London mob arming itself in defence of a Protestant England. The subject of this play, Wyatt, the son of the poet, tried to raise an insurrection against the Spanish marriage of the Catholic Mary I with the future Philip II of Spain in 1554. It did not succeed. The last line in the quotation from *Sir Thomas Wyatt* is especially illuminating: 'No, a Dondego is a desperate Viliago, a very Castilian, God bless us.' In the context of this violently xenophobic scene, *don* and *dego* form an alliterative term of abuse; a '*Viliago*' presumably means Vile Iago, and is precisely identified as Spanish, Castilian and desperate. Dekker's audience clearly knew that Diego and Iago were variants. It was precisely this kind of thinking which informed Burckhardt's negative view of the Spanish.[9]

Rowland's marginal glosses remorselessly and unscrupulously twist the anti-Spanish knife; from the Third Treatise: 'At home in his own country he did eat nothing else [but a cow's bony foot] (p.123); 'Small need to pick his teeth for any meat he had eaten' (p.127); 'Two and thirty maravedis is six pence in English' (p.135).

The vilification of the Spanish in Protestant northern Europe gave rise to a potent myth of Spanish cultural barbarism which continued to inform scholarship into the twentieth century. One of the main contributors to this 'black legend' was Burckhardt, whose seminal study of the Italian Renaissance is littered with anti-Spanish sentiment and prejudice.

Exercise

Read the following passage in which Burckhardt describes the impact of Spanish troops on Italy following the Sack of Rome in 1527, and comment on the language used to describe the Spanish:

> outrages like these were as nothing compared with the misery which was afterwards brought upon Italy by foreign troops, and most of all by the Spaniards, in whom perhaps a touch of oriental blood, perhaps familiarity with the spectacles of the Inquisition, had unloosed the devilish element of human nature. After seeing them at work, at Prato, Rome and elsewhere, it is not easy to take any interest of the higher sort in Ferdinand the Catholic and Charles V, who knew what these hordes were, and yet unchained them.

(pp.80–1)

Discussion

Burckhardt here alludes not only to the sacking of Rome by Charles's troops but also to the fact that the Spanish crown subsequently ruled most of Italy, including Milan and the kingdom of Naples, and for many years threatened the independence of Venice. In using the word 'oriental', presumably to refer to the long Muslim occupation of parts of the Iberian peninsula and consequent

---

[9] Curiously, according to the Oxford English Dictionary, the term of anglophone abuse '*dago*' originated in the south-western United States to indicate a man of Spanish parentage, and the earliest cited uses of the pejorative are 1888 and 1890. It may on the contrary be inferred that the pejorative went to North America with the first English Protestant settlers.

racial mixture, he insinuates that the Spaniards were not fully European and not fully civilized, although he elsewhere concedes that Muslim political and cultural hegemony was a feature of Italian cultural history too (see pp.312 and 314). ❖

Elsewhere Burckhardt blamed Spanish influence for preventing a full flowering of aspects of the Renaissance in Italy: 'It was the Inquisitors and Spaniards who cowed the Italian spirit, and rendered impossible the representation of the greatest and most sublime themes ...' (p.206). We learn, too, that 'Jews and Moors, who had taken refuge from the Spaniards at Ferrara, were now compelled again to wear the yellow O upon the breast' (p.311). Burckhardt regrets Spain's intervention, culturally and politically, in the Italian peninsula: Spain's influence was violent, inhuman and repressive.

Emotionally he was very hostile to the imperial expansion under Ferdinand and Isabella the Catholic and Charles V, which resulted in the Spanish empire, the first upon which, it was claimed, the sun never set. He regarded Spanish political and military hegemony in the sixteenth century much as many in the west recently regarded the Soviet Union's domination of eastern Europe.

During the course of the twentieth century this view of Spain, and its relationship to the Italian Renaissance, has been substantially revised by the work of scholars like Henry Kamen (1997) and Jeremy Lawrance (1990), who have produced a more nuanced and positive picture of Spanish society. In many respects *Lazarillo de Tormes* provides substantive evidence for this process of cultural rehabilitation. Though critical of many aspects of the social and religious culture of Spain in the sixteenth century, the mere fact of its existence, and its debt to Renaissance humanism, provides something of a corrective to Burckhardt's dark vision of Spain and the Spanish.

Western literary tradition: genealogy and innovation

Exercise

Read the following passage and consider Bjornson's argument for the importance of *Lazarillo de Tormes* in the history of western fiction.

> If *Lazarillo* reflects particular historical relationships as perceived by its anonymous author, it also established a precedent which would be followed under quite different circumstances in later picaresque novels. Besides delineating the major outlines of this myth [the rise of the low-born individual], the anonymous author contributed to the evolution of the modern European novel. Earlier works – anatomies of roguery like *Liber vagatorum* (1510) or jest books like *Till Eulenspiegel* (1515) – had

depicted low-life scenes and drawn upon popular anecdotes, but by sustaining a consistent pseudo-autobiographical perspective while allowing readers to glimpse the flaws and inadequacies of the narrator's personality, the author of *Lazarillo* achieved a much higher degree of artistic organisation and moral seriousness than did his predecessors. Furthermore, his extended portrayal of a lower-class character's life placed a new emphasis upon the primacy of individual experience and reflected a heightened interest in creating the illusion of verisimilitude, suggesting that the anonymous author of *Lazarillo* was among the first Europeans to seize upon the novel's potential as a serious form of literary expression.

(Bjornson, 1979, p.42) ❖

Nearly 50 years after *Lazarillo* first appeared, a work by Mateo Alemán (1547–*c*.1614) entitled *Guzmán de Alfarache* was published in Madrid in two parts (1599 and 1604) and achieved an extraordinary popular success. Although Alemán called the second part of his novel *Watchtower of Man's Life*, the work became popularly known as *Pícaro* (*Rogue*), because the lighter, racy and entertaining aspects appealed much more to the public. Guzmán was born in Seville, the illegitimate son of parents of low social status; his father was a usurer, his mother a prostitute. When his father died, Guzmán decided to venture forth. Perhaps not surprisingly 1605 saw the publication of *La Pícara Justina* (*The Female Rogue Justine*) by Francisco López de Ubeda, which quotes Alemán's novel and makes jokes of Lazarillo's witticisms. The vogue for such fiction was launched and translations rapidly followed. James Mabbe, who spent the years 1611–13 in Madrid, and delighted to call himself Diego Puede-Ser (James May-be), was translator of *The Rogue or the Life of Guzmán de Alfarache*, published in London in 1622/1623, and reprinted in Oxford in 1630 and in London in 1634. Ben Jonson wrote dedicatory verses. A chain of direct and verifiable influences leads from the Spanish picaresque through Lesage's *Gil Blas* (1715) and Smollett's *Roderick Random* (1748) but:

despite a continuity suggested by the recurrence of the picaresque myth, the first person narrative and the panoramic perspective, differences in social and literary conventions bring about a change in the picaresque hero and reflect points of view which are diametrically opposed to those commonly associated with the earlier Spanish novels.

(Bjornson, 1979, pp.12–13)

Lazarillo de Tormes was not the first (or last) book to entertain with stories of low life and practical jokes. Classicists nowadays claim that the novel, far from being datable to the economic rise of a bourgeoisie and a predominantly female reading public, had classical antecedents, such as Apuleius's *The Golden Ass* (second century CE), Petronius's *Satyricon* (first century CE) and Lucian's *Dialogues of the Dead* (second century CE), which in certain features anticipate rogue or delinquent fiction. These works were well known to Renaissance humanists, and their possible influence on the author of *Lazarillo de Tormes* cannot be excluded.

The book's significance is that it reworked such material in the form of a fictional autobiography or memoire-letter, that this form allowed the reader to access the narrator's mind and personality, that it highlighted characterization as an enduring feature of the novel, and that this illusion of autobiography and individual experience contributed to what we have later called the 'realist novel'. Reflect for a moment on the almost endless list of English novels called after the key protagonist, either in autobiographical form or dominated by the destiny of a single protagonist: *Robinson Crusoe, Moll Flanders, Jane Eyre, Tom Jones, Emma, Pickwick Papers* and thousands more. Within Spain and beyond, the fictional form grew to incorporate female personages and, as it evolved, jumped class to include young noblemen. We find novels with clear picaresque features adapted to philosophical, educational, even psycho-analytical studies: *Candide, David Copperfield, Ulysses...*

Lazarillo de Tormes is the sort of literary work that resists closure. Notwithstanding its concluding two paragraphs, the experience of reading the book denies us the sense of 'they all lived happily ever after'. Lots of questions come to mind:

- Is the eponymous hero of the book a moral agent or a product of relations of power in a particular society?

- Or is the narrator/hero a 'fictive' person who should not be considered to own his words and actions?

- Is the book a witty parody or burlesque, ridiculing those who seek glory and renown?

- Is the book evidence of a prudential self and a prudential ethic, a rhetorical posture that subordinates honesty to decorum?

- Who is the mysterious 'Your Worship'?

- What is the nature of his relationship with Lazarillo?

- What sort of authority does he have?

- Is the whole situation a bluff?

The book deconstructs all authority, even its own authority as a book. Why is this so?

Exercise

Read the article '*Lazarillo de Tormes*: the case of the purloined letter' by Peter Dunn (Reader, no. 24), and ask yourself on what grounds the book may be judged innovatory, modern and subversive. ❖

Dunn's argument takes the form of a public lecture: he sets out to surprise, tease and entertain. His pleasure in the sheer paradoxes of *Lazarillo de Tormes* leads him to make the following points:

- the book's structure does not allow resolution of a host of questions raised;
- there is parody of several modes of discourse, such as medieval writing on the three estates, chivalresque romance with the intervention of providence, confessional literature, depositional testimony before a court and epistolary conventions;
- the interior life of the narrator is unresolved and inexplicit;
- there are many gaps and omissions, matters of fact and causality are not clear or not known, and questions proliferate out of control;
- the text appears not to have been written for the public because its context is one of a private communication, but the Prologue, with its mention of writing to achieve fame, is predicated on an aesthetics of reader reception; the text is then, in a sense, written yet requires its readers to rewrite it;
- the matter ('*el caso*') giving rise to the communication is not precisely known, just inferred;
- the author is not known;
- the recipient is not known;
- Lazarillo appears to want to substitute his own agenda for that of his enquirer;
- the book is an act of masking rather than communicating.

There are then a self-consciousness and a range of narrative practices that anticipate a modern writer like Joyce or Borges. It could be said of *Lazarillo de Tormes*, as of *Don Quixote*, that it anticipated a very large number of the later experiments and developments in prose fiction.

Bibliography

All quotations from and line references to *Lazarillo de Tormes* are from Whitlock, 2000.

ALPERT, M. (1977) *Two Spanish Picaresque Novels*, Harmondsworth, Penguin.

BJORNSON, R. (1979) *The Picaresque Hero in European Fiction*, Madison, University of Wisconsin Press.

BURCKHARDT, J. (1990) *The Civilization of the Renaissance in Italy*, trans. S.G.C. Middlemore, Harmondsworth, Penguin; first published 1860.

CRUZ, A.D. (1999) *Discourses of Poverty: Social Reform and the Picaresque Novel in Early Modern Spain*, Toronto, Buffalo and London, University of Toronto Press.

DEYERMOND, A. (1993) *Lazarillo de Tormes, A Critical Guide*, London, Grant & Cutler.

EISENSTEIN, E.L. (1993) *The Printing Revolution in Early Modern Europe*, Cambridge, Cambridge University Press.

GRICE-HUTCHINSON, M. (1978) *Early Economic Thought in Spain 1177–1740*, London, George Allen.

HERRERO, J. (1978) 'The ending of Lazarillo: the wine against the water', *Modern Language Notes*, vol. 93, pp.313–19.

HMSO (1858) *Calendar of State Papers Domestic Series*, London, HMSO, vol. 15, pp.60–1, 62; 23 October 1623.

JONES, R.O. (ed.) (1966) *La vida de Lazarillo de Tormes*, Manchester, Manchester University Press.

KAMEN, H. (1997) *The Spanish Inquisition: An Historical Revision*, London, Weidenfeld & Nicolson.

LAWRANCE, J.N.H. (1990) 'Humanism in the Iberian peninsula' in A. Goodman and A. Mackay (eds) *The Impact of Humanism on Western Europe*, London and New York, Longman.

SHIPLEY, G. (1982) 'A case of functional obscurity', *Modern Language Notes*, vol. 97, pp.225–53.

WHITLOCK, K. (ed.) (2000) *The Life of Lazarillo de Tormes (La vida de Lazarillo de Tormes y de sus fortunas y adversidades)*, trans. D. Rowland, Warminster, Aris & Phillips.

Reader sources

Henry Kamen, Excluding the Reformation: *The Spanish Inquisition: An Historical Revision*, Weidenfeld & Nicolson, London, 1997, pp.83–101. (Reader, no. 21)

Javier Herrero, Renaissance poverty and Lazarillo's family: the birth of the picaresque genre: *Publications of the Modern Language Association*, vol. 94, 1979, pp.876–86. (Reader, no. 23)

Thomas Hanrahan, *Lazarillo de Tormes*: Erasmian satire or Protestant reform?: *Hispania*, vol. 66, September 1983, pp.333–9. (Reader, no. 22)

Peter N. Dunn, *Lazarillo de Tormes*: the case of the purloined letter: *Revista de Estudios Hispánicos*, vol. 22, 1988, pp.1–4. (Reader, no. 24)

CHAPTER FIVE

Did science have a Renaissance?

BY PETER ELMER

Objectives

The objectives of this chapter are that you should:

- be introduced to the wide-ranging debate among historians of science as to the nature and role of science in the Renaissance;

- examine, through selected case studies, examples of the new approach adopted by some historians to understanding developments in Renaissance science;

- gain an awareness of the way in which science was intimately related to other fields of human endeavour in the Renaissance, for example humanism, the visual arts, literature, philosophy.

Introduction

In his classic study of the Italian Renaissance, Jacob Burckhardt had relatively little to say about the role of science in this period (roughly the fifteenth and sixteenth centuries). Acknowledging his ignorance in this sphere (1990, p.192), he nonetheless characterized the era of the Renaissance as a period of slow, scientific advance, in which, as in all else, the Italians were pre-eminent. In writing in this vein, Burckhardt undoubtedly reflected a general attitude on the part of scholars in the nineteenth century towards the historical origins of western science. These views have continued to inform the writing of the history of science down to the present day and they thus constitute a good starting-point for this chapter, in which I wish to raise the issue of the place of science in Renaissance culture.

Exercise

Read Burckhardt, pp.187–92. What are Burckhardt's main presuppositions about the nature and practice of science in this period?

Discussion

First, Burckhardt takes it for granted that Italy was the home of scientific innovation. It was in the Renaissance, he infers, that Italians were first given the freedom to pursue scientific and philosophical speculations unimpeded by such barriers to free inquiry as dread of nature, slavery to books, and tradition. Equally important, however, is his assumption that religion and the institutional powers of the Roman Catholic church (which, by the way, he implies were more draconian and effective in northern Europe) were major impediments to a true understanding of the natural world. Finally, there is a suggestion that humanism was inimical to the pursuit of science, as it claimed the attention of intellectuals who might otherwise have been drawn to scientific investigation. ❖

In suggesting that the roots of modern science (which in true nineteenth-century vein Burckhardt characterizes as empirical and inductive) lay in the broader culture of Renaissance Italy, Burckhardt was helping to create a powerful tradition – some would say myth – which has continued to exert a strong influence on historians of science to the present day. Integral to this view is the idea that the progress of science from the sixteenth century to the present was both natural and inevitable, the product of visionaries – men like Nicholas Copernicus (1474–1543) and Galileo Galilei (1564–1642) in the field of astronomy – who were not afraid to challenge the scientific status quo. Consequently, historians of science who have accepted the 'whig' assumptions[1] underlying this perception have been tempted to see the period of the Renaissance as an important prelude to the era of the scientific revolution that occurred in the seventeenth century. They have viewed the Renaissance as a period in which few important discoveries were made, but in which, nonetheless, the foundations of a new approach to the natural world were laid. Of particular importance in this respect is the emphasis that scholars like Burckhardt have placed upon the role of individual genius in the field of scientific innovation, an attribution that bears obvious comparison to Burckhardt's view of the place and significance of the artist in Renaissance culture. This view of the scientist as inspired genius continues to permeate our understanding of the origins of western science. In the last 40 years, however, it has undergone radical reappraisal in scholarly circles. In what follows, I would like to present something of these new approaches, which will, I hope, provide a richer and more nuanced depiction of the place of science in Renaissance Europe.

---

[1] 'The "whig interpretation of history" was defined [...] as the tendency of historians to see the past as the story of the conflict between progressives and reactionaries, in which the progressives, or whigs, always win, and in so doing bring about the modern world' (Reader, no. 31, p.327).

Recent developments in the history of Renaissance science

Since the 1960s, it has become increasingly common among historians of Renaissance science to question the 'whiggishness' of much of the work of earlier historians in this field, and to propose instead new approaches for an understanding of the evolution of early modern science. In particular, there has been a movement away from what have been termed 'internalist' accounts of the history of science in favour of 'externalism'. The classic internalist view, which Burckhardt himself, unconsciously no doubt, espoused in his brief excursion into science, is predicated on the idea that science, or knowledge of the natural world, existed independently of other fields of human endeavour or systems of belief. Proper understanding of the natural world was thus dependent upon a logic, or system of reasoning, which was entirely unrelated to extraneous factors. Social or economic background, religious orientation, and political and cultural factors were simply disregarded as irrelevant to the historian of early modern science. In extreme cases, non-scientific factors such as religion might even be regarded as major obstacles to the pursuit and discovery of new scientific truths. This view is most famously epitomized by Galileo's humiliating submission to the Italian Inquisition in the seventeenth century, when he was forced by religious authority to recant his support for **heliocentrism**.

Today, however, historians of science are far more likely to reject this somewhat simplistic account of the onward march of science. Instead, it is now widely held that non-scientific factors played a definitive role in the advance of science. Particular emphasis is now placed in the period of the Renaissance on the critical role of religion, both positive and negative, in the evolution of new approaches to science. At the same time, the definition of what constituted science has been broadened to include a wide realm of ideas and beliefs that hitherto historians had considered to be unscientific. In relation to the period we are considering, the most significant development in this respect has been the 'discovery' of Renaissance magic, or **occult science** (alchemy, astrology and **natural magic**). Previously disregarded as pseudo-science or a remnant of medieval superstition, the occult tradition is now generally seen as one of the critical, formative influences on scientists in the age from Copernicus to Isaac Newton (1642–1727).

Despite the major differences between internalist and externalist practitioners of the history of science, they nonetheless share a common outlook – namely the desire to explain the roots of the modern scientific world-view in the science of the past. In recent years, however, even this fundamental assumption has been subjected to challenge by some who have questioned the whole notion of what it meant for the so-called scientists of the Renaissance to 'do science'. Central to this approach is a redefinition of early modern science, one that pays far greater attention to what the scientists of the period themselves thought they were doing when they studied aspects of the natural world. In the process, some historians have rejected the assumption of both internalists and externalists that science today is, by and large, the same pursuit as that practised by our Renaissance forbears, and have substituted a different set of assumptions, which reflect more accurately the motives and concerns of Renaissance scientists. Significantly, scholars who subscribe to this new approach have suggested that we ought to refer in future to these activities, not as science but rather, in line with Renaissance usage, as 'natural philosophy'.

There is little doubt that such an approach has led to numerous novel and fascinating developments in the history of early modern science. In the case studies that follow, we shall have an opportunity to look in more detail at this new methodology and to assess its success in accounting for early modern science. We will need to begin our investigation of Renaissance science, however, with a brief overview of scholarly work in the field over the past few decades.

The Renaissance and the scientific revolution

If the main object of studying the science of the past is to discover the roots of modern-day science, then the Renaissance would seem to constitute a poor starting-point. Critically, it provides few examples of the new empiricism, which most consider to be the defining characteristic of modern scientific investigation. The scientific revolution itself is usually regarded as a phenomenon of the seventeenth century, the preserve of such giants as Francis Bacon (1561–1626), René Descartes (1596–1650) and Isaac Newton. Only in two key areas does the Renaissance appear to have had a major impact on subsequent scientific developments: astronomy and anatomy. In the case of the former, the development of a theoretical heliocentricity by Copernicus and his followers proved surprisingly uncontroversial in the sixteenth century, thanks largely to the fact that most serious commentators simply rejected the hypothetical principles on which it was based. Anatomy, as we shall see, also underwent a revolution in the sixteenth century, with many of the assumptions of the ancients regarding the internal organization of the body challenged for the first time in two thousand years. But, as historians of medicine are only too eager to point out, the discoveries and writings of the anatomists made little or no impact on the practice of Renaissance medicine, which remained, by modern standards, ineffective in the face of most physical complaints and diseases.

In all other realms of Renaissance science, despite the growing interest in, and fascination with, the natural world, few examples of scientific modernity are apparent. For many historians of science, internalist and externalist alike, the failure of Renaissance science lay in the continuing domination of the university curriculum by the writings of the Greek natural philosopher, Aristotle (384–322 BCE). Scholasticism was first introduced into the curriculum in the late Middle Ages, and by the early sixteenth century it was the single most important influence on early modern science and its practitioners. For historians of science, it has long been associated with intellectual stagnation and retrogression. With its emphasis on book-learning, it appeared to provide no new routes to knowledge of the natural world. As long as it dominated the teaching of science in the universities, the prospect for scientific innovation looked gloomy.

During the 1960s, some historians of science began to challenge this rather pessimistic view of the place of science in Renaissance Europe. In particular, the pioneering work of Frances Yates (1899–1981) suggested that the revival of interest in occult science in the Renaissance marked the first stage in the creation of a genuinely scientific spirit of enquiry that highlighted the importance of observation and experiment. Supporters of the 'Yates thesis' (as it somewhat erroneously came to be known) argued strongly for a positive role for hermeticism (the collective term most commonly used to describe the various occult arts) and began to detect its influence at work among a number of scholars and scientists in the period. The 'Yates thesis', however, has its detractors, who claim that the obscure language and secretive tradition surrounding the occult arts are essentially antithetical to science as we understand it today (Vickers, 1984, pp.1–6, 95–163; Vickers, 1991, pp.51–93).

Another important development in the history of science in this period is the reassessment of the role of Aristotelianism as a catalyst for scientific innovation. As a result of the work of scholars like Charles Schmitt, it is now apparent that the ideas of Aristotle were never perceived by Renaissance scholars as a single, monolithic whole. On the contrary, there were many different 'Aristotelianisms', some of which challenged traditional scientific thinking, as well as promoting empirical approaches to the natural world (Schmitt, 1983;

Copenhaver, 1987). In the words of Eckhard Kessler, Renaissance Aristotelianism should no longer be seen 'as simply opposing and repressing new problems and new positions [in science], but rather as producing, or at least influencing them' (Kessler, 1990, p.142). In biology, for example, it was largely scholars working within the Aristotelian tradition who were to lay the foundations of the biological revolution of the seventeenth century that culminated in the work of William Harvey (1578–1657), the discoverer of the circulation of the blood. In medicine, too, a willingness to adapt revered ancient authorities such as Hippocrates (*c.*460–380 BCE) and Galen (*c.*129–*c.*200 CE), and to innovate within these traditions, is frequently cited as yet another example of this modernizing trend in Renaissance science.

The result of these new approaches to the history of science has been to create a more complex and sophisticated view of the origins of science in the Renaissance and of the scientific revolution. It is no longer orthodox or commonplace to posit a simple dichotomy between Renaissance science (backward-looking, book-bound and sterile) and modern science (forward-looking, empirical and productive). Instead, historians of science are beginning to come to terms with the paradox that, by looking backwards to ancient thinkers and modes of thinking, new approaches and discoveries in science were made possible. Gone is the traditional model, which characterized the age of the Renaissance and the ensuing scientific revolution as a battle between 'ancients' and 'moderns'. Despite the fact that no consensus has emerged to explain satisfactorily the relationship between an emerging new science and the Renaissance, most historians are now agreed that the period of the fifteenth and sixteenth centuries was seminal in fostering novel approaches to the study of humankind and the natural world. It is impossible to do justice to the vast range and erudition of recent scholarship on Renaissance science. We can, however, appreciate something of the flavour of modern research in this area by focusing on one particular aspect of sixteenth-century science: the Renaissance rediscovery of anatomy, which forms the basis of the following case study.

The anatomical revolution of the sixteenth century

In 1543, the same year in which Copernicus published his defence of heliocentricity, *De revolutionibus*, the Flemish-born anatomist, Andreas Vesalius (1514–64), produced his anatomical masterpiece, *De humani corporis fabrica libri septem* (*Seven Books on the Structure of the Human Body*).

Figure 5.1 Portrait of Andreas Vesalius, aged 28. Photo: from Andreas Vesalius, *De humani corporis fabrica* ... , 1543. Wellcome Institute Library, London

From the moment of its first appearance, *De fabrica* was lavishly praised, both for its beautiful woodcut illustrations and its medical iconoclasm. In the traditional history of science, Vesalius stands as an obvious example of the superiority of the 'moderns' to the 'ancients'. Vesalius was in the vanguard of the scientific revolution, in his willingness to break with the past and openly criticize the authority of Galen in matters relating to the physiology of the human body – or so it has seemed to most historians of Renaissance medicine. But it is not only Vesalius's conclusions that have led scholars to praise his achievements and to set him apart from his more conservative contemporaries; it is also the manner in which he set out to prove himself right, and Galen wrong. Vesalius was an avowed empiricist, adopting what we would clearly see today as methods of modern scientific investigation. He argued that the true function and structure of the human body could only be discovered by acute observation of the dissected body itself. Unlike Galen, whose experience of anatomy was confined to animals, Vesalius's observations were based on a wide sample of anatomized human cadavers, which were increasingly available for dissection in the sixteenth century. Moreover, by publishing the results of his research in a fully illustrated and easily accessible form (Figure 5.2), Vesalius guaranteed a wide and enthusiastic reception for his new insights into the human body. Vesalius, in brief, was a model example of a Renaissance scientist who had made a decisive break with the past and stood head and shoulders above his peers.

Figure 5.2 Dissected figure. Photo: from Andreas Vesalius, *De humani corporis fabrica ...* , 1543. Wellcome Institute Library, London

In recent years, this view of Vesalius and his place in the pantheon of scientific 'greats' has undergone radical revision. The anatomical revolution that he initiated has itself been the subject of much debate, particularly in relation to the role that anatomy played in the wider cultural history of the Renaissance. While no one has seriously challenged the significance or novelty of Vesalius's findings, it is now generally acknowledged that the impact of his anatomical investigations, and that of his successors, was largely inconsequential in terms of practical benefits in the art of healing. Indeed, despite Vesalius's clear refutation of many aspects of traditional Galenic physiology, learned medicine continued to depend heavily on ancient medical authorities, particularly Galen, throughout the sixteenth and seventeenth centuries. Anatomy thus provides an interesting case study for an examination of the place of science, and scientific innovation, in Renaissance culture. It also provides an opportunity to assess the merits of the various approaches to Renaissance science outlined in the section on 'Recent developments in the history of Renaissance science' above.

Exercise

Read 'The old and the new' by Nancy Siraisi in the Reader (no. 26). Without worrying too much about the specific details, how, in general terms, does what Siraisi has to say about anatomy relate to other aspects of Renaissance culture?

Discussion

Siraisi discusses a number of areas of Renaissance life and culture affected by, or impinging on, the vogue for anatomizing. The following are the main areas of intersection as I see them.

1 Humanism. Siraisi refers in particular to 'medical humanism or Hellenism', an aspect of the wider Renaissance interest in the rediscovery and re-evaluation of ancient texts (in this case, specifically the renewed interest in medical circles in the writings of those two founding fathers of western medicine, Hippocrates and Galen).

2 Art. Renaissance artistic styles and values were crucial to the anatomists who wished to spread their message to as wide an audience as possible.

3 Religion. Anatomy played an important subsidiary role in the promotion of religion and morality. Human anatomy 'was testimony to the benevolence and design of the Creator' (and was thus popular in both Catholic and Protestant circles). Note, in particular, Siraisi's allusion to the philosophical importance of anatomy and its consequent prominence in the medical curriculum of the reformed Protestant university at Wittenberg.

219

4   Drama. Siraisi's reference to the 'theatricality' of Renaissance anatomy and its indebtedness to notions of 'representation' and performance are highly suggestive of the Renaissance rediscovery of classical drama. The public nature of much anatomizing, and the creation of purpose-built anatomy theatres, testifies to its appeal to a wide audience beyond the narrow confines of the university medical schools.

5   Politics. There is also a hint that the spectacle of public anatomies provided an invaluable opportunity for governments to display and legitimate their authority. Cadavers of executed criminals were the chief source of bodies for Renaissance anatomists. Their ritualized dismemberment therefore offered rich opportunities for legal and political commentary. ❖

As Siraisi's brief overview of recent research on anatomy suggests, the anatomical revolution of the sixteenth century was deeply enmeshed in the social, cultural, religious and political life of the period. The suggestion here – and it is one to which we shall return – is that support for the new anatomical findings of Vesalius and others was conditioned as much by non-scientific factors as it was by purely scientific ones. The emphasis that scholars have recently placed on non-scientific aspects of anatomy is awkward from the narrowly internalist point of view. Just as puzzling is the stress that is now placed on the role of medical humanism in promoting scientific advance. Looking to the past for inspiration, we are now being informed, is not inconsistent with scientific progress.

How, we might ask, did medical humanism help to encourage initiatives like those of the anatomists? In the first place, it is now increasingly clear that the rediscovery of ancient medical texts, particularly those of Hippocrates and Galen, helped to foster a critical spirit of enquiry among many of the humanist-educated physicians of the sixteenth century.

Vesalius himself was steeped in the humanist tradition and owed an immense debt to his reading of Galen in the original Greek editions that first appeared in Europe in 1525. According to Andrew Cunningham, the failure of historians of science to recognize this debt has led to a catastrophic misreading of Vesalius's life and work. Cunningham has argued that what Vesalius really intended in his anatomical endeavours – in spite of his medical iconoclasm and rejection of Galenic anatomy – was to emulate the ancients, and in particular Galen (Cunningham, 1997). Cunningham's evidence rests not just on a reassessment of Vesalius's life and published work, and an acknowledgement of his deep commitment to the humanist

Figure 5.3 Title page of Guinter of Andernach's Latin translation of Galen, *Anatomical Procedures*, 1531. Photo: Wellcome Institute Library, London

programme, but also on the iconographical evidence found in *De fabrica*, in particular its celebrated title page (Figure 5.4). Here, we not only find Galen appearing as a prominent witness to the importance of Vesalius's work, but, as Cunningham points out, a full understanding of the complex meaning of this crowded scene is only possible through a thorough appreciation of humanist wisdom.

Figure 5.4 Title page of *De humani corporis fabrica*. Photo: from Andreas Vesalius, *De humani corporis fabrica ...* , 1543. Wellcome Institute Library, London

The famous woodcut of the anatomist Vesalius at work also hints at a further source of indebtedness on the part of the Renaissance anatomist to the classical past. The Renaissance anatomy theatre, in which the action takes place, almost certainly owed much to the sixteenth-century rediscovery of Greek architecture and drama.

COLISEVS SI   VE THEATRVM

Figure 5.5 Wood engraving of a theatre from the title page of Plautus, *Comoediae XX*, Venice, 1511. © The Trustees of the British Library, London

The construction of permanent and purpose-built anatomy theatres dates to the mid sixteenth century in Italy. Prior to this, dissections were carried out in either churches, private homes or temporary constructions that were dismantled after use. By the mid sixteenth century, however, the growth in popular demand to witness

Figure 5.6 Vitruvian architecture modelled on the human body, from John Shute, *The First and Chiefe Groundes of Architecture*, 1563. Royal Institute of British Architects, London

anatomical demonstrations required a more permanent solution to the problem of organizing such events. The classical architectural tradition, particularly that of Vitruvius (fl. 46–30 BCE), which emphasized the close parallel between perfect building form and the human body, provided the answer.

By the late sixteenth century, most of the medical schools of Italy (for example, those at Padua, Pisa, Pavia and Ferrara) possessed permanent and classical edifices for the performance of human dissections, many of which were designed by the anatomists themselves. We might note the conclusion of Giovanna Ferrari, in her study of the anatomy theatre at Bologna:

> The interest in the theatre design of the ancients that some anatomists displayed during the early Renaissance was no doubt dictated more by practical need than by any genuine philological interest. The fact, however, remains that in order to solve a new problem they fell back on an example provided by the ancient world, and they did so precisely at that moment at which reference back to ancient times was a cultural imperative. It should not be forgotten

that doctors, especially if they were physicians rather than surgeons, still underwent a training that had a great deal in common with that of literary scholars.

(Ferrari, 1987, p.86)

The emphasis on dissection as a form of public performance is also worthy of further consideration, particularly in relation to humanism and the Renaissance revival of drama. Just as the classical play was divided into acts and scenes, so too the anatomist's performance was divided into discreet phases, which were largely determined by practical concerns over the rate at which different parts of the body were subject to decay. In many instances, the audience was required to purchase an entrance ticket, 'bouncers' were frequently employed to ensure civil behaviour, and music was often performed before or during the performance to add to the sense of drama. It has even been suggested that it was the vogue for public anatomies in purpose-built theatres that provided a stimulus to the construction of permanent buildings for the performance of Renaissance drama (Heckscher, 1958, pp.43–4; Ferrari, 1987, pp.82–4).

The debt of Renaissance anatomy to ancient precedents and texts clearly suggests that the emergence of scientific 'heroes' or 'geniuses' like Vesalius owed more to the revival of antiquity than has previously been acknowledged. Moreover, anatomical instruction and medical advance were conditioned by a number of factors, not all of which were scientific in character. The public nature of anatomy is itself both intriguing and problematic. Why did Renaissance anatomists, and the university and civil authorities who allowed public dissections, remove such activities from the privacy of the classroom and professorial dwelling to the public domain? Is it possible that contemporary witnesses to these events, even the anatomists themselves, saw the prime function of the fad for anatomy as something other than the demonstration of scientific and medical truths?

There is a growing literature which suggests that this might in fact be the case. We now know, for example, that, in the vast majority of dissections, the explicit medical purpose of the anatomical demonstration was not to reveal new truths or disprove ancient falsehoods. Rather, the role of the anatomist was to use the dissected cadaver as a supplementary device to illustrate well-established truths (usually those found in the pages of medical authorities like Galen). Intriguingly, even after Vesalius, it was not widely accepted that the evidence provided by the dissected corpse was superior to that of revered medical texts. Underlying adherence to belief in the superiority of texts was the Renaissance preoccupation with order and hierarchy: in this case, the higher standing of the trained medical professor (whose medical qualifications rested on book learning above all else) over that of the mere surgeon–anatomist (who, in using his hands in the execution of his job, demonstrated his social and intellectual inferiority).

Of even greater significance in this respect, however, is the wide appeal of anatomies for all sections of the community, unlearned as well as learned, throughout Renaissance Europe. The fascination of the general public cannot be explained purely by reference to the medical or scientific significance of the work of the anatomist. Moral, political and religious considerations loom large and may well have taken priority for the anatomist, above and beyond those of science itself. A number of scholars have persuasively argued, for example, that public anatomies performed a political function, the dissection of the corpses of hanged criminals representing a powerful statement of the authority of the state in the preservation of divinely ordained law and order (e.g. Sawday, 1995).[2] It was not uncommon for the skeletons of dissected criminals to be reassembled and exhibited in the anatomy theatre, often with placards announcing their names and crimes. These developments went hand in hand with the emergence of the anatomy theatre as a cultural centre – a place, that is, which members of the public might visit for general edification. Those constructed in early seventeenth-century Holland, for example, certainly functioned along these lines, combining the attributes of a modern-day art gallery, library and centre for scientific research. Here were found all manner of natural curiosities (animals, plants and stones), as well as examples of human ingenuity (coins, paintings and scientific instruments). The one at Leiden (founded in 1597; Figure 5.7) contained the skins of exotic wild animals, the hand of a mermaid and the foot of a sea monster. It also contained diverse works of art, paintings of biblical, historical and allegorical scenes, including examples of the *vanitas* genre,[3] the object of which was to encourage the viewer to contemplate the transitory and fragile nature of human existence (Rupp, 1990). The coded messages implicit in such works of art demanded a humanist education to decipher them, which suggests once again the debt of anatomy to Renaissance humanism.

[2] For a critical reassessment of the approach of Sawday and others, see Park (1994).

[3] *Vanitas* (Latin, 'emptiness') describes a type of still-life painting commonly found in the Netherlands in the seventeenth century. The works included symbols and emblems intended to emphasize the transitory nature of earthly possessions and desires.

Figure 5.7 Leiden anatomy theatre, *c.*1609. Photo: Leiden University Library, Leiden

If the Renaissance obsession with anatomy derived in part from a moral imperative (the anatomist acting as an arm of the coercive state), it also owed something to the wider religious context of Renaissance Europe. In particular, two recent studies of the resurgence of interest in anatomy in northern Europe have focused on the relationship of Lutheranism to the vogue for anatomical reform and the work of Vesalius. That anatomy contained a strong religious dimension has long been evident. Many of the earliest dissections and autopsies, dating from the early fourteenth century in Italy, were carried out in churches. In addition, it was frequently urged by Vesalius and others that knowledge of the human body, created by the Deity in His image, must be conducive to belief in an eternal Creator. This commonplace of Renaissance thought was particularly attractive to the Protestant reformers who gathered

Figure 5.8 A *memento mori* skeleton figure, from Andreas Vesalius, *De humani corporis fabrica ...* , 1543. Wellcome Institute Library, London

around Martin Luther at Wittenberg in the first half of the sixteenth century. It was subsequently developed by one of Luther's most trusted lieutenants, Philipp Melanchthon, to the point where anatomy was destined to perform a central role in the reformed curriculum of the University of Wittenberg.

Exercise

Now read 'Wittenberg anatomy' by Vivian Nutton in the Reader (no. 27). What arguments does Nutton put forward to defend his thesis that Wittenberg anatomy was more concerned with theology than it was with medicine and science?

Discussion

Nutton insists that the medical purpose in the activities and writings of Wittenberg's anatomists went hand in hand with a higher purpose – to demonstrate the operation of the divine in the daily functioning of the human body. He notes that in the Wittenberg scholars' texts little attention was paid to anatomy in relation to disease and surgery, but every opportunity was taken to demonstrate that each person is not a chance collection of atoms but the work of a divine

Creator. Reformers like Melanchthon were keen to emphasize the moral lessons that might be drawn from the dissection of the human body, particularly in relation to the interaction of the body and the soul. Dissections might be used to point to the transitory nature of human life, to show the body as the temple or dwelling-place of the soul and to indicate that the order and function of the body are related to the order and function of the soul. ❖

We are, therefore, forced to confront the possibility that the vogue for anatomy in the Renaissance was motivated as much by moral and theological considerations as it was by the pure spirit of critical scientific enquiry. Without this religious dimension, it is difficult to see how, within the context of sixteenth-century Europe, Vesalian anatomy would have had the influence that it did on contemporary conceptions of how the body worked. In other words, Nutton's understanding of Wittenberg anatomy and its integration within the theological world-view of leading Protestant reformers like Melanchthon is a perfect example of the merits of the externalist approach to the history of Renaissance science.

The general acceptance in scholarly circles of externalist accounts of the rise of modern science marks a profound transition in the way in which historians view the origins of that movement. Nonetheless, the externalist approach is not without its critics, and not just from unreconstructed and old-fashioned internalists. In recent years, there has been a concerted effort on the part of some historians of science to raise even more fundamental issues concerned with how we attempt to see and interpret the science of the past. Integral to this approach is the idea that the categories that we use today to describe the activities of scientists, and the disciplinary boundaries that we take for granted, were themselves the product of nineteenth-century priorities and do not therefore accurately reflect the reality of the sixteenth century. Foremost among these boundaries is the one that is automatically assumed to exist between religion and science. Even externalists, who have argued for a more positive role for religion in the promotion of science, have tended to acknowledge, albeit subconsciously, this essential duality. But, has this led to a distortion of our understanding of past science? Cunningham has argued just such a case.

According to Cunningham, the polarization of religion and science was the obsession of men of the nineteenth century (he specifically implicates Burckhardt), for whom the topic carried great pertinence and weight. But this may not have been the case in the sixteenth century. Taking anatomy as an example, he has recently sought to demonstrate that the *chief* purpose of Renaissance anatomy was not the disinterested investigation of the structure and function of the human body (the orthodox view of historians of science), but rather the attempt to understand more fully the faculties and operations of the soul:

> This soul-obsession of sixteenth-century anatomizing obliges us therefore to look at such anatomizing in a new light. We will not be dealing with science on the one hand, and religion on the other, nor even with mixtures of the two in various proportions; but with an enterprise of investigating Nature which, unlike science today, was itself religiously informed and constituted.
>
> (Cunningham, 1997, p.202)

By putting forward this viewpoint, Cunningham wishes to transform conventional approaches to subjects such as the study of anatomy during the Renaissance. He also firmly believes that it might help to answer certain problems that have so far eluded historians of science of the 'old school'. One in particular that he highlights is: why did particular anatomists seek to revive ancient projects of anatomizing (e.g. Vesalius's emulation of Galen's approach to anatomy) *at this particular time*? For Cunningham, the answer lies not so much in the Renaissance preoccupation with classical precedent (important as this was in furnishing the anatomists with a material starting-point), but rather in religion. Religion provided the motivation and the ideological framework in which it made sense for Vesalius's contemporaries to indulge in dissection. Cunningham's enterprise thus consists of expounding the view that:

> in the Christian world the investigation of Nature, as represented by anatomizing, up to and indeed long beyond the sixteenth century, was an inherently Christian enterprise; that there was no way of investigating Nature, or reason to do so, without religious, or better put, pious, motives; that an individual's religious persuasion provided him with the 'spectacles' through which he saw Nature, and thus for what he saw Nature to be. My position is built on a different understanding from that held by most historians of science, of what kind of enterprise sixteenth-century investigation of Nature was: that it was 'Natural Philosophy', rather than 'science' in its modern understanding.
>
> (Cunningham, 1997, p.206)

Exercise Now read 'Luther and Vesalius' by Andrew Cunningham in the Reader (no. 25).

In a series of case studies, Cunningham attempts to show that the various approaches to anatomy developed in the Renaissance owed a significant debt to the religious environment in which the anatomist worked and lived. Here, he seeks to establish a relationship between Luther and Lutheranism on the one hand, and Vesalius and Vesalian anatomy on the other, which transcends the usual accounts of the success of the latter in sixteenth-century Europe. Make a note of the chief areas of similarity between the two men and their ideas.

Discussion

Broadly speaking, Cunningham sees two points of similarity: one relating to the two men themselves, their lives and careers, and potential points of intersection; the other concerned with a comparison of their respective beliefs and methods.

Of the former, much is made of the fact that both men were born and raised in northern Europe, whose socio-economic, political and urban context was fertile territory for religious and scientific innovation.

Of the latter, Cunningham suggests numerous ways in which the intellectual preoccupations of the two men bear close comparison. Just as Luther saw himself as a reviver of the primitive apostolic church, so Vesalius portrayed himself as a reviver of a purified Galenic medicine. Great play is also made of the comparison between Luther's stress on the singular authority of the Word of God, the Bible, in religion and the emphasis that Vesalius placed on the evidence of the dissected body, which he frequently referred to as a 'text'. Moreover, just as Lutheranism is depicted as a 'hands-on' faith, which encouraged lay involvement in religious worship and communion, so too Vesalian anatomy is predicated on the involvement of the audience in the process of dissection (often through actual physical contact with parts of the body). Finally, both Luther and Vesalius encouraged the use of pictorial and iconographic imagery as a means to get their messages across. ❖

On many levels, this is a compelling and wonderfully insightful analysis. But does it carry full conviction? Although Cunningham would dearly love to show that Vesalius was a closet Lutheran, the surviving evidence is both circumstantial and inconclusive. On the other hand, the close parallel between so many aspects of the two men's approaches to their respective callings is intriguing. Ultimately, for Cunningham, whether or not Vesalius was actually a Lutheran is immaterial. It is the fact that he acts like one, that consciously or not he sought to adopt and adapt the substance and style of Lutheran argument, which is of crucial importance. In the last resort, it is difficult to argue with Cunningham's overall assessment of Renaissance anatomy as an investigative procedure that owed as much to theology as it did to pure science. Moral and theological concerns lay at the root of the anatomists' quest and were clearly shared by the audience, both learned and popular, that crowded into the new anatomical theatres to witness public dissections. In order to understand the Renaissance preoccupation with anatomizing, we must therefore attend more closely to the cultural context in which it took place. For it is the belief of Cunningham and others that the agenda pursued by Vesalius and his colleagues was profoundly shaped by a whole range of factors, many of which had little to do with science in the modern sense of the word.

Renaissance natural philosophy

In rejecting much of the traditional internalist history of early modern science, revisionists have argued for a different nomenclature with which to describe the activities of Renaissance scientists. By referring to 'natural philosophy', it is argued, we stand a better chance of producing a less anachronistic and more accurate assessment of what it was that Renaissance scientists actually did. 'Natural philosophy' was itself the designation used by contemporaries to describe certain aspects of the traditional university curriculum. Subsumed within its title was the study of a range of disciplines that we would today recognize as scientific: astronomy, botany, biology and psychology. But students who studied these aspects of natural philosophy did so for a variety of reasons, ranging from a general desire to acquaint themselves with the broad sweep of human knowledge to preparation for specialist courses and degrees (e.g. in medicine). Many who studied such fields of learning went on to become clergymen or civil servants. Others were the sons of the gentry for whom a broad, general education was increasingly seen in the sixteenth century as an essential prerequisite for the acquisition of gentility.

The chief feature of Renaissance natural philosophy was its dependence on knowledge gathered from books. Scientific research that required hands-on experience was largely frowned upon, particularly since such activity was considered more appropriate for artisans than for the sons of the well-to-do. Book-learning, however, need not be an impediment to the advance of scientific knowledge – a point well illustrated by the recent emphasis that some historians have placed on the central role of humanism in the natural philosophical programme of the sixteenth and seventeenth centuries. The contribution of humanism to medicine – in particular, the rise of a learned and respected medical profession – has already been alluded to. In other spheres, humanism also played a significant part. In botany and zoology, for example, humanist-inspired scholars such as Conrad Gesner (1516–65) produced lavishly illustrated treatises that contained a wealth of scientific information. Much of this literature has been overlooked by historians of science, however, precisely because it does not fit the image of a modern scientific text. Gesner's encyclopaedic *History of Animals* (1551), for instance, is only now receiving its proper due (it was immensely influential in its own day) because historians are willing to see it for what it was, and not for what we think it ought to be. As with anatomy, so with Gesner's zoology, the prime purpose was not to convey an accurate, scientific account of animals, but rather to produce a series of pictures, or emblems, which might be used to convey complex moral, religious, political and other messages (Ashworth, 1990, pp.303–32). The Renaissance fascination with emblem literature eludes modern standards of rationality. In its day, however, it was widely employed, not least by artists and patrons who appropriated similar iconographical schemes for use in the visual arts.

Today, we are used to thinking of science, and scientific investigation, as a specialized pursuit, the preserve of self-appointed experts whose research is performed in purpose-built laboratories. In Renaissance Europe, such boundaries, both professional and locational, were largely non-existent. In part, of course, this reflected a feature of early modern science that we have previously encountered, its bookishness. But it was also an aspect of the wider socio-cultural and political context in which it was deemed appropriate to discuss and analyse the natural world. A prime example of this process is provided by the role of the court as a site of scientific endeavour and research.

Natural philosophy, the court and the role of patronage

In Book 2 in the series, we saw how the Renaissance court acted as a vital stimulus to developments in the visual arts, and how these in turn conveyed political messages, which reflected the priorities of the patron. At the same time, the court acted as an important source of patronage for scientific activity, shaping in the process the nature and direction of much scientific research in this period. Here, once again, we are faced with an unfamiliar scenario: the idea that somehow the generation of scientific knowledge was indebted to factors (political, cultural and institutional) that we would dismiss today as largely irrelevant to the pursuit of science.

From the earliest days of the Renaissance, it was common for powerful princes and rulers to designate specific areas of their courts for the collection of natural objects and exotica. Just as the anatomy theatre might contain diverse assemblages of works of art and other natural curiosities, so too the rooms of kings, princes and wealthy patrons frequently featured 'cabinets of curiosities' (Daston and Park, 1998). In most cases, this desire to assemble all manner of specimens from the animal, mineral and vegetable kingdoms reflected the Renaissance preoccupation with an occult natural philosophy that emphasized the hidden virtues of specific plants or minerals. In order to tap the power of natural objects, it was thought essential to arrange and order them in such a way as to enable them to attract supercelestial powers, which might then be used for the benefit of the patron. Ultimately, of course, such beliefs depended heavily upon the learned revival of magic and astrology, which was one of the main features of Renaissance science and is discussed in more detail in the following chapter.

Nowhere are these trends more apparent than in the court of the Italian princes. Not only were their buildings frequently designed and decorated to accord with contemporary astrological practice, but the day-to-day routines of the prince might equally be conditioned by such thinking. Leonello d'Este of Ferrara (1407–50), for example, was reputed to change his clothes every day of the week so that the colours might correspond to the planets ruling that day. Building works were often begun at astrologically propitious moments, and court festivals and theatrical performances frequently incorporated complex Neoplatonic and magical devices and symbolism, which only the cognoscenti were able to decipher (Rossi, 1991, pp.155–72; Greene, 1987, pp.636–59). On occasions, even princes themselves might indulge in these occult practices. When the essayist Michel de Montaigne (1533–92) visited Florence in 1581, he noted, for instance, that in one of the palaces of the grand duke 'he himself takes pleasure in working at counterfeiting oriental stones and cutting crystal; for he is a prince somewhat interested in alchemy and the mechanical arts, and above all a great architect' (Montaigne, 1983, p.66).

Similar preoccupations loomed large in the courts of the German princes, including those of the Holy Roman emperors. Here, a wide range of 'scientific' pursuits attracted princely patronage, particularly among the Protestant rulers of northern Germany. Mathematics, astronomy and engineering feature prominently in this respect. The court of the landgrave, William IV of Hesse (1532–92), for example, was renowned as a centre of excellence for the study of astronomy. Not only did he correspond with the renowned Danish astronomer, Tycho Brahe (1546–1601), but he was also closely involved in the manufacture of a variety of astronomical machines and clocks. Moreover, many of these activities were clearly motivated by utilitarian ambitions. Patronage of mathematics, both at court and in the new universities founded by Protestant princes in Germany, facilitated the state's growing determination to assess accurately its economic and political resources. Instruction in applied mathematics provided a firm grounding in map-making and surveying – vital features of government in war-torn and divided Germany. Above all, however, it proved invaluable when applied to mining and the metallurgical industries, which were the life-blood of many of the German states. A particularly fine example of such patronage in action is provided by Duke Julius of Braunschweig (1528–89), who both inspired and was directly involved in a project to create special machines to be employed in the mineral-rich mines of the Harz mountains (Moran, 1981, pp.253–74).

The court of Emperor Rudolf II

It is not difficult to see how the cases cited above might fit comfortably into an account of Renaissance science as empirical and progressive. Less satisfactory, however, from this point of view is the court of the Emperor Rudolf II (1576–1612), where concern for scientific pragmatism rubbed shoulders with a range of esoteric pursuits which, from today's perspective, defy easy assimilation. Rudolf's patronage extended to artists, astronomers and various practitioners of the occult arts.

Figure 5.9 Giuseppe Arcimboldo, *Emperor Rudolf II as Vertumnus*, c.1591. Skokloster Castle, Sweden. Bridgeman Art Library, London

It was at Rudolf's court in Prague that the celebrated astronomer, Johannes Kepler (1571–1630), an émigré from the Counter-Reformation in Graz, was to produce his most creative and original scientific work. Between 1600 and 1612, Kepler formulated his controversial three laws on the motions of the heavenly bodies, which appeared in print in 1609 with a dedication to the emperor. But Kepler's remodelled Copernicanism was imbued with ideas and beliefs that defy modern scientific logic. Throughout his career, he was attracted to mystical, quasi-scientific streams of thought, which owed more to a faith in a divinely ordered and harmonious universe than to simple scientific inductivism. Kepler was typical of the eclectic spirit of his patron, the emperor, who surrounded himself with men of learning from every field of Renaissance arts and sciences. More often than not, the aims and objectives of the artists and natural philosophers whom Rudolf employed coincided with the wider religious and political concerns of the emperor.

The court of Rudolf II, and the imperial patronage of scholars and practitioners from all avenues of human learning and the arts, suggests once more that, if we are to understand Renaissance science aright, we must acknowledge its complete integration with all other aspects of early modern life. Our contemporary definitions as to what constitutes science simply do not apply when attempting to decipher as complex a figure as Rudolf. In the late sixteenth century, Rudolf's court at Prague constituted one of the most important centres of free, intellectual debate in Europe (Evans, 1984). Scholars and artists from all over the continent were attracted there to ply their trade and demonstrate their skills before the emperor. During the 1580s, for example, two Englishmen, John Dee (1527–1608) and Edward Kelley (1555–95), were in residence when they attempted to persuade the emperor of their ability to communicate with angels. Dee was no crank or charlatan. He was the most senior natural philosopher at the court of Queen Elizabeth I (1558–1603), and was renowned throughout Europe as an *adeptus* – one steeped in the wisdom of the ancient philosophers, and whose skills ranged from applied mathematics to alchemical and other forms of occult wisdom.

Of all the arts that attracted the emperor's attention, the most influential was alchemy. This was described by Rudolf's biographer as 'the greatest passion of the age in Central Europe' (Evans, 1984, p.199), and the language and imagery of the alchemist's art were a recurring theme in Rudolfine Prague. The search for the 'philosopher's stone', a substance that might enable people to transmute base metals into gold, was an ancient one, indebted to medieval as well as Renaissance authorities. During the course of the sixteenth century, interest in alchemy was further boosted by the popular writings of Paracelsus (1493–1541) and his followers, who rapidly made converts throughout central Europe. The Paracelsians were not just committed to alchemical speculation but evolved a new school of medical thought, which was directly opposed to Galenism and which proposed a novel form of therapy based on the chemical preparation of medicines (iatrochemistry). As we shall see in the following chapter, there was also a religious dimension to Paracelsism, one that was peculiarly attractive to men like Rudolf. For not only did alchemists seek to regenerate metals through the use of the 'stone', but they also invoked it as an allegory for the spiritual and moral rebirth of mankind.

The search for a solution to the religious and political divisions in the Holy Roman empire ushered in by the Reformation was high on the agenda of Rudolf II. The emperor was temperamentally and ideologically averse to physical coercion as a means of settling the deep religious divisions within his vast empire, and was consequently attracted to ideas in the arts and the sciences that appeared to promise a 'magical' solution to the problems of his age. In particular, what the emperor sought was the goal of religious peace and political unity, and an end to religious extremism and inter-confessional conflict. Increasingly, in common with many of his contemporaries, he found a potential panacea for the ills of his age in the occult programme of astrologers, alchemists and natural magicians. The idea that harmony between men might be achieved through the alchemical exploration of the natural world is a distinctly odd notion from the vantage-point of the twenty-first century. Yet, in its day, such a belief exerted a tremendous grip on the minds of great intellects, including those whom today we might wish to classify as scientists. It clearly motivated the patronage of a man such as Rudolf. We can now better appreciate, perhaps, why politically powerful men like the emperor sought to surround themselves with all manner of natural objects, artificial devices and heavily symbolic works of art (such as those produced by the court painter, Giuseppe Arcimboldo (c.1530–93), see Figure 5.9). By collecting examples of the divinely created universe and displaying them in their unique relationship to each other in 'cabinets of curiosities' or specially designed rooms, patrons like Rudolf sought two goals. First, they looked to appropriate the 'magical' powers inherent in such objects and to use them for practical ends (e.g. as talismans). And secondly (and more importantly one suspects for Rudolf himself), they sought to restore religious and political unity in Europe through the contemplation of the natural world. Nature, they believed, as the creation of God, was fundamentally informed by the principle of cosmic harmony (Evans, 1984, pp.243–55).

Figure 5.10 The private natural history museum of Francesco Calzolari, from Benedetto Ceruti and Andrea Chiocco, *Musaeum Francisci Calceolari Iunioris Veronensis*, Verona, 1622. Bibliotheca Universitaria Bologna, Bologna

Galileo, the Medici, and scientific patronage in Renaissance Italy

I want to conclude this chapter on Renaissance science with a brief case study of one of the greatest scientific figures of the age, Galileo. In particular, we shall be looking at how Galileo's science and his own image of himself as a scientist may have been shaped by forces that on first reflection would appear to have little obvious relation to his scientific work – in this case, the court and the patronage of the Medici, the grand dukes of Tuscany.[4] Galileo is best remembered today as an astronomer who, through the invention of the telescope, was able to provide conclusive proof for the heliocentric hypothesis first put forward by Copernicus in 1543. For this and other

---

[4] The Medici were members of a Florentine family, who amassed great wealth from banking during the fourteenth and fifteenth centuries. In 1537, they acquired the title of dukes of Florence, and later grand dukes of Tuscany, transforming the republic into a principality.

Figure 5.11 Leoni Ottavio, *Galileo Galilei*. Biblioteca Marucelliana, Florence. Scala, Florence

achievements he rightly holds a prominent place in the pantheon of the scientific revolution. In traditional accounts, Galileo is portrayed as a 'modern' battling against the superstitions and prejudices of his age. Ultimately, under pressure from the Inquisition, he was forced to recant his scientific beliefs, an episode frequently invoked to epitomize the conflict between religion and science in early modern Europe. But his views lived on, popularized by later adherents, who pointed to the proofs he left behind in the form of his published works and the observations he recorded through his use of the telescope.

But is this an accurate assessment of Galileo the scientist? Recent research into what we might term the socio-cultural roots of his work as a natural philosopher has produced a different and, in many respects, more rounded view of the man and the world of learning he inhabited in the formative years of his career as a scientist. In particular, much has been made of his role as a courtier at the court of the Medici. This, it has been suggested, played as large a part in legitimating his scientific findings as did the actual 'scientific' proofs that appeared in his published writings (Biagioli, 1993). The court of a great prince – as we have seen with Rudolf II – offered more than just a convenient space, with salary, for the scientific courtier to indulge in research. In the case of Galileo, it may well have provided the vital boost to his status that enabled him to disseminate his proofs of the heliocentric system to a Europe-wide audience.

Exercise

Read 'Galileo's early career' by Mario Biagioli in the Reader (no. 30i). This provides a brief synopsis of Galileo's career up to 1610, prefaced by a summary of recent research into the status of mathematics in Renaissance circles.

1 Why was the study of mathematics accorded low status in the academies and universities of early modern Europe?

2 How did this affect Galileo's early career, and what strategies were available to him in order that he might overcome these barriers to professional advancement?

Discussion

1 There were two main barriers to the promotion of mathematics as a high-status subject in the universities of Renaissance Europe. First, an epistemological one, which stressed that mathematics was subordinate to philosophy and theology. The study of the physical dimensions of natural phenomena, along with the causes of change and motion in the natural world, was the domain of the philosophers. Those who taught mathematics lacked the intellectual status and authority with which to promote new theories in these studies. (This, Biagioli implies, was one of the reasons why Copernicus's attempt to reform astronomy was treated with indifference.) And secondly, underpinning the hierarchical deference of mathematics to philosophy lay the fact that the former was 'perceived as a technical ... discipline'. Put another way, mathematics was insufficiently 'bookish' in orientation, its practitioners frequently having to resort to practical applications of the subject (surveying, designing and building military fortifications, book-keeping, etc.) in order to make a living.

2 Galileo needed some form of social legitimation for his intellectual pursuits. For a trained mathematician like Galileo, who wished to overcome the institutionalized barriers to academic advancement and to promote his novel scientific conclusions, an obvious strategy was to seek legitimation through the auspices of the princely court. Here, the professional demarcation disputes, which consistently undermined the ability of mathematicians to be treated on equal terms with their colleagues in 'higher' faculties such as philosophy, no longer operated. Instead, professional legitimation lay in the gift of the princely patron, whose support alone was sufficient to bestow intellectual merit upon the client and his scientific endeavours. ❖

The process whereby Galileo made the crucial breakthrough from relative obscurity to court natural philosopher began in 1609. In that year, as a professor of mathematics at the University of Pisa (a

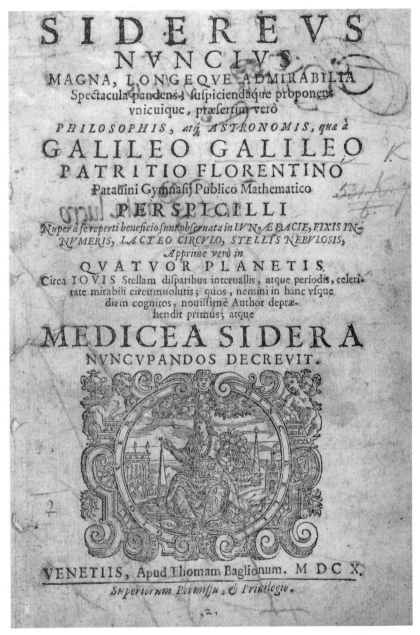

Figure 5.12 Title page of Galileo Galilei, *Sidereus nuncius*, 1610. © The Trustees of the British Library, London

Medicean foundation), Galileo used his new telescope to make a number of important astronomical discoveries. These were subsequently published in his *Sidereus nuncius* (*The Starry Messenger*) of 1610, which he dedicated to Cosimo II de' Medici (1590–1620).

The discoveries enunciated in this book subverted the traditional Aristotelian cosmology, which was firmly rooted in the geocentric system (although it should be pointed out that nowhere did Galileo explicitly declare himself in favour of Copernicanism). They included discussion of his observation of the imperfections of the moon (as a planet, it was held by Aristotelians to lie in a sphere above the earth immune from imperfection); his discovery of numerous new stars; and, most importantly, his discovery of four new 'planets' circling not the earth but the planet Jupiter, which he named the 'Medicean stars'. Within months of publication, Galileo was called to the court of Cosimo at Florence. Cosimo viewed Galileo's findings with approval, and he was rewarded with an honorary teaching position at Pisa (with few duties, and a large salary), as well as the title of philosopher to the Grand Duke himself.

Now Galileo was in a position to advance his controversial astronomical claims – in particular his hitherto suppressed support for Copernicanism – despite the fact that his new-found patron showed little interest in such speculations. Galileo was rewarded by Cosimo because he provided the Medici with a valuable gift, an exotic and powerfully symbolic present, which satisfied the political and cultural requirements of the new ruling house. The precise nature or scientific status of Galileo's work was neither here nor there. In order to appreciate this point more fully, we must look at the court of the Medici as it was newly founded in the mid sixteenth century by Cosimo I (1519–74). Only then can we truly appreciate the purpose of Galileo's strategy in dedicating his discovery of the Medicean stars to the recently established dynasty.

Exercise

Read 'Galileo and the Medicean stars' by Mario Biagioli in the Reader (no. 30ii). Then read the brief extract from Galileo's preface to *The Starry Messenger* in the Anthology (no. 88).

1   From a scientific point of view, what is distinctive about the language that Galileo uses in discussing his recent discoveries?

2   How might this have been shaped by the Medicean predilection for mythological and astrological speculation, as described by Biagioli?

Discussion

1   The emphasis in Galileo's dedication is not on the originality of his discovery nor its significance for astronomy, but rather on the fact of its confirmation of the destiny of the Medici, which had been prefigured in the stars. Galileo throughout places inordinate stress on the language of astrological determinism. His own discovery of the stars, he says, was no chance encounter but one predestined by the stars themselves: Galileo and the Medici had

been brought together by the stars, which had not been 'discovered', but rather 'encountered'.

2 The clear implication of Biagioli's analysis of the Medicean predilection for mythology and astrology is that Galileo's strategy of dedicating the planets to his patron was predicated on his full understanding of the meaning and significance that his patron attached to such emblems and devices. Only via the medium of the court could Galileo have acquired this knowledge and the subsequent opportunity to present his discovery in the appropriate manner. ❖

DI M. GIOVIO. 57

altroue il premio del pallio, con vn motto di sopra in lingua Spagnuola, NON BVELVO SIN VEN-CER. *che vuol dire; Io non ritorno in dietro senza vittoria, secondo quel verso, che dice,*

    Rhinoceros nunquam victus ab hoste redit.

E parue, che questa impresa gli piacesse, tanto che la fece intagliare di lauoro d'agimia nel corpo della sua corazza.

DOM. *Poi che voi hauete raccontate l'imprese di questi illustrissimi Prencipi della Casa de' Medici già morti, siate contento anchora di dir qualche cosa di quelle, che porta l'Eccellentissimo Signor Duca Cosmo, delle quali tante se ne veggono in palazzo de' detti Medici.* GIO. *Certo che il giorno delle nozze sue io*

           D 5

Figure 5.13 Capricorn over Florence, from Paolo Giovio, *Dialogo delle impresse militari et amorese*, 1574. © The Trustees of the British Library, London

What we are witnessing here, in the words of Biagioli, is an example of Renaissance 'self-fashioning', that process whereby a new persona is adopted using the existing social and cultural codes of the age. In this case, it is argued, Galileo successfully refashioned for himself a new identity – that of radical natural philosopher – by manipulating the environment in which he lived and worked.

In the process, it is urged, not only was Galileo the scientist indebted to the court and the demands of the patron–client network, but his scientific findings were themselves the product of powerful socio-cultural forces focused on the court:

> Galileo did not win over his audience by explaining the optical behaviour of the telescope, to prove that it did not deceive the viewers, or by introducing a full-fledged alternative epistemology to Aristotle's in order to legitimize the use of instrument-mediated sense data. Instead, he tried to bring to closure the debate over the reliability of the telescope ... by tying the Medici's image to his discoveries and by mobilizing the resources available through their diplomatic networks.
>
> (Biagioli, 1993, p.96)

Consequently, if we accept this argument, there are grounds for believing that it was not only Renaissance science that was formed by the wider social and cultural environment in which contemporary scientists lived. In many cases, social and cultural factors may even have dictated the fate of certain discoveries and inventions that have acquired in recent times a canonical status in the eyes of historians.

Conclusion

The case studies of Vesalius and Galileo clearly indicate that the process of medical and scientific innovation in the Renaissance was a complex affair. Recent accounts of such great thinkers have tried to elucidate their scientific work by construing it firmly within the context of contemporary social, religious and political concerns, rather than extracting and distancing these individuals from the society in which they lived and worked. In the process, we are led to the view that the creation of scientific knowledge is frequently contingent and conditional upon historically specific circumstances. No longer are men like Vesalius and Galileo reduced to the role of scientific geniuses working in isolation from, and in opposition to, the rest of the world. In place of the old dominant historiographical tradition in science, a new model of historical enquiry seeks to dominate the stage. In the words of one of its foremost practitioners:

> Putting hindsight behind them, today's historical scholars have sought to abandon time-honoured but question-begging 'before/after' explanatory models: from darkness to light, from error to truth, from superstition to religion, from magic to science. Instructed by cultural anthropology and by new trends in the sociology of knowledge, the accent nowadays is not upon plotting the triumphal progress of truth, but upon interpreting structures of belief.
>
> (Porter, 1991, p.3)

Looked at in this way, scientific knowledge is considered no different from any other form of knowledge: 'Historically understood, it is local, it is plural, it embodies interests, it mobilizes the claims of groups and classes, and, above all, it is recruited willy nilly, on all sides in wars of truth' (Porter, 1991, p.3). Consequently, for science to succeed, its practitioners had no choice but to engage with the world, a point graphically illustrated in the case studies of Vesalius and Galileo. Similar approaches have been extended to other 'scientific giants' of this era. Copernicus's preface to his masterpiece, *De revolutionibus*, for example, has recently been the subject of a brilliant study, which seeks to demonstrate the profound debt of Copernicus – a Polish cleric – to Erasmian humanism. This alignment was no empty gesture on Copernicus's part. On the contrary, it formed part of a complex strategy to seek the support and patronage of the reformist wing of the Catholic church in Rome, led by the man to whom the book was dedicated, Pope Paul III (1534–49) (Westman, 1990, pp.167–205). The fact that the publication of Copernicus's revolutionary hypotheses provoked relatively little debate in clerical circles in the years immediately after 1543 may be attributed, in part at least, to the success of Copernicus's original strategy.

A further consequence of this historiographical revolution is a tendency to view science, and its practice, in the Renaissance as no longer confined to well-established and mutually exclusive philosophical traditions. Most scientists of this period, we are increasingly aware, operated without concern for such boundaries and were far more eclectic in their approach than historians have hitherto acknowledged. The dominant scientific philosophies of the era – Aristotelianism, Neoplatonism and Hermeticism – were never precisely defined, and frequently overlapped. Moreover, individual natural philosophers characteristically borrowed from each tradition according to the need of the moment, seemingly unconcerned by any potential charge of philosophical inconsistency. This state of affairs has led one historian to refer to the sixteenth century as a 'century of confusion' in terms of its science (Hall, 1983, p.73). If so, then it is best acknowledged that the confusion is largely ours as we try to comprehend how men of the stature of Vesalius struggled to incorporate ancient systems of thought into their 'modern' approaches to science.

One final conclusion might be drawn from this brief foray into the realm of Renaissance science. Rather than thinking in terms of 'wrong' or 'correct' science, we might be better served by opting to accept the existence of numerous competing approaches to the study of the natural world in the Renaissance, each of which in its own way contributed to the emergence of new scientific knowledge and understanding. Today, the majority of historians of science no longer believe that modern science began when the authority of Aristotle, or that of the occult philosophers, was displaced. Correspondingly, modern scholars are far more sympathetic to the explanatory appeal and the inner logic of these bodies of thought than earlier accounts, which dismissed them as either erroneous or 'superstitious'. In considering an age that was so manifestly scarred by intellectual conflict and debate, we shall need to tread carefully if we wish to discriminate between 'good' and 'bad' science, and to allocate medals to proponents of the former. On current evidence, the distinction would appear to be historically inadmissible: a conclusion that we shall seek to put to the test in the next chapter when we confront one of the most problematic aspects of Renaissance science and culture, the fascination with magic, demonology and witchcraft.

Bibliography

ASHWORTH, JR, W.B. (1990) 'Natural history and the emblematic world view' in D.C. Lindberg and R.S. Westman (eds) *Reappraisals of the Scientific Revolution*, Cambridge, Cambridge University Press, pp.303–32.

BIAGIOLI, M. (1993) *Galileo, Courtier: The Practice of Science in the Culture of Absolutism*, Chicago and London, University of Chicago Press.

BURCKHARDT, J. (1990) *The Civilization of the Renaissance in Italy*, trans. S.G.C. Middlemore, Harmondsworth, Penguin; first published 1860.

COPENHAVER, B.P. (1987) 'Science and philosophy in early modern Europe: the historiographical significance of the work of Charles B. Schmitt', *Annals of Science*, vol. 44, pp.507–17.

CUNNINGHAM, A. (1997) *The Anatomical Renaissance: The Resurrection of the Anatomical Projects of the Ancients*, Aldershot, Scolar Press.

DASTON, L. and PARK, K. (1998) *Wonders and the Order of Nature, 1150–1750*, New York, Zone Books.

EVANS, R.J.W. (1984) *Rudolf II and His World: A Study in Intellectual History 1576–1612*, Oxford, Clarendon Press.

FERRARI, G. (1987) 'Public anatomy lessons and the carnival: the anatomy theatre of Bologna', *Past and Present*, vol. 117, pp.50–106.

GREENE, T.M. (1987) 'Magic and festivity at the Renaissance court', *Renaissance Quarterly*, vol. 40, pp.636–59.

HALL, A.R.(1983) *The Revolution in Science 1500–1750*, London, Longman.

HECKSCHER, W.S. (1958) *Rembrandt's Anatomy of Dr Nicholaas Tulp*, New York, New York University Press.

KESSLER, E. (1990) 'The transformation of Aristotelianism during the Renaissance' in J. Henry and S. Hutton (eds) *New Perspectives on Renaissance Thought: Essays in the History of Science, Education and Philosophy in Memory of Charles B. Schmitt*, London, Duckworth, pp.137–47.

MONTAIGNE, M. (1983) *Montaigne's Travel Journal*, trans. D.M. Frame, San Francisco, North Point Press.

MORAN, B.T. (1981) 'German prince practitioners: aspects in the development of courtly science, technology and procedures in the Renaissance', *Technology and Culture*, vol. 22, pp.253–74.

PARK, K. (1994) 'The criminal and the saintly body: autopsy and dissection in Renaissance Italy', *Renaissance Quarterly*, vol. 47, pp.1–33.

PORTER, R. (1991) 'Introduction' in S. Pumfrey, P.L. Rossi and M. Slawinski (eds) *Science, Culture and Popular Belief in Renaissance Europe*, Manchester and New York, Manchester University Press, pp.1–15.

ROSSI, P. (1991) 'Society, culture and the dissemination of learning' in S. Pumfrey, P.L. Rossi and M. Slawinski (eds) *Science, Culture and Popular Belief in Renaissance Europe*, Manchester and New York, Manchester University Press, pp.143–75.

RUPP, J.C.C. (1990) 'Matters of life and death: the social and cultural conditions of the rise of anatomical theatres with special reference to seventeenth-century Holland', *History of Science*, vol. 28, pp.263–87.

SAWDAY, J. (1995) *The Body Emblazoned: Dissection and the Human Body in Renaissance Culture*, London, Routledge.

SCHMITT, C.B. (1983) *Aristotle and the Renaissance*, Cambridge, Mass. and London, Harvard University Press.

VICKERS, B. (1984) 'Introduction' and 'Analogy versus identity: the rejection of occult symbolism, 1580–1680' in B. Vickers (ed.) *Occult and Scientific Mentalities in the Renaissance*, Cambridge, Cambridge University Press, pp.1–55, 95–163.

VICKERS, B. (1991) 'On the goal of the occult sciences in the Renaissance' in G. Kauffmann (ed.) *Die Renaissance im Blick der Nationen Europas*, Wiesbaden, Otto Harrassowitz, pp.51–93.

WESTMAN, R.S. (1990) 'Proof, poetics, and patronage: Copernicus' preface to *De Revolutionibus*' in D.C. Lindberg and R.S. Westman (eds) *Reappraisals of the Scientific Revolution*, Cambridge, Cambridge University Press, pp.167–205.

Anthology and Reader sources

Nancy G. Siraisi, The old and the new: *The Clock and the Mirror: Girolamo Cardano and Renaissance Medicine*, Princeton, Princeton University Press, 1997, pp.94–7. (Reader, no. 28)

Vivian Nutton, Wittenberg anatomy: O.P. Grell and A. Cunningham (eds) *Medicine and the Reformation*, Routledge, London and New York, 1993, chapter 1, pp.11–12, 16–26. (Reader, no. 27)

Andrew Cunningham, Luther and Vesalius: *The Anatomical Renaissance: The Resurrection of the Anatomical Projects of the Ancients*, Scolar Press, Aldershot, 1997, chapter 8, pp.216–36. (Reader, no. 25)

Mario Biagioli, (i) Galileo's early career and (ii) Galileo and the Medicean stars: *Galileo, Courtier: The Practice of Science in the Culture of Absolutism*, University of Chicago Press, London and Chicago, 1993, pp.5–8, 106–12. (Reader, no. 30)

Galileo Galilei, The Starry Messenger (1610): *Telescopes, Tides, and Tactics: A Galilean Dialogue about the Starry Messenger and the Systems of the World*, ed. S. Drake, University of Chicago Press, London and Chicago, 1985, pp.12–16. (Anthology, no. 88)

CHAPTER SIX

The 'dark side': occult philosophy, magic and witchcraft

BY PETER ELMER

Objectives

The objectives of this chapter are that you should:

- become familiar with some of the historical debates surrounding the place of science, magic and witchcraft in the Renaissance;
- assess and contextualize the role of demonology in Renaissance society.

Introduction

If Burckhardt struggled to find a place for science in his seminal study of Renaissance culture, he was positively bamboozled by the prospect of accounting for the revival of interest in magic and witchcraft in fifteenth- and sixteenth-century Italy (1990, pp.232–44). Burckhardt's rejection of what we might term, for the sake of simplicity, **occult philosophy** is, however, no longer held valid by the majority of scholars working in the field of early modern science. For a variety of reasons, it is now generally accepted that scholarly investigation of the **occult sciences** has helped to create a more rounded and historically sensitive picture of early modern culture and thought, and one less disposed to judge past beliefs from the perspective of the present. Critically, it is now commonplace to acknowledge the role which disciplines such as alchemy, astrology and natural magic played in the scientific work of such towering giants as Johann Kepler, Francis Bacon, Robert Boyle and Isaac Newton. Rigid boundaries demarcating 'science' from 'magic' or 'superstition' have generally disappeared from the vocabulary of historians of early modern science. Instead, we are increasingly urged to envisage the roots of the scientific revolution of the seventeenth century in the complex interplay of diverse scientific traditions and methodologies which proliferated in the Renaissance.

Though the debate over the origins of modern science, and the role of the occult sciences in that movement of ideas, continues to fascinate scholars of the period, new avenues of research have opened up other meanings and potential applications for the study of occult philosophy. In the previous chapter, for example, we saw how deeply integrated alchemy and astrology were in the rituals and practices of the court, and how these might even suggest solutions to the religious and political controversies of the age. No longer denigrated as relics of medieval superstition, the practice of alchemists, astrologers and natural magicians is now seen as a valuable historical resource for the exploration of cultural meaning in the Renaissance, one as frequently invoked by art and literary historians as it is by historians of science. In addition, study of such ideas has also proved an invaluable source for those historians interested in the intersection of popular and learned belief in the Renaissance. As we shall see in the two case studies in this chapter, it is no longer viable for historians to assume automatically that the 'people' were the passive consumers of an elite culture which conditioned their belief and everyday practice. Magic and witchcraft provide a useful corrective to this over-simplified view and help to demonstrate that the relationship between learned and popular culture in the Renaissance was one characterized by a greater degree of symbiotic cross-fertilization than was previously expected. In examining some of these issues through the medium of case studies of the Paracelsian revolution in medicine and Renaissance demonology, we should be better placed not only to provide a more accurate account of the origins of the scientific revolution in the Renaissance, but also to arrive at a more rounded and complete picture of the cultural vitality of early modern society.

Occult philosophy and Renaissance science

Study of the Renaissance preoccupation with occult philosophy was largely stimulated by the seminal research of Frances Yates in the 1960s. She concluded that the origins of the scientific revolution of the seventeenth century were firmly rooted in the resurgence of interest in what she termed hermeticism or the hermetic philosophy in the previous century and a half (Yates, 1964). Originating in the Neoplatonic academy of Marsilio Ficino at Florence, hermeticism was the study of the recently revived writings of the ancient seer Hermes Trismegistus (Figures 6.1 and 6.2), who, it was widely believed, was a contemporary of Moses and a distant intellectual ancestor of Plato.[1]

[1] The writings of Hermes Trismegistus were in fact the product of Christian Platonists working in the second and third centuries CE. They were not accurately dated until the early seventeenth century.

The hermetic texts were an eclectic mix of theology and magic which, according to Yates, encouraged an active approach to the study of the divine creation through the pursuit of what she saw as the quintessential sciences of the age: alchemy, astrology and natural magic. There now exists a copious literature in support of the so-called 'Yates thesis' which has dominated much recent work on the history of Renaissance science.

Figure 6.1 Jean Theodor de Bry, *Hermes Trismegistus (Ermete Trismegisto)*, engraving, from Jean-Jacques Boissard, *De divinatione et magicis praestigiis*, 1616. Reproduced in Pierre Mussard, *Historia deorum fatidicorum ...*, 1675, Geneva, Chovet, p.74. Photo: Mary Evans Picture Library, London

Figure 6.2 Pinturicchio, *Hermes Trismegistus Seated Beneath an Armillary Sphere While Talking with Astronomers*, from a fresco in the Borgia apartments in the Vatican, Rome. Photo: Alinari-Anderson, Florence

Inevitably, however, some scholars have rejected important elements of Yates's work, and that of her 'followers', and have called for a reappraisal of the role of hermetic or occult philosophy in early modern science. In particular, Brian Vickers has consistently sought to discredit Yates's original argument, contending that her 'thesis' is 'almost wholly unfounded' (1984, p.6). The core of Vickers's argument lies in his failure to detect in the Renaissance revival of hermetic and Neoplatonic thought any vestige of what we might consider today to constitute modern scientific method:

> We do not find the Neoplatonists studying the behaviour of falling bodies, taxonomising plants, or dissecting the human body simply to find out why these things are as they are. Their lack of interest in the physical world goes along with a positive distaste for quantification: Symbolic arithmetic, attributing moral values to numbers, was acceptable, but anything to do with measurement or computation was rejected as mundane or ephemeral.
>
> (Vickers, 1984, p.6)

Vickers's radical refutation of Yates is not shared by most scholars working in this field, though many have proposed subtle refinements to her original 'thesis'. Brian Copenhaver, for example, has suggested a number of modifications, including a plea for greater sensitivity among scholars to the terminology which should be employed in these debates. In particular, he has proposed that the adjective 'hermetic' should be applied exclusively to those texts (largely non-magical in character) which were supposedly written by Hermes Trismegistus, preferring in its place 'occult' as a descriptive term to encompass the various sub-branches of learning, such as alchemy, astrology and natural magic. In order to underline the point, he cites, for example, the way in which natural magic cuts across philosophical boundaries:

> no idea of natural magic susceptible to rigorous and detailed historical analysis can be said to be 'Hermetic', as opposed to 'Peripatetic' [i.e. Aristotelian] or 'Stoic' or 'Galenic' or 'Neoplatonic'.
>
> (Copenhaver, 1990, p.281)

Though problems also surround the use of the term 'occult' to describe the revival of Renaissance interest in magic and related beliefs, it is the formulation which I shall adopt throughout the rest of this chapter.[2]

While debate still rages over the validity of the 'Yates thesis', few historians would quibble with the view, popularized by Yates and others, that the occult sciences experienced a dramatic renaissance of their own in the fifteenth and sixteenth centuries. To a large extent indebted to the revival of Neoplatonism in fifteenth-century Florence, disciplines such as astrology and natural magic rapidly acquired an intellectual status and social prominence in the world of cultured and educated Italians. Such ideas are frequently encountered in the art of the period. It is important to remember, however, that *adepti* (skilled ones) in these arts were also serving what was perceived as an important technological

---

[2] The term 'occult' in Renaissance discourse simply refers to that which is hidden or unsusceptible to the normal methods of scientific investigation. It does not necessarily imply, however, magical or forbidden knowledge. Thus Aristotelian scholars, working within the traditional medieval system of natural philosophy, possessed a concept of occult causation which was entirely naturalistic and non-demonic.

function. Astrology and natural magic (e.g. the construction of talismans) represented a powerful resource with which to manipulate occult (hidden) forces in nature (Eamon, 1983). They were treated with the utmost seriousness by the vast majority of the educated populace and, in the case of astrology, formed part of the formal training of the learned physician. Much the same can be said for alchemy. Predicated on the belief that there was a natural hierarchy of metals (with gold at the pinnacle), the aim of the alchemist was to speed up, by art, the natural process whereby baser metals aspired to evolve into their higher forms. In addition, alchemy possessed potentially useful applications to the study and cure of disease. It was widely believed, for example, that the discovery of the 'philosopher's stone' (the mysterious formula which would convert base metals into gold) would also provide a universal cure for all human sickness.

Figure 6.3 Niccolò Fiorentino, *Giovanni Pico della Mirandola*, c.1495, medal, obverse. Photo: © The Trustees of the British Museum, London

As learned interest in revived occult science began to spread in the Renaissance, a lively debate ensued as to the legitimacy of various aspects of the work of its practitioners. Many of those who were initially attracted to the technological potential of alchemy, astrology and natural magic frequently repented and became its most trenchant critics (Borchardt, 1990). Others were clearly mindful of the very real dangers implicit in pursuing such studies. Something of the ambivalence of the age toward the occult arts is suggested by the case of the celebrated Italian scholar, Giovanni Pico della Mirandola (1463–94) (Figure 6.3). Of natural magic, he wrote, it had two forms:

> one of which depends entirely on the work and authority of demons, a thing to be abhorred, so help me the god of truth, and a monstrous thing. The other, when it is rightly pursued, is nothing else than the utter perfection of natural philosophy ... as the former makes man the bound slave of wicked powers, so does the latter make him their ruler and lord.

> (quoted in Burke, 1987, p.184)

Pico was in fact one of those who did, ultimately, speak out against the contemporary fascination with astrology. In doing so, he was almost certainly influenced by a growing current of religious opinion in late fifteenth-century Italy (and probably elsewhere in Europe) which was hostile to the impious and excessive claims of the various practitioners of the occult arts. Alchemy, astrology, natural magic and related practices were indeed susceptible to religious opposition on a number of grounds. Biblical prohibition of magic and divination weighed heavily with many critics, including charismatic and influential preachers such as the Franciscan St Bernardino of Siena (1380–1444) and Girolamo Savonarola (Paton, 1991). They, and many others, pointed to the destructive ends to which magic, for example, might be applied, invoking the spectre of witchcraft. Equally disturbing, moreover, was the fear that a number of magicians employed wicked spirits, or demons, to carry out their purposes. Throughout the Renaissance, accusations of demonism (the employment of evil spirits in the natural world), necromancy (raising spirits from the dead) and witchcraft (which characteristically assumed a pact with the devil) were commonly levelled against those who dabbled in the various branches of the occult arts. A good example is provided by the English **magus** John Dee (1527–1608) (Figure 6.4). As a young man studying at Cambridge, Dee acquired a reputation as an evil magician because of the spectacular mechanical devices which he created for a performance of a play by Aristophanes (French, 1972, p.24). His subsequent career as a natural magician –

Figure 6.4 Anon., *John Dee*, c.1594. Ashmolean Museum, Oxford

in particular his celebrated encounters with 'angels' – did little to dispel rumours in some quarters that Dee's magic was sinister and that the real source of his angelic wisdom was the devil and his minions.

The example of Dee also illustrates another important theme of recent historical scholarship in Renaissance occultism. Since the publication of the biography of Dee by Peter French (1972), it has been common to represent Dee as the archetypal Renaissance magus, a master of the occult arts, whose profound attachment to the hermetic revival heralded a new spirit of scientific enquiry. Though recent research into Dee has not sought to deny the influence of this tradition on him, it has nonetheless suggested a radical reappraisal of the nature and extent of its impact upon Dee's natural philosophy (Clulee, 1988). Two aspects of this work demand particular notice, not simply for the light which they shed on Dee, but also for their general application to the study of Renaissance science. First, close study of the sources of Dee's scientific preoccupations demonstrates the broad eclecticism of his scholarly interests. He was not exclusively, nor even primarily, a devotee of the refined Neoplatonic magic most commonly associated with the Renaissance. Among the various traditions upon which he drew, those of medieval and Arabic natural philosophers – the scholastic interpreters of Aristotle – were seemingly just as important as the more recently recovered writings on magic of the Neoplatonists. In particular, the natural magic of the English Franciscan Roger Bacon (1214–94) stands out as a major influence upon Dee throughout his long career. And second, there is the question of the purpose behind Dee's exploration of Renaissance natural magic. Now, we are told, his interest in such thought was not motivated by a 'scientific' impulse, or a desire to understand the natural world better, but rather by the idea of magic as a 'vehicle for spiritual illumination' (Clulee, 1988, p.236). For Dee then, the Renaissance magical tradition, and occult philosophy, was an important aspect of his eclectic and wide-ranging world-view, though one mainly confined to his religious search for truth:

> The more these concerns became predominant, the more he moved toward natural philosophy as theology and magic as religion. Whatever the possibilities for science were within various kinds of magic, as Dee understood it and its Renaissance sources, magic was religious and not scientific.
>
> (Clulee, 1988, p.237)

This brief excursion into the realm of esoteric systems of knowledge has suggested once again that any simple relationship between the emergence of modern science and the culture of the Renaissance is

Figure 6.5 *Scenes of Alchemical Activity Presided Over by Geber, Arnoldus of Villanova, Rhazes and Hermes Trismegistus*, from Elias Ashmole, *Theatrum Chemicum Britannicum*, 1652. This engraving, based on a fifteenth-century English alchemical manuscript, illustrates the eclectic nature of the Renaissance fascination with alchemy. Geber (fl. eighth century) and Rhazes (fl. ninth century) were Arab alchemists whose works were extremely popular in this period. Arnoldus of Villanova (c.1235–1316) was a Catalan physician. British Library, London

both elusive and ill-conceived. Traditional historiography, which assumed a lineal descent in western science from sterile scholasticism (medieval), through the occult revival (Renaissance) to the mechanical philosophy of Newton (modern), is increasingly viewed as overly simplistic. As the example of Dee implies, the research agendas of 'scientists' were frequently shaped to a frustrating degree by a wide-ranging philosophical eclecticism which owed as much to medieval precedents as it did to the innovations of Renaissance scholars. Equally frustrating from a modern perspective, we also have to wrestle with the possibility that 'men of science' like Dee were as likely to invoke magical texts, not for their technological content, but rather to assist in their religious and spiritual development. As we saw in the case of the appropriation of Vesalian anatomy in the Lutheran universities of sixteenth-century Germany (see Chapter 5), science was frequently inseparable from religion in the era of the Renaissance. In seeking to make sense of the Renaissance revival of the occult, we will need to display equal attention to the religious implications of such ideas if we are to arrive at a just estimate of its place in the scientific debates of the era.

Paracelsus and the Paracelsian revolution in medicine

Today, Paracelsus (*c.*1493–1541) is best known for his contribution to the advancement of medicine in the Renaissance. For centuries a forgotten figure, his rehabilitation in the annals of scientific progress is now largely complete thanks predominantly to scholarly interest in, and admiration for, his promotion of the virtues of chemistry in the production of drugs and chemical medicines (iatrochemistry). In addition, he has been widely applauded for the emphasis in his

Figure 6.6 Jan van Sorrel (attrib., after Quentin Massys), *Paracelsus*, Musée du Louvre. Photo: © R.M.N.

medical work on empirical techniques such as observation and experimentation, as well as for his wholehearted rejection of outmoded medical philosophies such as Galenism. For all this, however, Paracelsus remains a controversial personality whose life and writings are as much the subject of debate today as they were in his own lifetime. In this section, I would like to focus on some of these debates, particularly in order to illuminate a number of themes which were raised in Chapter 5. First, we shall investigate how Paracelsus's debt to what I have termed the 'occult' tradition in science may have hindered the subsequent acceptance of his medical philosophy, and how modern-day scholars have attempted to rationalize (some might say sanitize) it. And second, we shall investigate how yet others have argued for a different approach entirely – one which, like that applied to Vesalius in the previous chapter, seeks to reintegrate Paracelsus's medical and scientific thinking with other aspects of his thought, particularly his deep-seated commitment to radical religious reform.

Paracelsus: life and career

By no stretch of the imagination do the life and work of Theophrastus Paracelsus Aureolus Bombastus von Hohenheim – known simply to his contemporaries and later generations as Paracelsus – fit easily into the Burckhardtian stereotype of the Renaissance genius. Born at Einsiedeln in Switzerland, little is known of his early life and career. His father, also a physician, probably encouraged his interest in medicine. His life-long passion for alchemy was stimulated by his early contact with miners and the metallurgical industries of Carinthia, where he spent his early years and was educated in the mining schools of the Fuggers. Uncertainty surrounds his higher education. It has long been assumed that after graduating at Vienna in 1512, he spent a brief period in Ferrara, in Italy, where he was exposed to the latest currents of medical humanism.[3] No direct evidence exists, however, to support Paracelsus's supposed university training; and it is not inconceivable, given his views on conventional medical education, that if he did attend Ferrara, or elsewhere, his stay was short-lived. Throughout his writings, most of which remained unpublished in his own lifetime, Paracelsus displayed contempt for orthodox medicine and medical training, and frequently lauded the achievement of folk healers over and above that of trained physicians. Here, then, is a man whose learning was not greatly indebted to the contemporary fashion for

---

[3] Among those whom he heard lecture was Giovanni Manardi to whom Gianfrancesco Pico dedicated his work on witchcraft, *Strix* (1523). This work forms the basis of the second case study in this chapter.

Figure 6.7 Mine, woodcut, from Georgius Agricola, *De re metallica*, 1556. Reproduced from the English translation by H.C. Hoover and L.H. Hoover, New York, Dover Publications Inc., 1950

Unusual attitude

medical humanism, the bookishness of which was anathema to Paracelsus. He preferred instead to place his faith in knowledge derived from hands-on experience of disease and its cure.

For the vast majority of his life, Paracelsus travelled widely throughout Europe, stopping only briefly to exercise his craft as an 'alternative' physician. In 1524, he was practising medicine in Salzburg, and a year later was resident in Strasburg, where he made the acquaintance of numerous influential reformers and humanists. In 1527, he was appointed town physician at Basle, but again his restless disposition and uncanny knack of alienating those in authority led to his rapid departure after only ten months. Thereafter, he spent the rest of his life wandering through central Europe, preaching and practising his medical skills among the poor and the sick. All the while, he continued to write and to develop his unique medical philosophy – a strange synthesis of religious mysticism with various strands of occult wisdom – which, at his death in September 1541, remained largely ignored by the orthodox medical establishment. It was only in the generation after his death that his medical ideas, frequently shorn of their radical religious and political elements, came to acquire a wider audience and in the process to gain an aura of respectability and acceptance that was previously unthinkable.

Exercise

Read 'The philosophy, medicine and theology of Paracelsus' by Nicholas Goodrick-Clarke in the Reader (no. 29). What features of Paracelsus's work are shown to foreshadow later advances in scientific and medical thinking?

Discussion

Despite the real difficulties for the modern reader in coming to terms with the complex and mystical (some might be tempted to call it 'mystifying') nature of Paracelsus's thought, Goodrick-Clarke is clearly of the view that there is much in Paracelsus's way of thinking which is 'progressive' and pioneering. This manifests itself in two ways. First, through the stress which Paracelsus places throughout on empirical techniques (even when applied to what we might think of today as pseudo-sciences such as astrology), it is possible, the author argues, to see the beginnings of a new scientific methodology. This is in direct contrast to the dominant natural and medical philosophies of Aristotle and Galen, respectively, which are depicted as essentially theoretical, text-based and lacking in empirical verification.

And second, Paracelsus has laid the foundations of a new medicine – one far more likely to cure disease than Galenic prescriptions such as bloodletting and purging – based on the idea that the cause and cure of individual ailments lay outside the body. Paracelsus is thus seen as the founder of homeopathy (like cures like) and the originator of numerous other 'proto-scientific ideas' and medical initiatives including the use of antiseptics in the war against disease. ❖

It is also clear from this description of Paracelsus and his contribution to medical science that he was not entirely ill-disposed to certain habits of thought which we might think of as quintessentially 'Renaissance' in the Burckhardtian sense. Paracelsus's concept of the individual, for example, as essentially free and unconstrained by the social and political mores of the age, would appear to complement Burckhardt's views on the subject. It is also apparent in Paracelsus's assimilation of a number of key features of the Renaissance rediscovery and appropriation of Neoplatonic magic. Though Burckhardt, like the majority of his educated contemporaries, was unable to find a place for the Neoplatonism of Ficino in his concept of the Renaissance, twentieth-century scholarship has proved more generous. Ever since Yates first proposed in 1964 that the revival of Neoplatonism (including alchemy, astrology and natural magic) may have acted as a spur to scientific innovation, scholars have been keen to explore the implications of such a hypothesis. While this theory is not without its detractors, it is probably nonetheless fair to conclude that most historians of Renaissance science today readily admit that the revival of a magical world-view was responsible, among other factors, for encouraging new approaches to the natural world in the age before the scientific revolution.

Of particular interest in this respect to modern scholars has been the reception and fate of Paracelsus's work in the sixteenth century. For, whereas numerous elements of the programme of Ficino and the Florentine Neoplatonists were warmly received at the courts of Italian princes and popes, Paracelsus's therapeutics was largely greeted with irreverence and disdain. Indeed, in large parts of southern Europe, including Italy, Paracelsism went largely unnoticed. Even in central Europe, where Paracelsus's posthumous influence was greatest, it was not until the last two or three decades of the sixteenth century that his doctrines began to make significant inroads into learned culture and to acquire noble support. Why, we might ask, this delay, which contrasts with the enthusiastic response that Paracelsus's insights have received in the late twentieth century as a harbinger of medical and scientific change? Some clues, perhaps, can be found in those writings of Paracelsus that were published in his own lifetime.

Exercise

Read the two extracts from Paracelsus, 'On medical reform', in the Anthology (no. 89). What clues are there in Paracelsus's own writings as to why his medical philosophy was poorly received in his own lifetime?

Discussion

Putting to one side the 'truth' or 'falsehood' of the views which he expounded, there are a number of clear hints here as to why Paracelsism was treated with caution in learned circles. First, in *Das buch paragranum* (1529–30), the sheer ferocity of the attack on the medical establishment and its practitioners ensured a rough ride for Paracelsus. Not only does he deride the learning of orthodox physicians ('my shoebuckles are more learned than your Galen and Avicenna') and the universities where they gain their qualifications ('and my beard has more experience than all your high colleges'), but he also calls into question the whole hierarchical edifice of professional medicine. For Paracelsus, physicians are not made by the study of ancient writers, or the diplomas of the schools, but rather by God.

Second, in the extract from *De ordine doni* (1533), we witness Paracelsus's pronounced commitment to a reordering of society which, if not communistic in the modern sense of the word, was surely subversive of all conventional notions of hierarchy and social order. In Paracelsus's critique of contemporary society, money is seen as the root of all evil, which more often than not perverts the nobility ('You become profiteers, gamblers, debauchees, and whores from money') and creates a vice-ridden and immoral commonwealth. Interestingly, however, Paracelsus does not blame the nobility and princes, the leaders of society, for this corruption, but rather 'businessmen' and their associates, the growing middle classes, who cheat both rich and poor alike by 'inventing all sorts of rubbish and luxury'. Such views are to be found throughout Paracelsus's literary output and cannot have endeared him to the powers that be at a time when, in the aftermath of the Peasants' War (1525), Germany appeared to the ruling classes to be on the brink of revolution. ❖

Paracelsus's medical, social and political iconoclasm was clearly at the root of his failure to cultivate success for his new way of medicine. Nor were his aims advanced by the intemperate and bad-tempered language which he invoked in his struggle with the medical authorities. But the decisive factor in the official rejection of his medical philosophy was probably related to the uncompromising religious stance which Paracelsus adopted throughout his published writings, including those concerned primarily with medical reform. Indeed, as with Melanchthon's integration of Vesalian anatomy (see Chapter 5), some scholars argue for an approach to Paracelsus which demands that his science and medicine should be seen as an integral part of his wider theological worldview (Webster, 1993; Weeks, 1997). It is clear from contemporary reaction to Paracelsus that this approach informed much of the response to his writings in the sixteenth and seventeenth centuries. It also provides further evidence for the view that scientific and medical progress in this period was largely conditioned by criteria which were, by modern standards, non-scientific.

Exercise

Read the extract from Charles Webster, 'Paracelsus: medicine as popular protest', in the Reader (no. 28).

1   As you read the extract, make a note of those instances where the medical and scientific ideas of Paracelsus are characterized as essentially religious in tone and content.

2   To whom were these ideas most likely to appeal?

Discussion

1 In many respects it is difficult to single out individual items for comment since the thrust of Webster's argument is that the whole of Paracelsus's work and mission to reform medicine is infused with the passionate language of the religious zealot or prophet: 'the entire edifice of his scientific and medical writing is built on an explicit theological infrastructure'. Nonetheless, you will undoubtedly have noted individual instances of the debt of Paracelsus's science to religious concerns. Among those which I would highlight are his overwhelming dependence upon the Bible as the chief source and authority for his 'theology' or 'religion' of nature; the enunciation of his ideas within the context of an imminent second coming of Christ and the destruction of the old order (again, largely based on the book of Revelation); his pronounced anti-clericalism which, for Paracelsus, was comparable with his loathing for the established medical profession; and finally, the clear religious and moral character of those diseases (syphilis and plague) which he chose to highlight in his pamphlet war against the physicians.

2 It was clearly Paracelsus's intention to reach as wide an audience as possible in those few works which he did manage to publish in his lifetime. It goes without saying that the reaction of most professional physicians (i.e. those with university medical qualifications) was almost certainly hostile to Paracelsus's new medical philosophy. But it is also self-evident that the social, political and religious content of his writings guaranteed a lukewarm reception from those in authority, on both sides of the religious divide. The continual appeal to the inherent wisdom and righteousness of the people, particularly the poor, was bound to encourage the hostility of the wealthy and powerful, whose immorality was the main butt of Paracelsus's savage polemics. In this context, we might also note the use of simple woodcut illustrations in Paracelsus's published writings, as well as the use of German in the accompanying text. Not only did he often borrow ideas from the culture of the masses among whom he lived and laboured, but to a large degree they were the audience to whom his ideas were most frequently addressed. ❖

You may have noticed in much of the foregoing a number of close parallels between the work and thought of Paracelsus and that of the man with whom he has frequently been compared, Martin Luther. Like Luther, Paracelsus was a product of the religious and spiritual crisis which afflicted Germany and Switzerland in the early sixteenth century. Both men wrote in German, often using the coarse dialect of the common people, and neither was afraid to court controversy by appealing to the authority of the lowborn over and above that of their so-called superiors. Their use of the illustrated pamphlet and manipulation of popular excitement generated by prophetic and millennial literature both attest to this fact. At one stage, Paracelsus was even dubbed the 'Luther of physicians' by his opponents. There are, moreover, some interesting similarities between the ideas of the two men. Luther's doctrine of a universal priesthood of believers (the idea that all men contain within them the resources to arrive at a true understanding of God and salvation) has its parallel in Paracelsus's appeal to the innate wisdom of the poor and ignorant whose understanding of nature and medicine gave them a higher standing in his eyes than that of educated doctors. Likewise, both men wished to see a return to an earlier age of 'apostolic purity' which would wipe away the corruptions of the Middle Ages. For Luther, this meant the destruction of the 'paganism' and 'superstition' of the Roman Catholic church; for Paracelsus, the overthrow of the unchristian and corrupt 'paganism' of Aristotle, Galen and their modern followers.

Given such similarities in the characters, ideas and agendas of the two men, why, we might ask, did Paracelsism fail to make a significant impact in Lutheran Germany in the sixteenth century? Lutheranism, as we have seen with the case of Vesalius and Wittenberg anatomy, was certainly not uncongenial to medical innovation. Quite the reverse. And there was nothing heretical, per se, in the main plank of Paracelsist thought – the advocacy of chemical remedies in the cure of disease – which alone might account for such a negative response to the new medicine. Clearly, the explanation for the relative failure of Paracelsism to receive official acclaim in the sixteenth century lies outside the realm of pure science. Instead, we are forced to look to wider cultural factors to explain the slow response and only partial acceptance of the new medicine. So far, we have seen how the infusion of Paracelsus's medical agenda into a broader programme of social, religious and moral reform – one that sought in particular to appeal to those without power or wealth – undermined the success of that project. Paracelsus was, in fact, no Luther. His mysticism and deep sympathy for the revolutionary aims of the German poor in the Peasants' War of 1525 were anathema to the social conservative, Luther. Instead, Paracelsus's ideals were far more likely to appeal to the representatives of what has been termed the 'Radical Reformation', a movement which was in part inspired by Luther's stand against the papacy, but which extended his critique of the church to all aspects of society in the early sixteenth century. Throughout Paracelsus's life, and long after his death, the radical and subversive associations of his thought continued to exert a negative influence upon its reception. They were also used by his opponents to denigrate the name of Paracelsus, and to create an image of the man which continues, even in the present, to attract scholarly support.

Chief among Paracelsus's early detractors, and the contemporary most responsible for the creation of his poor image and reputation, was the celebrated humanist physician and natural philosopher Conrad Gesner (1516–65). Gesner's reaction to Paracelsus is, to a large extent, symptomatic of the response of the learned medical world to the Swiss iconoclast in the sixteenth century. On the surface, Gesner exhibited unrestrained antipathy towards the extremism of Paracelsus's language and thought, and rejected without reserve his social and religious teachings. Yet in private, he frequently conceded the usefulness of much of Paracelsus's medical doctrines, in particular his avowal of the benefits of chemically prepared drugs. And in his later work, he himself indulged in the new passion for chemistry and maintained cordial relations with a number of the most successful Paracelsian physicians of the age. By the middle decades of the sixteenth century, when Gesner was busy tarnishing the name and reputation of Paracelsus (including accusations of necromancy, drunkenness and general immorality), he was himself involved in the process whereby many of the aims of Paracelsus were beginning to achieve academic respectability (Webster, 1990).

The process was, however, a slow one. The chief contribution of men like Gesner was to discard the revolutionary premises upon which Paracelsus had built his reform programme, and to promote in their stead a refined version of Paracelsism which focused entirely on the practical advances of the new medicine. Repackaged and remarketed, Paracelsism (or, more accurately perhaps, Paracelsianism) proved widely popular and was now able to appeal to a broad spectrum of influential patrons, including princes and emperors. As we have seen in the case of Galileo in Chapter 5, princely patronage was often crucial to the reception and dissemination of scientific innovation. It was particularly critical in the case of Paracelsianism:

> A Renaissance prince could defy the entrenched authority of a medical faculty or corporation. He could give protection against the law. He could pay for the publication of books and guarantee them against censorship. He could provide resources – a laboratory, a professorial chair in his private university, a team of researchers, international contacts. And he could also provide power, wealth, and fame: to be in charge of the health of a prince [and] his alchemist, capable – at least potentially – of creating wealth by chemical transmutation, was a responsibility which, of itself, brought in rewards.

> (Trevor-Roper, 1990, pp.81–2)

In Germany and throughout much of northern Europe in the late sixteenth century, Paracelsianism (the refined, modified and sanitized version of the master's writings) thrived at the courts of princes. Just as the mathematician Galileo was able to avoid the censure of academics for overstepping their authority in natural philosophy by securing the patronage of the Medici, so too scores of Paracelsian physicians were able to circumvent the displeasure of the medical faculties by ingratiating themselves at the courts of princes. In time, they even infiltrated the universities. In 1609, Maurice, Landgrave of Hesse, as patron of the University of Marburg, founded there the first chair in chemistry. The first professor was the Landgrave's own chief physician, the Paracelsian Johann Hartmann (1568–1631) (Moran, 1990, pp.97–8). The medical doctrines of Paracelsus did acquire, belatedly, academic and social respectability, but not before they were shorn of their subversive religious and political connotations.

The case of Paracelsus, as I have outlined it here, is I think a useful reminder of the various problems which surround the proper scholarly evaluation of past scientists. In attempting to isolate what we would readily acknowledge today as the progressive elements in Paracelsus's thought, we run a two-fold risk. First, we radically distort the original meaning and intention implicit in Paracelsus's writings (in this case by failing to acknowledge Paracelsus's debt to religion in an age of spiritual ferment). And second, we fail to give due weight to the social, religious and political implications of those writings in accounting for the mixed reception which his medical ideas received in the sixteenth century. When due credit is paid to Paracelsus as he was, and not the semi-mythical figure of historical legend, a different, more complex, and in many ways a more satisfying picture emerges of the medical iconoclast. Gone is the image of the man as an archetypal Renaissance figure, the prototype of Faust, who single-handedly repudiated medieval authority and laid the foundations for a new empirical medicine. In its place appears an idiosyncratic and often obscurantist thinker whose medical interests were always subservient to his radical theological outlook. Not interested in book learning or the current vogue for humanist scholarship (despite associations with several humanist scholars), Paracelsus was hardly ever what one might consider in the Burckhardtian sense a product of the Renaissance. The key to Paracelsus is not to be found in the world of books and humanist scholarship. Rather, it is more likely to be located in that great period of religious upheaval and spiritual renewal that historians generally refer to as the German Reformation.

Renaissance demonology

Introduction

No matter how complex the scientific work of a Paracelsus or a Dee might seem to us in the present, we are still able, in the last resort, to acknowledge their contribution to the age in which they lived. The same, alas, is not true for the Renaissance preoccupation with witchcraft and its intellectual sub-discipline, **demonology**. Unlike other manifestations of occult philosophy, witchcraft has consistently failed to attract an empathetic response from those who have studied it closely, with, I shall suggest, unfortunate consequences. It is not only Burckhardt, writing in the middle decades of the nineteenth century, who exhibits incredulity in the face of explaining how cultured minds in the period could accept what he termed that 'great and revolting system', the persecution of witches (1990, p.335). Most modern scholarship on the subject is equally scathing. Writing in the introduction to a series of essays concerned with the place of the occult in the Renaissance, Brian Vickers memorably introduced the two essays on witchcraft thus:

> Of all the aspects of the occult, that connected with demonology and witchcraft seems the most difficult to come to terms with ... Studying the other occult sciences is difficult enough, given the proliferation of that literature and its frequent repetitiveness, but nothing is quite so disheartening, I find, as studying the literature of demonology. The records of the trials are unspeakably depressing, as much for the delusions of the victims as for the prejudices of the prosecutors ... As an intellectual and social phenomenon, too, witchcraft is harder to understand than any of the other occult sciences and has provoked an extensive controversy. Many more factors seem to be involved than with alchemy or astrology – social, legal, religious, psychological – and many of them are rather hard to pin down.
>
> (1984, pp.23–4)

In this concluding section, I hope to show how it might be possible to arrive at a different set of conclusions, through the study of a single demonological text, *Strix* (*The Witch*), by Gianfrancesco Pico della Mirandola. The object of this exercise is not to rehabilitate the reputations of those who engaged in the punishment of witches. Rather, it is envisaged as an exercise in what one might term historical empathy – an attempt, that is, to understand how it was possible for men of learning to rationalize the existence of extreme evil in their midst, and to persecute the same, in the name of sound government and true religion. In the process, I shall not be paying a great deal of attention to the social history of witchcraft, which has sought to discover the dynamic of witchcraft accusations in the inter-personal relationships which prevailed between accuser and accused. My aim, instead, is to focus on the ideological context of the so-called 'witch-craze' – an aspect of the process hitherto largely overlooked by historians – to determine what clues, if any, may be found in the texts of educated men to explain how belief in witchcraft achieved such prominence in the age of the Renaissance. If witchcraft is one aspect of the 'dark side' of the Renaissance, as many historians clearly imply, we ought at least to make the effort of understanding how it came to figure so prominently among some of the brightest talents of that age.

Renaissance demonology in context: Pico's *Strix* (1523)

Between about 1450 and 1750, approximately 50,000 people, mostly women, were executed in Europe for the crime of witchcraft. Many more were either tried and subsequently released, or were accused informally and dealt with without coming to trial. We now have a fair idea of who was accused (the witch was stereotypically female, old and poor), what they were accused of (usually *maleficium* or evil-doing, occasionally devil-worship or a combination of both), and the nature and frequency of the punishments which they suffered.[4] What is less clear is why learned and elite interest in the activities of witches should have grown so rapidly from the mid fifteenth century onward, given that belief in the existence of witches and demons was commonplace throughout the preceding era. From the mid to late fifteenth century, clerical and secular authorities increasingly called for a purge of such delinquents, and as the witch hunts gathered pace, so too did the tendency of commentators to systematize their findings in published demonologies.

The publication of these works has baffled modern-day commentators, not least because the authors of the demonologies frequently invoked a whole range of authorities, including the Bible, which betrayed sophisticated levels of learning and erudition. How could the Renaissance have spawned such monstrous errors which would lead to the executions of thousands of innocent persons? And how are we to make sense of this material?

Exercise

You should now read the abridged text of Gianfrancesco Pico della Mirandola's *Strix* (1523) in the Anthology (no. 90). Although we shall be focusing on particular sections and aspects of this text, I suggest that you read it through first as a whole to gain a general idea of the tenor of the work and the thrust of Pico's argument. You should also read, as a preparation to the main text, the analysis of Peter Burke in

---

[4] There is now a vast literature on witchcraft in early modern Europe. For a good, general overview of the subject see Levack (1993).

the Reader (no. 31), which provides helpful commentary on various aspects of Pico's work. What are your first impressions of this work? Does it fit your imagined stereotype of a demonology?

Discussion

Your first reaction is probably to concur with Vickers (above) where he expresses ill-concealed distaste for demonology. You will also probably have acknowledged, however, that the whole discourse is replete with classical knowledge and wisdom. It is not an easy read, even in its modern translation, but this suggests that in its own day it was intended for a highly educated audience. Do not worry too much at this stage if you do feel disoriented by its erudition and long-windedness. If nothing else, this provides further evidence of the nature of learned Renaissance discourse. ❖

In order to analyse and comprehend the meaning of this text, we should begin by saying something about the author and the immediate context in which he was motivated to write this demonology. Gianfrancesco Pico della Mirandola (1469–1533) was an Italian scholar and minor nobleman with close links to many of the most celebrated humanists of his age.[5] Chief among these was his famous uncle, Giovanni Pico della Mirandola, whose biography the admiring nephew wrote following the death of Giovanni in 1494. The close ties with his uncle undoubtedly opened doors for Gianfrancesco, who was personally acquainted with some of the most important figures in contemporary Italian cultural and scholarly life, including Marsilio Ficino, the poet Lodovico Ariosto and the Venetian printer Aldus Manutius. Pico's noble title, prince of Mirandola, involved him in considerable political and military intrigue throughout his adult life. His grip on the title and lands was always precarious and frequently broken. In 1502, for example, he was forced into exile, which lasted for nine years. During this time, Pico entered the military service of popes and the emperor, frequently appealing to both for support in his campaign to reclaim the title of Mirandola. It was also at this time that he made numerous visits to Germany, where he came into contact with some of the leading humanists of northern Europe. Not until 1514 did he secure his patrimony, following a deal which saw the principality divided into two halves. Further unrest and familial in-fighting were never far from the surface, however, and continued to dog Pico until his death, murdered at the hands of one of his nephews in 1533.

[5] For biographical information on Gianfrancesco Pico della Mirandola I am largely indebted to Schmitt (1967, pp.11–30). Schmitt's account of Pico's life and thought informs the analysis of Peter Burke in his 'Witchcraft and magic in Renaissance Italy: Gianfrancesco Pico and his *Strix*' (see Reader, no. 31).

The bare facts of Pico's life fit neatly the stereotypical image of Italy, its learning and politics, as described by Burckhardt in his classic study of the Renaissance (1990). Murder, intrigue and deceit intermingle with erudition and courtly patronage in equal measure. How, then, are we to make sense of Pico's publication in 1523 of a work which explicitly defended the existence of witches and witchcraft? Can we dismiss it – as Burckhardt himself tried to dismiss all such demonology and magic – as merely the product of fevered minds, temporarily deluded by the crude influx of ideas from north of the Alps (1990, pp.335–6)? And if not, what can the study of Renaissance demonology tell us of the society which produced such a literature? These are some of the questions we will address in the pages which follow. For the sake of simplicity, I shall discuss Pico's *Strix* by focusing upon the various sources of authority which he adduces to defend his view (expressed largely in the words of Phronimus and Dicastes) that witches exist and must be punished for their sins. These I have reduced to four headings: humanism; religion; natural philosophy; and popular culture. The relative significance of these authorities, both in the work itself, and in the wider European debate over witchcraft, will be discussed in the conclusion to this chapter. A final, and very important consideration, will be the extent to which we may wish to argue that *Strix* is a typical product of its genre or an aberration. Discussion of this point will form the focus of the conclusion.

Renaissance demonology and humanism

The question of the extent to which Renaissance demonology was indebted to the concurrent interest in humanism and humanist discourse is a central concern for scholars of witchcraft. As Peter Burke makes clear in the introduction to his discussion of Pico's *Strix*, the relationship of the two poses a fundamental problem to any student of the Renaissance, one which has continued to perplex scholars since Burckhardt first raised the subject in 1860. Burke suggests a number of useful ways in which it is possible to account for a shared interest in humanism and witchcraft in sixteenth-century Italy. Before we discuss these, however, we need to be clear as to the precise nature of the debt to humanism in a work like *Strix*.

Exercise

What evidence is there for *Strix* as a work of humanist scholarship? Though you will find evidence throughout the work to support this contention, you may wish to focus on Book One, which provides the fullest sample.

Humanism informs every aspect of the debate between Apistius (the sceptic) and Phronimus (the believer) in Book One. This is most evident in the frequent recourse of both men to examples taken from classical literature to bolster their arguments. Many of the authors will be familiar: Aristotle, Plato, Pythagoras, Homer, Pliny the Elder, Ovid, Virgil and Horace. But both men's learning is further accentuated by their citation of a host of 'lesser' writers – poets, philosophers, historians and others – who read like a roll-call of the literary pantheon of the ancient world.

The terms of the debate over the reality of witchcraft are thus set from the start within the context of a correct reading of the evidence of past authors. Both men, it is important to note, are well read in the literature of classical antiquity and both acknowledge each other's linguistic felicity in Greek, as well as Latin (note, for example, where Apistius congratulates Phronimus on his translation of Homer). The debate therefore begins as a contest of equals, and it is important for Pico to demonstrate that Apistius is in every respect able to appreciate the strength and substance of Phronimus's arguments in favour of the view that the classical world was infested with witches and demons. Apistius, just as much as Phronimus, is a man guided by humanist principles. He reads the poets and philosophers for moral edification and as a guide to correct social behaviour. ❖

The fact that Pico chose to situate his debate about witchcraft within the context of a dialogue between two men skilled in the language and craft of humanist endeavour is critically important to our appreciation of the work as a whole. As Burke suggests, the classical revival of tales of demons, gods and magic provided fertile ground for evidence of witchcraft in former times (see Figure 6.8). Allied to the contemporary vogue for philosophical magic and the occult arts, it is not perhaps surprising that men of Pico's learning equated the new wave of witch accusations and trials with a demonic renaissance (Burke, 1977, p.49). On the other hand, it is also important to point out that Pico was not a typical humanist (if such an individual ever existed). As Burke makes clear, Pico used his considerable knowledge of classical literature, as well as humanist methods of textual criticism and debate (for example, the use of the dialogue form), to undermine many of the humanists' most coveted aspirations. Thinly disguised as Phronimus, Pico met 'the humanists on their own ground in order to convert them' (Burke, 1977, p.44). But to convert them to what?

Figure 6.8 Dosso Dossi, *Circe*, Galleria della Villa Borghese, Rome. Burke speculates that this typically Italianate depiction of the classical witch Circe, dating from about 1520, may reflect general interest in such ideas at the court of Ferrara, where Dossi was active at this time (1977, p.37; Reader, no. 31, p.331). The treatment of this subject by Italian Renaissance artists is in stark contrast to that of northern painters (cf. Figure 6.9 below). Photo: Alinari-Anderson, Florence

Pico's religion

Despite the fact that it is the language of humanism which dominates the debate between Phronimus and Apistius, the promotion of humanist values is evidently not Pico's goal. While displaying an encyclopaedic knowledge of the classical world, Phronimus (Pico) nonetheless has little sympathy with its sordid, pagan practices and general irreligion. Not until the end of Book One do we encounter Phronimus's true motives in engaging with Apistius in this manner, when he turns his attention to religion.

Exercise

Read the section of Phronimus's long speech beginning: 'As regards the movement' to the end of his declamation (Anthology, no. 90, pp.376–8). What importance does Pico attach to religion and religious values in his attempt to prove the existence of witches and witchcraft?

Discussion

Critically, in the first paragraph, Phronimus (Pico) sets out to show that all sources of knowledge and authority, including 'poetry' (classical literature), philosophy and the arguments of lawyers, are flawed as a guide in this issue when compared with the authority of theology. The former are characteristically described as 'variable' or 'inconsistent' (i.e. capable of more than a single interpretation and therefore prone to dispute). The subject-matter of theologians, however, is singular and error-free. It alone is capable of providing irrefutable truths.

The ancient writers, poets, and philosophers unintentionally testify to the reality of witchcraft because they themselves illustrate at every turn how they were beguiled and deceived by demons. The classical world was seething with pagan irreligion and the worship of demons and devils. That this is no longer the case, and that the devil now has to make do with deluding 'wretched men and women', is entirely due to the Incarnation of Christ and the establishment of the Christian religion. Pious Christians, Pico implies, are not so easily seduced by the devil's wiles. ❖

Phronimus's view of witchcraft as religious apostasy sets the tone for much of what follows in Books Two and Three, particularly after the introduction of Dicastes at the conclusion of Book One. Dicastes, an ecclesiastical judge or inquisitor, has first-hand experience of the deceitful nature of witches. As the dialogue progresses, his theocentric approach to the problem of witchcraft predominates while both Phronimus and Apistius bow to his superior knowledge. Moreover, his skill resides not so much in eloquent speech and humanist learning as in a thorough knowledge of divine will as revealed in the scriptures, the works of theologians and the lives of the saints. While not ignorant of polished Greek and Latin, Dicastes, like Phronimus, favours the more substantial knowledge which can be derived from 'simple' theologians in preference to the 'refinement of words'. Among those authorities cited by the disputants, the Bible and St Augustine now take precedence (see Plate 8). There is even room for the inelegant prose of contemporary German theologians when Dicastes introduces evidence drawn from the *Malleus maleficarum* (*The Hammer of Witches*) (1486) to prove the sexual perversity and general bestiality of witches. One by one, Apistius's doubts are conquered. God's permission of evil and tolerance of evildoers is answered, for example, by recourse to the doctrine of free will and divine providence (God allows evil in order that a greater good may emerge). Witches, it follows, are allowed to exist because through the knowledge of their existence the faith of the godly is strengthened. Slowly but surely, Apistius is led to the same conclusion. His faith too is affirmed as he takes his leave of Phronimus and Dicastes.

Pico and natural philosophy

On the basis of the preceding discussion, it is fairly clear that the overriding influence on Pico in his espousal of the truth of witchcraft was that of the authority of the church and the scriptures. Though not altogether a surprising conclusion, it is nonetheless mildly disconcerting that a man of Pico's learning and connections should have so studiously ignored the claims of the natural philosophers to contribute to this debate. What can we learn from *Strix* about Pico's evaluation of natural philosophy?

Exercise

What evidence does Pico's *Strix* provide for the role of science, or natural philosophy, in Renaissance demonology?

Discussion

Pico conflates what we might think of as science with other fields of scholarly endeavour. The authority of poets in discussing natural phenomena is allocated equal weight with that of philosophers and naturalists such as Plato, Aristotle or Pliny the Elder. The Greek-born author Plutarch, for example, is cited as an authority for the scientific ingenuity of the poet Homer. Occasional references are made to a number of classical philosophers and writers on science (e.g. Pythagoras and Empedocles), but even where they are cited, their insights have little bearing upon the substance of the discussion. Even Aristotle – the undisputed monarch of Renaissance science – appears only fleetingly as a witness to demonic powers. ❖

The absence of scientific explanations in Pico's *Strix* is unsurprising in the light of his philosophical preoccupations. Pico was extremely hostile to the natural philosophy of Aristotle. Indeed, in 1520 he published one of the first detailed critiques of Aristotelianism in which he attempted to demonstrate that a philosophy or science based on evidence gleaned from sense data (i.e. the evidence of one's eyes and ears) was essentially fallacious.[6] Pico's rejection of Aristotelianism, or any other sense-based natural philosophy, was not, however, the product of an obscurantist mind. Pico was deeply

---

[6] Gianfrancesco Pico della Mirandola, *Examen vanitatis doctrinae gentium et veritatis christianae disciplinae* (*An Examination of the Futility of Pagan Learning and of the Truth of Christian Teaching*), 1520.

indebted to a tradition of philosophical scepticism, based largely on the writings of Sextus Empiricus (fl. *c*.200 CE), the revival of which he pioneered in the sixteenth century. Consequently, when Pico challenged the methodological assumptions of the Aristotelians, he did so by recourse to arguments which were as ancient and potentially authoritative as those which he attempted to supplant.

We are thus faced with an intriguing situation when we read Pico's *Strix*, for here is a learned treatise, informed throughout by a thorough-going philosophical scepticism, which aims to substantiate the existence of witches and demons. Unlike Montaigne, who was equally influenced by classical scepticism (see Chapter 8) and may even have read Pico's critique of Aristotle, Pico has no trouble in asserting the reality of diabolical witchcraft (Siraisi, 1990, p.214). How, we might ask, does Pico arrive at this surprising conclusion? To start with, we might wish to acknowledge the fact that any sense of confusion generated here by Pico's use of scepticism is ours and not his! Pico himself clearly saw no incompatibility between his belief in witchcraft and his espousal of philosophical scepticism. In addition, we cannot level a charge of ignorance or intellectual naivety against Pico. He was fully conversant not only with the Peripatetic tradition which formed the basis of university teaching, but also with more modern currents of humanist medicine and science which were beginning to take root in the academies of northern Italy. *Strix*, for example, is dedicated by Pico to one of the foremost medical humanists of his day, Giovanni Manardi (1462–1536), who was responsible, among other things, for encouraging the revival of a reformed and purified Galenism in medical teaching. Finally, we have the evidence of *Strix* itself to indicate the extent to which Pico's scepticism informed and shaped his credulity in the matter of witchcraft.

Exercise

1 What evidence is there in *Strix* to illustrate Pico's fundamental belief in the principle that one should not trust any concept of truth or reality based on sense data?

2 How does this affect Pico's view of witchcraft and the powers attributed to witches and demons?

Discussion

1 The answer, essentially, lies in the subtitle of the book: *On the Deception of Demons*. The emphasis throughout Pico's treatise – and it is one common to virtually every text written on this subject – is on the deceitful and illusory nature of the actions of demons and witches. What they claim to do, and what they can actually achieve, are more often than not poles apart. This is evident, for example, in three instances which take up a large part of the substantial debate between Apistius, Phronimus and

Dicastes: attendance at the witches' nocturnal meeting, or **sabbat**; demonic procreation with humans; and lycanthropy (or shape-changing). In all three cases, deceit and illusion are evident. In the case of the witch's presence at the sabbat, it was happily accepted by Dicastes that the witch might have been present in person at this gathering or that she might simply have been deluded. With respect to demonic sexual congress, the devil went to great lengths to hide the fact that he was incapable of engendering demonic offspring. Finally, in the case of people transformed into beasts, the devil was reduced either to a sophisticated form of prestidigitation or to working on the malleable human imagination in order to create the illusion of a real transformation.

Figure 6.9 Hans Baldung Grien, *Witches Preparing for the Sabbath Flight*, 1514, pen on red-brown tinted paper. Fonds Albertina, Vienna, Inv. 3221

2   Although it is not always clearly spelled out, it is evident throughout the discussion that the ability of the devil and his disciples to perform actions above and beyond the ordinary laws of nature is impossible. It is a consistent theme of all demonologies that only God can perform supernatural or miraculous feats. If the devil claims to have done so, as the testimonies of many convicted witches would seem to suggest, then it was the standard response of the prosecuting authorities that such actions were nothing more than clever deceits or fictions. As a spirit, the devil's knowledge of nature, and his ability to manipulate, but not alter, the laws of nature, was vastly superior to that of men. Consequently, though he might appear to perform miraculous feats, he was nonetheless constrained in the last resort by the same natural laws which all living creatures must obey. Pico's devil is no different. He is little more, in fact, than a magus – a supreme magician – who like his human counterparts was reduced to the use of trickery and illusion rather than indebted in any real sense to supernatural powers. ❖

Figure 6.10 *Three Witches Changing their Shape and Flying on a Broomstick*, woodcut, from Ulrich Molitor, *De lamiis et phitonicis mulieribus*, 1495, Cologne, Cornelius de Zurichzee. Photo: Mary Evans Picture Library, London

Demonology and popular culture

So far we have largely excluded discussion of the fourth figure in Pico's dialogue without whom there would have been no learned demonology: the witch. As Burke points out in his brief description of the four main actors in the drama, the historical attempt to resurrect the attitude of the accused in witch trials is highly problematic (1977, pp.44–8). In most demonologies, the figure of the witch appears as a characterless stereotype – old, female and poor – whose association with Satan rapidly alienates the sympathy of the reader. How typical, then, is Pico's witch? She is certainly female and old, though many of her co-accused are interestingly referred to as males. Burke's suggestion that a fair proportion of those accused of witchcraft in Italy were clerics (1977, p.46) is also borne out by incidental information found in *Strix*. The recent discovery of the trial records of the Mirandolan witches also sheds important light on the nature of popular witchcraft beliefs in the area of the Po Valley, much of this evidence tending to confirm the picture outlined by Burke (Biondi, 1984).

One particular aspect of the discussion in Pico's *Strix* which does impinge upon the important question of the relationship between popular and learned belief in witchcraft is the reference by the witch to the nocturnal visits to the 'Game of our Lady'. There is some suggestion in the dialogue that what might have been a relatively innocent pastime of some Italian peasant villagers (carousing, dancing, fornication, etc.) was transformed by the witch's

Figure 6.11 Depiction of Diana (the goddess of the night) seated in a chariot and greeting a fellow witch, an initial letter from the proclamation of the Inquisitor Camillo Campeggi, 2 January 1564. Modena state archive, San Uffizio, b.1

Figure 6.12 Franz Francken II, *An Assembly of Witches*, early seventeenth century, drawing, pen and ink, gray/brown wash. Photo: © The Trustees of the British Museum, London

interrogators into something more sinister. Certainly Phronimus testifies to the problem some of the latter had in making the evidence of the Mirandolan witches conform to the inquisitors' preconceived image of the sabbat (itself largely drawn from the *Malleus maleficarum*) when he suggested that:

> It may be fear or lapses of memory that cause witches to give such differing accounts of the Game, for they are mostly uneducated, rustic women. It's also possible that the discrepancies are to be ascribed to the demon's deception, which does not affect them all in the same way.

(Anthology, no. 90, p.376)

Other examples drawn from sixteenth-century Italy imply that such a process of acculturation[7] was indeed part of the cultural landscape at this time. The case of the *benandanti* cited by Burke (1977, p.48; Reader, no. 31, p.340), based on the research of Carlo Ginzburg, is particularly instructive since it demonstrates most clearly just how interested educated elites were in uncovering popular practices and rituals and reshaping them to fit their own preoccupations and ends (Ginzburg, 1983). Similarly, popular belief in '**white witchcraft**' – a perennial feature of European culture since the Romans – was also appropriated in this way, stigmatized as it was by the demonologists and others as a set of 'superstitious' practices that were seen as antithetical to the teachings of both Protestants and Catholics. Again, we see a glimpse of such thinking in *Strix* when Dicastes objects that there is no such thing as a good demon: 'we maintain that they are all malign'. It follows that in Pico's eyes there was no distinction between the acts of learned magicians, on the one hand, and the superstitious practices of folk healers or 'white witches', on the other. They were both equally abominable and diabolical in the eyes of God. It is perhaps worth noting in this context that Pico was also the author of influential treatises attacking popular and learned belief in prophecy and astrology (the latter, like *Strix*, dedicated to his friend, the medical humanist, Manardi).

Conclusion

I would like to conclude this chapter by focusing on two questions. First, what was the chief source or authority for Pico's demonological beliefs? And second, how typical were they in comparison to other demonologies of the time?

With respect to my first question, I have provided examples of the various ways in which Pico's work was shaped by his religious, philosophical and humanist outlook. Of these, religion, the authority of the Bible, and authorized theology were clearly paramount. They alone, in Pico's words, were capable of producing error-free knowledge and undisputed truths:

> What is false in nature is very often multiplex and diverse; what is truthful is founded on simplicity ... It can ... be observed in works of poetry, which are variable and inconsistent, and very frequently in histories in which two, three or more traditions are recorded. It is seen, too, in the ideas of philosophers and lawyers' responses. But

---

[7] Acculturation is the name given by historians to the process whereby it is believed the culture of the unlearned masses was slowly appropriated and reordered by those in authority in order to reinforce the social, religious and political status quo.

you will never observe this in the writings of theologians ... for there are never any discrepancies when theologians discuss those subjects which are their preserve – that is, the precepts and decrees that relate to faith and morality which are essential to our salvation.

(Anthology, no. 90, p.376)

The main concern which motivated Pico was essentially religious or spiritual in kind, and it permeates all of his writings. It comes as no surprise that one of the major influences on his life and thought was Girolamo Savonarola. Pico was a fideist, that is, he believed that Christian faith is always to be preferred before the uncertain truths of 'human learning', which are based on the error-prone evidence of the senses. Witchcraft is just one of a number of issues, hotly debated in the Renaissance, which for Pico provides a convenient vehicle for the expression of his profound faith in the authority of the church. In short, Pico was a Christian sceptic whose philosophical scepticism, paradoxical as it may seem, reinforced his religious faith. Whether this makes him a typical product of the Renaissance is open to debate. We might profit, however, from Charles Schmitt's verdict of the man and his relationship to the age in which he lived:

Pico ... was not entirely typical of his age; no man is. In a sense he was 'out of joint' with the Renaissance – at least with many interpretations of the Renaissance which have gained wide popular acceptance. He was a humanist, but not quite a Platonist, and certainly he did not write paeans on the abilities of man. He was a staunch Catholic, yet wholly unfriendly to Aristotle. He was closely tied to the Papacy, dedicated works to four pontiffs, rode into battle with the popes against their enemies, but wrote two works so critical of the organization and abuses of the Church that they are well-worthy of a Luther. In another sense, he was a typical representative of the Renaissance. He 'revived' the teachings of two ancient authors (Sextus Empiricus and John Philoponus), who were practically unknown at his time. He knew Greek well and applied all of the philological techniques of literary humanism to his critique of Aristotle.

What emerges from this whole complex picture of Gianfrancesco Pico is a strange mixture of new and old. Certain of his methods and techniques of criticism, certain of the philosophical doctrines which he rejects or calls into question mark him as a 'modern man,' forward looking and non-traditional. On the other hand, his most basic assumptions and his own conception of the world mark him as a traditionalist and as one who missed the significance of many of the more important elements of the modern civilization which was emerging during his own lifetime.

(Schmitt, 1967, p.9)

If we have difficulty deciding how typical Pico was as a product of his age, can we be any more certain as to the orthodoxy of his demonological beliefs? Again, we might need to temper any definitive answer with the use of a proviso. In many respects, Pico's *Strix* is unoriginal and canonical. It is also largely derivative of other, more celebrated (or infamous) tomes. Thus, it includes within its compass all the main features of demonological enquiry as expounded in the fifteenth century, including that most authoritative of texts on the subject, the *Malleus maleficarum*. The sabbat, or orgiastic gathering of witches and demons, is prominent throughout, as is the belief in transvection (moving objects and bodies through the air), lycanthropy and the existence of succubus and incubus (implying sexual intercourse between humans and demons). Equally prominent, though not fully spelled out, is the belief in the diabolical pact or covenant. In the eyes of the prosecuting authorities, admission of the pact was tantamount to a renunciation of the Christian faith. On these grounds alone, the ultimate punishment of execution was justified.

In other respects too, Pico's exploration of the crime of witchcraft was unexceptional. His citation of biblical precedents and reliance on established and revered authorities such as St Augustine was entirely commonplace. Where the emphasis in his work does deviate from the norm is suggested by the relative absence of arguments drawn from natural philosophical sources – an absence which we have previously acknowledged and accounted for. Recourse to legal argument is also largely absent – a deliberate omission in all probability, given that medieval canon law was highly ambivalent on the question of witchcraft, and how it should be punished. In the course of the sixteenth century, these elements of the demonologists' armoury would become a more central feature of their arguments as interest in the subject increasingly pervaded the scientific and legal debates of the era. Indeed, by the mid sixteenth century, as the most recent survey of the demonologist's craft has brilliantly demonstrated, interest in such issues permeated educated discourse in virtually every branch of learning (Clark, 1997). So much so that one is left to ponder whether the title 'demonologist' is something of a misnomer.

The idea of professional demonologists engaged in a learned pursuit with well-established disciplinary boundaries is, in fact, highly misleading. In its place, we might better envisage the debate about witchcraft taking place between theologians, lawyers, natural philosophers and even political theorists,[8] who, each in their own way,

---

[8] Both Jean Bodin, the celebrated French apologist for monarchical absolutism, and King James VI of Scotland and I of England were the authors of published demonologies.

were able to contribute to the debate. But if this was the case – and recent research points strongly to the close integration of witchcraft lore into every facet of Renaissance life and culture – then we may have inadvertently answered one of those concerns with which we began this chapter. For, under these circumstances, it would be very unwise of the historian to continue to express exasperation with, and to marginalize, issues which clearly grabbed the imagination of our educated forbears. Rather than seek to argue such beliefs away as the irrational fantasies of corrupt and perverted minds (note how frequently the prosecution of witches is referred to as a 'craze'), the challenge of demonology is rather to understand how it made perfect sense for intelligent men such as Pico to speak rationally of witches and demons. In the process, we may discover an image of the Renaissance which fails to tally with that created by Burckhardt and his successors over the last century and more. It might just, however, possess the virtue of authenticity: the Renaissance, warts and all.

Bibliography

BIONDI, A. (1984) 'Gianfrancesco Pico e la repressione della Stregoneria: Qualche Novità sui Processi Mirandolesi del 1522–23', *Mirandola e le terre del Basso Corso del Secchia della deputazione di storia patria per le Modenesi: Bibliotheca*, vol. 76, pp.331–49.

BORCHARDT, F.L. (1990) 'The *magus* as Renaissance man', *Sixteenth Century Journal*, vol. 21, pp.57–76.

BURCKHARDT, J. (1990) *The Civilization of the Renaissance in Italy*, trans. S.G.C. Middlemore, Harmondsworth, Penguin; first published 1860.

BURKE, P. (1977) 'Witchcraft and magic in Renaissance Italy: Gianfrancesco Pico and his *Strix*' in S. Anglo (ed.) *The Damned Art: Essays in the Literature of Witchcraft*, London, Henley and Boston, Routledge & Kegan Paul, pp.32–52.

BURKE, P. (1987) *The Italian Renaissance: Culture and Society in Italy*, Cambridge, Polity Press.

CLARK, S. (1997) *Thinking With Demons: The Idea of Witchcraft in Early Modern Europe*, Oxford, Clarendon Press.

CLULEE, N.L. (1988) *John Dee's Natural Philosophy: Between Science and Religion*, London, Routledge.

COPENHAVER, B.P. (1990) 'Natural magic, hermeticism, and occultism in early modern science' in D.C. Lindberg and R.S. Westman (eds) *Reappraisals of the Scientific Revolution*, Cambridge, Cambridge University Press, pp.260–301.

EAMON, W. (1983) 'Technology as magic in the late Middle Ages and the Renaissance', *Janus*, vol. 70, pp.171–212.

FRENCH, P. (1972) *John Dee: The World of an Elizabethan Magus*, London, Routledge & Kegan Paul.

GINZBURG, C. (1983) *The Night Battles: Witchcraft and Agrarian Cults in the Sixteenth and Seventeenth Centuries*, London, Routledge & Kegan Paul.

LEVACK, B.P. (1993) *The Witch-Hunt in Early Modern Europe*, 2nd edn, London, Longman.

MORAN, B.T. (1990) 'Prince-practitioning and the direction of medical roles at the German court: Maurice of Hesse-Kassel and his physicians' in V. Nutton (ed.) *Medicine at the Courts of Europe, 1500–1837*, London and New York, Routledge, pp.95–116.

PATON, B. (1991) ' "To the fire, to the fire! Let us burn a little incense to God": Bernardino, preaching friars and *maleficio* in late medieval Siena' in C. Zika (ed.) *No Gods Except Me: Orthodoxy and Religious Practice in Europe, 1200–1600*, Parkville, Victoria, University of Melbourne Department of History, pp.7–36.

SCHMITT, C.B, (1967) *Gianfrancesco Pico della Mirandola (1469–1533) and His Critique of Aristotle*, The Hague, Martinus Nijhoff.

SIRAISI, N. (1990) 'Medicine, physiology, and anatomy in early sixteenth-century critiques of the arts and sciences' in J. Henry and S. Hutton (eds) *New Perspectives on Renaissance Thought: Essays in the History of Science, Education and Philosophy in Memory of Charles B. Schmitt*, London, Duckworth, pp.214–29.

TREVOR-ROPER, H.R. (1990) 'The court physician and Paracelsianism' in V. Nutton (ed.) *Medicine at the Courts of Europe, 1500–1837*, London and New York, Routledge, pp.79–94.

VICKERS, B. (1984) 'Introduction' and 'Analogy versus identity: the rejection of occult symbolism, 1580–1680' in B. Vickers (ed.) *Occult and Scientific Mentalities in the Renaissance*, Cambridge, Cambridge University Press, pp.1–55, 95–163.

WEBSTER, C. (1990) 'Conrad Gessner and the infidelity of Paracelsus' in J. Henry and S. Hutton (eds) *New Perspectives on Renaissance Thought: Essays in the History of Science, Education and Philosophy in Memory of Charles B. Schmitt*, London, Duckworth, pp.13–23.

WEBSTER, C. (1993) 'Paracelsus: medicine as popular protest' in O.P. Grell and A. Cunningham (eds) *Medicine and the Reformation*, London and New York, Routledge, pp.57–77.

WEEKS, A. (1997) *Paracelsus: Speculative Theory and the Crisis of the Early Reformation*, Albany, NY, University of New York Press.

YATES, F. (1964) *Giordano Bruno and the Hermetic Tradition*, Chicago, University of Chicago Press.

Anthology and Reader sources

Nicholas Goodrick-Clarke, 'The philosophy, medicine and theology of Paracelsus': *Paracelsus: Essential Readings*, Crucible (The Aquarian Press), Wellingborough, 1990, pp.23–36. (Reader, no. 29)

Paracelsus, 'On medical reform' (1529–30/1533): (i) and (ii) *Paracelsus: Essential Readings*, ed. and trans. N. Goodrick-Clarke, Crucible (The Aquarian Press), Wellingborough, 1990, pp.72–4, 167–70. (Anthology, no. 89)

Charles Webster, 'Paracelsus: medicine as popular protest': *Medicine and the Reformation*, ed. O.P. Grell and A. Cunningham, Routledge, London and New York, 1993, ch. 3, pp.57–77. (Reader, no. 28)

Gianfrancesco Pico della Mirandola, *The Witch or On the Deception of Demons*: *Strix*, 1523, Bologna, copy held by the British Library. (Anthology, no. 90)

Peter Burke, 'Witchcraft and magic in Renaissance Italy: Gianfrancesco Pico and his *Strix*': *The Damned Art: Essays in the Literature of Witchcraft*, ed. S. Anglo, Routledge and Kegan Paul, London, Henley and Boston, 1977, ch. 2, pp.32–50. (Reader, no. 31)

CHAPTER SEVEN

'Out of my door you witch': *The Witch of Edmonton*

BY RICHARD DANSON BROWN

Objectives

The objectives of this chapter are:

- to develop your sense of the 'dark side' of the Renaissance by exploring *The Witch of Edmonton*[1] in the context of other representations of witchcraft in the Renaissance;

- to give you a more localized sense of the impact of the witch persecutions by focusing on a specific case in seventeenth-century England;

- to consider the effect of collaborative authorship on our response to a literary text and our ideas of Renaissance writers;

- to explore *The Witch*'s representation of witchcraft in relation to its concern with other crimes and misdemeanours within Jacobean society.

Your first task will be to read the play through carefully. Note that all quotations from *The Witch* in this chapter are from Corbin and Sedge's 1999 single-volume edition of the play.

Introduction: representing witches

In his poem 'Witches', Ted Hughes gives a vigorous sample of traditional witchcraft imagery: witches bargained their bodies with the devil; they went 'Dancing in Ireland nightly'; they spent these nights 'under the blackamoor spraddled' only to be returned 'Back beside their spouse by dawn/As if they had dreamed all' (1995, p.39). Hughes then questions the assumption of 'our science' that witches had 'dreamed' their nocturnal excursions. In Hughes's anti-rationalist rhetoric, 'small psychology' unwisely debunks folkloric accounts of

---

[1] For the rest of this chapter, for convenience I will usually refer to the play just as *The Witch*; this was, however, also the title of a play by Thomas Middleton (*c.*1613–16), and the two should not be confused!

witches' activities. He concludes: 'who's to know/Where their feet dance while their heads sleep?' (p.39).

The poem suggests that despite modern scepticism, witchcraft was (and is) genuine: the witch could have been simultaneously dancing in Ireland and sleeping beside her spouse – she could literally have been in two places at once. Hughes necessarily writes as a poet and not as a historian of witchcraft. Most historians preface their studies with cautious discussions of the relationship between the beliefs and practices they discuss and objective reality. James Sharpe, for example, negotiates a course between his desire not to write off 'the mental worlds of our ancestors' (1997, p.6) and a broader scepticism about the reality of witchcraft. As he puts it, the issue for the historian 'is not to show that people who believed in witchcraft were stupid; it is rather to explain how a wide variety of people ... were able to hold that belief' (p.7). You have just been engaged in a similar exercise in the detailed contextualization of Gianfranceso Pico della Mirandola's *Strix* in Chapter 6.

In this chapter, we are not concerned so much with how people sustained witchcraft beliefs or whether those beliefs had any basis in fact, but rather with how witches were represented on the London stage in the seventeenth century. So I am interested in Hughes's poem not because it tells me something that I did not previously know about witchcraft, but rather as a literary representation of witches. What excites him about witches is their ambiguous location between an urgent night-time world and the bedrooms they share with their slumbering spouses. As I've said, this is a rather traditional view of witchcraft. Hughes's witches are exclusively female, though, as was noted in Chapter 6, men too were accused of witchcraft in Renaissance Europe.[2] We can also see that, unlike a historian, Hughes shows no interest in the social factors which underpinned the persecution of witches. He represents his witches wholly in terms of folkloric images of night-flying and demonic sexuality.

As we have seen in Chapter 6, most witches in demonologies are described stereotypically; similarly, Renaissance writers – and I am thinking especially of *literary* writers like poets and dramatists – tend to give stylized images of witches that concentrate on their exotic qualities. The archetypal English depiction of exotic witches is in Shakespeare's *Macbeth* (*c*.1606), where their strangeness is repeatedly stressed:

---

[2] Men were always a small minority of those accused of witchcraft. Sharpe estimates that 90 per cent of witchcraft cases in England were against women, as against 80 per cent in continental Europe (1997, p.169).

> What are these
> So wither'd and so wild in their attire,
> That look not like th'inhabitants o' th'earth,
> And yet are on't? Live you? or are you aught
> That man may question? You seem to understand me,
> By each at once her choppy finger laying
> Upon her skinny lips. You should be women,
> And yet your beards forbid me to interpret
> That you are so.
> (1.3.39–47)

These witches are related to ordinary women – 'You should be women' – yet every detail about them upsets Banquo's already rattled sense of normality. Uncouthly dressed, emaciated and bearded, these figures look like parodies of women which Banquo therefore struggles 'to interpret'. Most English literary witches recall *Macbeth*: they are presented as physically and psychologically distorted versions of ordinary women, inhabiting marginal places like the 'blasted heath' where Banquo and Macbeth meet the 'weird sisters' (1.3.77, 32). Other good examples would be Edmund Spenser's Duessa from *The Faerie Queene* (1590–96) – a seductive enchantress compelled to reveal herself once a day in her true form as 'a filthy foule old woman' (Hamilton, 1977, p.57) – and Shakespeare's Sycorax – the mother of Caliban in *The Tempest* (*c.*1611), who, in Prospero's loaded account, was banished from Algiers and had sexual relations with the devil. Hughes's poem of 1960 fits with this recipe: witches embody the dangerously unfamiliar – they are the antithesis of ordinary women.

As you might expect, the Renaissance literary witch has antecedents in classical myth and literature. Gareth Roberts (1996) has traced this figure back to the first witch in western literature, the Greek poet Homer's Circe (*The Odyssey*, Book 10), whose sorcery is shown by her predilection for transforming men into pigs. But Circe is an attractive, though dangerous, figure, with whom Odysseus cohabits for a year. A more typically horrific descendant of Circe is the Roman poet Lucan's Erictho in his epic *Pharsalia*; John Marston dramatized her in his Roman tragedy *Sophonisba* (1604–6) as a compendium of lurid horrors: 'she bursts up tombs,/From half-rot cerecloths [shrouds] then she scrapes dry gums/For her black rites' (Corbin and Sedge, 1986, p.69). This is an important point: the Renaissance literary witch is more usually derived from classical texts than from contemporaneous demonologies. In his story 'The dialogue of the dogs' (1613), Miguel de Cervantes immediately defines his witch in terms of classical examples: 'She was so unique within her profession that the Ericthos, Circes, and Medeas, of whom I've heard that the history books are full could not rival her' (Lipson, 1998, p.283).

Exercise

Figure 7.1 is a woodcut from the 1577 edition of Raphael Holinshed's *Chronicles of England, Scotland, and Ireland* showing the moment at which Macbeth and Banquo meet the witches. Do they look congruent with Banquo's description of the witches from *Macbeth*? How would you describe them?

Discussion

Holinshed was the major source for *Macbeth*, but it is clear that Shakespeare hasn't tried to verbalize this particular image in the play. Unlike the alarming figures described by Banquo, the woodcut disarmingly presents three fashionably dressed sixteenth-century ladies accosting two equally elegant gentlemen out for a ride in the country. It's a long way from the battlefield atmosphere of Act 1 of *Macbeth*. ❖

The *Riverside Shakespeare* editors link the image with Holinshed's description of the witches as 'creatures of the elder world' by suggesting that the figures could represent the classical goddesses of destiny, the Fates (Evans and Tobin, 1997, p.1390). So although these well-appointed ladies are not the 'wild' figures described by Shakespeare or Marston, they are nonetheless stereotypical images. The represented witch is a figure remembered from reading rather than drawn from actual observation; in this case, the figure of the witch has become fused with ideas of classical deities.

Figure 7.1 The weird sisters meet Macbeth and Banquo, from Raphael Holinshed's *Chronicles of England, Scotland, and Ireland*, 1577, woodcut. By permission of the Houghton Library, Harvard University, Cambridge

But in the case of *The Witch of Edmonton* (1621) we are dealing with a radically different representation. Co-authored by William Rowley, Thomas Dekker and John Ford, this play is an almost journalistic account of a contemporary witch as an unexotic, poverty-stricken old woman. It dramatizes the story of Elizabeth Sawyer, who was prosecuted and executed for witchcraft in April 1621. The first record of the play's performance is at the court of James I on 29 December 1621, so the dramatists had worked quickly (Corbin and Sedge, 1999, p.5). Their major source was a pamphlet by Henry Goodcole entitled *The Wonderfull Discoverie of Elizabeth Sawyer, a Witch*, which was possibly published within a week of Sawyer's trial (see Harris, 1998, p.173, n.65). Goodcole was the chaplain at Newgate Gaol, and claims in the pamphlet that he was Sawyer's 'continual visitor' during her imprisonment (Corbin and Sedge, 1999, p.135). We are dealing, then, with a play located in a specific place (Edmonton in Middlesex) and time (the very recent past), staging the drama around the execution of a socially marginal Englishwoman. The contrast with the texts and images we've been looking at could not be stronger. Look again at Figure 7.1 and compare these statuesque and well-dressed witches with Sawyer's description of herself: 'I am poor, deformed and ignorant,/And like a bow buckled and bent together' (2.1.3–4). Shakespeare's equally 'deformed' witches are endowed with an exotic quality which is unlike any of *The Witch*'s descriptions of Sawyer: they are divorced from the sense of solid locality which defines Sawyer as the witch of Edmonton.

Yet this play is not just about the stereotypical image of witches as poor old women victimized by their communities (see Chapter 6). As well as the Sawyer narrative, the play includes two other plots, neither of which comes from Goodcole: Cuddy Banks's inept attempts to gain Katherine Carter's love through the assistance of the Dog, and the domestic tragedy of Frank Thorney's bigamous marriages. One of the major aims of this chapter will be to help you see that the play's representation of witchcraft is part of its wider concern with other and related misdemeanours. *The Witch* is not solely about witchcraft – as with so many other witch-related texts, witchcraft seems to be a vehicle for wider social and intellectual debate. As we have seen in the study of *Strix*, Pico della Mirandola's concern to prove the reality of witchcraft is related to his desire to attack humanism and to reassert the priority of Christian theology over pagan literature. In this case, the dramatists have taken a witch narrative and used it as an opportunity to develop what is cumulatively a subtle portrait of a provincial society. In that society, witchcraft is only one among a range of immoral activities. The play seems to suggest that compared with the predatory seduction of humble virgins by aristocrats, bigamy and murder, witchcraft is a less heinous sin.

Witchcraft in England

Through reading *Strix*, you have begun considering the intellectual background to the persecution of witches in early modern Europe. But as the studies of Sharpe and Robin Briggs (1996) have underlined, witch hunts differed from country to country. For example, the English legal processes surrounding witchcraft did not

Figure 7.2 Punishments for witchcraft, from *The Apprehension and Confession of Three Notorious Witches ... at Chelmsforde*, 1589. The Archbishop of Canterbury and the Trustees of Lambeth Palace Library

allow for the use of torture to extract confessions (Sharpe, 1997, pp.213–15), though popular forms of torture like the swimming test did occur in English villages (Reader, no. 32, p.349). Similarly, convicted English witches were executed by hanging rather than burning, which was the standard punishment elsewhere in Europe, including Scotland (Figure 7.2; Rosen, 1991, p.183).[3] *News from Scotland* (1591), a pamphlet which documents a case in which King James VI was centrally involved, goes to some lengths to explain to its English readers both the use of torture in the investigation of witchcraft allegations and the burning of the unfortunate Dr Fian (see Figure 7.3).

Figure 7.3 Frontispiece to *News from Scotland declaring the damnable life and death of Doctor Fian, a notable sorcerer, who was burned at Denborough in January last, 1591.* This woodcut was a schematic representation of a range of incidents from Fian's career. Bodleian Library, University of Oxford. Douce F 210

[3] Intriguingly, the play does refer to burning when Sir Arthur Clarington says 'Nay, if she be a witch, and the harms she does end in such sports, she may 'scape burning' (4.1.71–2). The legal position was that witchcraft activities were related to ordinary felonies, so that an accused witch who had used occult means to kill another person was technically guilty of murder and so received the standard penalty for that crime, hanging. The only circumstances in which an English witch could be burned were if she had used witchcraft to kill her husband which meant she was guilty of petty treason rather than felony (see Sharpe, 1997, p.90). The writer of a 1582 account of an outbreak of witchcraft at St Osyth in Essex, probably the examining justice Brian Darcy, argues that hanging is actually too merciful a punishment for convicted witches (see Rosen, 1991, pp.105–6).

Read 'Manifold impieties: the social setting' by Anthony Harris (Reader, no. 32), which explains the legal basis for the persecution of witches, alongside quotations from primary documents. ❖

This section will further consider what was distinctive about English ideas of witchcraft. First we shall look at an eccentric example of learned opinion which was a significant influence on the writers of *The Witch*, then explore the role of the witch's **familiar** in England, since this figure has such a distinctive profile in the play.

One of the liveliest English witch texts was paradoxically the work of a convinced sceptic, Reginald Scot. Scot is an Apistius ('unbeliever') who knows the arguments of Phronimus ('prudent') in detail (Reader, no. 31, p.329), yet shows no signs of being convinced by them – indeed, he goes so far as to write a massive book to refute them. Refreshingly for the modern reader, his *Discoverie of Witchcraft* (1584) at first seems to oppose traditional demonology with a robust common sense:

> If it were true that witches confesse, or that all writers write, or that witchmongers report, or that fooles believe, we should never have butter in the chearne, nor cow in the close, nor corne in the field, nor faire weather abroad, nor health within doores.

> (Nicholson, 1886, p.49)

Scot asserts that 'witchmongers' rarely try to tally their extravagant claims with objective reality – if 'the fables of witchcraft' (Nicholson, 1886, p.1) were true, there would never be any food on the table. Note how Scot's accumulating clauses dismissively imply that 'witchmongers' and 'fooles' are indistinguishable. Because of his scepticism, Scot offers what seem like modern explanations for witchcraft accusations: marginal figures are persecuted because they diverge from communal norms. In the following extract, Scot gives a classic portrait of the witch as a social outcast. I quote at some length partly because Scot's prose needs space to make its full impact, but also to give you a detailed view of English witches. You may need to read this a couple of times before moving on – like most Elizabethan writers, Scot liked long and complicated sentences!

> One sort of such as are said to be witches, are women which be commonly old, lame, bleare-eied, pale, fowle, and full of wrinkles; poore, sullen, superstitious, and papists; or such as knowe no religion: in whose drousie mindes the divell hath gotten a fine seat; so as, what mischeefe, mischance, calamitie, or slaughter is brought to passe, they are easilie persuaded the same is doone by themselves; imprinting in their minds an earnest and constant imagination hereof. They are leane and deformed, shewing melancholie in their faces, to

the horror of all that see them. They are doting, scolds, mad, divelish; and not much differing from them that are thought to be possessed with spirits; so firme and stedfast in their opinions, as whosoever shall onelie have respect to the constancie of their words uttered, would easlie beleeve they were true indeed.

These miserable wretches are so odious unto all their neighbours, and so feared, as few dare offend them, or denie them anie thing they aske: whereby they take upon them; yea, and sometimes thinke, that they can doo such things as are beyond the abilitie of humane nature. These go from house to house, and from doore to doore for a pot full of milke, yest, drinke, pottage [soup], or some such releefe; without the which they could hardlie live: neither obtaining for their service and paines nor by their art, nor yet at the divels hands (with whome they are said to make a perfect and visible bargaine) either beautie, monie, promotion, welth, worship, pleasure, honor, knowledge, learning, or anie other benefit whatsoever.

(Nicholson, 1886, pp.5–6)

<table>
<tr><td>

Exercise

</td><td>

1 How does Scot account for witchcraft accusations?

2 How would you characterize Scot's attitude to the people he describes?

</td></tr>
<tr><td>

Discussion

</td><td>

1 Scot gives two related explanations of why poor old women were particularly vulnerable to accusations of witchcraft. First, he suggests that these women are so physically and intellectually impoverished that their 'drousie mindes' become susceptible to the belief that they are witches. Second, because these women are so frightening and offensive to their neighbours, they become further convinced of their extraordinary abilities. In brief, Scot offers one explanation located in the mentalities of accused witches and another located in their communities.

2 Scot's own attitude is one of patrician disdain for these lower-class women. Notice how he focuses on their physical blemishes: 'bleare-eied', 'fowle, and full of wrinkles'. These women are 'miserable wretches' whose delusions can be explained by this educated writer but hardly sympathized with. Scot presents a generalized portrait of 'such as are said to be witches'; unlike Rowley, Dekker and Ford – who concentrate on making one witch a dramatically credible figure – he shows no interest here in particular cases. Rather, he maximizes the reader's sense of the deformity of alleged witches in order to rubbish the claims of demonologists. Just look at the sort of people these so-called experts accuse of being witches, Scot says: they're a miserable bunch, whose allegedly magical powers have done nothing to alleviate their poverty. ❖

</td></tr>
</table>

Scot's disdain incidentally highlights how far he was a writer of his time, rather than a precursor of modern scepticism. As well as concentrating on their physical shortcomings, Scot notes that these women are 'superstitious, and papists'. This implies that they are superstitious *because* they are Catholics. In Scot's overall argument, there is a strong connection between a belief in witchcraft and a belief in Catholicism, which paradoxically links his work with that of English demonologists who persistently viewed witchcraft as a function of residual Catholic beliefs and practices (Sharpe, 1997, pp.53–4). As an example of this tendency, Roberts notes that in 1586, the year she was tried for treason, three English poems identified Mary, Queen of Scots, 'as a witch and a seductive Circe' (1996, p.202). It is therefore an oversimplification to see Scot as an 'enlightened' thinker (Sharpe, 1997, p.54).

Nonetheless, Scot gives a fuller picture of the stereotypical witch. Female, old and poor, this figure is defined as a witch because of her own intellectual limitations and the social conditions in which she finds herself. *The Witch*'s portrayal of Elizabeth Sawyer draws on this kind of scepticism. Take her first soliloquy:

> Some call me witch,
> And, being ignorant of myself, they go
> About to teach me how to be one, urging
> That my bad tongue, by their bad usage made so,
> Forspeaks [bewitches] their cattle, doth bewitch their corn,
> Themselves, their servants and their babes at nurse.
>
> (2.1.8–13)

Almost like a modern sociologist, Sawyer insists that her badness is a product of social intercourse – she has been 'made so' by the 'bad usage' of her neighbours. By looking back at the neighbourly frictions described by Scot, you will be able to see that the dramatists' sense of witchcraft as a social misdemeanour has been informed by the *Discoverie*. Anthony Dawson, indeed, connects 'the scapegoat role [Sawyer] has been forced to play in the community' with the similar role of Shylock in Shakespeare's *The Merchant of Venice* (1989, p.80; see also Mateer, 2000, pp.346–50).

Yet scepticism was not the norm. Thousands of people like Elizabeth Sawyer were executed as witches during the Renaissance (see Chapter 6), and this persecution was supported by both elite writers and popular fears. Having read extracts from *Strix*, you can imagine the outrage Scot's *Discoverie* provoked among learned demonologists: James VI of Scotland asserted that his *Daemonologie* (1597) was partly written 'against [Scot's] damnable opinions' (Harrison, 1966, p.xi);

he is even reputed to have ordered the burning of remaining copies of the *Discoverie* when he became king of England in 1603 (Sharpe, 1997, p.55). While *The Witch of Edmonton* draws on Scot's thinking, there are many more English texts – both learned treatises like *Daemonologie* and popular accounts of particular witch hunts – which replicate the strategies of *Strix*. Goodcole's *Wonderfull Discoverie* is, as we shall see, a typical example of English demonology.

Before turning directly to Goodcole, we need to think about the familiar. Animal familiars were more prominent in English accounts of witchcraft than in continental ones; they constitute a leitmotif of witchcraft in England. What, then, was the function of these shadowy figures?

Exercise

Read *The Witch*, 2.1.106–91. How would you characterize the Dog's role in this exchange?

Discussion

The whole of this dialogue is extraordinary. A talking dog offers a socially outcast old woman revenge on her enemies in exchange for her 'soul and body'. You may feel that this is an early modern equivalent of science fiction – that it is a text which grafts the unknown or implausible onto a broadly realistic background. But the Dog is not an extraterrestrial being: as the devil he is already a part of Sawyer's mental world. (He later explains to Cuddy Banks that he is a spirit who is always on the look-out for opportunities to entrap unwary souls: 'Thou never art so distant/From an evil spirit but that thy oaths,/Curses, and blasphemies pull him to thine elbow' (5.1.137–9)). This scene presents the Dog as the devil in the act of seducing Sawyer into a diabolical pact. ❖

Read in this way, *The Witch* is reminiscent of Christopher Marlowe's *Doctor Faustus* (*c*.1588–9), in which Faustus 'bequeath[s] his soul to Lucifer' by signing it away in his own blood (Bevington and Rasmussen, 1995, p.153). The animal familiar would then be a different manifestation of the devil: where in *Doctor Faustus*, Lucifer (or the devil) appears as himself and through the demon Mephistopheles, in *The Witch*, he becomes the Dog. Writing more generally about the importance of familiars in England, Robin Briggs notes that: 'The animal familiars ... quite clearly performed the role of the Devil': taking the place of the devil, the familiar persuades his victim to become a witch (1996, p.29). Yet Briggs admits that English familiars exhibit 'striking peculiarities of detail'. The image of the Dog sucking Sawyer's arm is just such a detail. Figures 7.4, 7.5 and 7.10 show the range of creatures portrayed and identified as familiars in English witchcraft pamphlets; dogs, cats, toads, hedgehogs, rats: any of these could be potential wicked spirits. So as we read this passage – or

Figure 7.4 A devil-dog, from *The Examination and Confession of Certaine Wytches at Chensforde* [Chelmsford], 1566. The Archbishop of Canterbury and the Trustees of Lambeth Palace Library

especially if we are lucky enough to see it in the theatre – we sense that something out of the ordinary is happening. You might say that we experience similar feelings in reading or watching *Doctor Faustus*. But there are key differences. Marlowe's play is centrally concerned with the 'hellish fall' of a 'learned man': it dramatizes Faustus's intellectual journey from licit to illicit forms of knowledge (Bevington and Rasmussen, 1995, p.183). Though even a secular audience will be horrified by Faustus's 'fiendful fortune' (p.183), by the end of the play it should understand how he has moved from excelling in the study of 'divinity' to falling through the pursuit of 'cursed necromancy' (p.139). There is no such intellectual journey in *The Witch*: indeed, we could say that where *Doctor Faustus* dramatizes elite ideas of magic, the later play explores more popular ideas of witchcraft.

This is a good point to explore the issue, already touched on in Chapter 6, of the relationship between learned and popular conceptions of witchcraft. In his seminal book on Renaissance magic in England, Keith Thomas argued that where learned opinion focused on the notion that witches entered a pact with the devil, popular opinion was concerned with *maleficium*, or the witch's alleged ability to harm others through occult means (1973, pp.525–34). While learned writers constructed an intellectual understanding of the devil as the enemy of Christianity, the people involved in witchcraft persecutions – like Old Banks in *The Witch* – were motivated by the perception that their families and goods were under attack from

accused witches. More recently, historians like Barry Reay have
questioned this dichotomy, arguing that the intersections between
learned and popular beliefs are so complicated that neatly separating
them is impossible and misleading. In the context of this debate,
familiars demonstrate the cross-overs between apparently different
belief systems. As Reay puts it: 'The belief in familiars meshed
comfortably with theories of satanic influence through the agency of
demons and, whatever the origins of this popular superstition ... the
figure of the familiar remained central to English witch beliefs' (1998,
p.116). In other words, the familiar is indicative of both popular

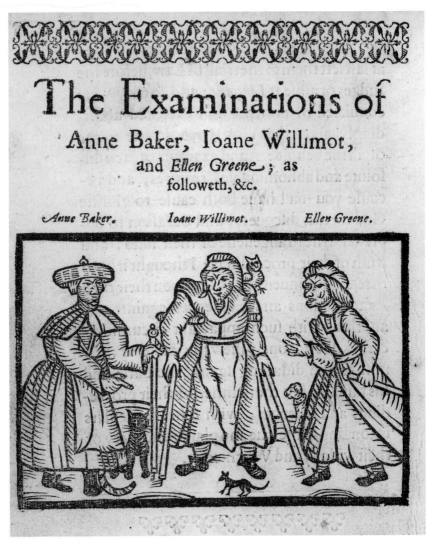

Figure 7.5 Witches with familiars, from *The Wonderful Discoverie of the Witchcrafts of Margaret and Philip Fowler*, 1619. © The Trustees of the British Library, London

NB

*priorities:
one's goods or one's soul*

superstition and elite ideas of demonic possession; but we can't unequivocally identify that belief as wholly popular or learned – it participates in both traditions. Literary texts like *The Witch* exemplify this kind of complication. Though Sawyer's demonic pact may remind us of *Doctor Faustus*, it does not follow that Rowley, Dekker and Ford are giving an exclusively learned representation of witchcraft. Rather, the echo of Marlowe more plausibly signals their work as popular dramatists since *Doctor Faustus* was one of the most popular and widely staged Elizabethan plays, while the scene crucially differs from its Marlovian prototype in centring on the figure of the demonic familiar. Like the familiar itself, *The Witch* shows the dense interconnections between learned and popular ideas of witchcraft.

This discussion could suggest that *The Witch* is simply a dramatization of its demonological source. Yet the play tells the story of Elizabeth Sawyer in radically different ways from the demonological tract. Let's now look at Goodcole's pamphlet to compare how the play and its source represent the demonic familiar.

Exercise

Read the complete text of Goodcole's pamphlet in Corbin and Sedge (1999, pp.135–49). The first half is a sketchy report of Sawyer's trial; the second half records Sawyer's confession, which Goodcole puts in the form of a dialogue because 'she was a very ignorant woman' (p.141). ❖

Now let's look in more detail at Goodcole's interrogation of Sawyer:

[Goodcole] In what shape would the Devil come unto you?

[Sawyer] Always in the shape of a dog of two colours, sometimes of black and sometimes of white.

[Goodcole] What talk had the Devil and you together ... what did he ask of you and what did you desire of him?

[Sawyer] He asked of me ... how I did and what he should do for me, and demanded of me my soul and body, threatening then to tear me in pieces if that I did not grant unto him my soul and my body ...

[Goodcole] What did you after such the Devil's asking of you ... and after this his threatening of you? Did you for fear grant unto the Devil his desires?

[Sawyer] Yes, I granted for fear unto the Devil his request of my soul and body; and to seal this my promise made unto him I then gave him leave to suck my blood ...

[Goodcole] In what place of your body did the Devil suck of your blood, and whether did he himself choose the place or did you yourself appoint him the place? Tell the truth I charge you, as ... [you] will answer unto the Almighty God, and tell the reason, if that you can, why he would suck your blood.

[Sawyer] The place where the Devil sucked my blood was a little above my fundament, and that place chosen by himself. And in that place, by continual drawing, there is a thing in the form of a teat at which the Devil would suck me. And I asked the Devil why he would suck my blood and he said it was to nourish him.

[Goodcole] Whether did you pull up your coats or no when the Devil came to suck you?

[Sawyer] No, I did not. But the Devil would put his head under my coats and I did willingly suffer him to do what he would.

(Corbin and Sedge, 1999, pp.143–4)

Figure 7.6 Henry Goodcole, *The Wonderfull Discoverie of Elizabeth Sawyer, a Witch*, 1621. © The Trustees of the British Library, London

Reading this passage immediately after *The Witch* 2.1, your first reaction is probably to think how close the play is to the pamphlet. Phrases like 'threatening then to tear me in pieces if that I did not grant unto him my soul and my body' are assimilated almost directly into the play. The closeness of play to pamphlet is another indication that Renaissance writers were not interested in the kind of originality prized by nineteenth-century critics like Burckhardt. It may also corroborate the idea that the play is a dramatic transcription of Goodcole. But there are other ways we can look at the relationship between these texts.

Exercise

What would you say is the major difference between Goodcole's account of Sawyer's relationship with the Dog and the presentation of that relationship in *The Witch* 2.1?

Discussion

The major difference which I notice is how the story is told, and therefore why it's being told. Goodcole claims he uses dialogue because of Sawyer's ignorance, implying that, had she been able to make a continuous confession, he would have preferred to record that. The dialogue makes us feel that Sawyer is being cross-examined again – it reminds me of Apistius's questioning of the witch in *Strix*. We could say that this constitutes a post-trial interrogation, confirming the legitimacy of the conviction. In the margins of the dialogue, Goodcole includes notes which explain why he asked particular questions. So the inquiry about 'what place of your body did the Devil suck' was intended 'to confirm the women's search of her' – that is, the question corroborates the evidence discovered on Sawyer's body during the trial. It seems to me that Goodcole needs to convince himself and his readers that Sawyer really was a witch and that her execution was justified. Note how mechanical and repetitive the dialogue is: the shape of Sawyer's sentences is very much dictated by the form of Goodcole's questions. His pamphlet makes no attempt to present her as an individual speaker: as in *Strix*, the witch's speech is only recorded to clarify that she is a spiritual outcast. In this sense, Goodcole's text exhibits the tendency for 'confessions to conform to the preconceived ideas of those who extracted them' (Thomas, 1973, p.617); Sawyer's confession, then, is shaped by Goodcole's interrogation. By contrast, the play is not recording a confession – the dramatists have no need to support Sawyer's conviction because they are staging her actions as reported by Goodcole. It is in the play rather than the pamphlet that Sawyer begins to emerge as a humanly credible figure: in this scene, she is assaulted by Old Banks then mocked by Cuddy and the other dancers, so that when she meets the Dog, the audience can understand why she is susceptible to this creature. Cumulatively this scene and the play as a whole seem to endorse Sawyer's own judgement that 'Tis all one/To be a witch as to be counted one'. ❖

leading the witness

You were probably also struck by the lurid quality in Goodcole's interrogation. This is most notable in his placement of the devil's mark 'a little above [Sawyer's] fundament', whereas the play locates it on her arm. The dramatists had to change this detail for practical reasons, yet it still signals an important difference between the play and its source. As I've suggested, Goodcole uses Sawyer's confession to corroborate the evidence against her. In the first half of the pamphlet, the devil's mark is described in more detail: 'a thing like a teat, the bigness of the little finger ... which was branched at the top like a teat and seemed as though one had sucked it, and that the bottom thereof was blue and the top ... red' (Corbin and Sedge, 1999, p.140). In fact, the court is persuaded of Sawyer's guilt on the evidence of a group of three 'grave matrons' of 'honest reputation', who conduct a physical examination of Sawyer which reveals a 'private and strange mark on her body' which is then identified as the mark of the devil (pp.140, 139). Though there is a temptation to feel that Goodcole's text records an assault by masculine authority (in the shape of both the court and the writer) on an isolated woman, we should remember that women actively participated in Sawyer's conviction. To the modern reader, this 'teat' seems to be extremely slender evidence on which to condemn someone to death: it did not occur to Goodcole, the court, or the women who strip-searched Sawyer, that this 'thing' could be as prosaic as a haemorrhoid. Jonathan Gil Harris explains the thinking underlying this passage: 'Goodcole's attention to these "markes" demonstrates how he regards Elizabeth Sawyer's body as a signifying text' (1998, p.129). By reading Sawyer's body, Goodcole confirms her guilt.

By contrast, *The Witch* does not lay such a disturbing emphasis on Sawyer's body. It rather suggests that her submission to the Dog is a product of her position as a social outcast. I would say that when we look at the play alongside its source we become aware of a contrast between psychological and physical representations of witchcraft. Now I'm not suggesting that Rowley, Dekker and Ford were convinced sceptics who wrote the play to send up Goodcole's pamphlet; since the first recorded performance was at the court of James I, it would be extremely unlikely that the dramatists would have gone out of their way to antagonize this powerful 'witchmonger'.[4] Nonetheless, the play's account of the relationship between witch and familiar is

---

[4] Though James was himself a demonologist, it's worth noting that the evidence about his behaviour as king is more ambivalent. As Sharpe notes: 'The problem with his legendary status as a witch-hunter ... is that despite his involvement in the trials of 1590–91 and his tract of 1597, James, at least as monarch of England, seems to have been more likely to intervene to save witches than to secure their convictions' (1997, pp.48–9). See also Anthony Harris's account of James's behaviour as king in the Reader (no. 32).

strikingly more subtle than the pamphlet's. Just look at how the dramatists expand Sawyer's remark in Goodcole that the devil 'asked of me ... how I did' into a portrayal of an intimate relationship. Though the Dog threatens her, he also uses an affectionate tone which is startlingly unlike the way Sawyer has been addressed up until this point. Compare the Dog's 'Come, do not fear, I love thee much too well/To hurt or fright thee' with Old Banks's refusal to let Sawyer gather his sticks: 'Down with them when I bid thee, quickly. I'll make thy bones rattle in thy skin else' (2.1.131–2; 21–2). Paradoxically, Old Banks treats Sawyer like an animal, while the Dog – apparently himself an animal – treats her with something like human warmth.

The Witch's psychology, then, lies in making the audience appreciate that Sawyer is vulnerable to the Dog because of her isolation: as well as threats of violence, he offers her an affection which is only hinted at in Goodcole's account. You could also look at the passage where Sawyer asks the Dog to 'Kiss me, my Tommy,/And rub away some wrinkles on my brow ... Let's tickle' (4.1.170–71, 174), which has no precedent in Goodcole. Though the Dog is presented as a genuine and terrifying supernatural being, the dramatists show their absorption of Scot's ideas by stressing that Sawyer's status as a witch has been manufactured within society as much as in the devil's schemes for world domination.

What, then, have we learned about witchcraft in England? Through looking at the work of writers like Scot and Goodcole, we have encountered a broad range of contemporaneous English witch beliefs. At one extreme, it was possible to believe with Scot that there was no such thing as witchcraft, or at least that witchcraft accusations were more a product of social interactions than supernatural interventions. I have suggested that *The Witch* registers the influence of this kind of scepticism. But equally, the intersecting lore surrounding demonic pacts and animal familiars was capable of leading to the conviction and execution of women like Elizabeth Sawyer on the basis of slender physical evidence.

And what about the familiars? By reading Goodcole alongside *The Witch*, we have seen that the familiars functioned in English accounts as manifestations of the devil. Yet I also hope you have a feeling for the oddness of these creatures and the thinking which transformed domestic animals into demons. Goodcole also points us in the direction of the connection between familiars and ideas of demonic sexuality. Commenting on Goodcole's interest in Sawyer's body, Sharpe sees 'an echo of that sexual prurience which was so manifest in some continental accounts of the witch's relations with the devil' (1997, pp.74–5). You will remember from *Strix* the witch's account of her sexual relations with the devil (Anthology, no. 90, p.382). In *The Witch* interest in the witch's body is replaced with an interest in the local processes which lead Sawyer into witchcraft.

Collaboration in *The Witch*

Our inquiry into English witchcraft beliefs has led us closer to the play itself, and I hope that this contextualization has incidentally stimulated your interest in *The Witch* as a work of literature. But before we analyse the play, we need to think about one of its most intriguing aspects: that it was written by three different dramatists. The title page of the first edition, which was not published until 1658, states that it was 'composed ... By divers well-esteemed Poets; *William Rowley, Thomas Dekker, John Ford*, &c'. That '&c' (see Figure 7.7) implies that even more writers may have been involved in the writing of the play. As you will remember from Book 2 in this series, post-Romantic critics like Burckhardt tend to view art as the product of solitary geniuses like Shakespeare and Leonardo da Vinci. A powerful play written by a committee of 'divers well-esteemed Poets' is a challenge to this view: if the greatest art is created by artists with almost divine gifts, then a collaboratively written work should hamstring the conceptions of each individual participant.

Exercise

What do you make of this problem? See if you can think of any successful works of art which have been written or composed by more than one person.

Discussion

Single authorship is more widespread than collaboration, or at least it seems to be. In the context of this series, *The Witch* is the only text to have been written collaboratively. Yet if we think of the work of Renaissance visual artists, we will quickly remember that masters like Leonardo were often helped by pupils and assistants, so that one painting could quite easily be the work of two or more artists. If we update our cultural references, we can point to twentieth-century examples of collaborative art: feature films, manufactured by large casts of writers, actors, designers, and directors; rock albums, often co-written by various musicians then polished for the public by producers. Though we habitually think of art as the product of a single intelligence, this post-Romantic ideal is only one among a broad range of creative strategies. ❖

Indeed, collaboration was widespread among English Renaissance dramatists. This is hardly surprising: since plays were written quickly to meet the public's demand for new material, collaboration would give hard-pressed writers breathing space as well as the opportunity to learn from working directly with their colleagues. To give you an idea of the speed at which plays had to be written, consider Shakespeare's career: between about 1590 and 1613 he wrote at least 37 plays – that is, just under two plays every year (Evans and Tobin, 1997, pp.78–87). Between 1598 and 1602, Dekker was apparently involved in the composition of an amazing 45 plays (Bentley, 1956, p.242). In the case of *The Witch*, since it was dramatizing 'A known true STORY' (title page), speed was of the essence. Once Elizabeth Sawyer lost her topicality, a play about her would lose its commercial appeal. You can see the same pressures at work in films based on true stories: the aim of the producers is always to release their versions before the story has been forgotten.

The London stage encouraged a culture of collaboration. Dekker worked widely with writers like Ford, Thomas Middleton, John Marston and Philip Massinger; Rowley seems to have been a specialist collaborator, writing with Middleton, John Fletcher and Thomas Heywood (Gurr, 1980, pp.219–25). Now you might be tempted to think – following a post-Romantic view of literary creativity – that none of the plays written in this way could be as good or coherent as solo-authored plays like *The Merchant of Venice*. This would, I think, be false reasoning. Though some plays like *Patient Grissil* (1600) by Dekker, Henry Chettle and William Haughton are not nowadays much read, we could equally point to major plays like Rowley and Middleton's *The Changeling* (1622), or Francis Beaumont and John Fletcher's *The Maid's Tragedy* (1610), which continue to be read and staged. It's also worth noticing that Shakespeare – in many ways the epitome of Burckhardt's conception of artistic genius (1990, p.205) – worked collaboratively himself. The late plays *Henry VIII* (*c*.1612–13) and *The Two Noble Kinsmen* (*c*.1613) were written with Fletcher; Shakespeare was possibly helped by persons unknown on *1 Henry VI* (*c*.1589–90), *Timon of Athens* (*c*.1607–8), and even *Macbeth* (*c*.1606). On this evidence, it looks as though our ideas of literary creativity need to be able to accommodate co-authored plays like *The Witch*.

So, who were the collaborators on this project, and what was their other work like? What are the implications of the way the play was written for our study of it – can we distinguish which bits were written by whom, and does collaboration undermine the text's coherence?

Even less is known about Rowley, Dekker and Ford than about Shakespeare. Their precise dates and places of birth are unknown, and the bulk of the information we have about these men is connected with their work as playwrights. Rowley and Dekker were both theatrical professionals. Rowley was known both as a playwright and as an actor from 1607 to his death in 1626; Dekker is first recorded as a playwright in 1598, and he continued to write plays, pamphlets and pageants until his death in about 1632. We know virtually nothing about their family backgrounds. It's important to understand that Rowley and Dekker were very different kinds of playwright from Shakespeare. Throughout his career, Shakespeare wrote for one company, of which he became a major shareholder; Rowley and Dekker lacked this extraordinary security of employment, both writing for different companies at different times. They were literary hired hands who had to work quickly and effectively to make ends meet.

Socially at least, Ford (*c.*1586–?1639) was a different kind of writer. He came from an aristocratic Devon family and during the first decade of the seventeenth century attended the Middle Temple, one of London's Inns of Court. These institutions were ostensibly colleges for trainee lawyers, but also performed a broader function as finishing schools for ambitious and affluent young men like Ford. John Donne and Marston, whose social origins were similar to Ford's, were also students at the Inns of Court. As Bentley notes, Ford's collaboration with Dekker (they worked together on four other plays between 1621 and 1624) is surprising in the light of 'what little is known of the two men and from the personal interests reflected in their works' (1956, p.244). Bentley's point is that Dekker tended to write popular plays centring on the exploits of citizen protagonists, like *The Shoemaker's Holiday* (1600), which appealed to audiences composed of similar people at public theatres like the Rose and the Red Bull. Ford's plays, on the other hand, seem to have been designed for the more aristocratic audiences of indoor playhouses like the Blackfriars and the Cockpit: it cost about six times as much to see a play at the Blackfriars as it did at the Globe or any of the other amphitheatres (Gurr, 1980, p.146). Ford's most famous play, *Tis Pity She's A Whore* (*c.*1629–33), is an elaborate revenge tragedy which recycles many fashionable intellectual ideas in its portrayal of an incestuous relationship between a brother and a sister. It was first performed at the Cockpit playhouse by Queen Henrietta's Men.[5] But it would be unwise to see this as clinching evidence for Ford's upward mobility as a dramatist – the title page of *The Witch* states that this play was also 'often [performed] at the Cock-Pit in *Drury-Lane*'. The wide repertoire of English Renaissance plays was capable of appealing to different audiences from citizen playgoers at the amphitheatres through to aristocrats at court and the indoor theatres.

[5] Both *Tis Pity She's A Whore* and *The Witch of Edmonton* were performed at the Cockpit playhouse or the Phoenix Theatre in Drury Lane; confusingly enough, there was another Cockpit, the Cockpit-in-Court. The Drury Lane Cockpit was built for the theatrical entrepreneur, Christopher Beeston, in 1617; the Cockpit-in-Court was built in 1629–30. Both buildings were probably designed by Inigo Jones (Gurr, 1980, pp.147–55).

So why did this gentleman work with these two popular writers? The simple answer is that we don't know, though we may speculate that Ford himself was hard-up and needed to learn how to write plays from working alongside professional playwrights. Being a gentleman has never been an insurance against poverty, and though Ford seems to have inherited money from his father, he may have had financial problems which forced him to write for the stage (Bentley, 1956, p.436). The seventeenth-century writers of *The Witch* are, then, inevitably rather shadowy figures to twenty-first-century readers.

We have an idea of why dramatists collaborated; the next issue to consider is how they worked together. It's important to be aware that there is little primary data about which dramatist wrote what in any given play. Often all the information we have is a title page, like that of *The Witch*, alerting us to the fact that the text was written collaboratively. This means that our sense of how these plays were written is constructed by scholars' research and guess work. For example, with Middleton and Rowley's *The Changeling*, on the basis of detailed readings of the play alongside the playwrights' other works, there is widespread agreement that Middleton wrote most of the main plot, while Rowley handled the subplot. By paying attention to the linguistic and narrative quirks of each writer, scholars have attempted to map the composition of such plays. In *The Changeling*, Rowley is partly believed to have written the subplot because the clown Lollio closely resembles a 'particular type of humorous figure' which is often found in his work – Nigel Bawcutt connects Lollio with Cuddy Banks (1958, p.xliii). You may detect a bit of circular reasoning here: arguing that Rowley wrote Lollio because he also wrote Cuddy depends on ascribing those parts of *The Witch* to Rowley, which is something which we can't unequivocally do!

Reconstructions of *The Changeling*'s composition suggest that each playwright took responsibility for a distinct portion of the play, but with both closely aware of what his partner was writing. This tallies with the surviving primary evidence of collaborative practices. In 1624, Dekker, Rowley, Ford and John Webster worked together on a play (subsequently lost) called *The Late Murder of the Son upon the Mother, or Keep the Widow Waking*. Like *The Witch*, this was based on real life stories: the domestic tragedy of a son who murdered his mother, and the tale of how a young rogue managed to deceive a wealthy widow into marrying him by keeping her 'dead drunk for about five days' (Bentley, 1956, p.254). Unfortunately for the dramatists and the Red Bull Theatre which staged the play, the widow's relatives were not amused and brought a legal action against the theatre. Dekker's evidence gives a fascinating glimpse of how playwrights worked together in the 1620s:

> this Defend[an]t [Dekker] sayth, that true it is, Hee wrote two sheetes of paper conteyning the first Act of a Play called The Late Murder in White Chappel, or Keepe the Widow waking, and a speech in the Last Scene of the Last Act of the Boy who had killed his mother.
>
> (Bentley, 1956, p.255)

Exercise

What attitude do you think Dekker displays to his work in this comment?

Discussion

Though this is evidence given to a court of law, rather than a writer discussing the finer points of literary composition for interested readers, it seems to me that there is something in these abrupt and unexpansive phrases which reflects Dekker's probable attitude to this lost play. He sounds workmanlike, as though the writing of this play has been one literary chore among the many others he had already carried out. *The Late Murder* sounds literally like a literary production. Dekker's comment also suggests a broader pragmatism which was characteristic of collaborative writing. As well as 'two sheetes of paper conteyning the first Act', he incidentally wrote a speech within 'the Last Scene' of the play – we can almost imagine the stumped Rowley, Ford or Webster turning to Dekker for help with the tricky task of writing an appropriate speech for a 'Boy' who has murdered his mother. There's something rather functional about this model of composition which contrasts powerfully with the later ideal that writing is an all-important task to which the writer dedicates body and soul. ❖

How have scholars divided up the composition of the play? As Corbin and Sedge summarize, it has generally been felt that Dekker was the project leader and wrote the scenes dealing with Elizabeth Sawyer. Rowley, the comic specialist, would have written the Cuddy Banks material, while Ford would have handled the Thorney plot (1999, p.6). Yet this putative division of labour is by no means as neat or persuasive as the account of the writing of *The Changeling*. There are many overlaps between the different narrative strands: the Sawyer and Cuddy Banks plots intersect (2.1; 5.1); the Dog crucially intervenes in the Thorney plot (3.3; 4.2). This suggests that the search for the individual 'hand' of a particular dramatist is probably fruitless. Though 1.1 reminds me of the beginning of *Tis Pity She's A Whore*, there is no external proof that Ford (rather than Dekker or Rowley) wrote it. If we can't identify the writer of a passage, we should then devote our energies to understanding the design of the play as a whole. The fact that plots and motifs overlap usefully signals the care with which the play has been put together. Despite Dekker's offhand account of the composition of *The Late Murder*, we are entitled to look closely at the dramatic design of *The Witch*.

This approach is congruent with Jeffrey Masten's recent attack on the thinking which underlies such attribution studies. Masten argues that collaboration was the rule and not the exception among English Renaissance dramatists. He suggests that the scholarly preoccupation with ascribing authorship is actively detrimental to our understanding of how these plays were written and the literary values they embody. Quite simply, once scholars try to label parts of *The Witch* as Rowley's or Dekker's or Ford's, they betray their feeling that the play *should* have been written by one of them. We then fail to see that the play was composed and produced through a complex series of collaborations. In Masten's terms, the text of *The Witch* that comes down to us is a deposit of collaborations not only between the dramatists, but also the actors, theatre managers, censors and publishers who were all successively involved in its writing, performance and publication (1997, pp.13–27).

What are the implications of the collaborative authorship of *The Witch* to our study of the play? The fact that collaboration was so widespread in Renaissance England leads us to question the Burckhardtian model of artistic creation. By trying to imagine the material conditions in which these playwrights wrought their play – what we might call the collaborative boiler room – we implicitly challenge later ideas of authorship. We have also seen that in practice it's difficult to determine who precisely wrote which parts of the play. I have suggested it was subtly constructed by its three writers. So instead of lamenting the fact that *The Witch* was not the work of one writer alone, we should approach it as a coherent piece of writing in its own terms: as a collaboratively written play script.

Studying *The Witch*

Our major concern in this section will be to look at *The Witch* as a complex representation of a local milieu, in which witchcraft is presented alongside related narratives about bigamy, murder and deception. This section will take the form of an exploration of the play's genre, language and location. Through this analysis, we should get closer to the 'dark side' of English Renaissance culture.

Locating *The Witch*: genre

The first issue to consider is what kind of a play this is, since genre is so crucial to the production of dramatic meaning (Mateer, 2000, p.333). As a preliminary to this, we need a sense of how the play is constructed.

Exercise

Quickly flick through the play. Write a brief summary of the major action which takes place in each Act.

Discussion

This is my summary:

Act 1 focuses exclusively on Frank Thorney, beginning after his clandestine wedding to Winnifride, then showing his entanglement in the proposed marriage his father wants him to make with Susan.

Act 2 presents Elizabeth Sawyer as a social outcast who enters a demonic pact with the Dog, while developing the Thorney plot as Frank marries Susan.

Act 3 stages the Dog's deception of Cuddy Banks before turning to Frank's murder of Susan, also supervised by the Dog. The act concludes with the arrest of Warbeck and Somerton on suspicion of Susan's murder.

Act 4 begins by simultaneously showing Sawyer bewitching her neighbours and providing a robust defence of her lifestyle to the Justice and Sir Arthur Clarington. Frank's responsibility for Susan's death is then revealed as he is haunted by her ghost.

Act 5 presents the Dog's desertion of Sawyer, quickly followed by her arrest; the final scene builds up to the executions of Frank and Sawyer. ❖

Such a summary gives a broad outline of the play's design. I'm struck by the speed of the action – no act has more than four scenes, while the longest scene is less than 300 lines (2.1). Through this exercise we can see the intermingling of the different plot lines throughout the play. Only Act 1 is concerned with a single narrative; after 2.1, the different plots jostle for the audience's attention as the tension in each of them escalates. For further information you should read the second extract from Anthony Harris, 'Instrument of mischief: tragi-comedy in *The Witch of Edmonton*' (Reader, no. 33), which gives a detailed summary of the play alongside an account of the dramatists' deviations from Goodcole.

But what sort of play is this? Let's start by looking at what the first edition of the play tells us about its genre.

Exercise

Look at Figure 7.7, the title page of the first edition of *The Witch*, published in 1658. In what ways is the play presented?

Discussion

By 1658, the three dramatists were long dead. So the presentation of the play was largely the responsibility of the publisher, Edward Blackmore. The idea of authors having copyright over their writings which extended beyond their deaths is of very recent origin: so long as Blackmore had a text of the play and no other bookseller could prove previous ownership of it, he was at liberty to print and present it as he saw fit. The title page describes the play as 'A known true STORY./Composed into/A TRAGI-COMEDY'.

The other information which the title page provides is the woodcut which depicts both the encounter between Elizabeth Sawyer and the Dog in 2.1 and Cuddy Banks falling into the pond in 3.1. It looks as though the woodcut explains what Blackmore means by 'TRAGI-COMEDY': the play deals with both the tragedy of a witch's demonic pact and the comic farce of a clown's deception. ❖

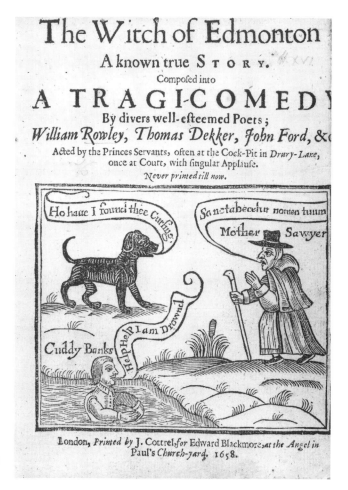

Figure 7.7 Title page of *The Witch of Edmonton* by William Rowley, Thomas Dekker and John Ford, 1658. © The Trustees of the British Library, London

Tragicomedy is a perplexing word, suggesting that *The Witch* is a particular kind of play: a self-conscious fusing of tragedy with comedy, which ultimately swerves away from a tragic outcome. Writing in about 1610, Fletcher used the term to describe his 'pastorall Tragie-comedie', *The Faithful Shepherdess*: 'A tragie-comedie is not so called in respect of mirth and killing, but in respect it wants deaths, which is inough to make it no tragedie, yet brings some neer it, which is inough to make it no comedie' (Bowers, 1976, p.497). As Fletcher indicates, there had been a vogue for such plays in the first decade of the seventeenth century: Beaumont and Fletcher's *Philaster* and even Shakespeare's *Cymbeline* (both 1609) have been seen as the most prominent examples of this kind of drama. But the term also has a resonance in Renaissance debates about poetry. In the 1580s, Sir Philip Sidney described tragicomedy as a 'mongrel' genre, crudely amalgamating the two genres but lacking the subtleties of either (Shepherd, 1973, p.135). Sidney was writing before the work of Shakespeare and Marlowe, and from the perspective of a humanist intellectual, devoted to a neoclassical conception of the form and function of drama (Mateer, 2000, pp.321–3). We could say that most English Renaissance drama is loosely tragicomic in that tragedies include comic material, while comedies can touch on the tragic – again, *The Merchant of Venice* is a good example of the mixing of modes characteristic of Renaissance English drama. Yet in contrast with *The Merchant*, *The Witch* is distinctly unclassical: it is located in England and makes no substantial reference to classical myth or literary ideas. As a technical term, 'TRAGI-COMEDY' is little help for understanding the play.

But is this how we should see the play – as a text which offsets Elizabeth Sawyer's tragedy with the 'harmless fun' of Cuddy Banks's escapades? My own view is that this is an inadequate description of *The Witch*. You may have noticed that the title page does not mention the Thorney plot: it implies that the play's central business is with the 'known true STORY' of 'Mother Sawyer'. Yet in studying the play the Thorney plot makes as much if not more of an impact than the Sawyer plot. Consider its centrality to the play's structure: Frank Thorney's tragedy is the major concern of seven scenes, while Sawyer appears in four only (Dolan, 1994, p.219). Now I'm not trying to argue that the play should really have been called *The Bigamist of Edmonton*; the issue is rather what kind of a play this is. The combination of the Thorney and Sawyer plots effectively makes *The Witch* into a darker play than the term 'TRAGI-COMEDY' implies. I would prefer to define it as a domestic drama. This was a thriving genre on the London stage through hit plays like the anonymous *Arden of Faversham* (*c*.1591) and Heywood's *A Woman Killed with*

Kindness (*c.*1607). Typically, such drama centres on unhappy marriages which result in adultery and murder in local milieux like Faversham in Kent, or in this case Edmonton in Middlesex. We might draw an analogy between texts like *The Witch* and television soap operas such as *EastEnders*. Like early modern domestic tragedies, soap operas depict ordinary people in ordinary milieux, often leavened with interludes of humour, while their central narratives focus on lurid interpersonal relationships and their frequently bloody-thirsty consequences. Instead of retitling the play, we need to understand why the dramatists combined witchcraft and bigamy plots in this tragic drama.

The literary language of *The Witch*

The most striking difference between *The Witch* and *EastEnders* is linguistic. *EastEnders* represents the speech patterns of contemporary East End Londoners; like all soaps, it aims to reproduce idioms which are familiar to its audience. By contrast, *The Witch* is largely written in blank verse, the form also used by Shakespeare. Blank verse is usually composed of unrhymed lines of five-stressed syllables; here are the play's first two lines with the stressed syllables emphasized: 'Come, **wench**, why **here's** a **bus**iness **soon** dis**patched**./Thy **heart**, I **know**, is **now** at **ease**. Thou **needst** not ...' . What impact, then, do the play's literary language and poetic form have on the way it treats its subject-matter? In this section, we will look at two different extracts to explore this question.

Let's reconsider Elizabeth Sawyer's first soliloquy:

> And why on me? Why should the envious world
> Throw all their scandalous malice upon me?
> 'Cause I am poor, deformed and ignorant,
> And like a bow buckled and bent together
> By some more strong in mischiefs than myself,
> Must I for that be made a common sink
> For all the filth and rubbish of men's tongues
> To fall and run into?
>
> (2.1.1–8)

Goodcole, as we have seen, underlined Sawyer's ignorance and suggested through his interrogation that she was scarcely capable of stringing two sentences together. This speech presents a radically different figure: an articulate verse speaker who deploys complex rhetorical questions to undermine the assumptions of the Edmonton community. Note the insistent rhythm of lines 6 and 7: 'Must **I** for

that be **made** a **comm**on **sink**/For **all** the **filth** and **rubb**ish **of** men's **tongues** ...'. This regular iambic rhythm (in which a stressed syllable follows an unstressed one) gives the speech a conviction and a dramatic authority which are at odds with the verbally impoverished figure described by Goodcole. Dawson indeed compares this speech with contemporaneous anxieties about the verbal power of women as exemplified in Goodcole's account of Sawyer cursing herself at her trial:

> Goodcole invokes divine nemesis and the traditional hierarchies of justice to turn Mother Sawyer's language against herself. In contrast the text of *The Witch of Edmonton*, by giving her voice dramatic as well as occult power, expresses its awareness of language and gender in a much less confident way, inflecting it with contradiction and ambivalence.

> (1989, p.82)

Such contradiction and ambivalence are evident especially if we consider the form of the speech as a soliloquy. This is one of the most stylized devices in English Renaissance drama, in which a character speaks alone on stage. Broadly, soliloquy is an expository device through which dramatists explored the dilemmas of their protagonists. Soaps like *EastEnders* never use it, precisely because it is theatrical and unnaturalistic: though real people may talk to themselves, they do not soliloquize. And in this case Sawyer is not talking to herself; rather, she is explaining her social position directly to the audience by the means of a formal speech. The soliloquy attempts to engage the audience with Sawyer and let them appreciate her socially marginal position. As such, there is something profoundly paradoxical about it. At one level, it exhibits a poetic and dramatic artifice which is far removed from the idioms of the real Sawyer; the woman interrogated by Goodcole would not have spoken like this. But equally, it is through the means of this formal contrivance that the dramatists can give a sense of the social and psychological complexity which leads to the demonization of Sawyer. As a dramatic character making a soliloquy, the Elizabeth Sawyer of *The Witch* is more like Shakespeare's Hamlet than Goodcole's ignorant old woman. In other words, Sawyer has progressed from a bogey-woman – an embodiment of human perfidy – to a more credible dramatic figure, whose words and actions are prompted by a range of stimuli.

Sawyer's soliloquies are, then, an important means through which the dramatists construct a plausible role. Let's have a look at a piece of dialogue from the Thorney plot to see if the play's literary language performs a similar function in that part of the play.

Exercise

Read *The Witch*, 4.2.1–50. How many different styles of speech do you think there are in this extract?

Discussion

I would say that there are three major styles of speech in this extract: colloquial, poetic and sententious. The first line of the scene is a good illustration of how blank verse can be broken up to give a sense of colloquial speech. Katherine's line has five stresses, but they vary from the more regular pattern of Frank's reply, aptly conveying a sense of her urgent concern for Frank's well-being: '**Broth**er, **Broth**er! So **sound** asleep? That's **well**./No, **not** I, **sist**er. **He** that's **wound**ed **here** ...'. As the scene continues, Frank veers away from the colloquial into a more poetic and metaphorical idiom: in lines 28–9, for example, he imagines age as a 'tottering bridge' across which an old man travels. Finally, the end of Frank's long speech turns from unrhymed verse into rhyming couplets as he considers what happens to the soul after death. Rhyming couplets in Renaissance plays usually signal that a character is talking sententiously or abstractly, as when Portia asks love to 'Allay' its 'ecstasy' in the successful casket scene of *The Merchant of Venice* (3.2.108–13), or indeed in the final lines of *The Witch* itself where the Justice concludes with a moralizing cliché: 'Join, friends, in sorrow, make of all the best./Harms past may be lamented, not redressed' (5.3.171–2). In this case, Frank tries to persuade himself that the soul is not judged after death: 'This were a fine reign,/To do ill and not hear of it again'. The rhyming couplets almost ostentatiously indicate to the audience that Frank is in the grip of a self-deluding fantasy. In contrast, Katherine's more prosaic reply ('I wish heaven/To pay – and so I know it will – that traitor,/That devil Somerton') aptly registers the spiritual reality shared by the characters of the play. ❖

But what about the dramatic purpose of this interchange – what is the poetic language doing here? I would say that this dialogue has two related functions. First, Frank's speeches betray his inner turmoil. Since this is the first scene in which he has appeared since killing Susan (3.3), his speeches indicate his preoccupation with the murder and its consequences. Indeed, Graham Greene used the couplet 'This were a fine reign./To do ill and not to hear of it again' as an epigraph to his 1938 novel *Brighton Rock*, whose central character, the gangster Pinkie Brown, is, like Frank, obsessed by the moral consequences of murder. Secondly, Frank and Katherine's dialogue prepares the audience for the extraordinary events of the rest of 4.2. After this extract, Frank is haunted by Susan's ghost, while Katherine discovers Frank's blood-stained knife and realizes his guilt. Frank's metaphysical speculations foreshadow the entrance of Susan's ghost and emphasize that the spirit world inhabited by the ghost and

Figure 7.8 Melvyn Hayes as the Dog and Ruby Head as Elizabeth Sawyer in the 1962 Mermaid Theatre production of *The Witch of Edmonton*. Mander and Mitchenson Collection, London

indeed the Dog (who enters invisibly before line 65) is inextricably linked to the 'real' world of the other characters.

In a related context, Marlowe's demon Mephistopheles remarks, 'Hell hath no limits, nor is circumscribed/In one self place, for where we are is hell' (Bevington and Rasmussen, 1995, p.154). Though the belief in ghosts was contentious among Protestant reformers, there was a widespread belief – dramatized by both *Dr Faustus* and *The Witch* – that the phenomenal world was continuously subject to the incursions of ghosts, spirits, angels and demons (Thomas, 1973, pp.701–11). While the Dog's presence throughout the play is a dramatic symbol of this belief, the beginning of 4.2 provides a poetic account of the same perception, balancing Katherine's orthodox belief in divine judgement with Frank's troubled ruminations. *The Witch* not only shows the interpenetration of two levels of reality through the appearance of Susan's spirit, it expresses that perception poetically: 'Why should not I walk hand in hand with death/To find my love out?'

What, then, do these extracts tell us about the literary language of *The Witch*? In both cases, poetic language is a vital part of the dramatic action. In Sawyer's soliloquy, rhetorical questions and the form of the soliloquy alert the audience (and the reader) to the complex factors which contribute to the protagonist's social identity as a witch.

Rowley, Dekker and Ford allow the audience to see Elizabeth Sawyer as a psychologically credible figure through the stylized, unnaturalistic language of English Renaissance drama. Similarly, in the dialogue between Frank and Katherine, poetic language draws attention to Frank's guilt and prepares the audience for the revelation of that guilt later in the scene. Language has the effect of allowing the audience to appreciate the gravity of Frank's predicament and to believe in the illusion of reality the play presents. It's also worth observing that while these extracts are drawn from different plots within the play – and so probably had different authors – that poetic language is used with a high degree of consistency. In each case, elaborate speech illuminates character and situation. We might make a final comparison with *EastEnders*. Television soap operas persuade their audiences of the plausibility of the events they present through representing a milieu that looks and sounds almost identical to ordinary streets and houses. By contrast, Renaissance plays like *The Witch* deploy an elaborate formal language to enable their audience to enter imaginatively into the events and experiences represented on stage. We now need to look in more detail at how the play – which after all would have been played on a bare stage with minimal props – gives its audience a sense of a specific locality.

Locating *The Witch* in Edmonton

Modern Edmonton is now a seamless part of the megalopolis London has become. Yet seventeenth-century London was much smaller, and Edmonton was a village on its peripheries. In the words of *The Merry Devil of Edmonton* (*c.*1601–4) – an earlier Edmonton-based play – the village was 'full seven miles from this great famous city' (McIlwraith, 1934, p.257). Figure 7.9 shows that Renaissance London was centred on the modern City of London alone. Hampstead and Highgate – now like Edmonton integral parts of North London – are here distant and undeveloped hilltops.

My point is not that Jacobean Edmonton was provincial in the way that, say, Carlisle was as a place far removed from London. Villages like Edmonton were distinct from the capital yet dependent on it economically. What's important for understanding *The Witch* is to see how its location informs and shapes the play. As Dawson puts it, 'The world depicted is rural England, the pressures and hierarchies are those of contemporary English village life' (1989, p.77).

Exercise

Reread *The Witch*, 1.2.1–36. What does this dialogue tell us about Edmonton and its inhabitants?

Discussion

In discussing the dowry Old Carter will pay Old Thorney if Frank marries Susan, these characters betray their divergent social origins.

Thorney claims Carter's offer shows him behaving 'like a gentleman', which Carter immediately rebuts: he behaves as an 'Honest Hertfordshire yeom[a]n'. From this dialogue we can see that the Thorneys are a minor gentry family entering into marriage negotiations with an affluent though humble 'yeoman' family. The implication is that the Thorneys desperately need the money Carter will give them; as Thorney later confirms to Frank 'If you marry/ With wealthy Carter's daughter, there's a portion/Will free my land' (1.2.137–9). The Carters' money will preserve the Thorneys' social standing.

Status also underlies the difference between Edmonton and London which runs through this dialogue. Note how keen Carter is to tell Thorney that financial dealings in Edmonton are just as proper as those in London and to sing the praises of the 'yeoman's fare' he offers his guests. Carter wants to impress Thorney – and wants Susan to marry the gentlemanly Frank – but he wants to accomplish this on his own terms as an unpretentious Edmonton yeoman. ❖

Figure 7.9 Wenceslaus Hollar, frontispiece to James Howell's *Londinopolis*, 1657. Guildhall Library, Corporation of London

So we can see that this sense of solid locality is a vital part of *The Witch*'s meaning: it is a play about delicate social gradations in a small place on the fringes of London. The Thorney tragedy in particular explores the tensions within that community through the strained ethical choices which underlie the characters' actions: Frank feels compelled to marry both Winnifride and Susan, unaware of Sir Arthur Clarington's earlier seduction of Winnifride. Like *Arden of Faversham*, the play presents the moral plight of its flawed protagonists within an enclosed milieu. Consider Frank's final moralization:

> Oh, that my example
> Might teach the world hereafter what a curse
> Hangs on their heads who rather choose to marry
> A goodly portion than a dower of virtues!
> (5.3.108–11)

This remark links back to the debate between Old Carter and Old Thorney: Susan's 'goodly portion' has lured Frank away from the impoverished 'virtues' of Winnifride. Frank's 'example' seems to provide the play with a convenient point of moral closure: he has transgressed social norms through avarice and ultimately murder; his story gives the audience an account of behaviours it should strive to eschew. But is this a convincing reading?

There are two major problems with this interpretation. First, Frank's bigamy is dictated by conflicting moral imperatives: he marries Winnifride because he believes he got her pregnant, while he marries Susan because he is under pressure from his father to save the family lands. We don't feel he goes through with the marriage to Susan because he is personally keen to get his hands on Carter's cash. A more apt moral might have been against lying, since Frank does have the option in 1.2 to tell his father that he is already married. Conversely, you may feel that Thorney bears some responsibility himself in forcing Frank to marry Susan. Part of the subtlety of 1.2 is in dramatizing the predicament of a character who is caught between what he has already done and a father who calls him 'a villain!/A devil like a man!' (ll.162–3) before really knowing one way or the other how his son has acted.

Secondly, this reading minimizes the role Clarington plays in Frank's tragedy. Jonathan Gil Harris makes a direct connection between Clarington's behaviour as a seducer and Sawyer's as a witch:

> 'satanic' behaviour in Edmonton is presented as emerging less from the incursions of the devil than from the existing class and patriarchal structures, which licence Clarington's *droit de seigneur* 'visitations' of Winnifride, or Old Banks's abusive promptings of Mother Sawyer.
>
> (Harris, 1998, p.137)

the instrument of the devil

This connection is also made in Act 5 by the application of the word 'instrument' to both Clarington and Sawyer. In less than 30 lines, he is 'the instrument that wrought all their misfortunes' while she is 'that instrument of mischief' (5.2.2; 5.3.21). In the close proximity of these related formulations, the dramatists endorse Old Carter's assessment that Clarington is 'worthier to be hanged' than Frank (5.2.6–7). The meaning of the play then becomes much more complex: can it just be a warning against avarice, or bigamy? Or rather, is its portrayal of social intercourse in a village setting cumulatively an indictment of the very social pressures which lead Frank to murder, and Sawyer to witchcraft? In this reading, the Edmonton of the play is a dysfunctional community because of the collapse in social morality typified by Clarington's seduction of Winnifride. Such a critique of the behaviour of the social elite is implied in Sawyer's description of 'Men-witches': 'Dare any swear I ever tempted maiden,/With golden hooks flung at her chastity,/To come and lose her honour, and being lost,/To pay not a denier for't?' (4.1.153–6). Clarington replies: 'By one thing she speaks/I know now she's a witch' (4.1.159–60). Sawyer, in other words, has accurately delineated his sin.

At this point I would like to return to the question of how the play links its different plots. The quotation from Jonathan Gil Harris makes one suggestion: it is unified through its concern with different kinds of 'satanic' behaviour – from the malevolent witchcraft of Sawyer to the equally destructive sexual egotism of Clarington. But there are other possibilities.

Exercise

Read 'Witchcraft and the threat of the familiar' by Frances E. Dolan (Reader, no. 34). What does Dolan see as the major connection between the different plots? Are you persuaded by her argument?

Discussion

Dolan argues that the play's central figure, spanning and unifying all three plots, is the Dog. He functions as an intermediary between the social and the supernatural, demonstrating that 'witchcraft is simultaneously about domestic *and* communal behaviours'.

To a degree this is a plausible and suggestive reading. Though Dolan doesn't spell this out, what the dramatists have done is to expand the familiar they found in Goodcole's pamphlet, whose activities centre on Sawyer, into a figure who menaces an entire community. So the Dog is an index of the paranoias of early modern England, as he explains himself:

Thou never art so distant
From an evil spirit but that thy oaths,
Curses, and blasphemies pull him to thine elbow.
Thou never tellst a lie but that the devil

All have the potential to be 'witches' ie to being harm to others. To be damned

Is within hearing it; thy evil purposes
Are ever haunted. But when they come to act –
As thy tongue slandering, bearing false witness,
Thy hand stabbing, stealing, cosening, cheating –
He's then within thee.
(5.1.137–45)

In this warning speech, the Dog summarizes the action of the play: he seduces Sawyer while she is cursing; he haunts Frank's 'evil purposes' from 3.3 onwards, while Cuddy Banks – to whom this speech is addressed – has also experienced his ability to deceive the unwary. The Dog is in short an incarnation of the belief in the devil as an ever-present threat to the human soul (for further discussion of this idea, see Thomas, 1973, pp.559–69). The play would then be unified by the sense that it is staging a vivid warning of the devil's involvement within the human community. ❖

Yet there are some reservations I would make about Dolan's presentation of the Dog: though he is the linchpin of the play's different plots, is he really as powerful a figure as Dolan implies? In this scene, it's important to see that, for all his satanic status, the Dog is worsted in his final encounter with the foolish Cuddy Banks, which is also his final appearance in the play. After hearing the Dog's account of his working methods, Cuddy defies him and threatens to 'beat thee out of the bounds of Edmonton' (5.1.207–8), an allusion to the ritual practice of tracing out and demarcating the boundaries of a parish once a year through hitting certain parts of the ground with sticks. This dialogue juxtaposes the different milieux of Edmonton – represented by Cuddy – and the London court to which the Dog aspires:

> *Dog.* ... I am for greatness now, corrupted greatness.
> There I'll shug in, and get a noble countenance;
> Serve some Briarean footcloth-strider
> That has an hundred hands to catch at bribes,
> But not a finger's nail of charity ...

> *Cuddy.* ... If thou goest to London I'll make thee go about by Tyburn, stealing in by Thieving Lane. If thou canst rub thy shoulder against a lawyer's gown as thou passest by Westminster Hall, do; if not, to the stairs amongst the bandogs, take water, and the devil go with thee.

> (5.1.196–200, 209–14)

As you can see from Corbin and Sedge's notes (1999, pp.125–6), not all these allusions are easy to explain. But the general sense is clear: the Dog wants to serve a courtier ('footcloth-strider') who is already morally 'corrupted'. In this atmosphere, he believes he will thrive. Cuddy's thumbnail sketch of London wittily recasts the Dog as a convicted criminal on his way to Tyburn for execution, or an indigent suitor trying to gain favour from a lawyer. A modern paraphrase of Cuddy's last sentence might be: '*You* think you're going to London as a courtier; *I know* you'll end up as a bum!'

At one level, the Dog's projected trajectory to court is the dramatists' reminder to their London and courtly audiences that they are not insulated from the devil – he is aware of their curses and 'evil purposes' too. But this dialogue also suggests that the Dog can be expelled from Edmonton, and then humiliated in London. Of course, a production of *The Witch* could so undermine Cuddy as a comic figure that the force of this speech is obscured – that would be a pity since it embodies such a robust antidote to the Dog's demonic paranoia. So this scene offers a double irony: first, the idea of the Dog's promotion to court reroutes the '"satanic" behaviour[s]' the play has depicted back to the London of the play's first audiences. But secondly, the power of the Dog is comically deflated by the ease with which Cuddy, the paradoxically clear-sighted dramatic fool, beats him out of Edmonton. In this devastating interchange, the playwrights invert our expectations of character and of place.

We now have two ways of explaining the combined plots of *The Witch*. Jonathan Gil Harris argues that the play is concerned with interrelated 'satanic' behaviours. Through representing witchcraft alongside Clarington's seduction of Winnifride, the play reveals its subversive sense of the inequality with which the law treats analogous crimes. Dolan claims that the play is unified by the Dog – the 'dangerous familiar' who menaces the inhabitants of Edmonton. I have just suggested that this reading needs modifying in the light of the fact that the Dog leaves the stage with his tail between his legs. Each of these readings provides a possible approach to the narratives which the play fuses. Yet you may not be satisfied with either of these explanations and may still be wondering how the playwrights expected their audiences to make sense of a script which amalgamates such apparently discrepant stories. In the final part of this chapter, I will compare *The Witch* with Shakespeare's *The Merry Wives of Windsor* (*c*.1597–1601) to help you see that the fusing of narratives about marital disharmony, witchcraft and deception is apparent in other, more celebrated, plays. Through this comparison, we should be able to see that witchcraft was not an arcane discourse in early modern England, but that it was rather an essential part of the verbal fabric of everyday life – and of the drama which attempted to represent that life.

The Witch and *The Merry Wives*

The Merry Wives is Shakespeare's most English comedy, rooted in its depiction of a town near London with which his audiences would have been familiar, and in a group of citizen characters. Like *Arden of Faversham* and *The Witch* itself, *The Merry Wives* is a domestic drama; unlike these plays, it treats marital disharmony comically rather than tragically. As David Crane suggests, it is a play 'about nothing significant' which energetically avoids any moralizing agenda (1997, p.10). As such, its complicated and detailed action is hard to summarize. If the play is 'about' anything, it is about the misadventures in Windsor of the anti-hero of the *Henry IV* plays, the bloated drunkard Sir John Falstaff. He attempts to seduce two citizen wives, Mistress Ford and Mistress Page, because he believes they are wealthy. But the wives are always several steps ahead of him, and trick him through a series of wickedly funny practical jokes. Alongside these deceptions, the play dramatizes Master Ford's paranoiac suspicions of his wife and a more traditional plot in which the Pages' daughter Anne is pursued by several suitors.

At first sight, you may think that this play can have little to do with *The Witch*. But I would suggest that what chiefly distinguishes the plays is their related plots and locations.

Exercise

Read the following extract from *The Merry Wives* (3.2) in which Master Page discusses his daughter's suitors.

> *Host.* What say you to young master Fenton? He capers, he dances, he has eyes of youth; he writes verses, he speaks holiday, he smells April and May – he will carry't, he will carry't – 'tis in his buttons – he will carry't.
>
> *Page.* Not by my consent, I promise you. The gentleman is of no having. He kept company with the wild Prince and Poins; he is of too high a region, he knows too much. No, he shall not knit a knot in his fortunes with the finger of my substance. If he take her, let him take her simply. The wealth I have waits on my consent, and my consent goes not that way.

(Evans and Tobin, 1997, p.340)

Why does Page object to Fenton? Compare his reasons with Old Carter's assessment of Warbeck in *The Witch* 1.2.80–85.

Discussion

Page and Carter object to Fenton and Warbeck as sons-in-law for essentially the same reasons. Fenton is 'of no having' financially; Page states that by consorting with 'the wild Prince' (that is, Prince Hal of *Henry IV*), Fenton reveals his social and moral untrustworthiness. Similarly, Carter characterizes Warbeck as 'A very unthrift ... one of the country's roaring-lads'. The only difference between Fenton and Warbeck is their backgrounds – Fenton is a minor courtier, while Warbeck is a 'country' prodigal, a rural counterpart to 'city ... rake-hells', or debauchers. ❖

So there are strong connections between these passages. In each case, the plays dramatize the frictions between fathers, daughters and putative sons-in-law. Such friction is based on the social and financial consequences of marriage. Since Carter and Page are investing their 'substance' in these young men, they are keen not to saddle themselves with profligate new relatives – Page threatens that if Fenton marries Anne, he will have to 'take her simply', that is, without a dowry. Both plays are partly concerned with the socio-economic anxieties of their protagonists, yet their handling of these plots is very different. Note how Carter is blithely confident throughout 1.2 of Frank's virtues and the soundness of the proposed marriage – the play's tragic irony is that both father and daughter have made a grotesque miscalculation. By contrast in *The Merry Wives*, Page is outsmarted by both Anne and Fenton; similar plot lines lead to different outcomes.

This point is also evident in the way Shakespeare's play handles the theme of witchcraft. As you can see from my plot summary, *The Merry Wives* does not have a 'witchcraft plot' in the way that *The Witch* does. However, witchcraft and witches are a significant presence within Shakespeare's Windsor. Like Edmonton, Windsor had itself been the site of a witch hunt in 1578. A pamphlet summarizing the cases was published in the following year; Figure 7.10 is taken from this text (Rosen, 1991, pp.83–91). The fear of witchcraft becomes explicit in 4.2, as Falstaff makes another attempt to seduce Mistress Ford. On this occasion, he is disturbed by the return of her husband, which forces Mistress Ford and Mistress Page to disguise Falstaff as 'the fat woman of Brainford' (Evans and Tobin, 1997, p.347). The joke is that Ford cannot stand this character who he swears is a witch. The scene is both extremely funny – presenting the ludicrous spectacle of the portly Falstaff cross-dressed – and darkly suggestive of the pervasive presence of witchcraft as an integral part of the social fabric of early modern England.

> *Ford.* Old woman? What old woman's that?
>
> *Mistress Ford.* Why, it is my maid's aunt of Brainford.
>
> *Ford.* A witch, a quean, an old cozening quean! Have I not forbid her my house? She comes of errands, does she? We are simple men, we do not know what's brought to pass under the profession of fortune-

telling. She works by charms, by spells, by th'figure, and such daub'ry [impostures] as this is, beyond our element; we know nothing. Come down, you witch, you hag you, come down, I say!

Mistress Ford. Nay, good, sweet husband! Good gentlemen, let him not strike the old woman.

[*Enter* Falstaff *disguised like an old woman, and* Mistress Page *with him.*]

Mistress Page. Come, Mother Prat, come give me your hand.

Ford. I'll prat [beat] her. Out of my door, you witch, you rag, you baggage, you poulcat, you runnion [scabby woman]! out, out! I'll conjure you, I'll fortune-tell you!

[*Ford beats him, and he runs away*] ...

Evans. By yea and no, I think the oman is a witch indeed. I like not when a oman has a great peard [beard]. I spy a great peard under his muffler.

(Evans and Tobin, 1997, p.348)

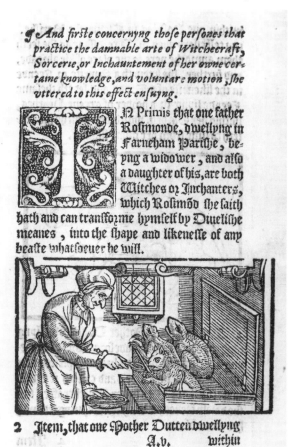

Figure 7.10 A witch feeding her familiars, from *A Rehearsall both Straung and True ... at Winsore* [Windsor], 1578. © The Trustees of the British Library, London

The comedy of this exchange lies in Falstaff's mistaken identity. He is not the old woman of Brainford (a village near Windsor), yet he paradoxically deserves the beating Ford dishes out to him because of his repeated attempts to seduce his wife. If we juxtapose this episode with *The Witch* 4.1, we can see that this boisterous comedy is not far removed from the violence simmering in that play's witchcraft plot:

> *All.* Are you come, you old trot?
>
> *Old Banks.* You hot whore, must we fetch you with fire in your tail?
>
> *First Countryman.* This thatch is as good as a jury to prove she is a witch.
>
> *All.* Out, witch! Beat her, kick her, set fire on her!
>
> *Elizabeth Sawyer.* Shall I be murdered by a bed of serpents? Help, help!
>
> (4.1.26–35)

This exchange dramatizes the popular tradition recorded by Goodcole as 'an old ridiculous custom' that burning the thatch from a suspected witch's house would force her to appear immediately (Corbin and Sedge, 1999, p.137). To the minds of the people of Edmonton, Sawyer's appearance is sufficient evidence 'to prove she is a witch' and to lynch her on the spot. Similar thought processes are evident in *The Merry Wives*: Ford bases his antagonism to the 'old woman' on the fact that she sells charms, while Evans corroborates Ford's judgement by asserting that 'she' must be a witch because 'she' has 'a great peard'. Though to the audience, this remark is richly comic because we know the 'old woman' is Falstaff, it is nonetheless indicative of the same thinking which is so graphically staged in *The Witch*. The accused figure looks or behaves like a witch, so she must be one. Note also the closeness of the language used by Ford and Old Banks to describe their witches: Sawyer is a 'hot whore' while Falstaff becomes a 'cozening quean', or in modern English, a 'cheating slut'. Once again, the accused witch is construed as a social outsider.

How, then, do these similarities help us to understand *The Witch*? *The Merry Wives* illuminates *The Witch* by showing that similar kinds of plot were often fused in plays set in distinctively English locations. Set in provincial towns on the edges of London, both plays explore tensions within the institution of marriage alongside presenting the figure of the village witch. The connection between plots about witchcraft and marital trauma should become easier to grasp. Because witchcraft was a significant part of seventeenth-century English social intercourse, domestic plays which staged 'real life' stories about the unhappy marriages of ordinary people frequently touched on witchcraft as a prominent anxiety of small communities. Old Carter and Page are concerned with how their daughters' marriages impact on their own wealth; similarly, Old Banks and Ford see witchcraft as a threat to their community which must be eradicated. Domestic plays like *The Merry Wives* and *The Witch* stage plots that look dissimilar but are unified by their dramatization both of a specific place and of the fears which afflict its inhabitants.

Conclusion: Renaissance drama and witchcraft

At the end of Chapter 6, Peter Elmer challenges us to accommodate learned demonology within our assessment of Renaissance culture. He argues that by looking at such disturbing primary evidence with an informed eye, we may come to a more accurate 'warts and all' image of the Renaissance, radically different from the less pock-marked portrait given by Burckhardt. In this chapter, we have looked at another manifestation of European witchcraft through the representation of Elizabeth Sawyer on the London stage. The question I want to consider now is how far we should see *The Witch* as a Renaissance play.

In many ways, it is difficult to view this play as a typical product of the Renaissance. Unlike *The Merchant of Venice*, *The Witch* lacks those pervasive allusions to classical myth and drama which make it easier for us to think of Shakespeare's play as part of the same broad culture which encompasses the work of Leonardo and Montaigne. Indeed, compared with other witchcraft plays like Marston's *Sophonisba*, *The Witch* is notably unclassical. Much of the analysis in this chapter is devoted to locating the play more firmly within indigenous English culture and beliefs. Does this mean then that we should not think of it as a play of the Renaissance?

Again, your answer will depend on how you want to define the Renaissance. If you use the term exclusively to describe the European recovery of classical culture within a given time frame, then *The Witch* will probably fall outside of your definition and you will be forced to find another way of accounting for it. But if you want to develop a more complicated picture of the Renaissance which can include demonological texts, and indeed texts which are noticeably unclassical, then you may wish to make a case for *The Witch* as a Renaissance play.

I think such a case can be made. As we have seen, the play is a cautious and critical reworking of its main source which ultimately views witchcraft, like bigamy, as a product of social pressures and interactions. For Rowley, Dekker and Ford, the devil underlies such interactions, but he is not without assistance from individuals and the society as a whole. In this sense the dramatists' attitude towards witchcraft is not unlike that of Montaigne (see Chapter 8). Though the dramatists were not as philosophically sceptical as Montaigne – they accept the broad outline of Goodcole's narrative – their play shows that Elizabeth Sawyer's demonic seduction takes place within a society which is itself morally problematic. We could also observe that the collaborative writing of *The Witch* gives us a different sense of the mechanics of the production of cultural artefacts in Renaissance Europe from Burckhardt. Moreover, though the play is ostensibly dissimilar from *The Merchant of Venice*, it nonetheless participates in analogous representational strategies by using a stylized literary language which paradoxically contributes to the construction of a theatrical illusion of reality. Through reading texts like this and *Strix*, our sense of Renaissance culture becomes more complex, as its previously pristine complexion becomes a little spottier.

Bibliography

BAWCUTT, N.W. (ed.) (1958) T. Middleton and W. Rowley: *The Changeling*, London, Methuen.

BENTLEY, G.E. (1956) *The Jacobean and Caroline Stage*, 5 vols, Oxford, Clarendon Press.

BEVINGTON, D. and RASMUSSEN, E. (eds) (1995) C. Marlowe: *Doctor Faustus and Other Plays*, Oxford and New York, Oxford University Press.

BOWERS, F. (ed.) (1976) *The Dramatic Works in the Beaumont and Fletcher Canon*, vol. 3, Cambridge, Cambridge University Press.

BRIGGS, R. (1996) *Witches and Neighbours: The Social and Cultural Context of European Witchcraft*, London, Fontana.

BURCKHARDT, J. (1990) *The Civilization of the Renaissance in Italy*, trans. S.G.C. Middlemore, Harmondsworth, Penguin; first published 1860.

CORBIN, P. and SEDGE, D. (eds) (1999) W. Rowley, T. Dekker and J. Ford: *The Witch of Edmonton*, Manchester and New York, Manchester University Press.

CORBIN, P. and SEDGE, D. (eds) (1986) *Three Jacobean Witchcraft Plays*, Manchester and New York, Manchester University Press.

CRANE, D. (ed.) (1997) W. Shakespeare: *The Merry Wives of Windsor*, Cambridge, Cambridge University Press.

DAWSON, A. (1989) 'Witchcraft/bigamy: cultural conflict in *The Witch of Edmonton*', *Renaissance Drama*, vol. 20, pp.77–98.

DOLAN, F.E. (1994) *Dangerous Familiars: Representations of Domestic Crime in England, 1550–1700*, Ithaca and London, Cornell University Press.

EVANS, G.B. and TOBIN, J.J.M. (eds) (1997) *The Riverside Shakespeare*, 2nd edn, Boston and New York, Houghton Mifflin.

GREENE, G. (1943) *Brighton Rock*, Harmondsworth, Penguin; first published 1938.

GURR, A. (1980) *The Shakespearean Stage: 1574–1642*, Cambridge, Cambridge University Press.

HAMILTON, A.C. (ed.) (1977) E. Spenser: *The Faerie Queene*, London and New York, Longman.

HARRIS, J.G. (1998) *Foreign Bodies and the Body Politic: Discourses of Social Pathology in Early Modern England*, Cambridge, Cambridge University Press.

HARRISON, G.B. (ed.) (1966) King James the First: *Daemonologie* (1597) with *News from Scotland* (1591), Edinburgh, Edinburgh University Press.

HUGHES, T. (1995) *New Selected Poems*, London, Faber & Faber.

LIPSON, L. (ed./trans.) (1998) M. de Cervantes: *Exemplary Stories*, Oxford and New York, Oxford University Press.

MCILWRAITH, A.K. (ed.) (1934) *Five Elizabethan Comedies*, London, Oxford University Press.

MASTEN, J. (1997) *Textual Intercourse: Collaboration, Authorship, and Sexualities in Renaissance Drama*, Cambridge, Cambridge University Press.

MATEER, D. (ed.) (2000) *Courts, Patrons and Poets*, New Haven and London, Yale University Press/The Open University.

NICHOLSON, B. (ed.) (1886) R. Scot: *The Discoverie of Witchcraft*, London, Elliot Stock.

REAY, B. (1998) *Popular Cultures in England, 1550–1750*, London and New York, Longman.

ROBERTS, G. (1996) 'The descendants of Circe: witches and Renaissance fictions' in J. Barry, M. Hester and G. Roberts (eds) *Witchcraft in Early Modern Europe: Studies in Culture and Belief*, Cambridge, Cambridge University Press.

ROSEN, B. (ed.) (1991) *Witchcraft in England, 1558–1618*, Amherst, University of Massachusetts Press.

SHARPE, J. (1997) *Instruments of Darkness: Witchcraft in England, 1550–1770*, Harmondsworth, Penguin.

SHEPHERD, G. (ed.) (1973) P. Sidney: *An Apology for Poetry*, Manchester, Manchester University Press.

THOMAS, K. (1973) *Religion and the Decline of Magic: Studies in Popular Beliefs in Sixteenth- and Seventeenth-Century England*, Harmondsworth, Penguin.

Reader sources

Anthony Harris, 'Manifold impieties: the social setting': *Night's Black Agents: Witchcraft and Magic in Seventeenth-Century English Drama*, Manchester University Press, Manchester, 1980, Chapter 1, pp.1–18. (Reader, no. 32)

Anthony Harris, 'Instrument of mischief, tragi-comedy in *The Witch of Edmonton*': *Night's Black Agents: Witchcraft and Magic in Seventeenth-Century English Drama*, Manchester University Press, Manchester, 1980, Chapter 7, pp.90–3, 95–7, 99–107. (Reader, no. 33)

Frances E. Dolan, 'Witchcraft and the threat of the familiar': *Dangerous Familiars: Representations of Domestic Crime in England 1550–1700*, Cornell University Press, Ithaca and London, 1994, pp.218–20. (Reader, no. 34)

CHAPTER EIGHT

Montaigne on Montaigne

BY ANTONY LENTIN[1]

Objectives

The objectives of this chapter are that you should:

- enjoy and engage with the *Essays* of Montaigne;

- develop an understanding of the nature and purpose of the *Essays*;

- consider from a different perspective – that of Montaigne – aspects of the Renaissance studied elsewhere in this series, including such themes as the reaction to Machiavelli's ideas on statecraft, scepticism, authority and religion, the Jews in Renaissance Europe, the European witch-craze, Renaissance medicine, political philosophy and classical writers;

- evaluate Montaigne's relationship to Renaissance humanism;

- be able to explore with confidence the essays of Montaigne that are not considered in this chapter.

Introduction

In this final chapter of the series we turn to a Renaissance text of world renown, the *Essays* (*Essais*) *of Michel de Montaigne* to which you were introduced in Book 1, Chapter 2. Montaigne's *Essays* are eminently browsable, 'one of Europe's great bedside books', as Michael Screech says (1991, p.xv), and the first objective of this chapter is to enable you to acquire a nodding acquaintance with as many of them as is reasonable in the space available. Passing reference, then, is made to most of the 107 essays (which range from a single page to nearly 200 pages). And particular essays, or extracts from essays, have been selected for study in greater depth in the teaching exercises, including Montaigne's short but suggestive preface, 'To the Reader', which was touched on in Book 1. Some essays are mentioned in order to bring out Montaigne's outlook on a variety of issues, while others are discussed more closely in order to focus on his attitude to themes discussed elsewhere in this series.

[1] My grateful acknowledgements are due to Peter Elmer, Lucille Kekewich, Jill Kraye and Nick Webb.

Unless otherwise indicated, all references to the *Essays* are to Michael Screech's 1991 edition, Michel de Montaigne: *The Complete Essays*. In the case of quotations from this edition, either the book and chapter number or the essay title will be given along with the page reference. Quotations in French are from the 1969, three-volume edition, Michel de Montaigne, *Essais*, with an introduction by Alexandre Micha. The Screech edition has been chosen for this study because, among other reasons, it is complete and also because it indicates the many successive revisions, additions and deletions which Montaigne made after publishing Books I and II in 1580 (see Screech, 1991, p.iii). Having these highlighted helps us to understand the evolution of the *Essays* as a distinctive and highly idiosyncratic genre. Screech also provides an informative introduction, helpful brief headnotes to each essay and an index of names. His introduction is particularly helpful in contextualizing and interpreting Montaigne's views on scepticism and religion (pp.xix–xliii), including those expressed in his longest essay, *An apology for Raymond Sebond*, which, as Screech notes, 'is centred on religious knowledge and doubt' (p.xxx) and 'is in a class by itself' (p.xx). You may not necessarily agree with Screech's conclusions, but you will find in his introduction a concise statement of one view of Montaigne's position by an acknowledged expert.

Partly because complete and authoritative editions of the *Essays* began to appear only in the early twentieth century, 'there is no such thing', Screech reminds us, 'as a definitive edition of the *Essays*' (p.xlix). Likewise, 'there is no one true reading of the *Essais*' (Coleman, 1987, p.12), no 'last word' on Montaigne. Despite all his revelations Montaigne remains protean, elusive, enigmatic and controversial. The moment one asks what were his views on religion (to take a prime example), contradictory responses spring to mind. The scholarship on Montaigne is enormous and still growing, and the *Essays* remain very much open to interpretation and reinterpretation.

Montaigne and the *Essays*

Montaigne's life

Michel de Montaigne (1533–92) was born Michel Eyquem de Montaigne at the château of Montaigne on the river Dordogne in the county of Périgord in Gascony, some 30 miles east of Bordeaux. The family had only recently been ennobled. His paternal great-grandfather and grandfather made their fortune from the sale of wine and salted fish; his grandfather acquired the estate and the title 'Seigneur (lord) of Montaigne' in 1477. His father, Pierre Eyquem de

LE SEIGNEVR DE MONTAIGNE

Figure 8.1 Anon., *Montaigne as Mayor of Bordeaux*, 1581–5, oil on panel. Musée Condé, Chantilly. Photo: E.T. Archive

Montaigne (who soon dropped the bourgeois name Eyquem), another successful merchant, became mayor of Bordeaux in 1554. His mother, Antoinette de Louppes de Villeneuve (Lopez de Villanueva) of Toulouse, almost certainly came from a family of *marranos*, converted Spanish or Portuguese Jews (the *marranos*, or 'new Christians', are mentioned in *Lazarillo de Tormes*). And, according to his standard biographer, Donald Frame, Montaigne was one-quarter Jewish (1965, p.28).

Montaigne's father, an enthusiast for the new learning of the Renaissance (II, 12, p.489), took unusual pains with his education. Montaigne actually spoke Latin before learning his 'native' French. He was sent to school at the prestigious new Collège de Guyenne at Bordeaux, which was staffed by humanist teachers, and then to the university there, where he studied philosophy, and then, possibly at Toulouse, law. After qualifying as a lawyer, Montaigne obtained a judicial post as a *magistrat* at Périgueux (1554) and then as a *conseiller* or member of the *parlement*, or high court, of Bordeaux (1557), where he served for thirteen years. By all accounts he was an honest judge: 'no man cared less for chicanery and legal technicality', wrote his friend, fellow humanist and lawyer, Étienne Pasquier (1529–1615) (Frame, 1965, p.58). In 1559 and again between 1561 and 1562 he attended the royal court at Paris. During his second attendance he was entrusted with a special commission by Charles IX, who in 1571 made him a knight of the Order of Saint Michael and in 1573 gave him the honorary title of gentleman of the king's bedchamber.

In 1563 Montaigne suffered a lasting blow in the death of a close friend whom he had met only four years earlier, Étienne de la Boétie (or Boëtie), a fellow *magistrat* and humanist, whose passion for Roman (particularly Stoic) philosophy profoundly influenced Montaigne. He wrote of this friendship in *On affectionate relationships*: 'If you press me to say why I loved him, I feel that it cannot be expressed.' Reviewing those words a dozen years later, he added, in a celebrated phrase, 'except by replying: "Because it was him: because it was me"' (p.212). He frequently mentions La Boétie in the *Essays*: even eighteen years after his friend's death, when travelling in Italy, he noted in his journal:

> I was overcome by such painful thoughts about Monsieur de la Boétie, and I was in this mood so long, without recovering, that it did me much harm.
>
> (Frame, 1983a, p.125)

In 1565 Montaigne married a wealthy Bordeaux heiress, Françoise de la Chassaigne, and in 1568, on the death of his father, he inherited his title and estates as 'Seigneur de Montaigne'. In the same year Montaigne published his own translation (from the Latin) of Raymond Sebond's *Natural Theology* (1484), a treatise on how knowledge of God is attainable by human reason alone, without the aid of revelation. (For Montaigne's adaptation of Sebond's prologue, see Screech, pp.lv–lviii.) Financially secure, Montaigne resigned his judicial post in 1570, formally quitting public life at the age of 37 to retire semi-permanently to the château of Montaigne. The tower of the château still stands (Figure 8.2). Montaigne made it famous for posterity by housing on the top storey the study–library (Figure 8.3) which he called the 'back of the shop' (I, 39, p.70), an expression intended to convey the idea of privacy, leisure, space and detachment for independent reflection. (For his description of the library, see *On three kinds of social intercourse*, p.933, and for the Latin inscription which he had painted on the library wall to mark his retirement, see footnote 14 below.) Here, in his forties and fifties, he devoted himself to what he considered the main achievement of his life, the *Essays*. From 1571 to 1580 he worked on the first two books, which were published at Bordeaux by Simon Millanges in 1580 (Figure 8.4).

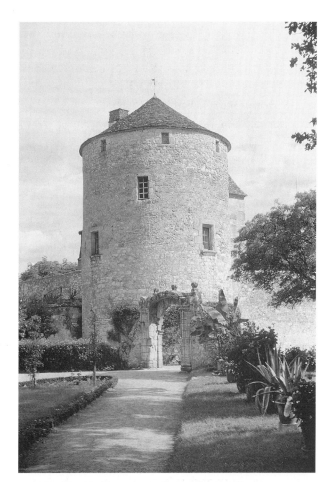

Figure 8.2 Library tower, château of Montaigne, Saint Michel de Montaigne. Montaigne's library was on the top storey, with views overlooking the countryside. Photo: René Lanaud

Figure 8.3 Montaigne's library, interior. Photo: René Lanaud

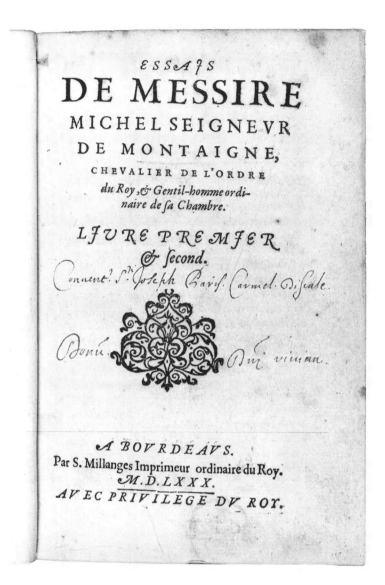

Figure 8.4 Title page of *Essais de Messire Michel Seigneur de Montaigne*, first edition, 1580, Bordeaux, Simon Millanges. British Library G.2344. Reproduced by permission of the British Library, London

Work on the *Essays* was periodically interrupted by important distractions in the form of military and political commissions. And then, from 1578, Montaigne began to suffer from kidney-stones. In search of a cure, he visited the most celebrated spas of France, Germany, Switzerland and Italy during 1580 and 1581, returning by command of Henry III to become mayor (or governor) of Bordeaux, where he had been elected for the years 1581 to 1582. (He was later re-elected to serve from 1583 to 1585. His period of office was no sinecure, his task being to keep Bordeaux, a mainly Catholic enclave in the largely Protestant province of Guyenne, loyal to the Catholic Henry III.) Montaigne's travels, during which he kept a journal, had afforded him new experiences and stimulated his imagination. In 1582 he published a second, revised edition of Books I and II of the

Essays with some 600 additions. He wrote Book III between 1586 and 1587 and published all three books in Paris in 1588 in an edition by Abel l'Angelier, which included the numerous additions to Books I and II mentioned above. While the first two books had been well received in France and Europe, the 1588 edition was somewhat less so: the critics were puzzled by the originality of Montaigne's final achievement.

In 1588, Montaigne took part in negotiations between Henry III and the Protestant leader Henry of Navarre, who had appointed him a gentleman of the bedchamber in 1577 and had twice visited Montaigne at his château. On the accession of Henry of Navarre as Henry IV of France in 1589, Montaigne offered him his services, but was too ill to take up a post and died at his home in 1592 at the age of 59. Montaigne had six daughters, all but one of whom died in infancy. In his last years he made the acquaintance of a young woman, Marie le Jars de Gournay, who profoundly admired the *Essays* and whom he made his adopted daughter and heir. He was revising his *Essays* and adding to them to the last. Marie de Gournay further edited them after his death, publishing in 1595 the edition from which most modern editions stem. Montaigne was buried at Bordeaux in what is now part of the university. The marble effigy on his tombstone shows him lying in full armour, the *Essays* on his chest, an inscription in Greek and Latin below (Figure 8.5).

Figure 8.5 Tomb of Michel de Montaigne, 1592, Bordeaux. Musée d'Aquitaine: Direction des Musées de Bordeaux. Photo © Musée d'Aquitaine Bordeaux – Jean-Michel Arnaud

Montaigne's preface 'To the Reader': his introduction to himself and his *Essays*

Exercise

'It is the only book of its kind in the world', Montaigne wrote of his *Essays* (II, 8, p.433). To find out why, please read his preface 'To the Reader' (p.lix) (and see Figure 8.6), which he added to the *Essays* in 1580 after he had completed the first two books. We took a preliminary look at 'To the Reader' in Book 1 of the series (pp.38–48). It provides an introduction to this unique collection, the subject of which, as he tells us, is Montaigne himself! But what is your reaction after reading it? What do you take to be Montaigne's intention?

Discussion

This is not a conventional preface, and if you are a bit puzzled, that is certainly what Montaigne intended! Our curiosity is tickled by Montaigne's nonchalant claim that the book was written not for 'the Reader' but for 'the private benefit of my friends and kinsmen' (so why publish it?). Montaigne states that he has not even bothered to please 'the Reader': 'I have not been concerned to serve you', softening this with what seems to be a dig at himself – 'nor my reputation'. This is immediately followed by an apparently innocent throw-away line: 'my powers are inadequate for such a design'. At this point the attentive reader (and Montaigne expects his reader to be attentive) does a double-take: is this conventional modesty or profoundly ironic? Montaigne goes blithely on to suggest that anyway his book is of no interest to the serious-minded reader; it would be a waste of time 'to employ your leisure on a topic so frivolous and so vain'. An odd sales-pitch, on the face of it![2] ❖

What kind of relationship does Montaigne establish with 'the Reader'? We are drawn in by a sense of paradox and irony, couched in a highly unconventional, unliterary and downright colloquial style. The sentences are short and direct. In the French, the unknown and anonymous 'Reader' is addressed in the familiar second person singular reserved for close friends (*tu–thou* in John Florio's translation of 1603[3]) as opposed to the polite form (*vous*) with which Montaigne addresses, for example, the Countess of Gurson, the noble dedicatee of *On educating children* (p.163; and see also pp.167, 168, where he addresses her as 'My Lady' (*Madame*)). For an altogether more conventional

[2] Jean Starobinski notes that if we look at the French of 'To the Reader', 'the *book is* named first and ... is kept present throughout the page by use of the locative pronoun '*y*', meaning 'there', i.e. in the book (1985, p.30). Four of these eight unobtrusive but insistent '*y's*', suggesting subliminal, or at least subtle advertising (and in Montaigne's case *self*-advertising), are omitted in Screech's translation.

[3] The 1603 translation of Montaigne's *Essays* by John Florio is published in The Museum Edition, Gibbons & Company, London, 1906.

AV LECTEVR.

EST icy vn liure de bône foy, Lecteur, il t'aduertit dés l'entree que ie ne m'y suis proposé aucune fin, que domestique & priuee: ie n'y ay eu nulle consideration de ton seruice, ny de ma gloire: mes forces ne sont pas capables d'vn tel dessein. Ie l'ay voué à la commodité particuliere de mes parés & amis: à ce que m'ayans perdu (ce qu'ils ont à faire bien tost) ils y puissent retrouuer quelques traits de mes conditions & humeurs, & que par ce moyen ils nourrissent plus entiere & plus viue, la cognoissance qu'ils ont eu de moy. Si c'eust esté pour rechercher la faueur du monde, ie me fusse mieux paré, & me presenterois en vne demarche estudiee. Ie veux qu'on m'y voye en ma façon simple, naturelle & ordinaire, sans contention & artifice: car c'est moy que ie peins. Mes defauts s'y liront au vif, & ma forme naïfue, autant que la reuerence publique me l'a permis. Que si i'eusse esté parmy ces nations qu'on dit viure encore soubs la douce liberté des premieres loix de nature, ie t'asseure que ie m'y fusse tres-volontiers peint tout entier, & tout nud. Ainsi, Lecteur, ie suis moy-mesme la matiere de mon liure: ce n'est pas raison que tu employes ton loisir en vn subiect si friuole & si vain. Adieu donc. De Montaigne, ce premier de Mars, mil cinq cens quatre vingts.

Cette preface corrigee de la derniere main de l'Autheur, ayant esté esgaree en la premiere impression depuis sa mort, a n'aguere esté retrouuee.

Figure 8.6 'To the Reader' (*Au lecteur*), prefatory page of *Essais de Michel Seigneur de Montaigne*, 1604, Paris, Abel l'Angelier. Montaigne added this preface in 1580, when he published Books I and II of the *Essays*. Reproduced by permission of the Syndics of Cambridge University Library preface, see his dedication 'To Madame de Grammont, Countess of Guiche' in *Nine-and-twenty sonnets of Estienne de La Boëtie* (pp.220–21), or his dedication of his translation of Raymond Sebond's *Natural Theology* to his father (p.liv).

As for paradox and irony, far from bidding 'the Reader' 'Farewell', Montaigne is inviting him to read on! That is the point of any preface. Or is his leave-taking meant to suggest the valediction of a man who, as he says, supposes that he has not long to live – 'having lost me (as they must do soon)'? At 47, Montaigne was conventional in the sixteenth century in depicting himself as old (see *On the length of life*, pp.366–9 and *On presumption*, p.729). He was obsessed by thoughts of mortality. Does he bid farewell on the assumption that 'the Reader', forewarned of the book's uselessness, will waste no more time on it? (For similar remarks at his own expense, see *On the affection of fathers for their children*, p.433, paragraph 1.) Does he mean – 'now read on'? Or – 'now don't read on'? If the latter, 'the Reader' will of course be tempted to do the opposite.

And what do you make of his assertion that, but for his 'respect for social convention', he would have shown himself 'wholly naked'? Here, as often in the *Essays*, it may be hard to state precisely what Montaigne does mean, how literally to take him. He is deliberately ambiguous, humorous, tentative and ironic. And that in itself makes 'the Reader' think. We suggested earlier that Montaigne is unliterary: down-to-earth, casual and offhand. In *On vanity*, he compares the *Essays* to turds – 'here ... you have the droppings of an old mind' (p.1070). But *is* he casual? Or does the preface suggest, despite all its disclaimers, 'the self-conscious pose of the author' (Conley, 1994, p.85), '*apparent* negligence' (Coleman, 1989, p.106)? John O'Neill refers to 'so selfish and indulgent a writer *as Montaigne sets himself to be*' (1982, pp.1–2; my italics).

Irony is certainly one characteristic of Montaigne's style, a clue to his outlook and a device both familiar and useful in the late Renaissance in which he wrote. At a fairly simple level, ironical, quasi-apologetic self-depreciation was customary in Renaissance prefaces (the equivalent of the 'unaccustomed as I am' of the after-dinner speaker) as a means of ingratiating the writer with his reader. But it goes deeper than that in Montaigne. Irony pulls us up short, makes us think twice, and ponder what exactly the writer is getting at. There seems in the preface to be some sort of underlying joke or sequence of jokes. But what kind of joke and for what purpose? And at whose expense? Montaigne's or that of 'the Reader'? Or both? As Pasquier suggested: 'He [Montaigne] meant deliberately to make sport of us, and perhaps of himself' (Frame, 1965, p.311). The reader must make up his or her own mind. Reading Montaigne, as many have found, turns out to be a two-way process of exploration: of Montaigne and of oneself. For while Montaigne states in the preface his intention to present a portrait of himself as an individual, he also tells us in *On repenting*, that 'every man carries in himself the complete pattern of human nature' (*la forme entière de l'humaine condition* – J.M. Cohen's translation (1958); for Screech's translation, see p.908).

What are 'essays'? Montaigne, the evolution of the *Essays* and Burckhardt's 'discovery of the individual'

'I myself am the subject of my book', Montaigne wrote in his preface, 'To the Reader'; and in the *Essays* he recorded the raw material of his existence, his sense-impressions and his mental reactions to a wide variety of stimuli. The three books of *Essays* contain what he called 'an account of the assays (*essais*) of my life' (III, 13, p.1224). So the *Essays* were, as we saw earlier, intended as a kind of self-portraiture. But what are 'essays'?

Montaigne invented the word 'essay' in its modern sense (as in the more finished *Essays* of Francis Bacon in the early seventeenth century, or of Richard Steele and Joseph Addison or Dr Johnson in the eighteenth). When in 1603 Florio published his English translation of Montaigne from the Italian version by Naselli, he followed Naselli's example by glossing the unfamiliar word 'essays' in an extended title not present in the French original: *The Essayes, or Morall, Politike and Militarie Discourses of Michael, Lord of Montaigne* (see Screech, p.xliv). A discourse (*discorso*) originally implied a loose, 'discursive' account, lacking formal structure. Ben Jonson wrote of 'Mere essayists! A few loose sentences, and that's all.' Bacon defined essays as 'dispersed meditations'.

But in French, too, the title *Essais de Michel de Montaigne* was equally strange and unfamiliar to contemporaries, and was differently interpreted by them. (Note that the French title is 'Essays', not 'The essays'.) What exactly did Montaigne mean by *Essais*? The word *essai* (from the late Latin *exagium*), derived from one meaning of the Latin verb *exigere* (to weigh, consider, examine) and had several overlapping senses: a test, trial, attempt or 'assay'; an experiment or experience; tasting, testing or sampling an item of food or drink for poison; and a piece of work by an apprentice craftsman (see Boase, 1935, pp.2–3; Frame, 1983b, pp.89–102).

Montaigne's *Essays* evolved gradually, originally without a definite plan. They began largely as a record of his reactions to his reading, which was mainly but not exclusively classical, with a strong leaning towards history and moral philosophy. The chapters are crammed with quotations in prose and verse (more than 1,300, not to mention passages that have been translated or paraphrased and incorporated in the text). In fact we could say that the *Essays* started life as an anthology of classical anecdotes and commonplaces, strung out with Montaigne's personal annotations (for an example of one such chapter, see *On the frugality of the Ancients*, p.345). Such miscellanies or 'commonplace books', as they were called, were well known to Renaissance readers. Erasmus was a famous compiler of commonplace books with his *Apophthegmata, Colloquies, Praise of Folly* and the *Adages*, which ran to 120 editions between 1500 and 1570.

Montaigne's readers, then, were used to this kind of book (though not to reading it in the vernacular instead of in Latin: this was an innovation in Renaissance Europe), and the *Essays* were welcomed as another example of a familiar genre. Pierre Charron (1541–1603), a canon of Bordeaux cathedral, who edited Erasmus's *Adages* in 1571, later adapted extracts from Montaigne's *Essays* in the more traditional form of a commonplace book, which he called *On Wisdom* (1601). Evidently Charron supposed that they would be more acceptable in that form. Even in their final version, Pasquier praised the *Essays* as 'above all ... a real seed-bed of fine and notable sayings' (Frame, 1965, p.311). Montaigne conceded that readers might well dismiss him as just another compiler of miscellanies:

> asserting that I have merely gathered here a big bunch of other men's flowers, having furnished nothing of my own but the string to hold them together.

(III, 12, p.1196)

Montaigne used to scribble his reactions to books in the flysheets and margins of the books themselves (an example of this is to be found in his copy of the Roman poet Lucretius, rediscovered in 1997[4]). Montaigne extended this practice by including such observations in the *Essays* and recording there his reactions to issues raised in his reading-matter.

Above all, however, Plutarch's *Moralia* (*Moral Works*), in the French translation by Jacques Amyot (1572), itself a classic of the French Renaissance, appeared just when Montaigne was embarking on his *Essays*, and served him as a model especially stimulating and attractive to his temperament. Montaigne placed Amyot 'above all our writers in French' and said of his translation of Plutarch: 'it is our breviary' (II, 4, p.408). He saw Plutarch's book first as a rich collection of reflections on life, classical history and ethics, and second as a literary genre, a loose framework in which to expatiate at leisure on a variety

---

[4] Montaigne's edition of Lucretius, with his marginal comments, has been published as *Montaigne's Annotated Copy of Lucretius* (Screech, 1998).

of miscellaneous topics – an 'essay' in the modern sense. Plutarch's approach, compared to the more formal studies of the Roman Stoic Seneca, which also served Montaigne as a model, was 'more detached and relaxed' (III, 12, p.1177). Indeed Plutarch, rather than Montaigne, was the real originator of the essay as a literary form, and Montaigne followed a tradition of Renaissance humanism in looking back to a classical model as an inspiration for his own activity.[5]

A glance at some of the titles in Montaigne's table of contents (pp.vii–xi) shows their random nature. The informal framework which he adopted – 'this confused medley', as he called it (I, 13, p.50) – allowed him to meander on as the fancy took him, stringing together his random reflections in a way that often takes him far from the ostensible theme of the essay (III, 9, p.1125). For this reason, though the *Essays* delighted, they also puzzled their first readers. Pasquier was struck by their apparent lack of form: 'you will find in him [Montaigne] several chapters whose heading bears no relation at all to the body, except the feet' (Frame, 1965, p.310). The *Essays*, wrote Pasquier, were not 'a flower-bed, arranged in various plots and borders, but a sort of diversified prairie of many flowers, pell-mell and', so he says, 'without art' (Frame, 1965, p.311). (See also *On idleness*, where Montaigne admits that his mind, when left to itself in his leisurely retirement, 'bolted off like a runaway horse', p.31.) Many of these early chapters were relatively uncontroversial, though Montaigne always approaches his material critically and invariably has something original and penetrating to say. Read, for example, his comments on a passage from Seneca in *One man's profit is another man's loss* (p.121).

From this position, however, Montaigne moved on a stage, when he came to revise both the *Essays* and his ideas on what they (and he) were all about. He returned to them repeatedly and obsessively, revising and adding on in great surges of creative and critical energy. In Screech's edition (see p.liii) we can follow this process and see what Montaigne wrote for his first edition of 1580 (marked 'A' in Screech), his alterations and additions in the 1588 edition (marked 'B'), and the further amendments and additions (marked 'C') that he made during the last four years of his life in the margins of an unbound copy of the 1588 edition (and on slips of paper when the margins were full!),

---

[5] At Rome, in 1581, Montaigne defended Amyot's translation in a discussion with his former teacher at the Collège de Guyenne, Marc-Antoine Muret (Frame, 1983a, pp.87–8). Without Amyot's translations of Plutarch, Montaigne's *Essays*, both in concept and form, seem to me inconceivable. A reviewer in 1584, Antoine du Verdier, stressed Montaigne's debt to Amyot's translation of Plutarch's *Lives* (1559) and *Moral Works* (1572). Friedrich describes Amyot's work as 'the most significant translation event of the French sixteenth century (perhaps of all French literature)' (1991, pp.71–2).

known collectively as the 'Bordeaux copy' (Figure 8.7). Montaigne intended publishing these amendments in a final edition on which he was working at the time of his death. On the frontispiece of the Bordeaux copy, he confidently added a quotation from Virgil: *viresque acquirit eundo* ('it gets stronger as it goes along'), suggesting that he saw the *Essays* as evolving and improving (Figure 8.8).

The *Essays* gradually evolved from their bookish models into something quite new, a form of self-portraiture, self-expression and self-understanding. While Book I contains only one chapter that is truly autobiographical in content, in Book II there are four. In *On*

Figure 8.7 Page of text with Montaigne's handwritten revisions and additions from Michel de Montaigne, 1588, *Essays*, I, 26, *De l'institution des enfants*, fifth edition, the 'Bordeaux copy', p.64, corresponding to pp.192–5 in the Screech translation. Bibliothèque Municipale de Bordeaux Collection Montaigne S.1238 Rés

346

Figure 8.8 Frontispiece of the 1588 fifth edition, the 'Bordeaux copy', with Montaigne's erasures and the quotation from Virgil: *viresque acquirit eundo* ('it gets stronger as it goes along'). Bibliothèque Municipale de Bordeaux Collection Montaigne S.1238 Rés

presumption, Montaigne made his first deliberate attempt at a self-portrait, and henceforth he regularly writes of himself, illustrating different assertions from his personal experience. In *On practice*, he explains:

> For many years now the target of my thoughts has been myself alone; I examine nothing, I study nothing, but me; and if I do study anything else, it is so as to apply it at once to myself.

> (II, 6, p.424)

All the chapters in Book III are autobiographical. For an example of how Montaigne later expanded a fairly commonplace chapter of 1580 into a more personal statement by the addition of a further passage, see *That our deeds are judged by the intention* (pp.28–9).

Montaigne used these 'trials', 'tests', 'attempts', 'experiments', 'experiences' or 'assays' to demonstrate to himself and his friends and relatives and to 'the Reader' the sort of person that he was. It was not autobiography in the sense of a sequential, chronological account of his life. It was more like a series of self-portraits painted at different moments and in different moods and settings, capturing different sides of his nature, and frequently reworked. 'It is my own self that I am painting', he declares in the preface. Montaigne frequently returned to the analogy between painting and autobiography (see *On presumption*, p.742, last paragraph, and note on the same page (footnote 39) the sentence which he included in his 1580 edition, and see also *On repenting*, p.907).

'An honest book' (*un livre de bonne foy*)?

'You have here, Reader, a book whose faith can be trusted.' With these words Montaigne opens his preface. A straightforward beginning, it would seem. And yet Screech has slightly expanded the original for the sake of clarity, and in so doing has given it a meaning not necessarily implicit in the original. The French says '*un livre de bonne foy*', literally 'a book of good faith'. Cohen translates this as 'an honest book'. This seems to me to be closer to the original, and to bring out a paradox worth thinking about. How can a *book* be 'of good faith'? A writer can be a man or woman 'of good faith'. A book may be *written* 'in good faith' by its author, because acting 'in good faith' is something that a human being, but *only* a human being can do. Why, then, does Montaigne describe his book in this way, unless he thinks of it, or wants 'the Reader' to think of it, as somehow a living thing, akin to a human being? For the *Essays* are consciously and overtly just that – the expression and reflection of a human personality, Montaigne's personality and a kind of other self. This at any rate was how he presented them, as 'a book of one substance with its author' (II, 18, p.755). When Henry III told him how much he liked the *Essays*, Montaigne replied: 'Then, Sire, Your Majesty must like me, if you like my book, for it is no more than an account of my life and actions' (Coleman, 1987, p.6).

The *Essays* are a living thing in the further sense that they continued to develop as Montaigne himself developed. 'My aim is to reveal my own self, which may well be different tomorrow if I am initiated into some new business which changes me' (I, 26, p.167). Few self-portraits can be, to quote the preface, 'more full, more alive,' even when, or perhaps especially when, the author is at his most meandering and apparently inconsequential (see, for example, the opening paragraph of *On liars*, p.32, or *On smells*, pp.353–4). He tells us about his physical appearance and quirks (for example, his clumsiness, laziness, poor memory, ignorance of elementary facts and indecisiveness in *On presumption*, pp.718–52, and his likes and dislikes, way of life, health and personal habits in *On experience*, pp.1126–269). Adding to the *Essays* and tinkering with them until he died, he went on revising them as he advanced through life, changing his mind as he underwent new experiences and entertained new thoughts and perspectives. (For his view of life as a process of flux and development, see *On repenting*, pp.907–8.)

Montaigne sought to arrive, if not at an expression of final absolute truth – scepticism taught him that that was impossible for any human being, whose judgement is fallible and whose conclusions should be tentative – then at as close and accurate as possible a record of himself, his character, thoughts and impressions, a picture of himself in his 'native form' (p.lix), just as he was at any given moment, including his 'defects'. He wanted to know himself better, to get closer to the truth about himself: that was the purpose of his revisions. In conventional autobiography the writer generally seeks, consciously or not, to make out a good case for himself, to make a favourable impression. As Montaigne notes: 'We are not so much concerned with what the actual nature of our being is within us, as with how it is perceived by the public' (III, 9, p.1081). Montaigne by contrast professes that he has no interest in defending himself, still less in making himself out as other or better than he is. For this reason, he says, he will not trouble to improve his style. In *On some lines of Virgil*, he tells us that 'I may correct an accidental slip ... but it would be an act of treachery to remove such imperfections as are commonly and always in me', because these are his *characteristic* defects, peculiar to him. If he 'corrected' them, he would be untrue to himself and falsifying the picture, whose virtue lies in its honesty. By including even his grammatical errors, he can reply:

> Am I not portraying myself to the life? If so, that suffices! I have achieved what I wanted to: everyone recognizes me in my book and my book in me.

> (III, 5, p.989)

He emphasizes this theme of truthful self-depiction in *On presumption*, where, admitting his many unheroic shortcomings, he concludes:

> But no matter how I may appear when I make myself known, provided that I do make myself known such as I am, I have done what I set out to do [and] cost me what it will, I am determined to tell things as they are.

> (II, 17, pp.741–2, 748)

In this sense, Montaigne wrote 'in good faith' and the *Essays* were an expression of that 'good faith', since they were the expression of what – by dint of 'assaying' – Montaigne felt he knew best – himself.

In the letter to Marguerite de Grammont with which he concluded the last essay of Book II (pp.884–7), he reverts to the same theme as in his preface 'To the Reader'. Preface and letter were written at the same time and were clearly intended to mirror and complement each other at the beginning and what was until 1588 the end of the *Essays*. In both, Montaigne wanted to introduce and explain his novel genre. The first dozen lines of the letter raise the same points as the preface: the book's function as a record of Montaigne's person and personality, 'the same mannerisms and attitudes ... those very same characteristics and attributes' which he showed in life. The third and fourth sentences are a variant of the fifth and sixth sentences of the preface: Montaigne insists that he puts no airs and graces in the *Essays*: they are 'sketched from nature', or, as we might say, they are 'true to life' or they are Montaigne 'to the life'.

Montaigne claims to write simply and naturally as the fancy takes him and in much the same manner as he speaks, that is, spontaneously. In his preface, as we have seen, he can sometimes appear quite abrupt and familiar with 'the Reader'. In *Reflections upon Cicero*, he claims that he has no small talk, and no skill 'in all those verbose compliments required by the rules of courtesy in our etiquette' (p.283). The implication again is that we can trust him to give us the truth, plain and unvarnished.

But, as we saw in Book 1 of the series in a discussion of Montaigne's attitudes to conventional portraiture, giving a 'true' picture of oneself is not so simple. (For Montaigne's appreciation of the diversity, waywardness and complexity of his and human nature, see *We reach the same ends by discrepant means*, pp.3–6, and *On the inconstancy of our actions*, pp.373–80.) Montaigne was acutely aware of the contrast between appearance and reality, between the public and private man, between projecting oneself 'in a studied gait' and in a 'simple, natural, everyday fashion, without striving or artifice' (p.lix), between imposing on others and deluding ourself, between self-deception and self-knowledge. It is a theme which continually fascinated him and which he explores in many chapters (see, for example, *On the inequality there is between us*, pp.288–99 and *On repenting*, pp.911–13).

In writing the *Essays*, then, Montaigne came to realize that man is complex and paradoxical. He was also convinced that giving an honest picture of himself in particular and telling the truth in general was a prime moral duty – 'the first and basic part of virtue' (II, 17, p.736).

But what is truth and how can we know it? This was another question which continually engaged his attention. Increasingly, he came to believe that human reason is fallible, far more than we normally realize. This raises the question of Montaigne's scepticism, to be discussed later in this chapter.

Self-portraiture, Renaissance 'glory' and the *Essays*

With Montaigne's bold claim in 'To the Reader' that 'I myself am the subject of my book', as Screech observes, 'he was defying one of the basic taboos of all civilised society and one of the great interdicts of European culture' (1991, p.24). The taboo on speaking well of oneself goes back at least to classical times, as we can see from one of Plutarch's *Moral Works*: 'How a man may praise himself without incurring envie and blame' (Figure 8.9). Plutarch's essay begins:

> To speake much of ones selfe in praise ... there is no man ... but by word of mouth will professe it is most odious, and unbeseeming a person well borne and of good bringing up; but in very deed few there be who can take heed and beware of falling into the inconvenience and enormitie thereof, no not even those who otherwise do blame and condemne the same.

As for the Renaissance, Burckhardt says of Benvenuto Cellini's autobiography that 'the reader often detects him bragging or lying' (1990, p.217). Can the same be said of Montaigne?

Étienne Pasquier observed of Montaigne that:

> while he gives the appearance of disdaining himself, I never read an author who esteemed himself as much as he. For if anyone had scratched out all the passages he used to talk about himself and his family, his work would be shortened by a good quarter, especially in his third book.

> (Frame, 1965, p.311)

The last sentence is undeniable. But what about Pasquier's assertions in the first sentence? It is remarkable that though the *Essays* relate to one man and his reactions to a random miscellany of topics, Montaigne is not usually felt to emerge as a bore or an egomaniac (you may, of course, disagree).[6] Among the characteristics of Renaissance individualism identified by Burckhardt is the pursuit of

---

[6] Among university students in the United States there are complaints that Montaigne 'talks too much about himself', is 'too jaded', 'too pessimistic', 'too male chauvinist', 'too intellectually radical and too politically conservative' – and 'elitist' (Henry, 1994, p.11). This suggests another good reason for studying him in the context of the Renaissance: to try to see him in his own time and on his own terms rather than in terms of the 'whiggish' march of progress or of the orthodoxy of 'political correctness' (see Insdorf, 1977).

Figure 8.9 Plutarch, 'How a man may praise himself without incurring envie and blame', *The Philosophie Commonlie Called the Morals Written by the Learned Philosopher Plutarch*, trans. Philemon Holland, 1603, London, Arnold Hatfield, p.301. Cambridge University Library, Huntingdon 21.6. Reproduced by permission of the Syndics of Cambridge University Library

'glory' (1990, p.104). Burckhardt points to its origins in Roman authors, whose writings, 'zealously studied' in the Renaissance, were 'saturated with the conception of fame' (1990, p.104). Dante prided himself on the novelty of his achievement. Petrarch admits to a desire for posthumous fame, but claims that he 'would rather be without it in his own day' (p.105).

What about Montaigne? The *Essays* are his claim to fame, but is that how he saw them? He was well aware of the originality of his achievement: 'it is the only book of its kind in the world', as he wrote (p.433). In 'To the Reader', however, he claims that his aim in writing is 'a private family one' and stresses that he has not been concerned with '*ma gloire*' – which Screech translates as 'my reputation' but which in the French means 'my glory' (as Florio translates it). Montaigne denies that he shares with the Roman emperor Tiberius a 'ridiculous' desire (the same as Petrarch's) for posthumous fame rather than fame in his lifetime, and claims: 'I have no wish to be better loved or better valued when dead than when alive' (II, 37, p.885). In *On giving the lie*, he offers an explanation of why, if the *Essays* were intended only for private reading by his family and friends, he had them published instead of circulating them in manuscript (p.754). And in *On vanity,* he states that 'my book I write for a few men and for a few years', claiming that had he wished to leave something more lasting he would have written in Latin, not in French, a language evolving so fast that it would (he predicts) be unrecognizable 50 years hence (p.1111). (It is true that Marie de Gournay, in her preface to the 1595 edition of the *Essays*, admitted that the French was already old-fashioned.) How convincing is his overall claim?

It was not that Montaigne was unaware of or uninterested in glory. He knew about its hold on people (I, 41, p.285) and on himself (see Figure 8.4, the title page of the first edition of the *Essays*, where he sets out his noble title and lists his honours). He himself prized military glory and a public career particularly highly, more so, apparently, than literary or intellectual repute. Out of all the chapters only thirteen make no mention of military matters. And he declared: 'I do believe that the most honourable vocation is to serve the commonwealth and to be useful to many' (III, 9, p.1078). Yet he also belittles his own role in diplomatic and political life, admitting: 'I cannot give an account of my life by my actions. Fortune has placed them too low for that; so I do so by my thoughts' (III, 9, p.1070).

He also asserts that writing the *Essays* and the study of himself has a practical application: 'Whatever I may be like, I have no desire to exist only on paper!' The purpose of his 'studies' is 'to teach me not to write but to act'; and his main occupation and purpose in life have been 'to make this self of mine worth something' (II, 37, p.885). One of his stated purposes, then, is self-exploration, self-discovery, self-development, self-understanding, self-realization. He hates the thought of being considered 'clever at writing but stupid and useless at everything else!' (p.885). He even dismisses his self-portraiture in the *Essays* as 'this silly nonsense' (p.885), and as we have seen in 'To the Reader', as 'a topic so frivolous and so vain' (p.lix). He disclaims any pretence at fine writing, doubting 'if I ought to use the term style for my formless way of speaking, free from rules and in the popular idiom' (II, 17, p.724).

Again, the question is how to take Montaigne's continual self-depreciation and his apparent modesty. (In *On vanity* he spends three to four pages talking down the *Essays*!, see pp.1070–71, 1091, 1126.) Clearly much of this is ironic. But is it modesty or false-modesty? To hold oneself out time and again as deeply modest is a contradiction in terms. As Pasquier suggests, his modesty, or apparent modesty, may be intended to screen the real pride which he takes in the *Essays* and to shield him from the charge of vainglory raised in the Plutarch essay quoted above. Montaigne was well aware that 'custom has made it a vice to talk about oneself and obstinately prohibits it, hating the boasting which always seems to be attached to any testimony about oneself' (II, 6, p.424). In *On giving the lie*, he claims that 'no suspicion of ostentation can fall upon me' (p.754) and in *On presumption*, he complains (as in 'To the Reader') of the artificiality of convention, 'the laws of etiquette, which do not allow a man to speak well of himself nor ill of himself', and hence serve as a hindrance to truth (p.718).

In *On glory*, Montaigne sets out arguments for and against the pursuit of glory, taken from the ancient philosophers. The latter were not all, with due respect to Burckhardt, 'saturated with the conception of fame'; or at any rate, as Montaigne shows, they valued fame differently. Or perhaps Burckhardt is right after all: Montaigne admits that even the Greek philosopher Epicurus, who appeared to disdain fame, sought it indirectly; and that Epicurus typifies the ambiguity of everyone who has thought and felt on the subject: 'within ourselves we are somehow double creatures' (p.704). We both despise the good opinion of our fellow men and crave it. In *On presumption*, Montaigne explores and analyses the concept of 'glory' still further. There is, he writes, 'another kind of "glory": the over-high opinion we conceive of our own worth', and which we demonstrate by 'presenting ourself to ourself other than we are' (p.718). Montaigne deplores such self-delusion, stemming from self-love and lack of self-knowledge.

'The study of man'

Exercise

Please turn to *On repenting*, and read from p.907 to the end of the penultimate paragraph on p.909. What does this passage add to our understanding of Montaigne's aims and achievements in the *Essays*?

Discussion

One reason why Montaigne does not, to most readers, emerge as a monster of egotism and self-absorption is his gradual realization that, while writing about himself, he was also ultimately writing about something else, of equal or greater interest and significance to 'the Reader' – humankind and human nature.

Montaigne perceived that while every individual is different and unique, each partakes of a common human nature. While each is shaped and differentiated from others by their own 'native form', at the same time, as we noted earlier in Cohen's translation, 'every man carries in himself the complete pattern of human nature'. Because of this affinity, everyone has something in common with every other, which, if we study ourself, we can identify in ourself and in that other, present and past, as Montaigne notes: in Socrates, in Julius Caesar, in the opposite sex, in the outsider and the outlandish, in Tamberlane the Great (leader of the Mongol horde), in the Jews of the ghetto in Rome, even in the recently discovered cannibals of South America. ❖

These considerations may help to explain why Pasquier, puzzled though he is at the peculiar form of autobiographical genre created by Montaigne, which by its very nature seems to be the embodiment of egotism, nevertheless concedes:

> I still cannot be offended when he [Montaigne] lets himself go and talks about himself. It is said in such a manner that I take as much pleasure in it *as if he were speaking of another*.
>
> (Frame, 1965, p.311, my italics)

Recapitulation: development of the *Essays*

The content and shape of the *Essays* changed over the years, and so, gradually, and perhaps imperceptibly to begin with, did their nature and purpose. To resume their various stages:

- The *Essays* began as a sort of commonplace book, a loose collection of Montaigne's comments on his reading, particularly of classical *sententiae* (moral maxims and reflections on human nature) and *exempla* (instances of praiseworthy conduct), many drawn from Plutarch. The genre was popular with Renaissance readers, but was not considered high literature, particularly when written in the vernacular.

- The *Essays* then developed into a more conscious and deliberate statement of Montaigne's reflections, a record of his states of mind and his thoughts on a variety of miscellaneous topics. The *Essays* became at once a means of self-expression and a highly original form of autobiography.

- As he revised and added to them, Montaigne realized that the *Essays* were also a record of change and development in himself, his personality and outlook; and that by making himself think more concentratedly and profoundly – and more honestly – he had turned them into a means of self-knowledge and self-education, which also broadened and deepened his human sympathies. He and his book became mutually creative ('a book of one substance with its author', as he says in *On giving the lie*, p.755). The chapters in Book III are fewer and longer than in Books I and II.

- Montaigne also realized that insofar as he was a human being, sharing characteristics with others, his account was of broader significance. The *Essays* were not merely a private memento for family and friends, they were a study of human nature, based on experience and fidelity to truth, and as such had an educative and moral value – for Montaigne and for 'the Reader'.

- The *Essays* also developed a pattern, or at any rate they led to a conclusion. According to Screech, *On experience* is not just:

  an essay which happens to come at the end: it is the last chapter of the third and last book of the *Essais* ... The last pages of the last chapter ... form the climax of all three books. They are the end ... of a long quest.

  (2000, p.13)

Montaigne on Renaissance beliefs and attitudes

Montaigne and Machiavelli

For all his normally relaxed and unbuttoned style and fondness for protracted reflection, Montaigne was no armchair philosopher. As mayor of Bordeaux, he held a position of political authority and was in personal danger during the civil and religious wars in a region fraught with strife, unrest and violence (see *On experience*, p.1184, second paragraph). 'I have gone to bed in my own home hundreds of times thinking that I would be betrayed and killed that night', he reveals (III, 9, p.1098). He went on important diplomatic missions to try to mediate among the rival parties and to bring peace to war-torn France. He was familiar with the ideas of Machiavelli, and, though he made no claim to be a political philosopher, in several chapters he expresses his thoughts on that central issue of politics and ethics, the conflict between the public and private man, the duties of the statesman and the claims of conscience.

Exercise

In France, the conventional view of Machiavelli, promulgated by French writers such as François Hotman and Innocent Gentillet, was that he deliberately advocated 'a policy of immorality' and gave encouragement to 'duplicitous politicians and others who achieve their goals by cunning' (Kekewich, 2000, pp.213, 249). Please read

On presumption, from p.734 (last paragraph) to p.737 (end of second paragraph), where, as Screech points out, 'Montaigne has Machiavelli's *Prince* in mind throughout' (footnote 31). What is Montaigne's attitude to Machiavelli's philosophy of statecraft?

Discussion

It is clear that Montaigne's understanding of Machiavelli's philosophy was the same as that of contemporaries such as Hotman and Gentillet. Montaigne abominates lying and dissimulation and argues that a statecraft based on duplicity is counterproductive. Even viewed from a practical rather than a moral angle, systematic duplicity seems pointless. In the long run, a ruler who is habitually deceitful loses credibility. Montaigne insists that 'might and violence can achieve something, but not always and not everything'. Conversely, popular support and loyalty are won by honourable conduct, by 'generosity and justice', not by deceit. (It is likely that the first two paragraphs on p.735 and especially paragraph two (which was added after 1588) were intended for the eyes of Henry of Navarre, heir to the French throne.) ❖

Exercise

Please read *On the useful and the honourable*, pp.891–906. In this essay Montaigne enlarges on his attitude to the conventional demands that political action makes on the integrity of public figures. He takes it for granted that the state is entitled to a man's service (p.899). What more does Montaigne indicate in this essay about his attitude to the ideas of Machiavelli?

Discussion

Montaigne refuses to compromise with his own nature and convictions. In his various political missions he tries to remain true to himself. Note again his insistence on 'my frankness, my simplicity and my naturalness of manner' as opposed to 'counterfeit artful frankness'. (This theme of self-consistency relates the essay to the aim of a natural and hence reliable self-portrait 'without striving or artifice' which he sets out in 'To the Reader'.)

Montaigne does not deny the reality and the efficacy of 'wiliness' in history and politics: 'that would be to misunderstand the world'. But alluding to the title of the essay, he 'differentiates between things useful and things decent' (*les choses utiles et les honnestes*). The word '*honneste*', as Screech reminds us (p.891), had connotations of 'decent' as well as of 'honourable' ('*un honneste homme*' would soon come to mean something close to 'a gentleman'). Montaigne's point – and he makes it by means of an ironic allusion to 'natural [bodily] functions' – is that not every useful action is decent or honourable. He describes the public executioner as 'an office as useful as it is shameful' (or 'dishonourable' – *charge autant utile comme elle est peu honeste* (*sic*)).

Montaigne makes the same point in respect of examples of 'treachery' in history. For his own part, he would refuse to undertake a political mission if it required him 'to tell lies, to be treacherous or to perjure myself ... (not to mention assassinations or poisonings)'. There are some actions which an honest man, *un honneste homme*, should be ashamed to perform: 'not all things are legitimate to a man of honour at the service of his king or of the cause of the commonwealth and its laws'.

Does Montaigne, then, rule out 'dishonourable' acts altogether? His penultimate paragraph on p.902 suggests that the good of the state may require them in exceptional circumstances. He understood and accepted, to some degree, Machiavelli's cynical realism; but he wished to marginalize these cases as 'dangerous examples, rare and sick exceptions'. There remains, perhaps, an unbridgeable conflict in the demands made on the integrity of the private and public man. ❖

Figure 8.10 Map showing France in the wars of religion, 1572–85. Adapted from Michel Péronnet, *Le XVIe siècle, des grandes découvertes à la Contre-Réforme (1492–1620)*, 1981, Paris, Hachette

Montaigne considered the same dilemma in other essays. In *On liars*, he expresses his abhorrence of lying. It is one of the few faults, like cruelty, at which he betrays real, passionate indignation. 'Lying is an accursed vice ... more worthy of the stake than other crimes', an offence against truth and even humanity, because 'it is only our words which bind us together and make us human' (p.35, and see Screech's headnote on p.32).

Montaigne, scepticism, authority and religion

Montaigne belonged to the first generation born after the Reformation, a generation subject to the unprecedented turmoil of the French wars of religion in the second half of the sixteenth century[7] (see Figures 8.10 and 8.11). His eldest sister, and for a time a

Figure 8.11 Map showing France in the wars of religion, 1585–1601. Adapted from Michel Péronnet, *Le XVIe siècle, des grandes découvertes à la Contre-Réforme (1492–1620)*, 1981, Paris, Hachette

[7] Historians distinguish eight successive wars between 1562 and 1598 (see Garrisson, 1995; Knecht, 1996).

brother, became Huguenots, as the French Protestants (mainly Calvinists) were called. His father-in-law was taken hostage by Huguenots. Another brother fought for the Huguenot Henry of Navarre, whom Montaigne too later supported. And Montaigne was directly involved in the political infighting of the wars as mayor of Bordeaux. Bordeaux was a city of some 50,000 Catholics with a Huguenot minority of around 7,000, a Catholic enclave under the control of the ultra-Catholic 'League' in an area of France increasingly under Huguenot control (see Figure 8.11). Montaigne kept the city loyal to the Catholic Henry III, while staying on good terms with Henry of Navarre, who became heir to the French throne in 1584. Montaigne's château, as he wrote, was 'situated at the very hub of the disturbances in our French Civil Wars' (II, 6, p.418). In 1569 he witnessed the siege of Mussidan, 20 miles away (I, 6, p.25). In 1586 the Leaguers besieged and captured Castillon, only five miles distant. Marauders and plague in 1586 and 1587 caused him to flee the château for six months. After his victory over the Catholics at Coutras in October 1587, Henry of Navarre spent the night at Montaigne's château. On his way to Paris in 1588 on behalf of Henry of Navarre, Montaigne was robbed by Huguenots and briefly put in the Bastille by the Leaguers.

He lived, then, under the impact, often violent, of the religious divide and of the Counter-Reformation, and the impact on him personally is clearly reflected in the *Essays,* though with characteristic self-depreciation he claims:

> how little it has cost me in terms of my life's repose and tranquillity to have passed more than a half of my days during the collapse of my country.

(III, 12, p.1185)

The St Bartholomew's day massacre (1572), which took place when Montaigne was embarking on the *Essays,* killed almost as many Protestants in Bordeaux as in Paris. Montaigne's horror at the civil wars and the excesses of both Protestants and Catholics is much in evidence, especially in Book III, Chapters 10 to 13 and in his final additions (the passages marked 'C' in Screech's edition). Attempts at religious pluralism in France did not bring peaceful coexistence. They provoked bitter disputation between Catholics and Huguenots, couched in what Sydney Anglo (1981, p.1) calls 'a rhetoric of hate', accompanied by a vicious circle of violence. 'All are alike in using religion for their violent and ambitious schemes', Montaigne notes, observing that 'Christians excel at hating enemies' (II, 12, pp.494–5). What was Montaigne's own position amid the contending rivalries?

In 1576, when he was well into the *Essays*, Montaigne designed a medal for himself, depicting a pair of scales in balance, symbolizing suspension of judgement. On one side of the medal was inscribed in French, *Que sçays-je?* (What do I know?). On the other side, in Greek, *epekho* (I suspend judgement), a watchword of the ancient sceptics (the word 'sceptic' comes from the Greek word '*skeptomai*', I examine).

The medal illustrates a problem with which Montaigne was continually exercised: what is truth and how can we ascertain it? He pointed out the problems of establishing historical truth, how difficult it is to ascertain exactly what happened in the past, even when we possess contemporary eyewitness accounts, as with many of the Greek and Roman historians. However reliable they appear, it is impossible to test their statements in 'our quest for truth', 'as in a judicial inquiry', by cross-examination of witnesses (II, 10, p.469). This reminds us of Montaigne's sixteen years of experience as a judge. Yet the problem of ascertaining the truth, he claimed, was, paradoxically, even more complex in his own day. As he put it: 'When I play with my cat, how do I know that she is not passing time with me rather than I with her?' (II, 12, p.505). We suggested earlier that what Montaigne felt he knew best was himself. But for all his profound introspection, he throws doubt even on that. In *On presumption* he admits 'I am most ignorant about myself' (p.720). From such evidence of scepticism and from his condemnation of the excesses of the warring Protestants and Catholics, we might suppose that his attitude was: 'a plague on both your houses!'

According to Burckhardt, religion in the Renaissance became 'an affair of the individual and of his own personal feeling' (1990, p.313). If this was true of Montaigne, then from his constant scrutiny of 'his own personal feelings' we might suppose that he sympathized with the Protestant belief in personal faith resulting from individual persuasion and conviction.

As the choice of words and image stamped on his medal suggests, Montaigne was much taken with the ancient philosophy of scepticism, or 'Pyrrhonism' (after the Greek philosopher, Pyrrho, third century BCE). Pyrrhonism was popularized by the Greek Sextus Empiricus (fl. *c.*200 CE), whose *Hypotyposes* or *Outlines of Pyrrhonism* became well known after its publication in France in 1562 in a Latin translation by the Huguenot scholar and printer Henri Etienne. Of the 65 philosophical maxims which Montaigne had painted on the ceiling beams of his library,[8] a dozen were taken from Sextus

[8] Fifty-seven of these maxims are published in Thibaudet and Rat, 1962, pp.1419–27. All 65 appear in the definitive study by Alain Legros (1999).

Figure 8.12 Latin and Greek inscriptions on the beams in Montaigne's library, château of Montaigne, Saint Michel de Montaigne. The first two inscriptions (top), from the Latin Vulgate, read: 'If a man think himself to be something, when he is nothing, he deceiveth himself', Galatians 6.3; and 'Be not more wise than it behoveth, but be ye soberly wise', Romans 12.3. Montaigne reproduced this in I, 30, *On moderation*, p.222. The third inscription, from the Greek writer Xenophon, quoted by Sextus Empiricus, reads: 'No man has known or will know anything for certain.' Photo: Alain Legros

Empiricus (including '*epekho*' and '*skeptomaï*') (see Figure 8.12). According to Richard Popkin, it was Montaigne who, of all Renaissance writers, 'felt most fully the impact of the Pyrrhonian theory of complete doubt, and its relevance to the religious debates of the time' (1979, p.42).

Pyrrho claimed that certainty of knowledge is unattainable. We should not say: 'this is so', but 'this seems so'. Montaigne summed this up as follows:

> If you can picture an endless confession of ignorance, or a power of judgement which never, never inclines to one side or the other, then you can conceive what Pyrrhonism is.
>
> (II, 12, p.563)

Montaigne agrees that wisdom lies in suspending judgement:

> Philosophy never seems to me to have a better hand to play than when she battles against our presumption and our vanity; when in good faith she acknowledges her weakness, her ignorance and her inability to reach conclusions.
>
> (II, 17, p.721)

Montaigne's Pyrrhonian scepticism features most prominently in *An apology for Raymond Sebond*, where he questions the ability of human reason alone, without God's grace, to apprehend religious truth. For a discussion of this, the longest chapter in the *Essays*, see Screech (pp.xx–xliii). Here we shall focus on some shorter chapters, where the influence of scepticism on Montaigne is also evident.

Exercise

Please read *That it is madness to judge the true and the false from our own capacities* (pp.200–4). Note the title, and the penultimate sentence in Screech's headnote. How does Montaigne, if he is a sceptic, reach this uncompromising conclusion?

Discussion

Montaigne begins by comparing credulity and its opposite, disbelief. He agrees that 'simplemindedness' and 'ignorance' lie at the heart of credulity, and that 'that is why children, the common people, women and the sick are more readily led by the nose'. The educated, however, who pride themselves on their judgement, are prone to the opposite 'vice' of incredulity: 'there is a silly arrogance in continuing to disdain something and to condemn it as false just because it seems unlikely to us'. But is this incredulity, the reluctance to take anything on trust, not precisely what the attitude of a Pyrrhonian sceptic, judging things on a balance of probabilities, is, or ought to be?

Not in matters of religion, is Montaigne's implicit answer. Or rather, in matters of true religion, what should be doubted is doubt itself! The true sceptic should have the modesty to suspend his judgement, not to exercise it in matters beyond the scope of his intellect, such as 'the frontiers and bounds of the will of God and the power of Nature'. A man who sees a river for the first time supposes it to be the ocean, simply because it is outside his experience. When, therefore, we encounter things which seem to us improbable, though vouched for by others, 'if we cannot be convinced, we should at least remain in suspense', particularly if our informants are 'people worthy of our trust'.

So we can scoff at chroniclers like Froissart and Gilles when they recount highly unlikely events; but when a reliable historian like Plutarch does so, we should be slow to dismiss his account. Likewise, we are free to reject Bouchet's accounts of so-called miracles, because his authority is not sufficiently reliable. But if the authority is that of Saint Augustine, then, however inherently improbable his accounts, we must accept them.

A Catholic must submit with implicit faith to the church's authority in everything. In Screech's words, 'he is not free to pick and choose among doctrines'. Montaigne objects to Protestantism precisely because Protestants do claim the right to decide for themselves, by the light of their own limited understanding, what to believe or not to believe: 'you are claiming to know the frontiers and bounds of the will of God'. This claim to know better than the church is in Montaigne's view a form of intellectual arrogance, 'a dangerous boldness of great consequence in despising whatever we cannot understand', which has led directly to France's religious and civil divisions and contributed to their ferocity and fanaticism. (See also *Judgements on God's ordinances must be embarked upon with prudence*, pp.242–4.) ❖

So Montaigne the sceptic turns out to be neither indifferent to religion nor sympathetic to Protestantism, but a conforming Catholic. *That it is madness to judge the true and the false* was cited in Montaigne's own time as proof of his Catholic orthodoxy according to the criteria laid down at the Council of Trent. (See *On prayer*, p.355 for a clear statement of his Catholic allegiance.) When he visited Rome in 1580–81, he submitted the *Essays* to the papal censor for approval. The censor detected in them only slight deviations from Catholic doctrine, and left it to Montaigne to decide whether or not to amend them (he did not!). The pope himself, Gregory XIII (1572–85), on receiving Montaigne in audience, complimented him on 'the devotion he had always borne to the church' (Frame, 1983b, p.75). (This was the pope who publicly celebrated the St Bartholomew's day massacre.) For long after his death, Montaigne's recommendations of unquestioning submission to the church were drawn on by apologists of the Counter-Reformation, such as his friend Pierre Charron. It was only later in the seventeenth century that the *Essays* came to be seen as dangerously ambiguous: they were placed on the Catholic Index of prohibited books in 1676.

In his own time, then, Montaigne was seen as a defender of the Catholic church, who consistently deplored what he saw as the 'presumption' of Protestants in claiming or even seeking to know God's will through the exercise of reason. In *On prayer*, he condemns one of the basic innovations of the Reformation – the translation of scripture into modern languages:

> How silly they are who think they have made it accessible to the vulgar simply by translating it into the vulgar tongues ... By bringing Scripture that little bit nearer they actually push it further away. Pure ignorance, leaving men totally dependent on others, was much more salutary and more learned than such vain verbal knowledge, that nursery of rashness and presumption.

(I, 56, p.359)

In his last essay, *On experience*, he points out the futility of biblical commentary and exegesis, an unending process which brings us no closer to truth and provokes incessant wrangling and strife, even among the Protestants themselves:

> I note that Luther has left behind in Germany as many – indeed more – discords and disagreements because of doubts about his opinions than he himself ever raised about Holy Scripture.

> (III, 13, p.1213)

Just because we are in reality so ignorant even of ourselves, it is all the more presumptuous in us to question the religious authorities.

> We must either totally submit to the authority of our ecclesiastical polity or else totally release ourselves from it. It is not for us to decide what degree of obedience we owe to it.

> (I, 27, p.204)

In *An apology for Raymond Sebond* he condemns Protestants for questioning religious dogmas beyond their understanding instead of taking them on trust. If the physical world, and even man himself, is unfathomable (and Montaigne was writing before the scientific revolution of the seventeenth century), how much more so are the mysteries of religion. His scepticism is underscored by relativism: 'We are Christians by the same title that we are Périgordians or Germans' (p.497). Pyrrhonian scepticism, then, leads Montaigne into comfortable acceptance of the state religion. In *On experience*, he writes: 'Oh what a soft and delightful pillow, and what a sane one on which to rest a well-schooled head, are ignorance and unconcern' (p.1218). The attitude of unquestioning conformism recommended by Montaigne is commonly known as 'fideism'.[9] But his irony is such that it is no wonder that he later came to be seen as subversive.

Montaigne and the Roman Catholic faith

Montaigne's account of himself as a conforming and practising Roman Catholic in *On prayer* is corroborated in his *Travel Journal*, a reliable source against which to test his assertions in the *Essays*, since, unlike them, it was not intended for publication and was discovered only in 1770. The *Travel Journal* records his frequent church attendance, including a pilgrimage to the famous shrine of Our Lady at Loreto. Was Montaigne, however, a true, a convinced believer, or was he a mere conformist, who privately entertained sceptical views on religion? Was he even a Christian? To explore this let us compare *That it is madness to judge the true and the false* (pp.200–4) with *In defence*

---

[9] Fideism is the belief that Christianity depends on faith alone since its truth cannot be demonstrated by reason. It was condemned as a heresy in the seventeenth century.

of Seneca and Plutarch (pp.817–24). A glance at the beginning of the second paragraph of the latter – Montaigne's reference to Protestantism as 'the Religion Allegedly Reformed' and the passage that follows in brackets – again confirms that he publicly places himself on the Catholic side.

At the foot of p.821 Montaigne again reverts to 'a major fault into which most people fall' and which is to him the 'major fault' of Protestantism, namely to place far too much reliance on human reason. For Montaigne the sceptic this is a form of naïvety and at the same time of arrogance and obstinacy, which has produced fatal results in France. (The words in brackets 'as I have said elsewhere' refer to *That it is madness to judge the true and the false.*) On p.820 (fourth paragraph) and p.821 (end of the first paragraph), Montaigne again emphasizes the horrible consequences of Protestantism to the Protestants themselves in 'these civil wars of ours', characterized (and indeed caused) by acts of 'obstinate resistance and of stubbornness even among the rabble' (i.e. the Huguenots, p.820), 'roasted or burnt for opinions which, without understanding or knowledge, they have taken from others' (p.821).

Exercise

Please read *In defence of Seneca and Plutarch*, from half-way down p.818 ('Now for Plutarch') to the end of the first paragraph on p.822. The question under discussion is the credibility of Plutarch's famous account of the Spartan boy who stole a fox-cub and hid it under his tunic, letting the fox gnaw away at his stomach, rather than reveal the theft. What is Montaigne's attitude to this account?

Discussion

Clearly, at one level, Montaigne's insistent critique of the Protestants' reliance on their own reason places him on the Catholic side. He reasserts that 'we must not judge what is possible and impossible according to what seems credible or incredible to our own minds'. But when he writes in defence of Plutarch (part of the title and the ostensible purpose of the essay) against Jean Bodin (1530–96), the learned historian, jurist and political theorist, while plausibly warning of the dangers of judging from our own experience, Montaigne does precisely that – and to considerable effect. To Montaigne, Plutarch is 'the most judicious author in the world'. In casting doubt on Plutarch's account of the Spartan boy's endurance, Montaigne says of Bodin, 'I find him a bit rash'. Bodin has come close to that 'major fault into which most people fall', of judging everything in the light of their own (limited) experience. To Montaigne, the episode is perfectly plausible. Plutarch's account is supported by evidence of what we know of Spartan attitudes generally (Montaigne gives several examples). Montaigne then turns on its head his argument about the dangers of relying on one's own experience. One man's experience may be different from another's and less restricted. 'By Bodin's standards it [the episode] is all miracle.' To Montaigne with *his* knowledge, 'the history of Sparta is full of hundreds of harsher and rarer examples', and the episode is entirely credible. He finds 'no great miracle' in it. 'I am so imbued with the greatness of those men of Sparta that not only does it not seem incredible to me as it does to Bodin: it does not even seem rare or unusual.' The probability of the episode is also confirmed for Montaigne by his own first-hand knowledge of people's fortitude under torture 'in these civil wars of ours'. ❖

Exercise

Rereading the same passage from *In defence of Seneca and Plutarch*, pp.818–22, consider how far Montaigne distinguishes extraordinary events from 'miracles' in the religious sense.

Discussion

Montaigne draws a clear distinction between the two. Extraordinary events, by definition, are rare, but they do happen and can be proved to have happened. Miracles, in the sense of occurrences outside the course of nature and beyond human experience, are not susceptible to verification by ordinary people, and, once authenticated by the church, must be taken on trust. ❖

Exercise

Please consider three more short passages:

1 *On the power of the imagination*, p.111, second paragraph, to p.112, end of first paragraph.

2 *On the art of conversation*, p.1067, last paragraph, to the end of that paragraph on p.1068.

3 *On experience*, p.1267, penultimate paragraph.

Does Montaigne seem to be affirming the reality of miracles in these three essays, or casting doubt on them?

Discussion

1 *On the power of the imagination*: Note here Montaigne's open disparagement of popular credulity, the superstition of 'the common people' and 'the power of the imagination'. He comments generally that the credulity of 'the common people' extends to 'miracles, visions, enchantments and such extraordinary events'. Either the events in question admit of a natural explanation (e.g. psychosomatic auto-suggestion) or they are purely imaginary. The witnesses are so credulous that 'they think they see what they do not see'. Paradoxically, Montaigne invokes the authority of St Augustine himself to discredit these supposed 'miracles'. The point of citing Augustine is Montaigne's way of distinguishing genuine miracles from unusual but natural phenomena. If St Augustine attests that he witnessed miraculous cures, we must take it on his authority that they really happened.

If, however, Augustine merely reports 'extraordinary events' without classifying them as miracles, or indeed indicates that they were imaginary, then, as with the accounts in Boucher, we are free to disbelieve. Montaigne uses Augustine's authority to protect himself from the charge of disbelief in genuine miracles; but he seems to come close to scepticism about the scars of St Francis. (In her 1595 edition of the *Essays* Marie de Gournay omitted the word 'miracles' from this passage.)

2   *On the art of conversation*: Montaigne here defends Tacitus, as he earlier defended Plutarch, but with this difference. In Plutarch's case, he argued for the truth of the extraordinary event. When considering Tacitus, he is clearly sceptical of Vespasian's 'miracle' cure, but rates Tacitus a good historian for recording popular beliefs without necessarily sharing them. The truth or untruth of 'popular beliefs' (in miracles) is a matter for 'theologians and philosophers as directors of consciences'. (Note also, at the top of p.1067, Montaigne's defence of Tacitus 'for being ignorant of the true religion'.)

3   *On experience*: In his last essay Montaigne sought to explain what he thought it meant to live like a human being. As you can see, he paid particular attention to this paragraph, retouching it after 1588. He is careful to distinguish genuine religious mystics, the apostles and saints, from 'the likes of us', whose 'supercelestial opinions' he disparages. ❖

In each of these passages (as in many others) there seems to be an underlying ambiguity. Certainly Montaigne recommends, or appears to recommend, unconditional submission to the authority of the Roman Catholic church and its dogmas (I, 27, p.204) without bothering our heads further – the 'soft and delightful pillow' of 'ignorance and unconcern' (III, 13, p.1218). As Screech points out, the notion, much favoured by Erasmus, of 'Christian Folly', that true godliness is to be found in the humble and the ignorant, was 'a major theme in Renaissance thought and had been long allied to scepticism' (pp.xxxii–xxxiii). Fideism was a perfectly acceptable intellectual stance in the late Renaissance. But Montaigne's reasons for submission are negative rather than positive: the unknowability of truth, the limits of reason, the relativity of experience, the horrors of the wars of religion. At the same time, he throws doubt on miracles not vouched for by the highest religious authorities, and deprecates religious zeal or mysticism, except in acknowledged holy men. Did he, then, recommend outward submission and conformity primarily for the sake of a quiet life and in the hope of restoring political and social stability to France? Did he privately entertain sceptical views on religion behind a mask of outward conformity? His biographer, Hugo Friedrich, writes of Montaigne's '*agnostic*, fideistic thought processes' (1991, p.81, my italics).

In *On repenting*, Montaigne appears to take issue with the Christian doctrine of repentance in the sense of a positive act of will to reform our being. This he considers unnatural. It does violence to our individual identity and to our common human nature. Only if touched by God's grace can we genuinely repent. Otherwise 'my doings are ruled by what I am and are in harmony with how I was made. I cannot do better' (p.916). Self-knowledge and rational conformity to one's nature are the safest guide to a quiet conscience. Montaigne is not repentant himself: 'If I had to live again, I would live as I have done' (p.920). Dorothy Coleman comments, 'this is a serene non-Christian attitude' (1987, p.79). Screech, however, in his headnote, distinguishes Montaigne's meaning of 'repentance' in the sense of 'denying the rightness of what one had formerly willed' from the solemn sacrament of repentance (p.907).

Montaigne's scepticism, condemned by the Catholic church in the late seventeenth century, was taken up by deists and freethinkers then and in the eighteenth century, including the *philosophes* (reformist intellectuals) of the French Enlightenment (Gendzier, 1967, pp.204–5). Critical of Christianity in general and of the Roman Catholic church in particular, the *philosophes* saw Montaigne as a precursor of modern scepticism. But we should consider how far this may be an anachronistic and over-simplified view of Montaigne as a conscious pioneer of scientific 'rationalism' and secular 'progress'.

The question of Montaigne's religious views remains highly controversial. One biographer, Gustav Lanson, wrote in 1948 that while Montaigne 'may have been a genuine believer, the book [the *Essays*] is unbelieving' (p.264). And in 1949 Friedrich maintained: 'Montaigne is faithful to the Church. But he does not derive his conservatism from agreement with the objective contents of the truths of Catholic doctrine' (1991 p.112). Fifty years later, the critic Harold Bloom agrees that 'whatever kind of writer Montaigne became, it would be grotesque to call him a religious one' (1994, p.148). Screech, however, both in his introduction to the *Essays* and in *Montaigne and Melancholy*, insists that Montaigne was always a convinced Catholic. Central to the debate is how to interpret Montaigne's 'delightfully paradoxical' *Apology for Raymond Sebond* (Screech, 2000, p.2). In his introduction to the *Essays*, Screech argues that Montaigne was a skilled theologian with a well-articulated philosophy of religion and that his 'scepticism' was at all times intended to defend Roman Catholicism. He denies that Montaigne subscribed to fideism. On the contrary, Montaigne is strictly orthodox, 'the authentic voice of post-Tridentine rigour' (2000, p.96).

Whatever the answer to this complex question, one thing clearly emerges: by separating the religious sphere from the secular, and expressly excluding Christian faith and doctrine from human speculation, Montaigne leaves himself free to range over everything else. Apart from in *An apology for Raymond Sebond* (admittedly a big exception), Christianity hardly features in the *Essays*. There is little biblical citation (Montaigne occasionally quotes from Ecclesiastes, 'that most sceptical of Biblical works' (Screech, 2000, p.4)) and scarcely any mention of Christ (see *On presumption*, p.728). Montaigne's heroes in the *Essays* are robustly secular, the heroes of classical antiquity – Alexander the Great, Scipio, the Younger Cato, Epaminondas, and, above all, Socrates (in *On cruelty* he describes 'the soul of Socrates' as 'the most perfect to have come to my knowledge', p.474).

Can these pagan predilections be squared with Roman Catholic orthodoxy? According to Screech, they do not of themselves make Montaigne a pagan. As Screech points out (pp.lviii–xix), Jacques Amyot, translator of Montaigne's beloved Plutarch, and himself bishop of Auxerre, declared that Plutarch was 'so consonant with Christianity that his books could more profitably be used to instruct Princes in their duties than Holy Writ itself'. Similarly in *On diversion*, Montaigne advised 'a young prince' against vengeance, not by invoking Christ's injunction to turn the other cheek, but by pointing out 'the honour, acclaim and goodwill he would acquire from clemency and bounty' (pp.940–41). Catholic theology acknowledged the classical tradition, in which many of its prelates were steeped, and a natural, secular morality which co-existed with Christianity. Screech contends that there was no necessary incompatibility between the two. The debate on Montaigne and religion continues.

Montaigne and the Jews: the outsider observed

Montaigne, as we know, was almost certainly of Jewish descent on his mother's side, though nowhere does he say so. In a series in which you study Shakespeare's *Merchant of Venice* (Mateer, 2000), written in about 1596, a dozen years after Montaigne visited Venice and the Jewish quarter of Rome, it is appropriate to consider Montaigne's attitudes to Jews.[10]

---

[10] On the Jewish dimension in Montaigne's thinking, Claude Rawson writes (sensibly to my mind) that the few references to Jews in the *Essays* 'don't suggest defensiveness, hostility, or any of the modes of denial or exacerbated sympathy which are the usual signs of embarrassed self-implication' (1994, p.112).

In *That the taste of good and evil things depends in large part on the opinion we have of them,* Montaigne gives an account of the expulsion of the Jews from Spain and Portugal (pp.55–6). In Spain, the Inquisition had been established in 1478 to root out Jewish converts who were not sincere in their Christianity. Among those whom the Inquisition burned at the stake in 1491 was Montaigne's great-great-great-grandfather (Frame, 1965, p.23). In 1492 those remaining Jews who refused to convert were expelled by Ferdinand and Isabella. Many went to Portugal, where they were first welcomed and then, by a decree of King Manuel in 1497, forced to convert under threat of expulsion. Of those who did convert, according to Montaigne, 'even today a century later few Portuguese trust in their sincerity or in that of their descendants' (p.56). Note that Montaigne's sympathies are with the exploited refugees for the 'inhuman treatment' which they have endured (p.55).

Renaissance attitudes towards practising Jews were usually critical and often hostile. As we were reminded in Book 2 of this series, the Jews were held collectively responsible for the death of Christ (Mateer, 2000, p.313). The English traveller, Thomas Coryate (*c.*1577–1617), visiting the Jewish ghetto in Venice in 1608, stirred up trouble by arguing on religion with a rabbi and his coreligionists, and 'earnestly bickering with them'. Forced to flee 'because I durst reprehend their religion', he was rescued by the English ambassador (the poet Sir Henry Wotton), in a passing gondola, who 'conveighed mee safely from these unchristian miscreants' (i.e. unbelievers) (McPherson, 1990, p.66).

Exercise

Please read the excerpt from Montaigne's *Travel Journal* in the Anthology (no. 91i) in which he recounts his visit to the Jewish ghetto in Rome in 1581. What does this account suggest of his attitude to Jews as compared to *That the taste of good and evil things depends,* pp.55–6?

Discussion

While in the essay Montaigne stresses the refined cruelty of the Portuguese authorities and the endurance of their Jewish victims (which follows and mirrors an example of Stoical suicide from Plutarch), what emerges from Montaigne's travel notes is his close interest in Jewish customs. He attends a Sabbath morning service in a synagogue. He witnesses a circumcision 'with great profit'. He is observant and non-judgemental. He notes that circumcision 'is the most ancient religious ceremony there is among men'. He makes comparisons and notes similarities and contrasts between Jewish and Christian practice without comment. The Jews worship on Saturday; at prayer in the synagogue they do not remove their hats; they wear prayer-shawls; they 'pay no more attention to their prayers than we do to ours, talking of other affairs in the midst of them'; at eight days old 'they give the boys a godfather and a godmother, as we do'; the operation of circumcision is without danger and 'the boy's outcry is like that of ours when they are baptized'. In sum, Montaigne is interested, sympathetic and open-minded. His interest is in both the variety and the unity of human custom: Jewish customs are different, but analogous to those of Christians. ❖

Montaigne and the European witch-craze

You will recall from Chapter 6 what Peter Elmer calls 'the Renaissance preoccupation with witchcraft and ... demonology'. The European 'witch-craze' was at its height when Montaigne wrote his *Essays*. Gianfrancesco Pico della Mirandola's *Strix* (*The Witch*) (1523) had reached its fourth edition by 1556. Far from being restricted to an ignorant peasantry, belief in witchcraft was shared by almost the entire educated elite: the clergy (Catholic and Protestant alike), the judiciary, popes and statesmen, and the universities, including humanist scholars and, notably in France, Jean Bodin. There was general agreement on the need to hunt down suspects and to put them on trial in order to identify and convict witches and eliminate them from society. The penalty for witchcraft was death by burning. The Catholic handbook on witchcraft, *Malleus maleficarum* (*The Hammer of Witches*), by the Dominican friars Sprenger and Kramer (1486), was still regarded as authoritative in Montaigne's time.

In France, witch trials became a major preoccupation during the civil wars, and there seems to have been a sharp increase in prosecutions in the 1580s and 1590s. In Bordeaux, in the 1560s and 1570s, when Montaigne was a member of the *parlement*, suspects were treated leniently and sent home 'to their parish priests and pastors, as if it had simply been a matter of hysterical delusions' (Boase, 1974, p.377). Between 1587 and 1593, however, witch hunts began in earnest and convictions rose. In these six years 368 persons were burned as witches in the district of Toulouse alone (Hale, 1994, p.448). Accusations commonly related to causing disease or death, of cattle or humans, and were attributed to dealings between the accused and the devil.

The commonest external indications of witchcraft, elaborated by churchmen and lawyers for judicial investigation, included, as Montaigne mentions, physical ugliness, immunity to pain in particular parts of the body and alleged flights on broomsticks (III, 11, p.1168).

Exercise

Please read *On the lame*, from p.1164, 'It is wonderful', to p.1169, 'also to me'. What does this essay suggest about the prevalence of belief in witchcraft and Montaigne's attitude to witchcraft? (Before answering this question, you may wish to recapitulate the discussion on Montaigne's attitude to miracles in the section above entitled 'Montaigne and the Roman Catholic faith'.)

Discussion

First, Montaigne gives his reactions to a particular supposed 'miracle'. He states emphatically that in the whole of his life he personally has never witnessed a miracle. The event in question turned out to be a practical joke carried out by some youngsters. Yet the whole neighbourhood had been in a stir for months, convinced that a ghost had appeared in the village and that other supernatural events had taken place. What calls for Montaigne's comment is the credulity and mass hysteria, 'the public's gullibility', including perhaps that of the judge who may condemn the young delinquents. The essay confirms that the wildest allegations of ignorant country folk were taken with the utmost seriousness by the judiciary and educated elite and that the law was readily invoked against witchcraft and related offences.

From here Montaigne makes the general observation, drawn from the sceptical philosophy, that we should be less prone to dogmatic assertion, that 'we should suspend our judgement, neither believing nor rejecting', but should preface our testimony by 'it seems to me that ...'. He goes on to mention the case of Martin Guerre, condemned to death, Montaigne suggests, on highly implausible evidence.

Montaigne then turns to convictions for witchcraft in his own neighbourhood – 'my local witches'. He emphatically does not deny that witches exist, since this is vouched for in the Bible: 'The Word of God offers us absolutely certain and irrefragable examples of such phenomena'. (For biblical authority, see Screech's footnote 12; and see also Chapter 6, where Peter Elmer stresses the paramount importance of scripture and theology as authority for the reality of witchcraft.)

Montaigne's point is that he finds the *evidence* in particular witch trials to be inadequate. 'To kill people, there must be sharp and brilliant clarity.' Even voluntary confessions by the accused, normally the best evidence against them, should be viewed sceptically, since there have been occasions when they have been proved to be false, or where, in Montaigne's opinion, the accused was deranged. Montaigne insists on weighing the inherent unlikelihood of the events testified to against the greater likelihood of falsehood or error in the witness. It is more likely that our imagination has run away with us 'than that, by a spirit from beyond, one of us humans, in flesh and blood, should be sent flying on a broomstick up the flue of his chimney'. His crowning observation is magnificently ironical (or is it?): 'After all, it is to put a very high value on your surmises to roast a man alive for them.' ❖

You may remember, from *On the power of the imagination*, Montaigne's contemptuous rejection of the popular belief that sexual impotence was caused by 'magic spells' (p.112). Montaigne concluded from personal observation that the causes were psychosomatic, in other words that they have a natural, not a paranormal explanation. This relates to an important point raised in Chapter 6, namely that according to canon law and to writers like Pico della Mirandola, witches, although they exist, cannot in fact do the things they claim to do.

Montaigne was not the first or the only writer to express scepticism about witch trials – Peter Burke cites like-minded Italians from the early and mid sixteenth century (1977, pp.40–1) But he does seem to have been a rare outsider in his own time and country, to judge from his account of the reactions of other people whom he describes as 'decent men' (or perhaps here 'honest men', '*des honnestes hommes*'), including 'a sovereign prince' (III, 11, pp.1168–9). In Chapter 6 it was shown, as we have emphasized, that belief in witchcraft figured 'prominently among some of the brightest talents of that age'; and Jean Bodin, in his *Demonomania* (1580), called for the punishment of those who disbelieved in witchcraft. Montaigne reacted ironically to such learned publications which gave scholarly support to the intensification of witch hunts: 'My local witches go in risk of their lives, depending on the testimony of each new authority [Montaigne in fact says 'author'] who comes and gives substance to their delusions' (III, 11, p.1166). The point here, again, is that although few doubted that witches existed (and Montaigne is careful to confirm that they do), the belief that they could perform supernatural deeds was itself based on 'delusions', since only God can perform miracles. Those who, like Bodin, saw confessions of witchcraft as authentic proof thus found themselves in a logical impasse, which Montaigne exposes, 'challenging', says Screech, 'deeply entrenched legal authority' (2000, p.159).

Montaigne and Renaissance medicine

Montaigne often refers to doctors and medicine. He had good reason to do so. Life was physically hazardous and often short. In 1586, he took care to stay clear of the city and temporarily fled from his estate when an epidemic of plague killed some 14,000 in Guyenne. Of the six daughters born to him between 1570 and 1583, all but one, Léonor, died in infancy.

Montaigne was 45 when he began to suffer, as his father had before him, from 'the stone' (renal calculus or kidney-stones). The sudden pain of 'the stone' (which Screech translates as 'colic paroxysms', p.xlvi) is one of the most agonizing known. Before the onset of his illness, Montaigne described physical pain as 'the worst disaster that can befall our being', admitting that 'of all men in the world' he shrank from it most (I, 14, p.59). 'The pain of a kidney stone is fierce', writes Guy Davenport in his foreword to Montaigne's *Travel Journal*, 'and in a male can be as sharp as birth pangs'. The 'colic paroxysms' consist of 'a severe nausea in combination with the feeling that one's back is broken and that one's bowels are about to move' (Frame, 1983a, p.viii). Solid calculi or pellets form in the kidney and bladder and in Montaigne's case sometimes passed out of the body through the penis. Montaigne describes his complaint as 'the worst of all illnesses, the most unpredictable, the most painful, the most fatal and the most incurable' (II, 37, p.860). He mentions that it was an illness which the elder Pliny said justified suicide (II, 3, p.399; see also *On diversion*, p.943 and *On experience*, pp.1240–4).

The conventional remedy for 'the stone' was to 'take the waters', i.e. to drink and/or bathe in medicinal mineral waters.[11] In 1580, shortly after publishing the first edition of the *Essays*, Montaigne set out on a long journey across Europe, taking the waters in 'virtually all the famous baths of Christendom' (II, 37, p.877), in France (Plombières), Germany (Baden), Switzerland and especially in Italy during 1581, in a vain search for a cure (see Figure 8.13).

Exercise

You should now read the extract from Montaigne's *Travel Journal*, which gives an account of the medicinal baths of La Villa, near Lucca (Anthology, no. 91ii). ❖

Taking the waters was regarded as unscientific and a waste of time by Paracelsus, whose theory of medicine, you will recall from Chapter 6, was based on a chemical theory with treatment by drugs. Montaigne mentions Paracelsus and the 'new' medicine in *An apology for Raymond Sebond* (p.643) and in *On the resemblance of children to their fathers* (pp.872–3). Paracelsus denounced the traditional Renaissance theories of medicine based on Galen (second century CE). Galen's texts were taught at universities and frequently republished: between 1490 and 1598 there were 660 editions. His authority was held in equal respect by Catholic and Protestant physicians, whereas the Paracelsians tended to be Protestant. (One such, Joseph Duchesne, became personal physician to Henry IV, and another, Théodore Turquet de Mayerne (a Huguenot refugee) to James I.) The Paracelsian theory of medicine, however, remained controversial.

---

[11] A fellow-sufferer from 'the stone', Claude Expilly (1561–1636), president of the *parlement* of Grenoble and a *conseiller du roi*, travelled to Vals, in the Vivarais, to take the waters in 1608 to 1609. Unlike Montaigne, whose stoicism he much admired and to whom he wrote a sonnet, Expilly was cured of the stone.

Figure 8.13 Montaigne's journey from Beaumont-sur-Oise, near Paris, to Italy and home, 1580–81

The University of Paris, the Sorbonne, denounced the University of Montpellier for questioning Galen's authority.

Exercise

Please read *An apology for Raymond Sebond*, p.643, paragraph 2. What does it tell us of Montaigne's attitude to Paracelsus and the 'new' medicine?

Discussion

Montaigne is sceptical and ironically humorous at the expense of both. He dismisses Paracelsus as 'some newcomer', who holds all past medical tradition as useless, indeed worse than useless, since it has allegedly 'merely served to kill people'. Montaigne jocularly dismisses Paracelsus's 'new empiricism' as an experience which he, Montaigne, might not survive. He concludes sceptically: 'believe nobody'. ❖

Montaigne's sceptical conservatism makes one think of his scepticism about the innovations of Protestantism, which, not being susceptible to proof, cannot be shown to be true and, given the age-old tradition of Catholicism, are most likely false. But does Montaigne hold traditional medicine in the same outward reverence as he does the Catholic faith?

Exercise

Please read *On the resemblance of children to their fathers*, pp.858–87, and refer to the extract from Montaigne's *Travel Journal* on medicinal baths (Anthology, no. 91ii). What are your impressions of Montaigne's attitude to conventional medicine?

Discussion

Montaigne gives examples of traditional medical theory. But he does not seem to find them of much use. Traditional treatment has not cured him of 'the stone', and in addition to the physical pain, there is the psychological 'weight of all the warning threats, inferences and complications which Medicine stuffs into our heads'. Furthermore, he asks, 'are the lives of doctors themselves so long and so happy that they can witness to the manifest effectiveness of their discipline?' Clearly, Montaigne does not have much time for doctors. He comes clean about his contempt for their dogmas and states that medical '"aid" is more often than not an impediment'. He concedes that his scepticism about conventional medicine may be hereditary (the only member of his family who did not share it died prematurely!); but experience has justified it. He is not against medicine, the art of restoring and maintaining health; far from it, he longs for relief from pain. 'Health is precious', since without it the other good things in life cannot be relished. It is simply that conventional medical theory and practice have done no good to him nor, so far as he can see, to those who follow its precepts, including doctors themselves and his beloved friend, La Boétie, 'who was worth more than the lot of them' and died under their ministrations.

He accepts the efficacy of herbal remedies for minor disorders, such as senna-pods for constipation. These he calls 'practices drawn from the natural world'. 'What I am suspicious of are the things discovered by our own minds, our sciences', i.e. general theories of medicine. These include new-fangled theories, such as those of Paracelsus (note Montaigne's distrust of drugs, even if properly compounded), as well as conventional medical science.

Diagnosis in the Renaissance was based on examination of urine and stools, their colour, consistency, smell, etc., though there were many different schools of thought about that too, as Montaigne notes. Hence, the 'ceaseless wranglings' of doctors 'over their diagnoses'. And hence too over treatments. Montaigne maintains that most of the world manages without medical science: it holds sway only in

Europe. Even in Europe, 'the common folk manage happily without it', as did the ancients before Galen. Practitioners of conventional medicine exercise a 'tyrannous authority' with their claims to superior knowledge.

Montaigne rejects as irrational the prescribing of outlandish potions, reminiscent, as he says of 'magic spells' (and indeed of the ingredients of the witches' cauldron in *Macbeth*), and the ritual incantations and choice of special times laid down for taking them, e.g. by moonlight. In any case, doctors constantly disagree among themselves: there are rival schools of medicine and contradictory medical advice (see *On experience*, pp.1231–7). The doctors cannot all be right. Montaigne questions the 'rational bases' of the accepted treatment for kidney-stones. (According to Screech, his account 'incensed some doctors' (1991, p.881, footnote 30).) ❖

Exercise

What are the sources of Montaigne's arguments about taking the waters in *On the resemblance of children to their fathers*, pp.858–87, and what is his conclusion?

Discussion

We know that Montaigne took some of his examples from Cornelius Agrippa's radical critique of conventional medicine in *On the Vanity of the Arts and Sciences* (1530). But he regards Paracelsus as simply one of the latest in a long line of rival disputants. Montaigne's main objections to conventional medicine are drawn from his own observation and experience. Having taken the waters in France and abroad, he concludes that by and large though the waters were 'useless', the treatment was 'at the very least, not dangerous even if it does no good'; and that ultimately patients are their own best physician, who 'allow themselves to be gently led by their feelings and by the counsels of Nature'. He admits that he takes no notice of doctors' advice or takes it only when he does not mind following it. He agrees that understanding of the human body through surgery and anatomy and of practical medical cures is likely to increase through 'our experimental knowledge'. ❖

During his stay at the baths of La Villa in Italy, Montaigne experimented, 'contrary to the rules of this region', by bathing where drinking was prescribed, and vice versa, to the horror of the locals, concluding in the *Travel Journal*, as in *On the resemblance of children to their fathers*, that 'if I judge rightly about these waters, they are not such as to do either much harm or much good' (Frame, 1983a, pp.124–5). Later in the *Travel Journal* he again observes that the doctors hold to opposite theories and give contradictory advice. This relates generally to the standard sceptic argument on the difficulty of attaining certain knowledge of anything.

In 'To the Reader', Montaigne, you will recall, explains that the *Essays* contain 'some traits of my character and of my humours' (*de mes conditions et humeurs*). In the original, both nouns are in the plural, because character is multifaceted and because personality itself is liable to change. The mention of 'humours' also relates to the medical and psychological theory founded by Galen and widely held in the Renaissance which explained an individual's physical constitution, character and mood as the result of the relative proportions of 'humours' generated in the body. To stay healthy it was thought necessary to maintain a balance between the 'humours' – hot and dry, cold and moist. Their combination (or 'complexion') formed an individual's 'temperament', which fell into four categories: sanguine, phlegmatic, choleric and melancholic. Excess of dry humours produced a choleric personality, too much moist led to melancholy. Montaigne's own 'complexion' was melancholic, tempered by sanguine (see Screech's note, p.433). In *On idleness*, Montaigne suggests that his voluntary retirement to write the *Essays* brought on mental instability rather than philosophic calm (pp.30–31).[12]

Montaigne refers briefly to his 'humours' in the *Essays* (see *How we weep and laugh at the same thing*, p.263, lines 8–10 and *On bad means to a good end*, p.775, first paragraph). It is difficult to determine from these short passages, however, how far he was convinced by the Galenic theory. The first passage summarizes the theory: 'there is said to be a variety of humours assembled in our bodies, the dominant one being that which normally prevails according to our complexion'; but does not make clear whether Montaigne shares the belief. The second passage, while explaining contemporary medical practice, also seems non-committal about the theory. And see *An apology for Raymond Sebond* (p.605, penultimate paragraph), where Montaigne questions whether commonly held beliefs, such as belief in Galen's authority, are based on a valid foundation.

Did Montaigne have a political philosophy?

Renaissance Europe saw much political theorizing, notably by Machiavelli and Francesco Guicciardini in Italy and Jean Bodin in France. Montaigne read the works of all three, and earlier we considered his attitude to one of them, Machiavelli. For these political theorists, the advantages and disadvantages of different forms of government – democracy, oligarchy, republic and monarchy – were a broad concern. But did Montaigne have a political

---

[12] Screech claims that writing the *Essays* was a means of 'exorcizing' the 'demon' of madness (1991, p.xiv). In *Montaigne and Melancholy* (2000), Screech examines Montaigne's interest in varieties of madness and ecstasy.

philosophy? Unlike Machiavelli, he was not an avowed political theorist, and his views on this, as on most topics, emerge at random from different chapters.

Exercise

Please read *On vanity*, pp.1082–8. What impression is given from this excerpt of Montaigne's notion of the ideal state?

Discussion

Clearly, Montaigne is no doctrinaire. He has little time for academic blueprints of the ideal society, like Plato's *Republic* (or, as Screech suggests in footnote 39, Thomas More's *Utopia*).

Montaigne argues that historically societies are formed and formalized at random, not by art or design. Institutions, laws and customs evolve around a living social organism; and however brutal its origins, 'human society remains cobbled and held together', and existing societies have proved 'as sound and as durable as any which Plato or Aristotle could ever have founded'.

A relativist, sceptic and pragmatist, Montaigne believes that, however unsatisfactory it may seem to the individual, 'the best and most excellent polity [i.e. political structure] for each nation is the one under which it has been sustained'.

The greatest danger to a state is revolution, which leads to 'injustice and tyranny'. 'Nothing crushes a State save novelty.' Minor defects in a state can be made good. But for Montaigne, radical reformers are men 'for whom cleaning means effacing, who seek to emend individual defects by universal disorder and to cure illnesses by death'. ❖

As with his religious philosophy (and religion and politics were particularly tightly bound up in sixteenth-century France), Montaigne's conclusions on politics stem from his experience and his scepticism. In *On presumption* (p.744), he claims there is nothing to choose between Machiavelli and his critics. Montaigne does not believe in 'political science' any more than in medical science. Political criticism is popular, but it leads to discontent and disorder, and is a form of presumption.

> It is easy enough to condemn a polity as imperfect since all things mortal are full of imperfections; it is easy enough to generate in a nation contempt for its ancient customs ... but as for replacing the conditions you have ruined by better ones, many who have tried to do that have come to grief.
>
> (II, 17, p.745)

Huguenot theorists, especially after the St Bartholomew's day massacre, developed theories of a 'social contract' between monarch and people, whereby kings were deemed accountable to their subjects, and if they failed to adhere to the 'contract' could legitimately be resisted as tyrants and ultimately deposed, if necessary by assassination. The Catholic League itself took a leaf out of the Huguenots' book to pressurize Henry III into making political concessions to the League (see *An apology for Raymond Sebond*, p.495 and footnote 19). By contrast, Montaigne belonged to a grouping of Catholic moderates known as the '*Politiques*', who sought an end to the wars through an accommodation with the Huguenots and a permanent settlement. Montaigne's attitude was one of conformity with the existing form of government and obedience to 'the powers that be' (see *On habit: and on never easily changing a traditional law*, p.136). In France, this meant acceptance of the traditional institution of monarchy and succession in the male line, whatever the faults of particular monarchs. A compliant Catholic, loyal as mayor of Bordeaux to the Catholic Henry III, Montaigne was on friendly terms with the heir presumptive, the Protestant Henry of Navarre, whom he looked on as a future deliverer and whom he offered to serve on his accession in 1589. In the final analysis, however parlous the state of the country, rebellion can never be justified. 'There is no system so bad (provided it be old and durable) as not to be better than change and innovation' (II, 17, p.745). In bad times one must hope for the best or pray to providence for relief. A conservative conclusion. (See also *On freedom of conscience*, p.759, second sentence.)

Montaigne and the classics

Burckhardt described humanists as 'those who acted as mediators between their own age and a venerated antiquity, and made the latter a chief element in the culture of the former'(1990, p.135). The Renaissance was an age when familiarity with the classics was the norm among the educated. Shakespeare, despite his 'small Latin and less Greek', was steeped in the classics (through translation); and from the frequency of his classical references, so, it may be assumed, was the educated section of his audience. Take, for example, the dialogue between Lorenzo and Jessica: 'In such a night ...', at the beginning of Act 5 of *The Merchant of Venice*, with its references to the loves of Troilus and Cressida, Pyramus and Thisbe, Dido and Aeneas, and Jason and Medea.

Burckhardt's expression 'a venerated antiquity' certainly seems an apt description of Montaigne's attitude to the classics. Here was a man evidently deeply moved at the thought of 'the greatness of mind and knowledge of those old Greeks and Romans' (p.194). (See *On vanity*, p.1128–32, for his pride at being made an honorary citizen of Rome during his visit in 1581.) In his *Travel Journal* Montaigne describes his visit to the Vatican library, where he examined manuscript copies of Virgil, Seneca and Plutarch, and later discussed the merits of Amyot's translations of Plutarch (Frame, 1983a, pp.85–6). Guy Davenport describes this episode as 'the emotional centre of gravity of the journal' (Frame, 1983a, p.x). Comparing his *Essays* to 'the products of those great fertile minds', he says not only that the ancients 'greatly surpass the farthest stretch of my imagination and my desires', but that they fill him with rapture: 'they leave me thunderstruck and throw me into an ecstasy of wonder' (II, 17, p.724). You may remember his veneration of the Spartans – 'I am so imbued with the greatness of those men of Sparta' (II, 32, p.819).

Even by Renaissance standards, Montaigne was exceptionally well versed in the Latin classics. This was because 'Latin is a native tongue for me: I understand it better than French' (III, 2, p.914). Following the direct method recommended by Erasmus, his father had brought him up so that he heard no language but Latin during his infancy, and 'I was six years old before I knew French' (I, 26, p.195). He was steeped in the verse of Lucretius and Horace (his joint favourites as poets, whom he quotes in the *Essays* 149 and 148 times respectively), Virgil (116 quotations), Catullus, Lucan and Terence (see *On books*, pp.460–61, and *On some lines of Virgil*). The *Essays* contain some 1,300 Latin quotations (for a breakdown of Montaigne's classical reading and quotation, see Highet, 1949, pp.188–90). Montaigne often quotes from memory (and hence sometimes inaccurately). He hardly ever identifies his source – writing 'without striving ['study' in the first edition] or artifice' as he claims in his preface. (And see *On books*, p.458, where he mischievously explains his practice of incorporating in the *Essays* unacknowledged passages from classical authors.)

He tells us in *On books* that his favourite prose authors were Plutarch and Seneca, whom he admires for both their style and their philosophy (though he knew Greek far less well than Latin, and, as we have noted, read Plutarch in Amyot's translation). In *In defence of Seneca and Plutarch*, he even claims that the *Essays* themselves are 'built entirely out of their spoils' (p.817). (There are up to 300 borrowings from Plutarch in the 1580 edition alone. For a close analysis, chapter by chapter, of these borrowings, see Isabelle Konstantinovic, *Montaigne et Plutarque*, 1989.) Certainly, as was noted earlier, Montaigne took the original form of the essay from Plutarch's *Moralia*, a supreme example of the Renaissance ideal of creative imitation of the classics.

Montaigne brings classical quotation into the *Essays* not as mere ornament, but as its very pith and marrow, an inexhaustible set of sources which prompt him to embark and enlarge on particular thoughts and topics. An interesting example of this is *On some lines of Virgil* (pp.947–1016), where nine lines from the *Aeneid* move him to elaborate on his sexual feelings. Montaigne believed that classical standards (or at least those of his favourite authors), in literature and life, were generally superior to those of his day; but for all his 'veneration' he treats the ancients almost as living men. Indeed, their whole value for him lies in their contemporary relevance (see *On vanity*, pp.1128–9). He makes the point that his own father is no less dead than the ancients, 'yet I do not cease to cherish his memory nor experience his love and fellowship in a perfect union, fully alive' (III, 9, p.1127). The classics serve him as a constant standard of reference. He continually looks back to and up to the poets, historians and moral philosophers of the ancient world. For him, even Aesop, author of the *Fables*, 'is an author of the choicest excellence, though few people discover all his beauties' (II, 37, p.869). Note his fascination throughout the *Essays* with several of the subjects of Plutarch's *Lives*: Alexander the Great and Epaminondas (*On the most excellent of men*); Cato the Younger and Julius Caesar (*The tale of Spurina*). See how he describes Cato: 'That great man was truly a model which Nature chose to show how far human virtue and fortitude can reach' (I, 37, pp.259–60).

What does Montaigne seek to learn from the ancients? In a nutshell, practical moral philosophy. How a man may live honourably, especially in such troubled times as the wars of religion. How he may be an honest man (the French for which, *un honneste homme*, you may remember, came to approximate the new aristocratic notion of the 'gentleman') and how a boy should be brought up to become one (see *On educating children*). Look at the sources which he quotes in *On glory*. They are identified in Screech's footnotes (pp.702–17) and include Aristotle's *Nicomachean Ethics*, Cicero's *De finibus* (*On the Chief Good*) and *De officiis* (*On Duty*) and the *Moral Works* of Plutarch and Seneca. These and the other authors whom he quotes represented the main 'schools' of classical moral philosophy – Aristotelian (or Peripatetic), Platonic, Stoic and Epicurean.

Montaigne and Neostoicism

The two main schools of moral philosophy predominant in the ancient world, the Stoic and the Epicurean, offered answers as to how a man should endure adversity. The Renaissance saw a strong revival of interest in Stoicism, and Montaigne's own marked interest in it is clear from the *Essays*, particularly in Book I (see *That the taste of good and evil things depends in large part on the opinion we have of them*, pp.52–72, where he presents an array of examples of Stoic endurance).

How a man should live included the question how he should die, something with which Montaigne (in common with many Renaissance thinkers) was also much concerned. Montaigne was often obsessed by thoughts of death. La Boétie's death and the manner of his dying made a lasting impression on him. Violent death was a constant possibility during the wars of religion, as he noted in *On practice*, pp.418–20 (an account of how he was knocked off his horse and nearly killed); and see *On vanity*, p.1098. And one of the essays is entitled *To philosophize is to learn how to die*. That death was often in his thoughts is also suggested in 'To the Reader', where he states that the *Essays* are intended as a memorial to himself. Montaigne also refers frequently to suicide.

Exercise

Please read *A custom of the Isle of Cea*, pp.392–407 and assess Montaigne's attitude to suicide.

Discussion

The essay falls into two parts, with arguments for and against suicide. These seem to be equally weighted; at any rate Montaigne does not say which side he comes down on. He cites numerous examples from ancient history in favour of suicide, and seems, like the Stoics, to consider it an act of supreme nobility and courage: 'death is the prescription for all our ills'; and when life becomes unendurable, he claims, we have God's permission to end it. He also argues that just as it is no crime to dispose of or destroy our own property as we see fit, so we are free to do away with ourselves. ❖

Note too Montaigne's Stoical entry in the *Travel Journal* for 24 August 1581 when, after painfully expelling a huge kidney-stone, he observes:

> There is no other medicine, no other rule or science, for avoiding the ills, whatever they may be and however great, that besiege men from all sides and at every hour, than to make up our minds to suffer them humanly, or to end them courageously and promptly.

(Anthology, no. 91, p.401)

Screech argues that there was no real conflict between the Roman Catholic condemnation of suicide and Montaigne's admiration for it, and that Montaigne 'is simply following – in detail – Renaissance theologians' (2000, p.44).

Montaigne was particularly affected by the exemplary suicides of Socrates and Cato (see *On judging someone else's death*, pp.686–91 and *On Cato the Younger*, pp.259–61), and also of Seneca, the main Latin writer on Stoicism, who, condemned to death by Nero on a trumped-up charge, cut his wrists and bled to death. Montaigne, who described the scene at length (*On three good wives*, pp.846–9), clearly found it edifying. He felt real enthusiasm for Seneca's writings: 'Seneca's virtue is so evidently alive and vigorous in his writings' (II, 32, p.818), not least for what he wrote about contempt for death. Contrasting Seneca's style with that of Cicero, he writes that Cicero 'cannot put

Figure 8.14 Peter Paul Rubens and workshop, *The Death of Seneca, c.*1615, oil on panel, Museo del Prado, Madrid

heart into you: he has none to give. But Seneca rouses you and inflames you' (II, 31, p.811; see also *On fleeing from pleasures at the cost of one's life*, pp.245–6 and *A custom of the Isle of Cea*, pp.398, 399).

Interest in Stoicism was common in the troubled, strife-torn Europe of the Counter-Reformation. During the Spanish campaigns to reduce the Netherlands to political obedience and religious uniformity, the Fleming Justus Lipsius (1547–1606), much admired by Montaigne and himself an admirer of the *Essays*, preached 'a Christianized Stoicism' in his immensely popular book *On Constancy in a Time of Public Evils* (1584) (Hale, 1994, p.210). Montaigne wrote that in the French wars of religion Tacitus had much to say of use to 'a sickly troubled nation like our own is at present' (III, 8, p.1066). In the face of adversity beyond their control, men sought peace of mind and stability in the cultivation of a self-mastery and personal dignity patterned on the ancients; and the Flemish painter Rubens (1577–1640), a devout Catholic, found inspiration in the death of Seneca, depicting him in quasi-religious overtones (Figure 8.14).

Yet moved though he was by classical examples, Montaigne also knew from experience and observation that Stoic self-control was sometimes a counsel of perfection and a physical impossibility. The will is not always as much in control of our actions as the Stoics claim: some actions are purely involuntary (see *On constancy*, pp.48–9 and *On drunkenness*, p.388).

The maxims on the ceiling of his library suggest that Montaigne was more open-minded and eclectic, and less decidedly Stoic, than was once supposed. Of the 20 of these maxims which Montaigne cites in the *Essays*, none was drawn from Stoic authors.

Until recently, scholars held that there were three distinct phases in the development of Montaigne's philosophical outlook, corresponding to each of the three books. According to this view, Book I reflects the influence of Stoicism, Book II of Scepticism (particularly *An apology for Raymond Sebond*) and Book III of Epicureanism. While the books do lend themselves to such an interpretation, it is also clear that this reading is too rigid in that each book contains elements of all three philosophies. Montaigne was affected by each according to his reading and his mood. At the same time, in terms of Montaigne's outlook, a clear line of overall development can be traced across the *Essays*.

While moved by heroic examples of Stoicism, Montaigne, after completing Book I, showed himself increasingly dissatisfied with Stoicism as a rounded, humane philosophy of life. He criticises it (and other classical schools of philosophy) in *An apology for Raymond Sebond* and, describing the Stoics as 'the most glowering sect' (III, 9, p.1106), begins to feel his way towards a philosophy less demanding, less rigorous and austere. In the end he comes to find unadulterated Stoicism too artificial. The lives of his classical heroes 'have many traits which I embrace more with esteem than emotion' (III, 9, p.1101). To refer again back to his preface, he seeks a philosophy which he can accept and follow 'without striving or artifice'. At the very end of his final essay, *On experience*, he suggests what such a philosophy might be.

Exercise

Please reread *On experience*, from the last paragraph on p.1256 to p.1269. Remember Screech's comment on the significance of these last pages (p.xliv, last paragraph). How would you categorize Montaigne's final expression of a philosophy of life?

Discussion

If Screech is right, Montaigne consciously reserved this last essay as his final word to 'the Reader', as a counterpart to his preface. He seems to advocate an eclectic balance of Stoicism and Epicureanism, rather than a rigid 'either ... or'. He commends the pleasures of life and defends the scholars of the Sorbonne from the charge that they enjoy their food and drink too much. 'That is how the sages lived ... mildly and happily submit to the laws of our human condition, to Venus and to Bacchus ... relaxed and approachable'. His classical examples, the elder and younger Cato, Epaminondas and above all Socrates, alternated Stoic endurance with ease of mind and body. Montaigne recommends acceptance and enjoyment of life, the practice of moderation and serenity. He claims that 'our most great and glorious achievement is to live our life fittingly' (*nostre grand et glorieux chef-d'oeuvre, c'est vivre à propos*).

At the end of the essay, Montaigne maintains that this same outlook holds good for him in old age. He rounds off the essay (and the *Essays*) with a quotation from Horace, in which the poet prays to Apollo for an old age of material content and good health, physical and mental, and the ability to enjoy music and poetry. (Screech writes of Montaigne's 'full and joyful acceptance of life', p.xvii.) ❖

Montaigne and humanism

Born in the 1530s, Montaigne was shaped by the Renaissance and, in turn, he helped to shape its progress in the late sixteenth century. His father welcomed scholars to the château, being an enthusiast for Renaissance humanism and 'all ablaze with that new ardour with which King Francis I embraced letters and raised them in esteem' (II, 12, p.489). While the term 'humanism' did not appear until the nineteenth century, the word '*humaniste*' was current in France in Montaigne's boyhood, and the ideas of 'humanism' had a definite meaning for him and his contemporaries.[13] To begin with a very broad concept of 'humanism', among the quotations on the rafters of his library was the well-known line from Terence: *Homo sum: humani a me nil alienum puto* ('I am a human being: I consider nothing human to be outside my range of interests'; also cited in *On drunkenness*, p.388). As the titles of his essays suggest, Montaigne was interested in human experience in all its variety and multiplicity. Let us, then, attempt to assess his place in the Renaissance by measuring him against some of the accepted definitions of humanism.

P.O. Kristeller defines the core of *studia humanitatis* as 'grammar, rhetoric, poetry, history and moral philosophy' (1961, p.10). While Montaigne professed aversion to the first two, he drew his favourite reading from the last three, which, he believed, afforded insights into human nature and guides for conduct.

[13] The word '*humaniste*' first appeared in French in 1539 (Aulotte, 1990, p.8). Montaigne uses the word once, in its modern sense (*On prayer*, p.361). Jean-Claude Margolin denies Montaigne a place among French humanists by restricting French humanism to the period 1480 to 1540 (1990, p.166). P.O. Kristeller includes Montaigne among 'the greater humanists' (1961, p.19).

As we have seen, Montaigne was a beneficiary of Renaissance classical learning and a transmitter of classical culture and values. Going into retirement to devote oneself to literary and philosophical pursuits was itself a classical ideal (see *On solitude*, p.270). That Montaigne entered upon his library retreat in 1571 with such associations in mind is clear from the rather self-conscious Latin inscription which he painted on his library wall to mark the occasion[14] as well as from the maxims on the rafters. His attitude to the classics thus largely overlaps with Peter Burke's definition of humanism as 'the movement to recover, interpret and assimilate the language, literature, learning and values of ancient Greece and Rome' (1990, p.2).

From boyhood, Montaigne mixed with scholars: 'my house has long been open to erudite men' (II, 12, p.489), and he attended a prestigious school, staffed by humanist scholars. He was not himself, however, a professional scholar, and his respect for that quintessential Renaissance profession was pointedly qualified: 'I like learned men myself, but I do not worship them' (p.489). A fluent Latinist, he played no part in the erudite classical studies of his day. He edited no classical texts, though the annotations on his recently discovered copy of Lucretius show that he could have done (Screech, 1998). He was not proficient in Greek, which he read mainly in translation. Above all, he wrote in French. Coleman therefore concludes that 'Montaigne was not really a "classical scholar", that is, he was not a humanist in the Renaissance sense of the term' (1987, p.29).

Like all the humanists, Montaigne had Latin literature at his fingertips. He surpassed them all in his ready ability to apply it imaginatively to a variety of contemporary contexts and situations: see his use of lines from Virgil in *On idleness*, pp.30–31 and *On some lines of Virgil*, pp.958–9. He was also well read in Renaissance literature, both in neo-Latin poets like Buchanan,[15] and writers in the vernacular such as the Italians Pietro Bembo, Petrarch, Boccaccio, Ariosto and Castiglione, and the French authors Marguerite of Navarre (daughter of Francis I and grandmother of Henry of Navarre), Rabelais, Marot,

---

[14] The inscription reads: 'In the year of Christ 1571, at the age of thirty-eight, on the last day of February, anniversary of his birth, Michel de Montaigne, long weary of the servitude of the court and of public employments, while still entire, retired to the bosom of the learned virgins [i.e. the Muses], where in calm and freedom from all cares he will spend what little remains of his life now more than half run out. If the fates permit he will complete this abode, this sweet ancestral retreat; and he has consecrated it to his freedom, tranquillity and leisure [*otium*]' (Frame, 1955, pp.35–6).

[15] George Buchanan (*c.*1506–82), Scottish humanist and Latinist, taught Montaigne at the Collège de Guyenne, at Bordeaux, where Montaigne performed in his Latin plays. Buchanan later became tutor to the future James I of England (see Mateer, 2000, pp.235–6).

Ronsard and du Bellay (the last two he describes as 'close to the perfection of the Ancients', II, 17, p.751).

A 'liberal' education

In *On schoolmasters' learning* and *On educating children*, Montaigne cast doubts on the aims of a humanist education, or what he felt it had been reduced to in his day, and certainly on its methods. He questions two of its basic pillars, as defined by Kristeller: grammar and rhetoric, and shows little interest in philology (though see *On thumbs*, pp.784–5). He objected, in J.A. Symonds's words, 'that scholars occupied themselves with the form rather than the matter of the classics' (Kekewich, 2000, p.54). Montaigne was not interested in the ancients for their grammar. He goes so far as to say that 'Greek and Latin are fine and great accomplishments; but they are bought too dear' in terms of time, effort and practical usefulness. 'I would prefer first to know my own language well and then that of the neighbours with whom I have regular dealings' (I, 26, p.194).

Unlike Valla in the previous century, Montaigne professes to find rhetoric affected, artificial and false. The Paris fishwives speak as vividly as 'the finest Master of Arts' (I, 26, p.190); Montaigne says he wishes he could limit himself to the vocabulary of the Paris market of Les Halles (I, 26, p.194). He preferred the so-called 'silver age' Latin of Seneca (and, we may add, Tacitus), precise, pointed and epigrammatic, to the more elaborate stylistic structures of the 'golden age' Latin of Cicero, whom he sometimes found 'boring' and in whom, he said, 'most of the time I find nothing but wind' (II, 10, p.464). He admits to 'my audacious sacrilege in thinking that even Plato's *Dialogues* drag slowly along stifling his matter' (II, 10, p.465). Montaigne himself often wrote long, discursive and reflective sentences as the *Essays* became a form of thinking aloud. As the *Essays* progressed, however, and nowhere more than in 'To the Reader' and in the last chapter, Montaigne's sentences become shorter, his language more 'down-to-earth', salty and crude (p.1256; see also p.1231, where he puts this down to being a soldier and a Gascon, and *On educating children*, p.193, for his description of a 'simple and natural' style).

For Montaigne, content and right thinking are more important than 'style'. The result of education should not be to produce learned scholars, but 'to have become better and wiser' (I, 26, p.171); and to nurture a 'well-formed rather than a well-filled brain' (I, 26, p.168); not about book-learning but about character, self-knowledge and the good life. The aim of education should be 'to teach him [the student] to know himself, and to know how to die ... and to live

[well]. Among the liberal arts, start with the art which produces liberal men' (I, 26, p.178). 'I would rather be an expert on me than on Cicero' (III, 13, p.1218, and see also the following paragraph).

The humanist as gentleman (*honneste homme, gentil'homme*)

Like Castiglione, whose *Book of the Courtier* (1528) was in demand throughout the sixteenth century, reaching its third French edition in 1585, Montaigne claimed to write as a man of the world, a 'courtier' (I, 26, p.193) and, as we have seen, a 'gentleman' (*honneste homme, gentil'homme*) and 'a professed soldier' (III, 9, p.1090), not as a scholar, ivory-tower recluse or religious thinker. He respected learning, but not the learning of 'schoolmasters' (see *On schoolmasters' learning* and *On educating children*, p.190); and his ideas on education as experience of life and training for life emphasized military qualities and the active, outdoor life rather than professional, sedentary and bookish pursuits (see *On educating children*, pp.163–99 and *On the vanity of words*, pp.341–4), though he loved reading and considered it 'the best protection which I have found for our human journey' (III, 3, p.932).

Montaigne sees the 'gentleman' as cultivated but debonair, 'an able man not an erudite one' (I, 26, p.168), accomplished but spontaneous, amiable and sociable, skilled in dancing, fencing and horsemanship (Montaigne loved riding, and said that some of his best ideas for the *Essays* came to him on horseback). In a word, he cultivates that quality of spontaneous polish which Castiglione called *sprezzatura* (and which Shakespeare suggests in Ophelia's evocation of Hamlet: 'The courtier's, soldier's, scholar's eye, tongue, sword', 3.1.150). Montaigne's gentleman wears his learning lightly. Contrasting the Spartan virtues of brevity and bravery with rhetorical exercises, literary skills and preciosity, Montaigne sought 'to re-emphasise the central importance of moral philosophy (and its handmaiden, history), and to restore thereby the urgency of the original humanist movement' (Supple, 1984, p.271).

Montaigne's combination of 'retirement' (*otium*) with interventions in public life suggests a commitment to the classical and Renaissance ideal of public service (*negotium*). But even as mayor of Bordeaux, he had measured views about the extent to which public duty should be allowed to impinge on private life, and on the need to strike a balance between them (see *On restraining your will*, pp.1136–9, 1155, 1158). A man should 'wish his country well (as I do) without getting ulcers about it' (III, 10, p.1149).

Montaigne, Europe, humankind and humanity

Though he made only one foreign trip, Montaigne was alive to the wider world and to the benefits of exposure to it. He loved Rome and Venice as much as Paris. He relished travel as an educative experience, which supplemented his reading and fed his curiosity, his relativism and his tolerance. His *Travel Journal* records that on leaving Austria for Italy in 1580, he would as readily have gone to Poland or Greece, such was his appetite for new places and peoples, and his eagerness 'on all occasions to talk to strangers' (Frame, 1983a, p.51).

> I know of no better school for forming our life than ceaselessly to set before it the variety found in so many other lives, concepts and customs, and to give it a taste of the perpetual diversity of the forms of human nature.

> (III, 9, p.1101)

You may recall that one meaning of '*essai*' was trying or tasting food or drink. Montaigne made a point of trying out local custom and conforming with it throughout his travels. He thought conversation 'the most delightful activity in our lives' (III, 8, p.1045), and he relished intellectual challenge and controversy: 'No premise [actually 'proposition'] shocks me, no belief hurts me, no matter how opposite to my own they may be' (III, 8, p.1046).

Montaigne devoured contemporary travel books and accounts of hitherto little known societies.

> [Not only is China] a kingdom whose polity and sciences surpass our own exemplars in many kinds of excellence without having had any contact with them or knowledge of them [... but its] history teaches me that the world is more abundant and diverse than either the ancients or we ever realized.

> (III, 13, pp.1215–16)

As for the infidel Turks themselves, still the traditional and hated enemy of Christian Europe, Montaigne holds out 'the discipline of the Turkish armies' as an object-lesson to 'our young men': 'for it has many superiorities and advantages over ours' (III, 12, p.1180, and see also *Against indolence*). The simple life-style of the Tupinamba Indians of Brazil suggested to Montaigne, in contrast to prevailing contemporary opinion, 'that there is nothing savage or barbarous about those peoples, but that every man calls barbarous anything he is not accustomed to' (I, 31, p.231, and, for a striking catalogue of contrasts with European custom, see *On habit: and on never easily changing a traditional law*, pp.126–7). Indeed, the lifestyle of the Tupinamba Indians suggests to Montaigne the 'golden age' of classical mythology. You may remember his reference in 'To the Reader' to 'those peoples who are said still to live under the sweet liberty of Nature's primal laws'.[16] One of his aims in writing about 'primitive' peoples (whom he probably idealized) was no doubt to prompt reflections closer to home about the barbarities of the wars of religion.

Montaigne was an 'elitist', proud of his (not so ancient) noble title. See the title page of the first edition of the *Essays* (Figure 8.4). In the portrait of him as mayor of Bordeaux (Figure 8.1), the title '*Le Seigneur de Montaigne*' (Lord of Montaigne) is painted across the top of the canvas in large capitals, with the Montaigne coat-of-arms featuring prominently just below on the left. Montaigne wears the Order of St Michael around his neck. He complained in *On rewards for honours*, pp.428–31, that the order was too freely awarded. Montaigne was mocked as a snob by the French critic Joseph Scaliger; and a neighbouring noble, Pierre de Brantôme, twitted him that true noblemen, as doughty warriors, do not write books. Montaigne set out to prove such criticism ill-founded.

He was proud of being a Frenchman (and a Gascon), fascinated by concepts of 'glory', yet a European in his sympathies: 'I reckon all men my fellow-citizens, embracing a Pole as I do a Frenchman, placing a national bond after the common universal one' (III, 9, p.1100); and while he disdained 'the mass of ordinary people', especially in the early chapters, he became ever more open (especially towards the end of his life) towards the common man and the common 'humanity' of all human beings (see *On the inequality there is between us* and *On physiognomy*, p.1178, first paragraph). When he came to revise his earlier reference to 'the common people', he added in 1588, ambiguously but significantly and perhaps self-inclusively: 'and virtually everybody is in that category' (II, 12, p.490). On the last page of his final essay, *On experience*, he stresses that even 'upon the highest throne in the world, we are seated, still, upon our arses' (p.1269). By the time he wrote Book III, his favourite term of judgement and of praise is 'human' (*humain*, which also means 'humane').

Montaigne was a humanist in another sense: in his championship, in a cruel, intolerant and fanatical age in France and Europe, of 'humanity', even amid war itself (see, for example, *On the useful and the honourable*, p.904). His imaginative sympathies are wide and reach out to victims of all kinds: on children and corporal punishment see *On educating children* and *On anger* (pp.809–10); on women accused of witchcraft see *On*

---

[16] In *The Tempest* 2.1, Shakespeare reproduces a passage from *On the cannibals* (p.233) practically *verbatim* in Gonzago's 'utopia'. This is his one undoubted borrowing from Montaigne.

conscience and *On the lame*; on disabilities see *On a monster-child*; on the Jews see *That the taste of good and evil things depends in large part on the opinion we have of them*; on the South American Indians and the Incas, oppressed by the Conquistadores, see *On the cannibals* and *On coaches* (pp.1032–7). See also *On cruelty* (pp.480–88) where Montaigne states his 'cruel hatred of cruelty, as the ultimate vice', and shows his sympathy for animals and the natural world and *On experience* where he is concerned for 'our human condition' (p.1259).

Conclusion

'What do I know?' (*Que sçay-je?*) was the inscription chosen by Montaigne for the face of the medal which he designed for himself. And this reflects his sceptical approach to many subjects. While Montaigne was not always indirect and sceptical (he showed strong feeling on some subjects, especially cruelty and lying), he certainly favoured the sceptical approach, the 'soft pillow' of doubt (III, 13, p.1218). He seldom comes up with quick or simple answers. He approaches a question from different angles. He *weighs* the evidence, *tests* it against his own *experience*, and *feels* his way *discursively* towards conclusions, often expressed in *tentative* terms. (All the words italicized express different aspects of an '*essai*'.)

But what do the *Essays* add up to? Does Montaigne's many-sided and somewhat elusive approach mean that he had few convictions of his own? I think not. As we make our way through the *Essays*, what seems to emerge is not so much a set of answers as of attitudes, and the image of a particular man – well-read, reflective, infinitely curious and observant, detached and quizzical. From his library tower, Montaigne used his sceptical approach as a vantage-point from which to survey developments in post-Reformation France, where the learned were so quick to jump to conclusions, to take sides, to dogmatize in 'a rhetoric of hate' (Anglo, 1981, p.1) and to feed the flames not merely of intellectual disputation but of the sectarian strife which prevailed throughout Montaigne's adult life in the bloody wars of religion. In these circumstances, writing the *Essays* was at once a form of personal escapism, an absorbing creative pastime, and a means of reacting to developments. The *Essays* suggest that, far from indifferent to events around him, in his own highly individual and human way, Montaigne responded fully.

If, as Burckhardt held, the discovery of the individual was a characteristic of the Renaissance, then Montaigne may be considered a prime candidate for the description 'Renaissance man'. As a Latinist, lawyer, administrator, sometime royal adviser, and European traveller, the expression 'universal man' seems applicable to him. He was certainly steeped in the classics of antiquity, which was an accepted badge of Renaissance humanism. At the same time he was a free-ranging spirit, with an inexhaustible and open-minded curiosity about other people and peoples. These attributes and experiences he drew on in his life-long study of the individual, through the close and candid exploration of one man – himself. In the idea and form of the 'essay', which he invented (or re-invented) and adopted as the medium of his self-expression, and which evolved into the *Essays of Michel de Montaigne*, he produced a unique and original creation and a classic of the French and European Renaissance.

Bibliography

ANGLO, S. (1981) 'A rhetoric of hate: political polemic in late sixteenth-century France' in K. Cameron (ed.) *Montaigne and His Age*, Exeter, University of Exeter, pp.1–13.

AULOTTE, R. (1990) 'Montaigne et l'humanisme' in *Montaigne: penseur et philosophe, (1588–1988), Actes du congrès de littérature française*, Paris, Librairie Honoré Champion, pp.7–15.

BLOOM, H. (1994) *The Western Canon*, London, Harcourt Brace.

BOASE, A.M. (1935) *The Fortunes of Montaigne: A History of the Essays in France, 1580–1669*, London, Methuen.

BOASE, A.M. (1974) 'Montaigne et les sorcières. Une mise au point' in *Culture et politique en France à l'époque de l'humanisme et de la Renaissance*, Turin, Accademia delle scienze, pp.375–80.

BURCKHARDT, J. (1990) *The Civilization of the Renaissance in Italy*, trans. S.G.C. Middlemore, Harmondsworth, Penguin; first published 1860.

BURKE, P. (1977) 'Witchcraft and magic' in S. Anglo (ed.) *The Damned Art: Essays in the Literature of Witchcraft*, London, Routledge & Kegan Paul.

BURKE, P. (1990) 'The spread of Italian humanism' in A. Goodman and A. McKay (eds) *The Impact of Humanism on Western Europe*, London, Longman, pp.1–22.

COHEN, J.M. (ed.) (1958) Montaigne: *The Essays*, Harmondsworth, Penguin.

COLEMAN, D. (1987) *Montaigne's Essays*, Cambridge, Cambridge University Press.

COLEMAN, D. (1989) 'Montaigne's text: "Neglegentia diligens"' in P. Ford and G. Jondorf (eds) *Montaigne in Cambridge. Proceedings of the Cambridge Montaigne Colloquium 7–9 April 1988*, Cambridge, The Burlington Press, pp.103–13.

CONLEY, T. (1994) 'The *Essays* and the visual arts', in P. Henry (ed.) *Approaches to Teaching Montaigne's* Essays, New York, The Modern Language Association of America, pp.84–9.

FRAME, D.M. (1955) *Montaigne's Discovery of Man: The Humanization of a Humanist*, New York, Columbia University Press.

FRAME, D.M. (1965) *Montaigne: A Biography*, London, Hamish Hamilton.

FRAME, D.M. (trans.) (1983a) *Montaigne's Travel Journal*, Stanford, Stanford University Press.

FRAME, D.M. (1983b) 'But what are essays? Montaigne read in 1580', in *Actes du Colloque International Montaigne (1580–1980)*, Paris, Librairie Nizet, pp.89–102.

FRIEDRICH, H. (1991) *Montaigne*, ed. P. Desan, trans. D. Eng, Berkeley, University of California Press; first published 1949.

GARRISSON, J. (1995) *A History of Sixteenth-Century France*, Basingstoke, Macmillan.

GENDZIER, S.J. (ed./trans.) (1967) *Denis Diderot's The Encyclopedic Selections*, New York, Harper Torchbooks.

HALE, J. (1994) *The Civilisation of Europe in the Renaissance*, Atheneum edition, New York, Macmillan.

HENRY, P. (ed.) (1994) *Approaches to Teaching Montaigne's* Essays, The Modern Language Association of America, New York.

HIGHET, G. (1949) *The Classical Tradition: Greek and Roman Influences on Western Literature*, Oxford, Clarendon Press.

INSDORF, C. (1977) *Montaigne and Feminism*, Chapel Hill, University of North Carolina Press.

KEKEWICH, L. (ed.) (2000) *The Impact of Humanism*, New Haven and London, Yale University Press/The Open University.

KNECHT, R.J. (1996) *The Rise and Fall of Renaissance France*, London, Fontana.

KONSTANTINOVIC, I. (1989) *Montaigne et Plutarque*, Geneva, Droz.

KRISTELLER, P.O. (1961) *Renaissance Thought: The Classic, Scholastic, and Humanist Strains*, New York, Harper Torchbooks/ The Academy Library, Harper & Row.

LANSON, G. (1948) *Les Essais de Montaigne*, Mellottée, Paris.

LEGROS, A. (1999) *Essais sur poutres. Etude et édition critique des sentences de la 'Librarie' de Montaigne*, Studies on Montaigne and the Renaissance, Chicago, Garamond Press/Didier editions.

MARGOLIN, J-C. (1990) 'Humanism in France', in A. Goodman and A. McKay (eds) *The Impact of Humanism on Western Europe*, London, Longman, pp.164–201.

MCPHERSON, D.C. (1990) *Shakespeare, Jonson, and the Myth of Venice*, London, Associated University Presses.

MATEER, D. (ed.) (2000) *Courts, Patrons and Poets*, New Haven and London, Yale University Press/The Open University.

MONTAIGNE, M. de (1969), *Essais*, with an introduction by Alexandre Micha, 3 vols, Paris, Garnier-Flammarion.

O'NEILL, J. (1982) *Essaying Montaigne: A Study of the Renaissance Institution of Writing and Reading*, London, Routledge & Kegan Paul.

POPKIN, R.H. (1979) *The History of Scepticism from Erasmus to Spinoza*, London and Berkeley, University of California Press.

RAWSON, C. (1994) 'Noble observer', *The Yale Review*, vol. 82, no. 1, January, pp.110–25.

SCREECH, M.A. (ed./trans.) (1991) Michel de Montaigne: *The Complete Essays*, Harmondsworth, Penguin.

SCREECH, M.A. (ed.) (1998) *Montaigne's Annotated Copy of Lucretius*, Geneva, Droz.

SCREECH, M.A. (2000) *Montaigne and Melancholy: The Wisdom of the* Essays, London, Duckworth; first published 1983.

STAROBINSKI, J. (1985) *Montaigne in Motion*, trans. A. Goldhammer, Chicago, University of Chicago Press.

SUPPLE, J.J. (1984) *Arms Versus Letters: The Military and Literary Ideals in the 'Essais' of Montaigne*, Oxford, Clarendon Press.

THIBAUDET, A. and RAT, M. (eds) (1962) Montaigne: *Oeuvres complètes*, Bibliothèque de la Pléiade, Paris, Gallimard.

Anthology source

Michel de Montaigne, from his *Travel Journal* (1581): (i) and (ii) *Travel Journal*, trans. and with an introduction by D.M. Frame, North Point Press, San Francisco, 1983, pp.80–3, 152–5. (Anthology, no. 91)

Glossary

all'antica in antique or classical fashion.

Alumbrado also known as 'illuminists'; a movement in the Spanish church inspired by mystical notions that focused on the individual's communion and union with God. Initially supported by a number of powerful patrons, lay and ecclesiastical, it was ultimately proscribed and persecuted in the general backlash against religious heterodoxy following the Lutheran schism.

Anabaptist term used to describe those who subscribed to the radical wing of the Reformation. The term literally means 'to baptize again' and is indicative of the radicals' belief in the need for those seeking divine grace to be re-baptized into the 'true church' as adults, i.e. at an age when a person is sufficiently learned in the scriptures. There were various 'anabaptist' congregations or sects (the term itself was coined by their opponents), who tended to veer away from conventional forms of church government. Some were also influenced by messianic and charismatic preachers.

anamorphosis distorted image which, when viewed from a certain angle or with the use of a mirror, appears regular and properly proportioned.

anti-clericalism opposition to the excessive wealth and authority of the church. The movement has its origins in the **Middle Ages**, and is generally felt to have been a contributory factor in the origins of the Reformation.

apostolic church church of the apostles following the death of Christ. It became a by-word for simplicity and a model for generations of would-be church reformers.

autos de fé literally, 'acts of the faith'; a judicial act or sentence of the **Spanish Inquisition**, usually performed in public, whereby persistent offenders were put to death by burning. It was particularly used in the 1550s and early 1560s in Spain to destroy the threat of Lutheranism and any other form of heresy.

Bohemia during the fourteenth century the kingdom of Bohemia was one of the most important in Christendom. Its capital, Prague, was the home of the imperial government of Emperor Charles IV. During the fifteenth century, however, it went into decline and suffered much from internal religious divisions engendered by the **Hussite** revolution.

bull papal order or edict that carried the full authority of the church; so named after the *bulla*, or seal, that was attached to the document.

cabala name given to a wide range of Jewish mystical writings or commentaries on the Old Testament.

chapter body of canons of a collegiate or cathedral church, who were responsible for the day-to-day administration of the cathedral and its precincts.

christocentric theological world-view that places the teachings of Christ at the centre of its outlook. Erasmus's work is often held up as an exemplary form of this type of thinking in the late medieval church.

Church Fathers (or patristics); the early leaders of the Christian church in the centuries immediately following the death of Christ, whose writings were frequently invoked as authoritative in the **Middle Ages** and Renaissance. The two most cited were St Augustine and St Jerome.

Colloquies series of dialogues first published by Erasmus in 1519. In this extremely popular book he contrasted and parodied the various aspects of human nature, in both their social and their religious guises, as well as advocating the essential liberty of mankind.

communion in both kinds Protestants allowed the laity to partake of both the bread and the wine at communion (Catholics reserved the chalice, or wine, for the clergy).

Complutensian Bible multi-volume, polyglot version of the Bible produced at Alcalá in the 1510s.

conciliarism belief that the authority of church councils overrode that of popes. The idea was widely supported by lay authorities in Europe in the late **Middle Ages**, particularly those that wished to secure greater control over clerical appointments and taxation.

confraternities groups of laymen committed to the espousal of charitable and pious works. They were often organized around guilds or specific occupations and underwent something of a revival in the period immediately preceding the Reformation.

Consilium ... de emendanda ecclesia report of a committee of senior Catholic clergymen into the state of the church; inaugurated by Pope Paul III in 1537.

converso literally a convert, used in the Spanish-speaking world almost exclusively to denote a Jewish or Muslim convert to Catholicism or a person or family of such ancestry.

demonology academic study of witchcraft and diabolism, including those practices and beliefs that were characteristically ascribed to witches in the early modern period.

Diet of Worms meeting of the German princes and emperor at the city of Worms in 1521. Although the meeting was called for other reasons, it was here that Luther was given his final opportunity to recant.

Doric oldest, strongest and simplest of the three Greek orders of architecture.

ecclesiastical benefices posts and offices held by clergymen.

eirenicism peaceful attempts to seek reconciliation among the various Christian faiths of early modern Europe.

Erasmianism general name given to the views held by Erasmus and his followers, which favoured a moderate, humanist-inspired, reform of the Catholic church.

eucharist sacrament of the Lord's Supper, or communion, deriving from a Greek word meaning 'to give thanks'.

familiar spirit in an animal form, such as the Dog in *The Witch of Edmonton.*

Gothic art form of the **Middle Ages** characterized by an absence of classical features. Examples include: in architecture the use of the pointed arch, and in writing the use of Germanic as opposed to Roman or italic script.

Great Schism period of division in the Catholic church which lasted from 1378 to 1417. It was prompted by the removal of the papacy from Avignon to Rome and spawned several claimants to the papal tiara. It was also responsible for popularizing **conciliarism** among some high-ranking churchmen.

grotesque artistic depictions of human beings and animals characterized by distorted or fantastic designs.

heliocentrism belief that the sun lies at the centre of the universe and is orbited by the planets, including the Earth.

hermits individuals, sometimes priests, who chose to live in poverty and seclusion.

Hussites followers of Jan Hus (1369–1415), a **Bohemian** cleric who repudiated both the authority of the papacy and various doctrines of the Catholic church, including transubstantiation. He was subsequently condemned and executed at the Council of Constance in 1415. His followers were also known as Utraquists (from the Latin, *utraque*, meaning each or both); they too advocated **communion in both kinds**.

Index created in 1559 in order to determine what Catholics could, or could not, read. It was not limited to religious literature, but included works on a variety of subjects including science and popular literature.

Inquisition body first established by the papacy in the **Middle Ages** to eradicate heresy and promote orthodoxy.

Inquisitor officer of the **Inquisition**.

journeymen workmen who had served their apprenticeships and worked for masters in their chosen occupations for a set wage.

late medieval revival of mysticism during the late **Middle Ages**, a greater emphasis on mystical strains of religious devotion is evident, as popularized, for example, in the work of the early fifteenth-century monk Thomas à Kempis, whose *Imitation of Christ* was widely read. Kempis was a member of the Brethren of the Common Life, a Netherlandish order that encouraged religious introspection and the pursuit of spiritual enlightenment.

liberal arts the traditional curriculum of the late **Middle Ages** and Renaissance consisted of the trivium (grammar, rhetoric and logic) and the quadrivium (arithmetic, geometry, astronomy and music), otherwise known as the seven liberal arts.

Lollards followers of the English medieval theologian and reformer John Wycliff (1320–84). Like Hus in Bohemia, Wycliff rejected a number of central beliefs of Catholic orthodoxy. His followers were persecuted throughout the fifteenth century in England, but Lollard cells were still in existence immediately prior to the Reformation and may have assisted the reception of Luther's ideas in England.

lunettes crescent-shaped or semi-circular spaces in a ceiling or dome decorated with paintings or sculptures.

magus master, or one deeply learned in the occult sciences.

Marian cults organized groups committed to the worship of the Virgin Mary.

Middle Ages roughly, the period from the fall of the old Roman empire (*c.*450 CE) to the onset of the Renaissance (*c.*1450).

Münster site in 1535 of an **Anabaptist** uprising in Germany that led to the temporary establishment of a utopian religious community. It was brutally crushed by the authorities and thereafter Münster became a by-word for religious extremism and social anarchy.

natural magic branch of Renaissance natural philosophy dealing with the study of obscure natural phenomena that were not susceptible to normal modes of explanation, e.g. the ebb and flow of the tides, the special properties of certain plants and stones, etc.

nepotism the conferring of lucrative offices or posts on one's relatives, a practice rife in the medieval church.

nominalism strain of thought in late medieval **scholasticism**, which, in opposition to **realism**, argues against the existence of universal or abstract concepts as nothing more than mere words or names (hence 'nominalism'). Such thinking was to play an important part in theological debate in this period.

non-residence description of those clergy who, for one reason or another, did not reside in the place of their post or benefice.

occult philosophy term used interchangeably with **occult sciences** to describe the study of alchemy, astrology and natural magic.

occult sciences see **occult philosophy**.

Ordinary book containing the order of divine service and the mass.

pardoner person licensed to sell papal pardons or indulgences. This corrupt practice was a focus of attack during the Reformation.

physiognomy art of judging human character from close inspection of the features of the face and the form and shape of the body. In the Renaissance it was closely associated with the study of astrology.

Piagnoni Italian followers of the Florentine priest Girolamo Savonarola who kept alive his preaching and message in the first half of the sixteenth century.

picaresque from the Spanish '*picaro*', which means a rogue or delinquent, the term describes a sub-genre of prose fiction dealing with the adventures of rogues. It is usually episodic in form.

priesthood of all believers term used to describe Luther's view that all people were equally capable of reaching salvation without the intercession of a separate priestly caste. In theory, this meant that anyone might become a priest, although in practice Luther limited entry to the Lutheran priesthood to those who were educated and well versed in the scriptures.

putti (singular, *putto*) representations of children or cherubs in Renaissance art.

Radical Reformation development of Luther's religious views that led to an outright rejection of much of the traditional organization and beliefs of both the Catholic and mainstream Protestant churches. Its leaders tended to be anti-authoritarian, charismatic preachers who advocated a complete secession from what they saw as the corruptions of institutionalized religion.

realists advocates of realism, one of the most important philosophical schools of thought in the **Middle Ages**. Realists believed in the existence of universal or abstract concepts, and were later opposed by **nominalists**.

recusant loyal Catholics who refused to attend the services of the Church of England as laid down by law and thus risked punishment in both the secular and ecclesiastical courts. Not all Catholics, however, openly defied the law in this way. Many remained outwardly obedient to Anglicanism while continuing to uphold Catholic beliefs and practices in private. Some high-church Anglicans also sympathized with certain elements of the old faith and sought reconciliation between the two religious denominations.

regular clergy clergy who were members of religious orders.

rentier literally one who makes an income from property or investment, and consequently as a pejorative, someone living on a frozen or declining unearned income and who does not work.

Rosary form of prayer or set of devotions to the Virgin Mary. The establishment of orders devoted to the worship of Our Lady became very popular in parts of northern Europe in the late fifteenth century.

sabbat nocturnal gathering of witches at which it was widely assumed by demonologists that the devil was present in person. In the accounts of writers on witchcraft, feasting and revelling were accompanied by special rites and ceremonies in which the devil was worshipped by his human acolytes, the witches, and demons.

Sack of Rome desecration and conquest of Rome by the troops of Emperor Charles V in 1527. This was an attempt by Charles to bring Pope Clement VII to heel, but it backfired badly, causing much revulsion among the other Catholic powers and princes of Europe.

Sacred Host wafer of bread consecrated by the priest during the celebration of the **eucharist**. During the fifteenth century many pilgrimage sites grew up around churches in which the Sacred Host was said to have bled and other miracles were performed.

scholasticism may be broadly defined as the dominant ideology of medieval Christian thought, based as it was on the revival and application of the doctrines of Aristotle to the teachings of the church. It was essentially a philosophical movement that sought to prove religious, scientific and other truths through the application of the logical methods of Aristotle. Its founder and chief spokesman was the Dominican, St Thomas Aquinas (d.1274).

serfs rural labourers who were not completely free but tied to the manor of their birth by the requirement to perform certain services for their lord. Serfdom was no longer a feature of much of western European society, although it could still be found in many parts of eastern Europe in the sixteenth century.

sgraffito decorative technique in which a surface layer of paint or plaster is cut or incised to reveal a contrasting layer of colour.

simony act of buying or selling ecclesiastical offices; it derives from the biblical figure, Simon Magus, who offered money to the apostles Peter and John in return for the gift of the Holy Spirit (Acts 8.18–19).

spandrels triangular spaces beneath the curves of an arch and the surrounding rectangular moulding or framework.

Spanish Inquisition established in 1478 by Pope Sixtus IV at the instigation of the joint sovereigns of Spain, Isabella and Ferdinand. Its initial purpose was to ensure that *conversi* remained loyal to the

Catholic church. Unique in Europe, it was under the strict control of the Spanish monarchy, who appointed an Inquisitor-General to co-ordinate its activities.

Spanish realism term 'realism' used here in a restricted sense to signify faithfulness in rendering the precise details, be it in painting or in words. In practice, a painter or writer so characterized depicts the sordidness of life without any evasion.

spirituali unofficial movement within the Catholic church which promoted the cause of religious reform and spiritual invigoration in the church.

tableaux vivants literally, 'living pictures', these were re-enactments or representations of well-known scenes from the Bible that were usually performed in the open air and in public on popular feast days and religious holidays.

tragicomedy Renaissance dramatic genre which fuses elements of tragedy and comedy.

Tridentine relating to the Council of Trent.

Tuscan simplest and least ornate of the five orders of classical architecture.

Visigothic literally West Goths, one of several Germanic tribes who overran the western Roman empire, and who controlled the Iberian peninsula in the fifth and sixth centuries until the Muslim invasion of 711. The surviving Christian kings of the north of Spain claimed lineal descent, and the legitimate right to reconquered Spain, hence in the Spanish-speaking world 'Visigothic' nowadays carries nuances of antiquity and legitimacy.

white witchcraft description of those magical practices used by wise men and women that were intended to produce beneficial effects, e.g. the discovery of lost property, healing charms, etc.

Acknowledgements

Grateful acknowledgement is made to the following sources for permission to reproduce material in this book:

Figure 1.3: Hay, D. (1986) *The Age of the Renaissance*, Guild Publishing. Reproduced by permission of Thames and Hudson Ltd. © 1967 & 1986 Thames and Hudson Ltd.

Figure 2.1: Greengrass, M.A. (1998) *The Longman Companion to the European Reformation, c.1500-1618,* Pearson Education Limited.

Figure 8.13: Frame, D.M. (1965) *Montaigne: A Biography,* Hamish Hamilton Limited.

Every effort has been made to trace all the copyright owners, but if any have been inadvertently overlooked, the publishers will be pleased to make the necessary arrangements at the first opportunity.

Index

ıs'